THE VATICAN,
THE BISHOPS AND
IRISH POLITICS
1919–39

DERMOT KEOGH

Lecturer in Modern History
University College Cork

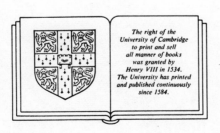

The right of the
University of Cambridge
to print and sell
all manner of books
was granted by
Henry VIII in 1534.
The University has printed
and published continuously
since 1584.

CAMBRIDGE UNIVERSITY PRESS

Cambridge
London   New York   New Rochelle
Melbourne   Sydney

Published by the Press Syndicate of the University of Cambridge
The Pitt Building, Trumpington Street, Cambridge CB2 1RP
32 East 57th Street, New York, NY 10022, USA
10 Stamford Road, Oakleigh, Victoria 3166, Australia

First published 1986
Reprinted 1988

Printed in Great Britain at the University Press, Cambridge

Library of Congress catalogue card number: 85-5915

British Library cataloguing in publication data

Keogh, Dermot
The Vatican, the bishops and Irish politics 1919–39.
1. Catholic Church – Political activity
2. Ireland – Politics and government – 1922–1949
I. Title
322′.1′09417   JN1415

ISBN 0 521 30129 7

CONTENTS

ILLUSTRATIONS

ABBREVIATIONS

AAA	Armagh Archdiocesan Archives
Amigo	Archbishop Amigo Papers
Byrne	Edward Byrne Papers
CAB	Cabinet
Cahill	Edward Cahill Papers
DAA	Dublin Archdiocesan Archives
DE	Dail Eireann files
DO	Dominions Office
EC	Executive Council (Cabinet after 1937)
FF	Fianna Fail
FG	Fine Gael
FitzGerald	Desmond FitzGerald Papers
FO	Foreign Office
Hagan	John Hagan Papers
Hales	Donal Hales Papers
ITGWU	Irish Transport and General Workers' Union
Kirby	Tobias Kirby Papers
Logue	Cardinal Michael Logue Papers
McGilligan	Patrick McGilligan Papers
MacRory	Cardinal Joseph MacRory Papers
Magennis	Peter Magennis Papers
MP	Member of Parliament
O'Donnell	Cardinal Patrick O'Donnell Papers
PRO	Public Record Office, London
PRO, Dublin	Public Record Office, Dublin
RTE	Radio Telefis Eireann
S	Provisional Government, Executive Council and Cabinet files
SE	Seanad Eireann
SPO	State Paper Office, Dublin

Abbreviations

TD	Teachta Dala (Member of Parliament)
UCD	University College Dublin
Walsh	William Walsh Papers

PREFACE

Any historian writing on the theme of Church and State in Ireland must
first acknowledge his or her debt to the four scholars who have been
working extensively in this field for many years. Mgr Patrick Corish of
Maynooth has inspired many by his writing and his teaching.[1]
Professor Emmet Larkin is one of two American scholars who have
published a series of monographs of quality and originality in the area.[2]
Professor David Miller has produced the standard book on the Catholic
Church between 1898 and 1921,[3] a fine piece of work given the archival
limitations under which it was written. Professor John Whyte has
contributed most directly in the area covered by my work.[4] I am deeply
indebted to all four for the indirect way in which they have influenced
me.[5]

The person who originally inspired the subject of this study was the
late Maureen Wall, of University College Dublin. It was she who first
suggested in 1969 that John Hagan, the Rector of the Irish College in
Rome from 1920 until his death in 1930, might have privately exercised
a significant influence over the direction of Irish politics and on the
personality of Eamon de Valera in particular; as in so many other cases,
she was accurate. His private papers are one of the richest sources for the
study of modern Irish history.

As a doctoral student and now a colleague of Joe Lee, I have been
fortunate to benefit over the past eight years from his advice and
encouragement. Without his support and infectious enthusiasm for the
subject of history I would never have gone to Florence. I am very
grateful to Anne and Joe for their support at crucial moments. I have
also been privileged to enjoy the friendship and supervision of
Desmond Williams, the most outstanding modern historian in the
country; he has given generously of his time and shared both his
archives and knowledge with a newcomer. He is a man with a unique
sense of history and of time. Equally, I would like to thank Dr Kevin

Kennedy, Dublin Archdiocesan Archivist, for his help that has extended far beyond the bounds of his archival duties. There are few people who are as much at home in French, German or Italian Church history as he is. In this regard, I would also like to thank warmly Geoffrey Hand and Margaret MacCurtain for their help and friendship. A special word of thanks to Deirdre McMahon, who shaped this book in a very direct way.

I would like to thank both the Cardinal Archbishop of Armagh, Dr Tomas Ó Fiaich, and the late Archbishop of Dublin, Dr Dermot Ryan, for granting me access to ecclesiastical sources in Dublin, Armagh and Rome. In all three archives, I enjoyed hospitality and courtesy which made the research all the more enjoyable and memorable. My thanks also to Bishops Eamonn Casey of Galway, Dominic Conway of Elphin, Patrick Lennon of Kildare and Leighlin and Michael Harty of Killaloe.

The Department of Foreign Affairs might take note of such a liberal ecclesiastical archival policy. Although granted permission to see material in 1977 by the then Minister of Foreign Affairs, Dr Garret FitzGerald, I have not as yet succeeded in having the decision acted upon by the Department concerned. However, I have learned that some – if not most – of the relevant files may have been assigned for 'Confidential Destruction' in 1940, when there was fear of invasion. Tracing the authorisation for such a decision may prove an interesting task for the historian. However, the general obstructionism of departmental policy has been superseded by the helpfulness of many retired and serving diplomats. I would particularly like to thank Drs F. H. Boland and Cornelius Cremin for giving long interviews.

The progressive attitude of the Department of the Taoiseach stands in marked contrast to the tardiness of Iveagh House. Successive Taoiseachs are to be applauded for their archival policy: Liam Cosgrave, Jack Lynch, Charles Haughey and Garret FitzGerald. I am also particularly grateful to Catherine Meenan, Richard Stokes and Frank Dunlop for their help. Dr Garret and Mrs FitzGerald kindly allowed me to consult family papers in their busy household. Mr Charles Haughey made files on the constitution available to me. Mr Liam Cosgrave spoke to me at length about his time in office and about the career of his father. Mr Maurice Moynihan and Col. Dan Bryan both gave me extensive interviews and many insights.

Sadly, a number of people who gave me extensive assistance in the research of this book have not lived to see its publication. Both Sean MacEntee and Frank Aiken allowed me to intrude a number of times on the peace of their retirement and gave generously of their time and knowledge. The late Denis McDaid, former Rector of the Irish College, Rome, spoke and wrote of his experiences for me. I also greatly valued the help of another Rector of the Irish College who died recently, the urbane and cultured Bishop of Ferns, Donal Herlihy. His wit and wisdom will be missed, as will the contribution of Bishop Birch of Kilkenny. It was with great regret that I learned of the sudden death of my thesis supervisor, Professor Walter Lipgens. Although he might have been happier with another subject, he was most supportive and encouraging.

I would also like to thank the former Rector of the Irish College in Salamanca, Alexander J. McCabe, who, like Bishop Herlihy, was a gracious guide to the events and personalities of the 1930s. A number of civil service and clerical sources who have helped in the research of this book prefer to remain anonymous; my thanks to them for their substantial help.

I wish to record my thanks to the following: Mr Pat Quigg, Beatrice Doran, Nora Brown, Finola O'Donovan, Ned Fahey of University College Cork library; the staff of the National Library of Ireland; Professor R. Dudley Edwards and the Archives Department, University College Dublin; Ken Hannigan and David Craig and Gay Gaynor of the Public Record Office; Desmond Byrnes of the Taoiseach's office library; the staff of the Library of Congress, Washington and of the Italian State Archives, Rome; the Instituto Luigi Sturzo in Rome; Ms Nancy Emmick, San José State Library; the staff of Stanford, Hoover and Berkeley libraries; and Mr Kenneth Humphries, of the European University Institute, Florence.

In Italy, I would like to thank Francesco and Gioliolla Margiotta Broglio; Brian Coughlin of the Carmelite Order and the Dominican Community at San Clemente; the Rector and staff of the Irish College and Robert Graham SJ. Mrs Kathleen McKenna Napoli was a gracious host.

In the United States, I would like to thank the Fulbright Commission and Professor Jim Walsh for affording me the opportunity to spend a semester at San José, Stanford and Berkeley, where this manuscript was completed. My thanks to Mrs Agnes Peterson, Director of the Western European Collection, at the Hoover Institution and the staff of the National Archives, Washington.

My thanks to Paul Hurley of the *Word*; Liam Moher and Fergus O'Callaghan of the *Cork Examiner*; Stephen O'Byrnes of the *Independent*; and Pat Cashman of the *Irish Press* for supplying photographs and illustrations for this book. Joe Carroll of the *Sunday Tribune* was very helpful on the background to recent events.

I am also grateful to Dr Miriam Hederman O'Brien, Katie Kahn-Carl, Professor Patrick Masterson, and Frs Michael Sweetman SJ and Oliver Trainor. Special thanks to Mattie and Madelaine MacNamara.

I would like to thank Veronica Fraser and Charlotte Wiseman for their patience and skill in the typing of the many drafts of this book. I would like to thank also four post-graduate students, Gerard Brockie, Sheila Crowley, Micheal Martin and Bernadette Whelan, who have helped me with this text.

Finally, it is the custom of another generation to thank a wife for patiently typing manuscript drafts; but I am most indebted to Ann for her intellecual support and critical appraisal of this work at all stages. My thanks to Eoin, Niall, Aoife and Clare for their tolerance, patience, sacrifices and unfailing good humour during the long preparation of this book, which has involved me in a constant round of travel over the past nine years. My regret is that my father did not see the finished work. In the course of my research I have interviewed many leading politicians, church figures and academics in Ireland and abroad. They cannot be held responsible for the ideas and views expressed in this book.

Badia Fiesolana,   DERMOT KEOGH
Florence 1976–9;

University College Cork,
San José and Stanford,
California 1980–5

INTRODUCTION

It probably came as no surprise to many that the head of the Roman Catholic Church, Pope John Paul II, should have received such a warm welcome on his visit to Ireland in 1979: the three days, 29 September to 1 October, witnessed scenes of mass enthusiasm unparalleled in the history of the state. Over 1.2 million people attended the papal Mass in the Phoenix Park, Dublin, while over 400,000 were present at the Liturgy of the Word near Drogheda later the same day. At a special youth Mass in Galway, the congregation was over 300,000 and the ceremonies at the Marian shrine of Knock were attended by only a slightly smaller number. There were 40,000 at the old monastic ruins of Clonmacnoise, 60,000 at the national seminary of Maynooth and over 300,000 at Limerick. That, of course, did not include the thousands who assembled at the airports for the Pope's arrival and departure, and the people who thronged the streets of Dublin for the motorcade through the city.

Such figures may be considered small by international standards, but the population of the entire island was only 4.8 million, some 3.3 million of whom lived in the Irish Republic. The papal visit was both an occasion for 'national' celebrations and an opportunity to itemise what constituted Irish identity. The crossed tricolour and papal flags on many houses, the intermingling of the green, white and orange with the yellow and white in streets festooned with bunting and ribbons, was a vivid illustration of the traditional relationship between Irish Catholicism and nationalism. The last occasion the state witnessed such scenes of public fervour was at the Eucharistic Congress in 1932.

This phenomenon can be expressed in another way. The virulence of continental anti-clericism is quite foreign to recent Irish history. In contrast to the political activities of 'Catholic' southern Europe, their 'anti-clerical' counterparts in the country once referred to as 'the island of saints and scholars' were rather more genteel in their demeanour

1

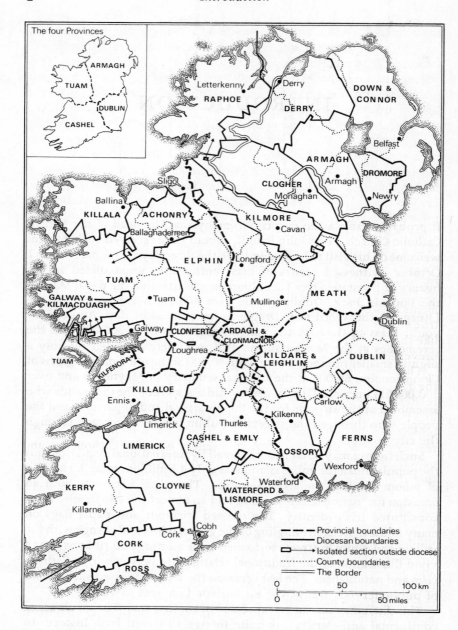

Fig. 1 (Map) Provinces and Dioceses of Ireland (*Irish Catholic Directory*)

towards the Catholic Church.[1] Despite what many of the hierarchy may have thought politically at the time, late nineteenth-century revolutionary Irish nationalism lacked a dominant Jacobinist content: 'the people know no patriotism except hatred for their rulers' was the rather graphic description of the popular content of radical nationalism by the Bishop of Kerry, David Moriarty, in 1868.[2] The same bishop attacked the Fenian leaders following an abortive rising, in 1867, describing them from the pulpit as criminals and swindlers deserving of God's most withering and blighting curse, for whom 'eternity is not long enough, nor hell hot enough'.[3] Pope Pius IX had great sympathy with the Irish bishops in their fight against radical nationalism. He told the special British envoy to the Vatican, Odo Russell, in January 1870, how he pitied the members of local hierarchy who were 'constantly exposed to "bastonato" from the Fenians', who were 'the Garibaldians of England'.[4] While Cardinal Paul Cullen of Dublin never used the same colourful language as Moriarty to describe his feelings, he saw in the growth of Fenianism the cloaked advance of the anti-clerical and anti-religious philosophy which was at the base of continental oath-bound movements. It was only a question of time before the Fenians showed 'their true colours'.[5] Successive generations of Irish bishops believed that – like their continental counterparts – they faced a growing challenge of preventing a cleavage developing between Church and people.

This book deals almost exclusively with the post-1916 period, when the rise of radical nationalism placed growing strain on the fragile relationship between the bishops and revolutionary leaders. It examines the reasons why politicians were often critical of the hierarchy – or opposed to an individual bishop – but rarely anti-clerical. Part of the reason may be that there was a closeness between Catholicism and nationalism which quickly resulted in the defusing of public conflict through immediate effective private representations. The closeness between political and religious institutions – clandestine or otherwise – did not allow misunderstandings to develop and fester. Moreover, there was never political unanimity on the bench of bishops and that was quite widely known in high political circles.

It is important to state what this book is not: it is *not* a study of priest and people in twentieth-century Ireland. The temptation to stray into that area – no matter how attractive – has been avoided. The broader theme, although part of the original doctoral thesis on which this book is based, will be dealt with in another volume. This book is a study in diplomatic and political history. It is a study of Irish ecclesiastical and lay leaders and elites in the period from 1919 to 1939.[6] These dates have not been arbitrarily chosen. The year 1919 marks the setting up of Dail Eireann and the outbreak of violence between 'physical force' nationalists and British government forces. The year 1937 sees the adoption of a new Constitution based on the political philosophy of Eamon de Valera – the only surviving commander of the 1916 Rising. At one level, this book examines the response of leading churchmen to the rise of separatist nationalism and treats of the political divergences, for example, between William Walsh of Dublin and Michael Logue of Armagh. An analysis of the complicating role of the Papacy in Irish politics is viewed through the extensive correspondence of the Rector of the Irish College in Rome, John Hagan, and the reports of British envoys to the Vatican. The Roman dimension in Irish Church–State relations reveals the interaction between secular and ecclesiastical politics. Hagan will be seen as a central figure in both spheres, not adverse to taking a highly unpopular and controversial stance. He is one of many figures who will illustrate the central thesis of this book, that the leadership of the hierarchy was never a political monolith.

The role of the British mission to the Vatican and of the part played by Cardinal Gasquet and other members of the English community in Rome will also be examined. The exaggeration of British influence at the Vatican was a persistent Irish clerico-nationalist tenet of the period. Conversely, there was the tendency to underplay the lobbying power of the Irish in Rome by men like Hagan.

Large sections of this book deal with political manoeuvrings in Rome; this serves as a backdrop to evaluate the development in Church–State relations in Ireland throughout the 1920s and 1930s. In the pre-Free State years, there is the constant fear of Vatican intervention in Ireland and the development of episcopal attitudes towards nationalist and state violence. In this period also, there is the forging of friendships between men like de Valera and leading members of the hierarchy, friendships that are strained beyond breaking point with the outbreak of civil war. On the Free State side, friendship between Archbishop Byrne of Dublin and President William Cosgrave is also strained during the Civil War over the policy of executions and government policy towards hunger strikers.

The extensive range of personal papers and ecclesiastical and government archives used in this study will shed new light on the complexities of the shifting relationship between political and ecclesiastical leaders in the years 1922 and 1923. It is to be hoped that the new evidence will help undermine simplistic doctrinaire attitudes concerning one of the most bitter episodes in modern Irish history. The secret role played by some bishops will come as a surprise to many who hold to the popular view that the hierarchy virtually acted as a 'State Church'.

Fundamental to an understanding of post-independence Church–State relations is a knowledge of the web of friendships built up between leading clergymen and prominent politicians during 'the Troubles'. They proved to be of a most enduring nature. John Hagan, the Rector of the Irish College, the Superior General of the Carmelites, Peter Magennis, and Archbishop Daniel Mannix of Melbourne are but three of the most prominent names associated with de Valera and Sean T. O'Kelly. They reflect the radical and comparatively unknown side of Irish Catholicism. But that system of relationships between de Valera and the clergy extended from the higher echelons to the humble curate, like Fr Tom Power of Clogheen, or the Cistercian monks of Mount Melleray. Such friendships even survived the strains of Civil War. In other words, the Catholic Church reflected the political divisions in Irish society and there was far less indiscriminate hostility to republicans than has hitherto been believed.

It is in this context that three chapters have been devoted to the growth in Church–State relations under Cosgrave and Cumann na nGaedheal. It would be virtually impossible to cover every aspect of Church–State relations in the late 1920s. This book does not attempt that task. There is a pressing need for monographs to be written on a subject such as the Catholic Church and the development of the educational system.[7] Controversies over legislation on divorce, censorship, etc., are sketched in an attempt to paint a broad picture of the emerging political competition between de Valera and Cosgrave.

Hagan's patronage of de Valera is an important new factor in understanding the development of Church–State relations in the late 1920s and 1930s. The Rector's theory that de Valera represented a moderate wing of republicanism may not have had much episcopal support in late 1923. But when de Valera founded Fianna Fail, with the intellectual support of Hagan, his stock rose in episcopal circles. When he entered the Dail in 1927 – again heavily under the influence of Hagan – de Valera was seen to be well on the road to respectability. By the end of the 1920s, Fianna Fail had demonstrated to some leading clergymen that Church interests might be better served by replacing Cosgrave with de Valera. Although Hagan did not live to witness the accuracy of his analysis, the 1937 Constitution demonstrates clearly the orthodoxy of de Valera.

A note of caution. This book deals with the various Vatican institutions involved in the conduct of diplomacy. Western European administrative models do not transfer so readily to the workings of the Papacy. The Cardinal Secretary of State is appointed by the Pope and he automatically resigns on the death of the Pontiff. In this study Pietro Gasparri held that office from 1914 until 1930, when he was succeeded by Cardinal Eugenio Pacelli, the future Pius XII. Gasparri, therefore, served two Popes, indicating a major degree of continuity in foreign policy between Benedict XV and Pius XI. The Secretary of State is not a Foreign Minister in the secular democratic political sense. He is identified with the Pope and works closely with the Secretary for Extraordinary Ecclesiastical Affairs. Moreover, the Secretary of State and his Office are not exclusively responsible for relations with other countries. The Congregation of Propaganda Fide (now named the Sacred Congregation for the Evangelisation of Peoples) was important in this area, as was the Congregation of the Holy Office, with a former Secretary of State, Cardinal Rafael Merry del Val, acting as secretary for the early part of this study. As will be seen, the relationship between Merry del Val and Gasparri was a complicating factor in a decision-making process which was restricted to a relatively small number of people.

Chapter I

WILLIAM WALSH AND THE ANGLO-VATICAN TRADITION

O, he'll remember all this when he grows up, said Dante hotly – the language he heard against God and religion and priests in his own home. Let him remember too, cried Mr Casey to her from across the table, the language with which the priests and the priests' pawns broke Parnell's heart and hounded him into his grave. Let him remember that too when he grows up.[1]

James Joyce was nine years of age when 'the priests and the priests' pawns broke Parnell's heart', according to Mr Casey in the famous Christmas dinner scene from *A Portrait of the Artist as a Young Man*. The occasion may have been reminiscent of many dinner parties in 1890–1 where the table was divided between those who supported and those who opposed Parnell and where the Irish were often referred to by one side as a 'priestridden Godforsaken race'. The Irish bishops were 'Lord Leitrim's horsemen', the betrayers of Ireland:

Didn't the bishops of Ireland betray us in the time of the union when bishop Lanigan presented an address of loyalty to the Marquess Cornwallis? Didn't the bishops and priests sell the aspirations of their country in 1829 in return for catholic emancipation? Didn't they denounce the fenian movement from the pulpit and in the confession box? And didn't they dishonour the ashes of Terence Bellew MacManus?

In the conversation at the Joyce household, Mr Casey – who had repeatedly attacked the bishops for betraying Irish nationalism – also protested vigorously to Mrs Riordan – the defender of the Church – that he was no renegade Catholic: 'I am a catholic as my father was and his father before him and his father before him again when we gave up our lives rather than sell our faith.'

But moments later, as the situation deteriorated and tempers became even more frayed, Mr Casey, in response to Mrs Riordan's remark, 'God and religion before everything . . . God and religion before the world', was prepared to shout 'Very well then . . . if it comes to that, no God for

7

Ireland . . . No God for Ireland . . . We have too much God in Ireland
. . . Away with God . . . Away with God I say.' That outburst
encapsulated the dilemma in which many of the most important
members of the hierarchy believed the Catholic Church had been placed
in 1890–1: how was it possible to keep Mr Casey – who claimed that he
was a good Catholic and that his ancestors had been persecuted for the
faith – in the Catholic Church? The political situation was so volatile that
Mr Casey could *at once* claim loyalty to the Catholic Church *and* shout
'no God for Ireland . . . we have too much God in Ireland.'[2] That was the
challenge facing the hierarchy from the early 1890s – a challenge that
was felt all the more acutely in a later period of revolutionary
nationalism.

One of the Irish Catholic bishops who was most aware of the volatility
of the political situation in the early 1890s was William Walsh, the
Archbishop of Dublin – referred to as 'Billy with the lip' in the *Portrait*
dinner scene. He had the Mr Caseys very much in mind as he shaped his
domestic pastoral policy in the last two decades of the nineteenth
century. Walsh, who was to remain the single most important Roman
Catholic ecclesiastical leader in Ireland until shortly before his death in
1921, had written thus to his close friend Tobias Kirby, the Rector of the
Irish College in Rome, about his fears for the future of religion in the
country:

As I often remarked to Your Grace, the people of Ireland, Catholics as they are,
might easily enough be brought into the same state of mind that now so
manifestly prevails throughout the people of Italy, France and other so-called
'Catholic' countries. The same influence is at work which has wrought such
mischief there. We must be careful now lest we incur any share of the
responsibility.[3]

Walsh was a highly intelligent ecclesiastical politician. He was an
academic of considerable standing with specialist knowledge in the
fields of theology, law, economics and the natural sciences. As President
of Maynooth and as Archbishop of Dublin from 1885, he had adopted a
series of controversial stances on agrarian and national questions. He
never enjoyed the full confidence of the government, while he also had
some difficulties with the Vatican. At the height of the Parnell crisis,
Walsh had occasion to write to Kirby:

We are still in the midst of our difficulties here – the prospects of an amicable
solution being now apparently further off than ever. It would be well if Your
Grace would tell any persons who presume to offer you advice about the details
of Irish affairs, that they had better keep to matters of which they are capable of
forming an opinion. *Above all, let them look at home.* We here mean to strain
every nerve to keep our people safe from such a fate as that which has befallen
the Catholics of Rome and Italy.[4]

1 William Walsh, Archbishop of Dublin 1885–1921

Walsh was determined to keep Mr Casey from reaching the point where he would openly and soberly shout in public 'No God for Ireland'. In the late 1880s, Pope Leo XIII had complicated the relationship between the hierarchy and nationalists by issuing a rescript against the Plan of Campaign.[5] Walsh remained both personally very upset by the document and pessimistic about the position in which the bishops had been left by the move:

During the present pontificate, at all events, the old feeling of confidence can never be restored. The people of course submit with respect to the explanation given by the bishops as to the authority of the Holy See in moral questions, but they are now shrewd enough to know that the exercise of that is a matter of discretion; they cannot see why it should have been exercised against them, and in no way against the landlords whose treatment of them is at least equally characterised by injustice and want of charity.[6]

The difficulty of keeping Mr Casey from moving to the point where he would shout 'No God for Ireland' had been made all the more difficult by the intervention of the Vatican. Walsh was convinced that the rescript, which had been issued following the visit of Mgr Persico of the Vatican to Ireland, was inspired by the British government.

Over the following thirty years Walsh, as de facto leader of the Irish hierarchy, strove to prevent the emergence in Ireland of a secularised anti-clerical society. Keeping Mr Casey in the Catholic Church meant having to remain close to the political leadership of Irish nationalism. It also meant keeping the Vatican out of Irish politics. There was nothing surer to send Mr Casey into the arms of anti-Catholic revolutionaries and radicals than to *perceive* the Vatican as acting at the behest of the British. That remained a constant in the Archbishop's thinking. He also opposed any idea of sending a permanent papal nuncio to London on the same grounds. The way in which both Walsh and the Catholic hierarchy were treated over the Plan of Campaign by Rome had a considerable bearing on the development of episcopal policy towards the Vatican and Irish politics in the post-1916 period.

There were other factors which contributed to Walsh's generally critical attitude toward the Vatican in the latter part of the nineteenth century. Unlike most international organisations, the Vatican, in his view, was neither efficient nor capable of conducting business in modern European languages other than Italian.[7] Official Church documents sometimes did not reach Ireland until after they had appeared in the British press. That placed the local hierarchy at a considerable disadvantage.[8] While that situation may have improved in the early twentieth century, some prominent members of the hierarchy remained convinced that Rome did not treat the Irish Church with the respect that it deserved.

A seemingly trivial example will illustrate the sense of hurt felt by members of the Irish hierarchy over the apparent incapacity of some members of the Vatican to understand the nature of the Irish Church. There was the feeling that Ireland was viewed in Rome as being on the periphery of Europe, not simply geographically, but also in terms of ecclesiastical importance. On the occasion of Leo XIII's jubilee, a present of vestments and altar plate was sent to the Irish Church. The quality of the gift left something to be desired. Walsh wrote to Kirby that the present reflected 'a strange notion in Rome of the condition of our Irish Church'.[9] The Archbishop added:

In the city of Dublin alone, we could in 24 hours bring together from the city churches a really fine show of vestments and of altar plate – far exceeding in every respect the whole of their collection taken together. Still of course we must do our best . . . I had been strongly pressed by a number of our priests to put in a few dozen really [good] vestments, chalices of our own so as to try in this way to save the Holy Father's reputation. But I heard this could not be kept secret, and then the remedy would be worse than the original evil. Many of the bishops will be very much annoyed. Still, as I have said, we must make the best of it.

The vestment incident was symptomatic for Walsh of the basic misconception which the Vatican held about the Catholic Church in Ireland. The changing of a Pope and the replacement of senior Vatican personnel did not affect the situation significantly. Walsh was heavily influenced by his personal experiences in the 1880s and 1890s when he perceived that the Vatican was vulnerable to British lobbying.

The Archbishop of Dublin, ever respectful of the Papacy, sought the greatest possible freedom from the Vatican, where matters of faith and politics shaded into each other. He was a modern, progressive prelate anxious to introduce changes essential to the more efficient administration of the Church and determined to build a better working relationship with all the Roman congregations.[10] The episcopal 'governmental' system lent itself to influence by strong personalities; in Ireland the hierarchy met twice a year while a standing committee met four times (see Appendix I). Walsh was a powerful force on both bodies. Often, however, he chose to lead by example. On one occasion there was a motion before the Maynooth meeting of the hierarchy criticising as undignified and inappropriate the growing use of bicycles by clergy by seminarians. The Archbishop, always a man who believed in taking daily physical exercise, rode the thirty miles from his residence in Dublin to Maynooth not in a carriage but on a bicycle. He made his point and the motion was dropped. Reluctantly, some of his fellow bishops had to agree that the time had come for the Church to regard the bicycle as a fitting mode of transport for clerics – even archbishops.

2 Mannix, Queen Mary and Walsh during Royal visit to Maynooth, 1911

But Walsh did not always have things his own way. The three remaining archbishops were also powerful figures. Moreover, individual bishops – despite the fact that they might preside over small dioceses – could also wield considerable authority by force of personality and specialist knowledge. It might have been expected, however, that the Cardinal ought to be the leader of the Church in Ireland. That was certainly true in the ceremonial sense. By virtue of ability, personality and administrative talent Walsh ought to have been made Cardinal. He was not. That honour went in 1893 to the Archbishop of Armagh, Michael Logue (1840–1924).

Logue was much more conservative politically than Walsh – a factor which was to prove a regular source of friction between Armagh and Dublin. The Cardinal caused general annoyance when he dined with Queen Victoria at the Viceregal Lodge in 1900 and received King Edward VII and King George V and Queen Mary at Maynooth in 1903 and 1911 respectively.[11] It was not that Logue was openly hostile to an emerging nationalism; but he lacked the intellectual subtlety and diplomatic finesse of Walsh. The Cardinal was blunt and sometimes too plain-spoken.

As an indication of how lasting the effects of the events of the 1880s were on Irish ecclesiastical society, over thirty years later an ecclesiastical protégé of Walsh wrote from Rome to the then Minister of External Affairs, Desmond FitzGerald:

The Vatican . . . is fed from these islands by a constant flow of correspondence in denunciation of Ireland, anonymous or deriving from all sorts of individuals whom we can here estimate at their proper worth, but whose credit is not so accurately gauged at a distance. Such letters numerously exist in the Roman Archives and helped to guide Leo XIII's unfortunate incursion into Irish politics of the eighties. Their opinion was preferred to that of loyal Irish Churchmen like Dr. Walsh and Dr. Croke who were reproached and snubbed instead of being called into counsel. It is as if English statesmanship should be directed by the Earl of Northumberland and the correspondence of the *'Morning Post'* and *'Daily Mail.'* In such circumstances Leo XIII sent us Perrico [*sic*].[12]

The Persico mission cast a long political shadow. The author of that statement was Fr Michael Curran, a long-serving secretary to Archbishop Walsh before being given the position, in 1920, as Vice-Rector of the Irish College in Rome.

Although somewhat removed from the Irish situation, that institution and its rectors were to play a central role in Irish ecclesiastical politics. If Mr Casey remained in the Catholic Church from 1916 to 1921, then it was due in no small part to the activities of two men who were strong supporters of Archbishop Walsh and his ideas.

Between 1905 and 1930, the Irish College in Rome had two of the most distinguished rectors in the history of the institution. Michael O'Riordan was perhaps the more brilliant of the two. He held the post from 1905 until his death in 1919. O'Riordan's major publication was *Catholicity and Progress in Ireland*, which was a response to Sir Horace Plunkett's *Ireland in the New Century* – a liberal unionist's view of the Irish question.[13] The Limerick-born priest showed an interest in politics,[14] but he never became involved as did his successor John Hagan, or John O'Hagan as he was sometimes called.

O'Riordan remained a staunch supporter of the Irish Parliamentary Party and of its leader, John Redmond, whom he once incorrectly introduced to Pius X as the holder of Daniel O'Connell's old Clare seat: 'You have a worthy predecessor,' replied the Pope, 'follow him in everything'. But if O'Riordan stood for the Irish Parliamentary Party, his successor represented another political generation, part of which embraced the creed of radical nationalism. John Hagan, who was Vice-Rector from 1904 to 1919, was much more politically committed than his predecessor. In 1913, he outlined his ideas on Home Rule in a pamphlet published in Italian with the sub-title *L'Autonomia Irlandese*.[15] After 1916, Hagan's political education was orientated more towards the radical nationalists.

One historian has written of Hagan that 'perhaps fatherland, while receiving its due meed, was dominating faith a little'.[16] In the political world of 1919–20 it was difficult for Hagan to see where one sphere stopped and another began.

As far as the Vatican and Ireland were concerned, Hagan was reared in the Walsh tradition. He was a member of the Dublin archdiocese and a friend of the Metropolitan. If anything, his experience in Rome led him to hold a more exaggerated form of the Walsh Irish–Vatican thesis.

Hagan was convinced that Irish interests at Rome had been neglected through the centuries due to the absence of a full-time representative at the Vatican. From the Anglo-Norman invasion of 1169 onwards 'almost for five hundred years, I am afraid that England took good care nobody but an Englishman should represent or misrepresent Ireland, or speak of it to the good people of Rome'.[17] Michael Curran, who became Vice-Rector of the Irish College in 1920, shared that view also. He felt that in the 1880s an 'anglophile, anti-Irish spirit possessed the Vatican'. Leo XIII was 'anti-Irish until, perhaps, the closing years of his pontificate and his attitude towards England was always more than conciliatory'. There were three factors, according to the former secretary of Archbishop Walsh, which made Leo XIII 'pro-English'. First, he was impressed by the liberal attitude towards Catholics there, in comparison to the situation in other European countries. Secondly, he maintained 'a passionate desire to achieve the conversion of England'. That was based on the Pope's 'over-sanguine estimate of the effects of the Oxford movement and the strength of the High Church feeling for the recognition of the validity of Anglican orders'. Finally, the spread of the Catholic Church in the English colonies during the period 'coincided with these other factors and supplied another reason for a full, political understanding with England'.[18]

Hagan agreed with Curran that that attitude continued to prevail during the pontificate of Benedict XV (1914–22) when the Pope 'could not look with a very favourable eye on Irish turbulence such as it was sedulously presented to him'.[19]

But just how extensive was British ecclesiastical and political influence at the Vatican? Until 1914, Britain had continued to depend for her representation at the Vatican on occasional 'missions', and on the impact of influential English clerics living in Rome and working within the various congregations. The Rector of the English College was in much the same position as Hagan, while the lay British community in the Italian capital gave the Foreign Office considerable scope for further lobbying. There were, of course, visits to the Vatican by the members of leading English Catholic families.[20] The British, however, were not nearly as well organised in Rome as Hagan believed.

The First World War necessitated a more formal British presence in

Rome, although the idea of full diplomatic relations was completely ruled out. This was provoked by the growing concern in London over the alleged strength of German and Austrian influence at the Vatican; and when Pius X died on 20 August 1914 – within three weeks of the declaration of war – a leading English Catholic, Sir Henry Howard, was charged with representing the King at the enthronement of the new Pope, Benedict XV.[21]

Howard remained in Rome as Envoy Extraordinary and Minister Plenipotentiary 'on special mission' and he was replaced by the Irish-born Count de Salis on 21 October 1916. The latter was a personable and able career diplomat who nevertheless found it difficult to strengthen the standing of his mission to the satisfaction of the Foreign Office, and 'it was commonly said that no one in London heeds him'.[22] De Salis was acutely aware of the negative Foreign Office attitude and commented caustically that they 'think in London that a Catholic British Minister spends his time kneeling to His Holiness when he has an audience, but, as a matter of fact he often spoke very frankly to him, and it would be no good having a minister who did not speak frankly. The Vatican see it and know, and know that this is the only way to get on'. Moreover, there were some in London who thought that the Secretary of State was 'a querulous old woman in petticoats', but many had seen 'what a strong individuality he possessed'. De Salis was in the unenviable position of trying to convince the Foreign Office that his assignment was a demanding one from the diplomatic point of view and called for much the same approach as any other 'ambassadorial' posting. But some members of the Irish community in Rome felt de Salis was in a more privileged position than the accredited envoys to the Vatican. Curran outlined the Irish nationalist viewpoint thus:

Apart from her political, economical and social influence, she has in Curia a Legation with all its officials (respectable spies in the camp, entertainments, machinery for propaganda, etc.). She has two Cardinals (one an ex-Secretary of State), the Dean of the Rota (a cardinalatial post) and a dozen prelates in positions from Mgr. Stanley (drawing actually – *incredibile dictu* — an Italian benefice) down to Dom Philip Langdon O.S.B. Nothing of an international character is done but she hasn't her representative.[23]

Curran's assessment was somewhat exaggerated. The former Secretary of State under Pius X, Cardinal Merry del Val, was strongly pro-British, although his real power passed with the death of his patron. Nevertheless, he continued to carry weight as Secretary to the Congregation of the Holy Office – a post he took over in 1914. His replacement as Secretary of State, Pietro Gasparri, was not a strong admirer of his predecessor. The rivalry between both men was to work well to the advantage of the Irish in Rome. The fact that Merry del Val was pro-British and the sternest critic of Hagan in particular – although disconcerting at times – was not entirely to the disadvantage of the Irish. 'Tell me what side del Val is on and Gasparri and Benedict XV will be on the other side' is far too crude a maxim to apply in the circumstances. But neither the Pope nor Gasparri was overly inclined to be accommodating to a man whose zeal had once questioned their orthodoxy. Hagan was not as vulnerable as he might have thought for as long as he had del Val as a critic, Cardinal Cajetan de Lai of Consistorial was very much in the Merry del Val camp, as was Cardinal William Van Rossum of Propaganda.

But the ecclesiastic 'most responsible' for organising British diplomatic initiatives against Ireland was Cardinal Francis Aidan Gasquet, an authority on Reformation England, and Archivist of the Holy Roman Church. Gasquet had been made a cardinal in May 1914. He had resided in Rome since 1908, when he was nominated to head the Pontifical Commission for the revision of the Vulgate. The Cardinal often took time off from his more scholarly pursuits when the war broke out; the Benedictine monastery of San Calisto 'became a second centre of allied propaganda in the city'. According to a member of his own order, Gasquet 'from the beginning had been an uncompromising champion of the cause of the Allies, and insisted on the absolute necessity of a British diplomatic representative at the Vatican'. He was assisted in his work by his polyglot secretary, Dom Philip Langdon. Both did much 'to dispute the supremacy of the central powers in ecclesiastical circles in Rome, and to ease the approach of British visitors to the Holy See'.[24] Gasquet was no admirer of radical Irish nationalism. He had a mischievous sense of humour. The following is typical of the Irish Tale this capital raconteur used to tell: 'An Irish bricklayer was carrying a hod of bricks to the top of a high building. He went up all right but whether through nervousness or other causes could not find his way down. "Pat", called out the Foreman, "Why don't you come down?" "I can't find my way", says Pat. "Why don't you come down the way you went up?" "Faith and I'll not", said Pat, "sure I came up head first."'[25] Another tale the Cardinal was fond of telling concerned the Irishman caught cursing the Italians. His sister remonstrated: 'But remember the Pope is an Italian', to which he replied: 'Sure don't I know that; but he isn't half as infallible as he would be were he an Irishman.'[26] On another occasion, Langdon came to the Cardinal's study to tell him that Hagan had been spreading a rumour that he was being paid £900 a year to work against Home Rule. 'For £900!!! I would work against Home Rule for half that amount', retorted Gasquet.[27] Hagan would not have been rolling in the aisles at these particular examples of Gasquet's humour.

Initially, both Hagan and Gasquet were on friendly terms. First signs of open conflict between the Vice-Rector and the Cardinal came when both met at the church of San Silvestro in 1914. Gasquet expressed genuine bewilderment at the hostile behaviour of the Irish College toward him. For example, they had not attended his elevation and took no part in the celebrations. A few days afterwards, Hagan set out his grievances to the Cardinal; up to 1910, he had tried to show his 'regard and esteem' for Gasquet and he was at pains to interest Irish bishops in his work on the Vulgate. Reluctantly, he had to take up 'a different line, simply maintaining a friendly attitude and no more'. The initial break between the two men dated from 1910, when Gasquet had an audience at the Vatican on returning from England. Afterwards the Cardinal had 'related how he had drawn attention to the danger it was feared Home Rule would bring to the Faith in Ireland'. Hagan's source was a person who had been present in San Anselmo that evening. At the time, Hagan had pointed out 'how ungracious such an argument sounded from an Englishman's lips'. Following that, the Secretary of State began to mention the existence of such fears to five Irish bishops, who returned home 'carrying with them abiding feelings of irritation at the doubts they had heard expressed in the Secretariat of State concerning the future of the Faith in a self-governing Ireland'. Hagan also claimed that Gasquet had represented Walsh of Dublin as opposed to Home Rule.

Moreover, at his elevation to the cardinalate, Hagan wrote that both he and the Rector of the Irish College did not attend any of the celebrations as a protest against the implication in his address that he claimed to represent England and Ireland. Hagan stated his position bluntly to Gasquet:

I have no fault to find with any man for being an anti-Home Ruler or anti-Irish. I am glad to count among my friends those who may be described as both the one and the other. I hold strong views myself, and I bear no ill-will to those who support the other side, no matter how warmly, provided they play the game. But, when the game took or appeared to take, the form of utilizing the Faith for party purposes there was only one alternative, and that was to be on guard so as to be ready when the time should come to counteract an influence which I could not but regard as unfair and injurious to the best interests of my country.[28]

The following day Gaquet sent a polite letter of reply. He appeared genuinely bemused by the vehemence of the attack. Without going into details, he denied that he had ever used any influence against Home Rule for Ireland:

It is absolutely inconceivable to me how people invent their statements . . . I may say, that *never* either by word of mouth or by letter have I been asked by any layman or ecclesiastic, whether English or Scotch, to do this [raise the danger of Home Rule to the Faith in Ireland]. Had I been so asked I should certainly have refused on the principle, that much harm has been done in our countries by bringing Ecclesiastical authority in politics, that I would never be the means of so doing.

Gasquet felt that it ought to be of no concern what people thought of him, 'but I have so many good Irish friends and have received so much kindness at the Irish College and from yourself personally, that I fear I am not saint enough to say "I don't care". Let us consider the incident closed and believe me.'[29] Hagan neither forgave nor forgot.

Gasquet could also offend the devotionalism and piety of some Irish clerics, as he most certainly did when the Archbishop of Sydney, Dr Kelly, asked while they were travelling together if His Eminence might avert the dangers of the route by reciting the *Itinerarium*, only to receive the reply: 'Never heard of it'. When it was then suggested they say the Rosary the answer remained the same.[30] The Benedictine scholar was a much more complex character than Hagan realised. After the 1916 Rising, on 28 April, Gasquet made the following entry in his diary:

I had an audience with the Pope. He talked about Ireland: the state of insurrection at present, but he seemed quite to understand that the present troubles in Dublin are nothing. He talked a good deal as to the relations between Irish and English and seemed to know the feeling of the Irish College. I told him that I believed nothing would content them unless Archbishop of Dublin (Walsh) was made a cardinal and that for my part I thought, if possible, it would be a good thing. He said it was quite out of the question at present.[31]

The idea of Gasquet proposing that a well-known nationalist like Walsh should be made Cardinal would not have been suspected by anyone in the Irish College. Yet when there was some talk of the Rector of the Irish College, O'Riordan, becoming an archbishop, Gasquet was aghast and entered in his diary: 'This would be most inopportune and give a very bad impression in England. I sent at once for Gainsford. Wilson came and I urged him to go at once unofficially to Mgr Pacelli [later Pius XII] to represent the matter.'[32] O'Riordan was never made an archbishop. It is unlikely, but it is impossible to say with certainty, that Gasquet's intervention was decisive.

It is not surprising that Hagan should have exaggerated British influence in Rome. Because of his preoccupation with 'intrigue' from one quarter, he did not stop to evaluate carefully the relative political strength of the Irish Church lobby at the Vatican. The Catholic Church, apart from the British Commonwealth, was the one international institution which had a liberal sprinkling of Irishmen in senior positions throughout the world. The Irish were strongly represented in the national hierarchies of America, Australia, New Zealand and Canada. There was Cardinal O'Connell of Boston, and Archbishop Daniel Mannix of Melbourne.[33] Others will be mentioned later. The lay and clerical voice of the Irish *diaspora* could be loudly heard in Rome, at times, with a succession of prelates continually passing on *ad limina* visits. The Vice-Rector of the Irish College had a very staunch ally in the Superior General of the Calced Carmelites, Peter Magennis, who came to Rome in 1919. Before his appointment, he had spent a number of years in the United States, where he had befriended members of a new generation of Irish nationalism. The 1916 Rising and the execution of the leaders, followed by the internment of hundreds of men in Frongoch (Wales) and other camps, had helped change the direction of Irish politics. The initiative had slipped away from John Redmond, John Dillon and the Irish Parliamentary Party. Magennis was in New York to welcome the influx of post-1916 political activists. He had played a leading role in the Friends of Irish Freedom since soon after his own arrival in the United States in 1911.[34] The Carmelite Friary in New York was a centre of political activity. It was also a place where men could find temporary accommodation before becoming established. Liam Mellowes was a regular visitor at the Friary and one of Magennis's closest political friends. He also got to know other prominent nationalists at 29th Street: Sean Nunan, Harry Boland, Liam Pedler and Eamon de Valera. Soon after the latter's arrival in the United States in 1919 Magennis moved to Rome.[35]

Hagan and Magennis were the cornerstone of Irish nationalist representation in the city. They were also joined by Patrick Murray, the Superior General of the Redemptorists from 1909 to 1947. The latter was, as Hagan puts it, 'most correct all these stormy years'.[36] He did not involve himself very deeply in Irish political affairs but, when called upon, he did perform some services in a discreet fashion.

The heads of the various Irish houses in Rome, Dominicans, Franciscans, Carmelites and Augustinians, came to the Irish College at least once a week for afternoon tea. It was an occasion when religious and more mundane matters were discussed, sometimes in a rather spirited and robust manner reflecting the various differences of opinion and allegiances on the Irish question. These men, particularly Murray and Magennis, who represented international organisations, had to be extremely careful lest the Irish question might become a cause of friction within their orders.

Hagan's political point of view was not accepted unquestioningly, and divisions within the Irish communities in Rome intensified following the 1916 Rising. A telegram was sent signed by many of the leading members of the Irish ecclesiastical community, voicing disap-

3 Monsignor John Hagan (Right)

4 Most Rev. Dr Peter Magennis, Superior General of the
Carmelite order 1919–31

proval at the armed revolt in Dublin.[37] Among those who signed was the Superior of the Irish Christian Brothers. That order had a large school at Marcantonio Colonna which was founded in 1900 to help combat 'proselytism' in the city. Hagan regarded that mainly 'anglophile' community as containing the 'most active of pro-British propagandists'. There was a strong animus between himself and Evangelist Thayne, a 'pro-British' Christian Brother who worked at the Vatican. The Superior of the Christian Brothers at the time was a Waterford man, Brother Michael Costen, who was a supporter of the Irish Parliamentary Party leader, John Redmond.[38] A decade earlier this Home Ruler would have been regarded as a nationalist. But that was a category which had narrowed following 1916, and as far as Hagan and many others were concerned, Costen, and those who continued to think like him, were simply 'pro-British'. But there were many other Irish religious like Costen in Rome who were slow to accept the emerging Sinn Fein movement. Among those groups were numbered Canice O'Gorman, an Irish Augustinian who later became Commissary General of his order. The latter was a very close friend of Hagan's until a personality clash, which was badly exacerbated by political differences, put them in opposite camps. There were many others who shared O'Gorman's views, a former prior of San Clemente called Nolan, a Jesuit named Edmund Power, a Fr Irwin of the Discalced Carmelites and some senior members of the Franciscans and Redemptorists. The political differences and tensions evident among the Irish ecclesiastical community in Rome simply reflected the divisions felt at all levels in Irish society. The hierarchy had failed to issue a joint pastoral condemning the Rising. Even if the bishops were not scheduled to meet again until October, a statement could have been issued by the Standing Committee (see Appendix I). There is evidence to show that some bishops outrightly condemned the nationalists. Only one bishop, however, said anything that might be loosely interpreted as a justification. The significant thing is that of the thirty-one bishops and auxiliaries, twenty-two remained silent, including the Archbishop of Dublin.[39] Walsh did not make a pronouncement about an event that took place largely in his own archdiocese. Walsh and other leading members of the hierarchy might have been placed in a much more difficult position if the Rising had not been followed by widespread internment and the execution of the leaders. The threat to introduce conscription was met with stiff episcopal opposition. That issue quickly brought support from the Irish *diaspora* in the United States and Australia. Between 1916 and the general election of 1918, some members of the Irish hierarchy moved slowly away from the dwindling Parliamentary Party.[40]

Some members of the hierarchy had been centrally involved in efforts to find a political solution in the post-1916 period. But the Irish Convention of 1917 had not proved to be a success. Home Rule had been placed on the Statute Book in 1914. But partition looked the most likely outcome in the post-1916 period; the hierarchy had good cause to fear the possible effects of this solution for Catholicism in the north of the country.

On 14 December 1918, people went to the polls in Ireland and Britain for the first time since the general election of December 1910; the new Irish electorate was about 1.9 million compared with 690,000 eight years earlier, while it was estimated that some 800,000 of the new voters were women. The fight was between the John Dillon-led Parliamentary Party which held some eighty seats going into the contest, and Sinn Fein – a relatively untried coalition of variegated nationalists who had shown good electoral form by winning three by-elections since 1917. The minuscule Labour Party had decided to stand down in the election in order to leave the way clear for an open fight on the national question.[41]

The Sinn Fein manifesto found its way to the Irish electorate in censored form. But the objectives could not be expunged: they were to establish an independent state by withdrawing all MPs from Westminster and to set up a constituent assembly in Dublin. All efforts were to be made to 'render impotent the power of England to hold Ireland in subjection by military force or otherwise'. Finally, the nationalists hoped to appeal to the Peace Conference 'for the establishment of Ireland as a free nation'.

When the pleas for 'untrammelled national self-determination' were put before the electorate, the result was a victory for Sinn Fein.[42] The Parliamentary Party, which began with eighty seats, was left with six, while Sinn Fein had seventy-three. De Valera defeated the opposition leader John Dillon in his home constituency of North Mayo, taking a seat he had held for over thirty years. Twenty-six unionists were returned; all but three of them were in the North. When Dail Eireann convened on 21 January 1919, only twenty-seven of the sixty-nine deputies representing the seventy-three Sinn Fein seats answered the roll. Over thirty of that number were involuntarily absent from the proceedings for the simple reason that they were 'fe ghlas ag Gallaibh', in jail in other words. Among those were included some of the most prominent names in the movement. That fact, in itself, is of great importance; it meant that documents passed unanimously at this first session had not been scrutinised by the main Sinn Fein leaders. A semi-clandestine government was set up in Dublin. Eamon de Valera, the only surviving commander of the 1916 Rising, was in jail. In his absence much of the day-to-day running of affairs rested on the shoulders of men like William T. Cosgrave in Local Government, Michael Collins in

Finance and Cathal Brugha in Defence. The various departments were housed in trade union offices, city-centre basements and private houses. The Minister and Ministries were constantly on the move in order to avoid detection.

On the same day as the first Dail met in Dublin, Dan Breen and a small band of gunmen shot two policemen dead in Soloheadbeg, County Tipperary, and stole their cargo of explosives: 'What were they but a gang of deserters, spies and hirelings?', Breen wrote later of the RIC – a force composed almost entirely of Irishmen.[43] About that particular ambush, Breen wrote: 'Our only regret was that the escort had consisted of only two Peelers instead of six. If there had to be dead Peelers at all, six would have created a better impression than a mere two.'[44]

But for the Vicar General of Tipperary, Mgr Arthur Ryan, the dead 'Peelers' were 'two of my own dear Tipperary flock, murdered in cold blood on one of our public roads while performing a public duty in protecting civilian property . . . We should show publicly our abhorrence at this inhuman act; we must denounce it and the cowardly miscreants who have been guilty of it.' The Archbishop of Cashel, John Harty, also denounced the attack as 'cold-blooded murder'. At Sunday Mass, the parish priest of Soloheadbeg, John Slattery, said he was glad to know 'the occurrence had met with the condemnation of every person in that parish'. It appears that constables O'Donnell and O'Connell were popular in the area. Both men were in their early fifties. The former was a widower with four children who had lived in Tipperary for over thirty years. The curate in Soloheadbeg described them as 'two inoffensive, kindly policemen'. O'Connell had helped nurse many of his colleagues during the 1918 influenza epidemic. In view of the fact that the incident is considered to have been the opening of the 'Anglo-Irish war', it is quite interesting to quote the local pro-Sinn Fein curate, William Keogh: 'They read with horror of the crime of the Bolsheviks of Russia, but nothing they had done was worse than this frightful outrage which had been committed at our own door.' As far as the incident could be related to Sinn Fein, he concluded: 'Ireland's enemies would try and saddle this crime on the new popular movement striving for her independence, but in that they were wrong. The leaders of the movement were far too logical and Godfearing to countenance such crimes. No party in this country would be more pained by the crime or condemn it more strongly than the leaders of that movement.' Fr Keogh may well have been quite correct. While few would have agreed with Dan Breen's 'cowardly' unilateral action at Soloheadbeg, there was a growing ambivalence among nationalist leaders towards the use of physical force.

There were to be many more Soloheadbeg-style ambushes of

policemen within the following two-and-a-half years. That violence was to be repeatedly condemned by members of the hierarchy as murder. There was an entirely separate issue of how the hierarchy, apart from the campaign of violence, viewed Dail Eireann. Although Logue was not over-enthusiastic, Walsh of Dublin showed as much public support for a purely political cause as he had shown on other occasions in the past. Bishop O'Donnell of Raphoe, soon to become Coadjutor Bishop of Armagh and Cardinal in 1924, was also very much in support of the Walsh view. The degree to which the hierarchy was converted to Sinn Fein remains to be documented elsewhere. There were bishops, such as Charles O'Sullivan of Kerry, who were never reconciled to Sinn Fein. But the leadership of the hierarchy, as represented by Walsh, was cautiously supportive of Sinn Fein moderates. The leadership of the movement was staunchly Catholic. Many prominent politicians associated with Sinn Fein and Dail Eireann were well known in clerical circles. Eamon de Valera had been educated by the Holy Ghost Fathers at Blackrock. He had pursued his academic career as a teacher of mathematics in clerical-run institutions like Carysfort, Rockwell, Belvedere and Maynooth. De Valera had once considered studying for the priesthood. There were other men who were staunch Catholics among the Sinn Fein leaders. William Cosgrave, a long-standing member of the Dublin Corporation, a member of the Irish Volunteers and a 1916 veteran, was Minister for Local Government. He, too, was a devout Catholic. That was certainly so in the case of Sean T. O'Kelly, the speaker of the Dail. Richard Mulcahy in National Defence, Michael Collins in Finance and Arthur Griffith in Home Affairs were also conservative Catholics although that is not how they were perceived by their English co-religionists. They had not been alienated from religion despite their pursuit of radical political objectives.

In so far as Walsh could take credit for this, along with his fellow bishops, the fact remained that the leaders of the post-1916 movement had not been alienated from either religion or from the Church. On the contrary, some exhibited feelings of great devotion. Mr Casey – now a radical nationalist – had been persuaded against shouting 'No God for Ireland'. When Walsh died in 1921, de Valera said: 'Although I had not met his Grace so very often, I felt for him something of the intimate personal affection of a son for a father. You can scarcely realise what confidence it gave to me, a novice, during the three or four years I have been in public life, to feel that there was always one at hand on whom I could rely for ripe counsel and wisdom in any hour of need.'[45] One of the major difficulties in the attempt to establish moderate political control over the somewhat loosely-knit Sinn Fein movement in early 1919 was that many of the most prominent political leaders were in jail. De Valera

5 Eamon de Valera, under guard before his court-martial in Dublin, 1916

was among those who had been picked up in 1918 and was lodged at
Lincoln. There he met a prominent Russian politician who got to know
the Irish leader very well. The Russian seemed to like him very much
but he made one major criticism of him years later: de Valera was too
much influenced by the clergy and the teachings of the Church.[46]
Meanwhile, in Rome, Hagan and O'Riordan viewed the development of
political events at home with considerable interest. The Parliamentary
Party had been swept away by a Sinn Fein movement which was viewed
with suspicion at the Vatican. There were fears that radical Irish
nationalism had been influenced by Bolshevism. Soloheadbeg and other
acts of violence signified the possible drift of Sinn Fein towards
extremism. Hagan interpreted his role in Rome as having a broad
political dimension. He was of the opinion that he should try to correct
many of the biased reports – as he viewed them – which appeared in the
Italian press concerning his country. He also believed that he had the
task of informing the Vatican 'objectively' about the political developments in Ireland.

    When O'Riordan died in 1919, it might have been expected that

Hagan should succeed automatically to the position of Rector. That would make the agent of the Irish bishops a staunch Sinn Fein supporter, with all the complications that that might include. The transfer of power proved awkward. The details are not relevant. But Hagan's promotion was far from automatic. There was major disagreement among the archbishops. Even after his appointment was confirmed in 1920 Logue remained unhappy about Hagan's political views and activities.[47] That disquiet was shared at the Vatican. But Hagan had his episcopal supporters as well as critics. The new Rector was from the Dublin archdiocese. He was a Walsh appointee. During the next ten years he proved a wise choice for those who supported the sensitive and highly subtle political approach of the elderly Archbishop of Dublin. Cardinal Logue and some of the more elderly bishops never lost their misgivings about that appointment. Hagan became agent for the Irish bishops in Rome. But at all times he was a *free* agent.[48]

THE PAPACY, THE BISHOPS AND THE ANGLO-IRISH WAR, 1919–1921

The years 1919–21 are three of the most written about in recent Irish history; from a Church/State point of view they are as misunderstood as they are central to an analysis of politico-ecclesiastical, institutional and personal political relations in the early decades of the State. There has been a tendency to accentuate the confrontational dimension, the clashes between clergy and activists over the use of violence, and the condemnations of the hierarchy as a body or individually. This is not surprising. Perceptions have been shaped by the reminiscences of activists, while no Irish bishop of the period has written his memoirs. But despite the harshness of the confrontations – and they were many and frequent – the parochial nature of Irish politics allowed for relatively close contact between politicians and prelates. Many members of the hierarchy were in a position to make the distinction between the *politicians* and the *gunmen*; prominent leaders of Dail Eireann were less than happy with the 'Soloheadbeg syndrome'. Very few in the Dail went so far as to reject the use of violence totally. But as the violence of the British authorities increased, and the law was brought into disrepute, bishops and nationalist politicians were to move closer together. Hagan was one of the main architects in preserving the delicate balance and harmony between the hierarchy and the politicians during this period. His actions will help explain – in part at least – the continued loyalty of the leadership of Dail Eireann to the Catholic Church even at moments when the bishops were seen to be making statements of an unhelpful nature. There was never any real fear of a rupture between the nationalists and the Church because it was well known in political circles that the tensions and divisions experienced within the leadership of Sinn Fein were reflected, albeit in a more modified form, on the bench of bishops. There were few people in a more privileged or vulnerable position than Hagan who knew in the fullest way possible of the tensions, ambiguities and antagonism within

29

the Irish hierarchy. That knowledge Hagan used to good advantage to preserve harmony between Church and State. Like his patron, Archbishop Walsh, the Rector of the Irish College was among a group of influential clergymen who realised that the events of 1919–21 would be of crucial importance in the history of the island. The Catholic Church had to stand close to the political process and not make the mistakes of the 1880s, when Vatican intervention soured relations unnecessarily between priests and people. There was not so much a need to cultivate the new leaders as to stay close to them and influence the direction of their thought where necessary. That was no great hardship for a man like Hagan and other like-minded clergymen. Their political ideas were more developed – if not more advanced – than some of the main ideologues of Sinn Fein. Irish politicians seldom strayed from the womb of the Catholic Church, where privately they were bound to find some support and shelter.

De Valera escaped from Lincoln jail in February 1919. He made his way back to Dublin, where he was first hidden in the home of Dr Robert Farnan. He was then moved to a distillery on the south side of the city. Arrangements were then made for him to hide for a while in the grounds of Clonliffe College, the seminary for the Dublin archdiocese. De Valera was taken at night to a side gate and admitted by Fr Michael Curran, one of the Archbishop's senior secretaries. He was given a room in the gate-lodge of the Archbishop's residence. Walsh is alleged to have known nothing about the visitor.[1] But it is probable that, for diplomatic and security reasons, he *chose* not to know anything about the matter. During de Valera's stay in the gate-lodge he never met the Archbishop. He had the company of Michael Curran, who was transferred to Rome as Vice-Rector of the Irish College in 1920. If the Archbishop had sought advice on politics from that source at the time, he would have found his secretary surprisingly knowledgeable.

In his Clonliffe hiding-place, de Valera spent most of his time revising a document entitled 'The case for Ireland's independence' which was to be 'presented' at the Peace Conference. The historical section had been written by two Jesuits, the Professor of Education at University College Dublin, Fr Tim Corcoran, and the historian Fr John McErlean.[2] The man chosen for the assignment in Paris was Sean T. O'Kelly, the speaker of the Dail and a member of Dublin Corporation. He was a devout Catholic, an ardent cultural nationalist, and a relatively good French speaker. (His wife, Cait, taught French at University College Dublin.) He was also charged with inviting President Woodrow Wilson to come to Dublin to accept the freedom of the city. Furnished with letters of introduction from the Lord Mayor, O'Kelly arrived in Paris on 7 February, and managed to secure a room at the Grand Hotel with the help of an English commercial traveller whom he had met on the train.[3]

6 From revolutionary to President: de Valera poised to start a football match between Wexford and Tipperary at Croke Park, Dublin on 6 April 1919 two months after escaping from jail; the proceeds went to the Republican Prisoners Fund (*Irish Independent*)

7   Sean T. O'Kelly, head of Dail Eireann mission in Paris, on his way to deliver an appeal to Clemenceau in 1919

Although O'Kelly's assignment was supposed to have been of short duration, he remained on the Continent for the next three years at the head of a Sinn Fein 'diplomatic' mission. Under O'Kelly, a network of 'envoys' was established with operational headquarters in Paris.

One of Kelly's first recruits was a Cork man, Michael MacWhite, who had served during the war in the French Foreign Legion and had been awarded the *croix de guerre*. He was still an officer in the French army when they met in Dublin, in 1919; MacWhite was in political sympathy with Sinn Fein – he had written for Arthur Griffith's paper years before when living in Denmark – and he agreed to smuggle back nationalist documents in his puttees.[4] In Paris, MacWhite secured the publication of some of the documents. He remained in the diplomatic service and, in 1938, served as the first Irish envoy to Italy.

The staff at the Paris 'office' was augmented by the arrival of Joseph Walshe, an ex-Jesuit seminarian who had completed his MA in French under Cait O'Kelly, and another University College Dublin graduate, Sean Murphy. From their somewhat accidental involvement in 'diplomacy', both men were to go on to help establish the diplomatic service of the Irish Free State. Walshe was a gifted linguist, while Murphy was perhaps the more intelligent of the two recruits. The small staff were quickly overburdened with work and at different times George Gavan Duffy and Erskine Childers were sent out to give assistance with propaganda work.[5]

Apart from Childers, one of the main architects of the Irish propaganda campaign was Desmond FitzGerald, a philosopher, poet and journalist, who had considerable experience in Fleet Street. He was an obvious choice to make the necessary contacts among pressmen abroad and take over the running of a copy service in Dublin. FitzGerald, who had been in the GPO in 1916, was also quite well known in London literary circles. He was a founder of the 'Imagist' school of poetry in 1908 along with Ezra Pound and F. S. Flint. The latter was an experienced journalist on whom FitzGerald could rely for introductions.[6]

When FitzGerald took over the Department of Publicity, he found that pamphlets were its main means of propaganda. He changed the policy completely by replacing the weekly list of 'acts of aggression committed by the British in Ireland' with a daily bulletin.[7] The editors of the agencies, Exchange Telegraph, Press Association, Reuter, etc., had explained to FitzGerald that they were bound to print the stories that were reported but they would also send out any other *bona fide* reports they could get. FitzGerald proposed using the wire of the *Freeman's Journal* to send about 300 words a day to the agencies as a counterblast to reports from other sources.[8]

The first issues of the *Irish Bulletin* appeared on 11 November 1919, and it did not miss an issue despite having to move 'office' rather hurriedly thirteen times; and it carried on after the truce on 11 July 1921. The first editor of the clandestine news-sheet was FitzGerald and he was replaced by Erskine Childers after his arrest. Arthur Griffith contributed to it regularly but Frank Gallagher, who later became editor of the *Irish Press*, did most of the writing. In the early stages, Robert Brennan also helped out.[9] An effort was made by Dublin Castle to start a bogus *Irish Bulletin*, but after a few feeble efforts which were produced on captured machinery, it folded up. In no sense could the *Bulletin* be seen as a counter-weight to the news agencies but it was received by many influential journalists, who saw it at least as 'the other side' of the story.

The newsletter was posted in batches to addresses in Liverpool and other centres and redistributed from there. Consignments were also sent to the United States and, of course, to Paris, where Sean T. O'Kelly was operating his office. London remained the most important propaganda centre; Art O'Brien, with support from Dublin, ran a self-determination movement and made repeated efforts to influence the resident international press corps.[10]

In Berlin, an American lady married to a German had started a German–Irish society and she carried on Irish propaganda somewhat ineffectually until 1921, when John Chartres was appointed envoy with Dr Nancy Wyse-Power as his chief assistant. In Madrid, Maire O'Brien set up an office; Brussels and Berne were covered from Paris (MacWhite was later transferred to Switzerland, where Annie Vivanti had already been stationed), as were Austria and Czechoslovakia. What little propaganda work was done in Scandinavia was carried out by Gearoid O Lochlainn, who lived in Denmark; Gavan Duffy also visited Scandinavia.[11]

Sean T. O'Kelly drew support from whatever political source he could find. He recruited Benito Mussolini and his newly-formed Fascist movement to the cause of Sinn Fein, despite the fact that the Blackshirts were responsible for so much street violence in Italy. O'Kelly had also enlisted the support of the literary figure, Annie Vivanti, who was a friend of both Gabriele D'Annunzio and Mussolini. She was married to John Chartres, a shadowy figure who was one of the Sinn Fein envoys. In Italy, O'Kelly attracted the support of the Partito Popolare, led by the priest Luigi Sturzo, who was to visit Ireland briefly in 1925 following his departure from Rome for exile.[12]

Irish affairs received sympathetic coverage in the Christian Democratic daily, *Il Popolo*. But Sturzo kept a more reserved position than some of his fellow deputies on the Irish question. The Fascist press was also strongly pro-Sinn Fein. The Rector of the Irish College, John Hagan, had particularly good relations with the editorial staff of *Il Popolo* and Mussolini's paper, *Il Popolo d'Italia*. In fact, one source has suggested that Hagan used to write quite frequently for the Fascist press on Ireland and that the copy used to be sent through a monsignore.[13]

The Rector of the Irish College was held in very high esteem by the restricted group of nationalist leaders who were privy to the fact that Hagan was giving unstintingly of his time and expertise in the service of the clandestine government. George Gavan Duffy, who was helping out with propaganda work at the Paris office, wrote in appreciation:

I know what your presence and position and influence in Rome have meant to us and to John Bull and I am more than delighted that he has been unable to interfere successfully against you who are the very spirit and voice of Ireland at the Vatican.[14]

For the head of the Irish mission in Paris, Hagan was a man who had rendered a 'valuable service' in Rome 'for so long'.[15]

The Vatican had sent observers to Paris; they were Bonaventure Cerretti and Paschal Robinson. The senior diplomat was Cerretti, who had visited Ireland in late 1918. He had spent a number of years as an envoy in Australia and in Washington where he had got to know members of the hierarchy in both countries, many of whom were either Irish or of Irish origin.[16] Robinson had been born in Dublin, and had worked as a journalist before joining the Franciscan order. Both men were gifted diplomats who were quite sympathetic to Ireland. But they were in Paris to represent Vatican interests and lobby the Peace Conference delegates. Article 438 of the Versailles Treaty determined what was to be done with the German colonies. The question of Catholic missionary interests had to be protected. There was also the problem of Palestine.[17] Neither of the Vatican envoys had much free time to attend to the representations of Sinn Fein.

Hagan had written to O'Kelly just after his arrival in Paris, advising him to see Cerretti. He called, leaving his card. When he did not hear anything, O'Kelly called again only to find that both men were 'out'. He then left a note requesting an appointment but it, too, went unanswered. Hagan intervened. A friend of the Rector's saw Cerretti in Paris and suggested that he should see the Sinn Fein envoy. They finally met on 15 June 1919. O'Kelly found him 'most apologetic for the previous disappointment . . . most pleasant, kind, courteous, and very sympathetic'. The talk lasted nearly half an hour and ranged over a number of topics which Hagan had suggested ought to be raised.

Cerretti agreed that there was biased coverage in the Vatican press relating to the affairs in Ireland but he assured O'Kelly that 'this arose not from any hostility to us but purely from want of knowledge'. He told O'Kelly that many people 'in and around his headquarters' — including those who ran the newspaper — had the impression 'for a long time that Sinn Fein was synonymous with Bolshevism'. Cerretti rejected as without foundation reports that a papal nuncio might be sent to Ireland. O'Kelly took the opportunity to raise the lessons of the Persico mission and 'how such an appointment would be regarded by our friends [the bishops] at home'. Cerretti showed himself to be 'a firm believer in the right of peoples to self-determination, and said that if the big peoples here were logical or consistent they should have seen to it that this right be given to Ireland'.[18] O'Kelly regarded the meeting a great success, but it is probable that he was being far too optimistic in his assessment of Cerretti's position. The Vatican envoy was in no sense a Sinn Fein partisan, but he was sympathetic and he knew the background to the Irish question – as did Paschal Robinson. Cerretti was a close friend of the Secretary of State, Gasparri, and he was also respected by Pope Benedict XV. Moreover, Cerretti was one of Hagan's most valuable contacts and sources of information at the Vatican.

A few days before the hierarchy met at Maynooth, on 21 October 1919, O'Kelly wrote to Hagan that they were expecting 'a big outpouring of British propaganda against Ireland in anticipation of the scheme "of settlement" which Lloyd George's latest committee is preparing and we are taking all possible measures to try and counter this advance'. In 1920, Lloyd George proposed a Bill which was to set up two parliaments in Ireland, one in Belfast and the other in Dublin, and there was also provision for a Council of Ireland, to be made up of representatives from North and South. It was envisaged that the Council of Ireland would vote itself more powers by degrees and that ultimately there might only be one parliament in Ireland. But before these provisions were announced, O'Kelly was telling Hagan that he saw no reason for compromise:

All recent communications from home tell us however that there is no fear as to what the attitudes of the people at home will be no matter what the nature of this new scheme may be. The spirit of the people was never better and all sides at home are reported to be more determined than ever not to be misled and not to be content with Home Rule nonsense of the usual Georgian kind.[19]

At Maynooth, the growth in political violence and the deteriorating situation in the countryside was on the agenda. Owing to illness, the Archbishop of Dublin did not attend either the Standing Committee or general meeting. His absence was of considerable political consequence. Cardinal Logue wanted to ensure that a firm statement would be issued on the state of the country. In response, the Standing Committee had drawn up a draft which dealt with the general state of unrest in the country, the increasing crime and the 'circulation of novel opinions'. The following day, there was 'considerable discussion' on the statement – probably a euphemism for sharp division. Some prelates felt that the bishops had to speak out on the questions of unrest, increasing crime and the 'circulation of novel ideas', while others felt that a statement would depress the friends and encourage the enemies of the Irish cause. Some of the bishops, who supported the latter position, argued that a statement at that time would be 'inopportune'. The matter was put to a vote and the bishops were found to be evenly divided on the question. As a consequence the matter was dropped.[20]

In the following months, the violence in the countryside increased. By the middle of 1920, the IRA had killed fifty-five policemen and wounded seventy-four more. Some 340 vacated RIC barracks had been destroyed, 104 damaged; of those still garrisoned, 12 were completely destroyed and 24 damaged in guerrilla attacks.[21] There were a number of incidents which highlight the lack of quarter being shown by either side in the struggle. In March, an elderly constable with twenty-four years' service in the RIC was returning from the funeral of a murdered colleague in Tipperary when he was shot in a Cork street. Within hours, a group of men with blackened faces carried out a reprisal raid on the home of the Lord Mayor, Tomas MacCurtain, and killed him in bed. The Bishop of Cork, Daniel Cohalan, wrote some months later to a politician friend, encouraging him to see that the matter was raised in the Commons. There he wanted his 'offer or challenge' repeated that '*if an independent, trustworthy commission is set up, positive convincing evidence will be submitted that District Inspector Swanzy was implicated in the murder of Lord Mayor MacCurtain*'.[22]

Two months before that shooting, the hierarchy had issued a joint statement highly critical of government policy and actions which had been modified substantially from what had been originally proposed to the general meeting of the bishops in October 1919. The bishops blamed the government for the state of the country: 'The principle of disregarding national feelings and national rights, and of carrying everything with the high hand, above the head of the people, has, we are sorry to say, brought about the dreadful confusion and disorder from which the country, unhappily, suffers, and which we view with deepest distress.' The 'legitimate demand of Ireland' had been denied and 'every organ for the expression of her national life had been ruthlessly suppressed, and her people subjected to an iron rule of oppression as cruel and unjust as it is ill-advised and out of date'. The result is 'violent collisions and retaliations between exasperated sections of the people and the forces of oppression growing ever more serious, and eventuating too often in the most sorrowful tragedies on both sides'. The bishops appealed for 'an undivided Ireland to choose her own form of government'. That statement marked a victory for the bishops, who had argued in October against a strong statement likely to alienate nationalists. The blame for the violence in the country was placed squarely on the shoulders of 'the advocates of military rule in Ireland'.[23] It is quite important to note that the bishops were not in favour of singling out the nationalists exclusively for blame. The fault ultimately lay, according to the January statement, with the government.

Cardinal Logue was almost certainly not pleased with the final wording. He was quite explicit about how he felt when confronted by the deteriorating political situation:

Not within living memory can we find in Ireland such calamitous conditions as exist at present. Drastic repression on one side, retaliation on the other; a military regime rivalling in severity even that of countries under the most pitiless autocratic government; on the other side lawlessness, retaliation and crime such as any man guided by God's law must regret and reprobate . . . it is not only our duty but our interest to unite in a determined effort to discourage and root out lawlessness and crime from our midst.

But the ailing Archbishop of Dublin, Walsh, did not take quite the same view as the Cardinal. He followed the logic of the January statement, although he chose to use much more direct language. His Lenten pastoral for 1920 was pessimistic in tone, stating that the situation in the country gave more cause for 'apprehensions than hopes', where 'people were now shut out by law from employing methods of seeking redress which, they will know, were in the past fully recognised as constitutional' and it would be 'unreasonable, and indeed impossible, to expect that they can rest content with such a state of things'. Walsh had made his own position even clearer six months earlier. On 10 November 1919, two weeks after a meeting of the national conference of Irish bishops which he could not attend owing to ill health, he sent a cheque for a hundred guineas to Cardinal O'Connell of Boston for the Dail loan – an international effort to collect money to fund the activities of the clandestine government. He did so because 'none of our papers dare publish the fact'. He told the Cardinal:

We are living under martial law, and amongst the numerous devices to which our present Government has had recourse in its foolish attempts to crush the national spirit of our people, is the issuing of sundry military orders. In one of these they have given notice to the editors or managers of our popular newspapers of the fate that awaits any newspaper venturing to publish the names of contributors . . . All this has had its natural effect – the driving of disaffection underground, with no less natural result than an outlet in crime. The 'competent military authority' does not seem to realise that there is no possible remedy for this lamentable state of things, so long as the source of all the evil, the present system of military rule, is maintained.

Walsh was supported in his views by the Archbishop of Tuam, Thomas Gilmartin, who said that if a people thought that they were being misgoverned then they had a 'right and a duty' to seek a change provided, of course, they kept within the moral law: 'In this country at present people are engaged in a struggle for the natural right of self-government. I call it a natural right, for a distinct nationality such as we are, has a natural right within the limits of the moral law to govern itself. In such a struggle, strong passions must be aroused and individuals may lose sight of the moral axiom that the end, no matter how noble, does not justify immoral means.' Archbishop John Harty of Cashel left his flock in little doubt as to what he felt about the competence of Dublin Castle:

We are living under a government which has proved itself an abject failure. Neither based on the consent of the nation, nor working for the good of the community as a whole, it has trampled on the will of the people, and has upheld the ascendancy of a pampered minority. Furthermore, it has excelled in acts of repression and coercion. History tells us that where such a system reigns, the laws of God are set aside. Coercion and crime go hand in hand, and peaceful citizens are made the victims of the vicious circle . . . The remedy for the Irish upheaval is obvious, since freedom is the best solvent of political disorder.[24]

The depth of feeling on the bench of bishops – and it is quite clear that by April 1920 there was a division within the hierarchy on the political question – reflected the intensity of political emotion in the country. Ireland had been denied the opportunity to select the form of government appropriate to her needs. There was the prospect of partition, which was not welcomed by the bishops. On 13 April, the Standing Committee of the Catholic Hierarchy passed a resolution demanding that persons who had been detained in prison and not brought to trial ought to be treated with marked humanity. The resolution concluded: 'The cry we utter today is the cry of humanity.'[25]

Meanwhile Sean T. O'Kelly had concluded his personal assignment in Paris. He sent a letter of resignation to the Minister for Foreign Affairs, Count Plunkett, in early 1920. Before returning to Ireland, he decided to spend a few weeks in Rome with his friend at the Irish College. He arrived on 9 February, when he was confined to bed for fourteen weeks. O'Kelly was very seriously ill. He was nursed back to health by the Little Sisters of Mary, known popularly as Blue Sisters, who worked in the college.[26]

Hagan learned in May 1920 from a Vatican contact that a document had been prepared condemning Irish nationalist violence. The sources are very vague on the author of the alleged 'fulmination'. The task may have been assigned to Cerretti, the Secretary of the Congregation for Extraordinary Ecclesiastical Affairs, or a number of opinions may have been sought in the preparation of the document. While it is not known how far advanced was the preparation, it is more likely that Hagan was as well informed as ever about what was happening in the Vatican. The

Rector gave the impression that the document was soon to be sent to the Pope for his approval before it was to be forwarded to the Irish hierarchy. Hagan encouraged O'Kelly to request an audience with the Pope as a matter of priority. He was quite reluctant to do so but then decided to proceed on the basis that he was speaker of the Dail. O'Kelly next went to see Cerretti, which might lead one to believe that he was the source of Hagan's information. He instructed O'Kelly to draw up a paper presenting the nationalist case. Cerretti also tutored him in the type of questions he was likely to receive from Benedict XV. The audience was to take place on 12 May 1920. Hagan immediately agreed to draw up the draft document. He may have been helped in his task by Magennis.[27] But when O'Kelly read the draft he recoiled at the directness of the language and sentiments expressed by the authors. O'Kelly had had a similar fit of nerves when he read Tom Johnson's draft of the Democratic Programme – the statement of Dail Eireann Social principles and aspirations – at the beginning of 1919. But on this occasion he had a little more cause for anxiety.

Hagan's draft referred to 'much water with not a little blood' flowing under the bridges in recent years, as Ireland strove for self-determination based on 'the noble principles laid down in Your Holiness's peace note to President Wilson'.[28] He argued against 'ill-considered' acts or pronouncements which could cause pain to 'our Catholic people at Rome and the fifteen or twenty missions of Catholics of Irish blood' who formed 'a powerful factor in civil life' and were the 'backbone' of the Church in America and Australia. He referred to the damage done to Irish Catholicism by the intervention of Leo XIII in the 1880s and to the 'anti-Irish bias' in the Catholic press of Rome – in particular, the *Osservatore Romano*. Hagan also used a comparison with Poland: 'we have lost homes and land, have been reduced to poverty and have had to seek a living under alien flags'. Because of its historic traditions and of its sufferings, Poland – a country whose cause the Pope had championed – had endured: 'I need not waste time in pointing out that on both grounds [suffering for the faith and historic tradition] Poland's claims are small indeed in comparison with those of Ireland.'

The Rector went much further than any of the Irish bishops in his draft when he referred to the 'real or pretended outrages' by nationalists:

Ireland is an armed camp occupied by a large army of British troops and all the appliances of modern warfare; that the people are subjected to every sort of provocation that they cannot take the field, but as long as human nature is human nature, individuals or sections of the community can hardly be restrained if in revenge for savage acts of repression they take the law into their own hands and wreak vengeance that is within their grasp. But there is not the slightest proof that the Sinn Fein organisation has any responsibility for these deeds.

There is something touchingly naive about that statement. When Fr Keogh rejected any likely connection between Sinn Fein and the Soloheadbeg killings in early 1919, there was an excuse for confusion. That was the first attack by nationalists in the Anglo–Irish war. But events had moved on rather swiftly since then and the IRA were in the field. Nevertheless, Hagan's draft points to the fact that he wants to have it believed that there was a radical distinction between the political wing of Irish nationalism and its 'physical force' counterpart. The Rector seemed to imply that acts of violence were nothing more than popular reaction to 'savage acts of repression'. Hagan was furious when O'Kelly rejected the document; he tore up the typed version but a written draft has survived. Both Curran and O'Kelly set about drafting a more moderate expression of the nationalist case. In the new document, Ireland was described as a Catholic nation 'enslaved by a Protestant power', denied its freedom by the machinations of continental anti-clericalism and freemasonry. The authors applauded the 'unswerving neutrality' which the Pope had 'observed in the struggle of the Irish nation for the preservation and extension of our beliefs'. When the document was finally ready, O'Kelly took it to Cerretti, who may have made further suggestions to amend the text. O'Kelly was then coached on the various questions to expect from the Pope and tutored on what answers would be the most appropriate.[29]

O'Kelly went to the papal audience on 12 May 1920 in 'fear and trembling'. He was with Benedict XV for nearly three quarters of an hour. The Pope was well informed about the Irish situation and expressed great concern about the ambushing and killing of RIC men. He did not appear to be too impressed by Sinn Fein arguments in defence of the use of violence. According to O'Kelly, Benedict suggested 'that we should go out and fight them openly with our men, armed and uniformed'. In no sense was that papal approval of Sinn Fein violence. He admonished the Irish envoy on two occasions during the audience: 'Ireland has every right to its independence, Ireland has every right to fight for its independence but remember my words, be careful of the methods you use.' He added: 'I think you should not shoot police and I think you should consider this question of ambushes.' As the audience drew to a close, O'Kelly insisted – as he had been instructed by Cerretti – that the Pope should read the document he had prepared on the Irish case. Benedict reluctantly agreed to take the paper. There was no condemnation issued by the Vatican.[30]

But rumour of such a move died slowly in Rome. The visit of the

British Cabinet Minister, A.J. Balfour, a month later was sufficient to give new life to denunciation fears. De Salis wrote to the Foreign Secretary, Lord Curzon:

I had indeed some occasion to speak on the subject [Irish–Vatican denunciation] before, when I found it necessary to relate to Mgr. Cerretti at the Secretariat of State how, according to what a distinguished Australian bishop of Irish origin had told me, a certain Irish prelate has assured him as a positive fact that negotiations had been going on through this legation between His Majesty's Government and the Vatican for the conclusion of a bargain detrimental to Irish interests. The Bishop had begun by admitting himself convinced of the absurdity of such an idea; I had given him leave to think what he liked about myself but asked him whether he was free to call in question an assurance given to the Holy See or to suggest the possibility of discreditable action on their part. Mgr. Cerretti showed annoyance and said he had told the Irish prelate himself that there was absolutely no grounds for his suggestion and suspicions; that should have been sufficient for him.[31]

It is probable that this is a reference to Hagan. But it could also have been — although this is rather unlikely — any one of the prelates who travelled to Rome for the beatification on 23 May 1920 of Oliver Plunkett, who had been hanged, drawn and quartered in 1681.[32] There was every possibility that the occasion could be turned into a nationalistic celebration. The visiting Irish prelates were aware of the draft condemnation, which the Vatican had not released. Obviously, some of the Irish bishops had made their feelings on the matter known to Vatican authorities during their stay. Nationalist sentiment was running high in Rome. De Salis reported to the Foreign Office that although it was commonly accepted that Plunkett was unjustly executed, there was just a hint that the whole affair was being given something of a contemporary flavour by political figures in Rome.[33] An unfortunate incident occurred a few days before the ceremonies which tended to reinforce the point made by the British envoy. The incident was headlined in *The Times* as 'Irish intrigue in Rome, story of an anonymous letter'.[34] Mgr Stanley, an English canon of St Peter's, was scheduled to officiate at the beatification Mass. This was a matter of coincidence. He received an anonymous letter beginning 'you old blackguard'. Another letter, 'with even more objectionable expressions', according to de Salis, was received by Merry del Val. The British envoy went to see the Cardinal and expressed the hope that he would not take the matter too seriously 'as such incidents were a daily occurrence in Ireland'. '"That", he said, "is just what Cardinal Logue had been here to tell me. I have accordingly asked him whether he was satisfied that such things should happen every day among his flock."' *The Times* report discounted the interpretation that the letter was the

8 Sean T. O'Kelly and Oliver St John Gogarty in St Peter's Square on 23 May 1920 on the occasion of the beatification of Archbishop Oliver Plunkett. (Courtesy of Fr J. Dempsey, PP, Garristown, Co. Dublin)

work of a Sassenach *agent provocateur* as finding 'no credence anywhere'. De Salis reported that the Vatican had a shrewd suspicion of who wrote the letters and was exceedingly displeased. Suspicion immediately fell on Hagan, who contemptuously dismissed the rumours. It is certain that Hagan had not written either letter. But the

minor incident demonstrates the charged nature of the political
atmosphere in Rome around the time of the beatification.

The beatification was a joyful occasion for the Irish in Rome.
O'Kelly was present in St Peter's Square. To his surprise, when the
ceremonies were over, he found himself surrounded by Irish seminaries
who pressed him to make a short address from his motor car. The
incident did not go unnoticed by Vatican authorities or by the Pope.
O'Kelly decided to follow the example of the French Ambassador who
gave a reception after the canonisation of Joan of Arc. The 'government
of the Irish Republic' would follow suit. The year 1920 had been set aside
for English-speaking bishops to make their *ad limina* visit to the Pope.
That meant there were many other important prelates of Irish extraction
in the capital, including Cardinal O'Connell of Boston. The reception
was set to take place in the Grand Hotel on 27 May. O'Kelly had the task
of persuading all the Irish bishops, including Cardinal Logue, to attend
what was, in effect, a propaganda coup for Dail Eireann. With the
assistance of the Lord Mayor of Dublin, Larry O'Neill, and the
promptings of Hagan and Curran, the Cardinal said he would
participate. O'Kelly has left this account: '"Oh dear", said the Cardinal
hesitantly, "I thought you, Lord Mayor, had more sense . . . I suppose if
I have to go I had better say I will go. I will go alright." He added, "I
don't know what you are dragging me into. I don't know what trouble I
am going to get out of this. But anyhow, I will go."' O'Donnell of
Raphoe, once a strong supporter of the Parliamentary Party, also agreed
to go. He told O'Kelly that the votes of the Irish people (1918 election)
had decided the issue 'and that he would go to the party being given in
the name of the government of the Irish Republic'.

The reception seemed to have gone off quite well although it was
marred by the late arrival of Cardinal Logue, who had 'forgotten' his
snuff-box and had to return to the Irish College to collect it. He arrived
into the hall to find the Bishop of Clonfert, Thomas O'Doherty, singing
the nationalist song 'Wrap the Green Flag around me' with 'great verve
and enthusiasm'.[35] O'Kelly then said a few words in Irish and English,
under the 'republican' flag: 'At the end of a couple of hours, the
orchestra struck up "The Soldiers' Song", and 600 men – archbishops,
bishops, prelates, priests, doctors, lawyers, university professors,
students of the Irish College, Propaganda and American Colleges, of the
Franciscans, Carmelites, Dominicans, Augustinians, the Irish Christian
Brothers – sang the stirring anthem amid enthusiastic scenes.'[36]

In another incident, which may not have come under the notice of the
Vatican, Cardinal O'Connell of Boston spoke at the Irish Dominican
house of San Clemente.[37] Logue and other bishops were in attendance
along with many of the most prominent members of the Irish religious

community in Rome. The Cardinal said in his speech that the hierarchy should 'stand with their people'. It was the duty of the bishops to 'place themselves at the head of those who were in the battlelines'. Such sentiments were often uttered by clergymen of Irish extraction who lived far from the whiff of grapeshot. Those closer to the action tended to be more discerning.

The Grand Hotel reception should not be taken as representative of the normal behaviour of the Irish hierarchy. There were major political divisions on the bench of Irish bishops. Those divisions were to grow in the latter part of 1920, as unease over the moral basis for the more violent actions of the IRA increased. It was difficult to sustain the view that the growing violence in the country was due exclusively to the aggression and repression of the civilian population by the British.

In the light of what was happening in Ireland, it is little wonder that de Salis reported that 'some scandal had arisen' in Rome as a result of the gathering, which was 'in striking contrast to the solemn dignity with which ecclesiastical receptions are conducted in Rome'. It was no accident that the 'goings on' of the Irish were reported in *The Times* on 29 May. On 2 June a leading article in the same paper asked whether the Vatican 'realised what feelings such an open act of sedition is calculated to produce in loyal British subjects'. There was a semi-official response from the Vatican on 10 June, claiming that it was in no way responsible for what might be done privately among Irishmen, lay or ecclesiastical. No members of the curia were present. In fact, the only non-Irish ecclesiastics to attend the Grand Hotel meeting were Mgr Tizi, a general factotum at the Irish College, and Mgr Salotti, the principal advocate in the cause of Oliver Plunkett.[38] De Salis tried to explain to the Foreign Office that the Vatican was not free to chastise the clergy or members of the hierarchy in the area of politics:

The clergy in various countries are left free, as I have frequently had occasion to explain, to follow their own idea in political matters and this liberty has been freely used by ecclesiastics of the new states formed in the course of the recent struggles. In this case there have been unseemly demonstrations in Rome itself and the impartiality with which the Vatican aims at surrounding itself has been invaded.[39]

If it is possible to rely upon O'Kelly as a source in this respect, Benedict XV does not appear to have been too upset by the incidents. But some curia members, such as del Val, might have been expected to have been annoyed rather than terribly surprised by Irish behaviour. Before leaving Rome, O'Kelly was summoned to the Vatican on 28 June for a private audience with the Pope. Benedict had been following recent local events among the Irish community with a keen interest. He had witnessed, from his private rooms in the Vatican, the commotion in the square on the day of the beatification and remarked on the fact to a surprised O'Kelly. He enquired about the reception and O'Kelly explained that it was a meeting attended by clergy from Rome and the Irish *diaspora*. The Pope seemed quite satisfied, and according to O'Kelly, said: 'You had every right to hold such a reception. I don't know what right anyone has to object to your doing so . . . I know what to say to the people who are trying to make trouble.'[40]

Had Curzon realised that the Pope was so well disposed towards the Irish, he might not have tried in July to have an apostolic visitor sent to report first-hand on the situation. There was little possibility of changing the direction of Irish politics through the intervention of the local bishops. After the Grand Hotel episode, the Foreign Office may have mistaken the *bonhomie* of the bishops and O'Kelly in Rome for political solidarity. The hierarchy was, in fact, very deeply divided since 1919 on the question of Irish politics. It was, however, united in its opposition to the idea of any direct intervention in Irish politics by the Vatican. De Salis reported discouragingly:

At one moment the despatch of a special delegate to Ireland to report on the situation came under consideration, but here there was considerable reluctance on the part of Cardinal Gasparri himself. The facts seemed to be sufficiently notorious, and enquiry by a delegate could go very near to an investigation into the political condition of the country. Ultimately, after a delay, the whole question was submitted to the Congregation of Foreign Affairs. As to what happened I do not profess to be able to speak with certainty.

While the political nature of the Irish problem made it particularly difficult for the Vatican, de Salis felt that, as crime was being committed, it was right to warn the faithful that they could not take part in a political movement unless and until sinful methods were abandoned:

Such was more or less the view favoured in London and, as far as I can form an opinion, the Congregation was not inclined to reject it; in that case it would be due to higher authority that it was not definitely adopted. Such an explanation is at least plausible. The attitude consistently maintained by Benedict XV, the conviction, the fixed idea of his policy that the part of mediator was the one which the Pope could best play, may well have stood in the way of his taking a step which his advisers favoured.[41]

The suggestion that the Pope had opposed an idea favoured by his advisers might well have been a rationalisation, on the part of de Salis, for his own inability to influence Vatican policy towards Ireland. But it is much more likely that Benedict XV, with the support of Gasparri, saw no reason to depart from established policy in such a sensitive area. The Pope might act as an intermediary favouring a peace initiative; but he would not intervene unilaterally.

Curzon had even greater cause for apprehension when it was learned that Archbishop Mannix of Melbourne – by now an ardent nationalist who was far less prudent than even the most 'imprudent' of the Irish bishops – was intending to visit the United States and Ireland while on his way to Rome for his *ad limina* meeting with the Pope. Controversy followed Mannix. As President of Maynooth, in 1909, he had been involved in the dismissal of the noted Gaelic scholar, Fr O'Hickey, from the teaching staff.[42] That did not endear him to the cultural nationalists of the day. In Australia, he had developed 'a taste for politics', which brought him into conflict with the Labour Prime Minister, William Hughes, particularly on the question of conscription. The 'very violent language' used by the prelate in the course of the controversy brought warnings from the departing apostolic delegate, Mgr Cerretti, and his successor, Mgr Cattaneo. He was urged to use 'prudence and moderation'.

In summer 1918, Hughes asked de Salis to request Mannix's recall from Australia, otherwise the Australian government would be compelled to take action themselves:

To this the assent of the Vatican was by no manner of means to be obtained. Though his language was disapproved of in Rome, Dr Mannix had not brought himself within reach of deprivation under the Canon Law: his employment in Rome was out of the question, while his transfer to Ireland was scarcely the solution desired by anyone. The Cardinal Secretary of State insisted that the further use of violent language after the receipt of the Vatican warnings was not supported by evidence.[43]

A former governor of Tasmania, Western Australia and New South Wales, Sir Gerald Strickland, had suggested the move to the Pope at an audience in late 1919, saying he 'thought the agitators in Ireland were so numerous and virulent that one more or less would be hardly noticeable'.[44]

That line may well have been delivered rather flippantly, but there was concern at the Foreign Office in summer 1920 that that might be all too likely a prospect. Walsh was very ill and the archbishopric of Dublin was likely to fall vacant within a few months. It was rumoured that Mannix's name would be put forward for the most important ecclesiastical post in the country. Moreover, it was no secret that he would have liked to return to Ireland. De Salis was instructed to advise the Vatican of the undesirability of appointing a person of known anti-British sentiments to Dublin. He was further instructed to inquire whether it would be possible to find a post for Mannix outside the United Kingdom.

De Salis did not particularly like raising this matter. He was informed by Gasparri that Archbishop Walsh was still very much alive and that there was an auxiliary, Mgr Edward Byrne, 'whose claims to the succession were . . . when the see became vacant, considered to be well-founded'.[45] The groundless rumour of the Mannix 'candidature' still persisted into late July, when de Salis wrote that the suggestion had 'not even the appearance of probability'.[46] In the intervening period, Mannix had made some extreme nationalistic statements in the United States. In response, a Foreign Office official, Alexander Cadogan, had minuted on 22 July:

The Vatican ought to be in a position to prevent him from openly preaching sedition and conducting a campaign with the avowed object of promoting ill feelings between England and America. Count de Salis should call serious attention to the utterance and performance of the Archbishop and express the very definite hope that the Pope will signify his disapproval of his political activities. I hope we shall not allow the Archbishop to land in Ireland.[47]

De Salis came under the most intense pressure from the Foreign Office to get results at the Vatican. The envoy had written that he could not get the Vatican to prevent Mannix from going to Ireland. One Foreign Office official appeared so upset about the 'weakness' of the envoy's performance that he did not see much point in having a representative at the Vatican if he could not take measures to safeguard their interests. Curzon found de Salis's reply 'profoundly unsatisfactory' and as 'reflecting neither credit on Count de Salis nor on the Vatican'.[48] The British envoy was instructed to hint at a break in Anglo-Vatican relations if Mannix were to be appointed. The much-maligned envoy responded that the Vatican was 'alive to the absurdity' of any such appointment. He considered it inadvisable to contemplate playing the strongest diplomatic card 'to prevent what is not going to happen. It is not a card you can play very often.'[49] De Salis found it extremely difficult to convince his superiors in London that the Vatican was not in a position to stop Mannix making political statements, while the rumoured appointment of the Archbishop of Melbourne to Dublin was simply outside the bounds of possibility. Nevertheless, some people at the Foreign Office remained very critical of Vatican inaction:

What we object to is the systematic and avowed preaching of hatred and vilification by the Archbishop. It is impossible to make us believe that the Vatican could not stop this if it wanted to. It does not want to, and we take note of this, just as we noted the Vatican's persistent refusal to condemn the German outrages in Belgium.[50]

Mannix was prevented from landing in Ireland. He was arrested aboard a passenger liner as it lay off Cobh; he was taken by destroyer to Penzance, from where he was allowed to travel to London. The Archbishop remained in England, where his travel was restricted, until

March 1921.[51] His presence was a source of some discomfort to Cardinal Bourne and a number of English bishops. Meanwhile, in Ireland the violence intensified in the latter half of 1920 as the authorities tried the roughest tactics to counter the attacks of the IRA. From June to December 1920, 122 policemen were killed, compared with 55 from January 1919 to June 1920. Over 150 were wounded while nearly 50 troops had died in action.[52]

One of the many people arrested during this period was Terence MacSwiney, the Lord Mayor of Cork. He had replaced the murdered Tomas MacCurtain. MacSwiney was convicted by court-martial and sentenced to two years' imprisonment. He went on hunger strike and died in Brixton prison on 25 October 1920 after a fast lasting seventy-four days.[53] His ordeal had attracted international attention and protest meetings were held in many countries. In Italy, MacSwiney was supported by both Mussolini and the Partito Popolare.[54] In Ireland, the case gave rise to considerable reflection on the morality of hunger strikes. In prison, MacSwiney had been visited by Bishops Cohalan of Cork, O'Sullivan of Kerry and Browne of Cloyne as well as by a number of English prelates of Irish extraction.

Less than a week before the death of MacSwiney, the Irish bishops met in Maynooth and discussed the deteriorating situation in the country. The statement released afterwards was one of the most forceful documents ever issued by the hierarchy. In the first paragraph, emphasis was laid on the failure of government as the cause of the violence. It was not easy, the bishops stated, for the pastors of the flock to uphold the Law of God and secure its observance when repression was rampant in a country: 'Where terrorism, partiality, and failure to apply the principles which its members have proclaimed, are the characteristics of government, the task is well-nigh impossible . . . Ireland is now reduced to a state of anarchy.' The Press was 'gagged', the 'right of public meeting interdicted, and inquests suppressed'. The pastoral outlined the behaviour of the military, indiscriminate raids and arrests in the darkness of night, prolonged imprisonments without trial, savage sentences from tribunals that commanded and deserved no confidence, the burning of houses, town halls, factories, creameries and crops. All this was to pave the way for want and famine and was carried out by men 'maddened with plundered drink and bent on loot' who had established in the country 'a reign of frightfulness which, for murdering the innocent and destroying their property, has a parallel only in the horrors of Turkish atrocities, or in the outrages attributed to the Red Army of Bolshevist Russia'. The bishops stated that when Ireland was 'still crimeless' they had warned the authorities of the consequences of using 'oppressive measures'. But the warning was in vain. Before the

9 Guests of the nation: British forces in Cork, 1920 (*Cork Examiner*)

First World War, and 'especially before the drilling and arming of Ulster', Ireland, 'however insistent on reform too long delayed, was in a state of order and peace'.

But how was the hierarchy to formulate a condemnation of nationalist violence without bringing political differences to the fore? The solution was rather sophisticated. A line stating 'Needless to say, we are opposed to crime, from whatever side it comes' was included and then the pastoral went on to quote Cardinal Logue's eloquent condemnation of the murder of a policeman which had been published two months earlier. The passage reinforced the main argument of the pastoral that the violence in Ireland was the result of 'living under a harsh, oppressive, tyrannical regime of militarism and brute force' – the words used by Logue. Two months after the Cardinal had written those lines the hierarchy agreed that the situation had become much worse: 'Men have been tortured with barbarous cruelty. Nor are cases wanting of young women torn, undressed, from their mothers' care in the darkness of night.' All that was taking place in the South while 'the carnage of sectarian riots on a vast scale has been allowed to run its course in the cities and towns of Ulster'. The hierarchy questioned the wisdom of setting up a separate state where such sectarianism was rife: 'It is not hatred of coercion that operates in Ireland, but partiality for the North-East.'

The pastoral also referred to the 'brutal treatment of clergymen', and the exclusion of Mannix was described as 'one of the most unwise steps that purblind and tyrannical oppression could take'.

The continued imprisonment of MacSwiney was regarded as cruel. The bishops urged people to remain steadfast in their faith: 'It is for a nation of martyrs to cultivate constant self-restraint. Our people were a great Christian nation when pagan chaos reigned across the Channel. They will remain, please God, a great Christian nation when the new paganism that now prevails there has run its evil course.'[55] Pastorals from the national hierarchy have rarely been characterised by such forthright language. But the bishops were meeting at a very tense political moment. There was sectarian violence in the north-east of the island, military and nationalist violence in the south, while Terence MacSwiney was fast approaching death. The Lord Mayor had been on hunger strike for nearly seventy days on 19 October, the day of the Maynooth meeting. On the same occasion, the hierarchy also took the unusual decision to set up a publications committee, of five bishops and the President of Maynooth, which was funded by each diocese. Its mandate was to see that the statements coming from the bishops were circulated widely in Great Britain, Europe, America and Australia. This wide circulation of their views was a dominant feature of many of the pastorals and statements at the time. Close contact was established with hierarchies in Europe and especially in America.[56]

As has often happened before in Irish history, funerals became the occasion for huge public protest. On 20 October 1920, the *Freeman's*

10 Vigil outside Cork jail for hunger striker Michael Fitzgerald, who died in
1920 (*Cork Examiner*)

Journal carried pictures of crowds outside Cork jail following the death
of Michael Fitzgerald; he was an untried prisoner from Fermoy who died
after a long hunger strike. While the coffin 'lay in state' in the church of
SS Peter and Paul, a British officer carrying a revolver entered it and
ordered Canon O'Leary to read a notice stating that only one hundred
people could walk in procession behind the coffin. A large crowd had
gathered outside when six lorries of soldiers and an armoured car took
up position near the church. The officer in charge said his orders were to
fire if more than a hundred followed the coffin. Such was the
atmosphere in the city. The funeral followed without incident at
Fermoy. The tension in the country was reflected in an editorial in the
Freeman's Journal (21 October 1920) entitled 'The Shame of it', where
the paper castigated the Chief Secretary, Hamar Greenwood, for
justifying 'reprisal' raids by the military around the country:

'Reprisals are justified (loud cheers).' Such was the verdict of the House of
Commons last night . . . What hope has Ireland from such a House . . . The
present government in Ireland can do no wrong . . . We are with T. P.
O'Connor when he says that between the Irish and the English there should be a
real bond of friendship. There is. But we have no feeling of friendship for a
government that send men along country roads firing at random into hedges,
ditches, and fields. They admit this is done.

The parish priest of Ennistymon, A. J. Nestor, felt compelled to defend
his parishioners; he rejected Greenwood's assertion that locals knew
beforehand that an ambush was to take place at Rineen, County Clare. 'I
say this is an outrageous falsehood', he wrote. In a climate of moral

outrage at the policy of 'reprisals' which had brought the law into disrepute, the popular Lord Mayor of Cork, Terence MacSwiney, died in Brixton jail on 25 October 1920. The following day, the *Freeman's Journal* departed from usual practice and gave over the front page to a black-bordered picture of the man who had 'died for Ireland'. This usually staid paper reflected the mood of public opinion in an editorial entitled 'Life Ever-lasting':

How inexplicably horrible and detestable are the actions of the men who forced him to do that which we all deplore. We would not change places with any one of these palace politicians. There are no words within our vocabulary which fitly express our contempt and loathing of the time-servers who saw this great man go to his death, and stirred not a hand to save him. And all we have said of Alderman MacSwiney applies in full measure to those other Irish heroes who, too, are fighting the good fight.

And that from a paper which opposed the use of physical force. The crass stupidity of British policy provoked greater ambivalence towards the use of violence in an ever-widening circle throughout the country. The same paper had been outraged on 20 October by an incident in the House of Commons when reference to the 'suffering, noble Lord Mayor of Cork' was 'received with laughter'. Despite the censorship, the *Freeman's Journal* published a stinging editorial headed 'Second-Raters' in which a plea was made to employ constitutional methods to secure national objectives:

No great social revolution in modern times has been gained by force. Therefore, force is no remedy. The British government can be beaten by the exercise of brains and the pressure of economic force. We have them at our command. 'Black and Tans' will not conquer or appease Ireland. Why? Because they represent a method of government that never in the history of the whole world has ever been a success. You may take men out of their beds and shoot them. That does not conquer a race, or instil into their hearts a fear of their oppressors. We get back to the need for only one – only one – first class man to tackle the Irish question. Where is he? He must be found. Why not find him? his name is not Lloyd George or Winston Churchill, or Bonar Law and it is certainly not our present feeble Chief Secretary, Sir Hamar Greenwood . . . Second Class!!!! How long, Oh Lord! How long have we to suffer these unspeakable ineptitudes? All Ireland must cry out against the vile fact that we have to tolerate such control. Again we say Oh, Lord – how long?

MacSwiney lay in state at St George's Southwark, where the incumbent, Amigo, proved much more sympathetic to the cause of the dead Lord Mayor than Bourne of Westminster. Archbishop Mannix led the cortege through the streets of London to Euston station. The Catholic editor of *The Times*, Wickham Steed, had expressed his paper's disapproval of government policy in the handling of the hunger strike:

11   Crowds line street in Cork to pay their last respects to Terence MacSwiney, who died on hunger strike in Brixton on 25 October 1920 (*Cork Examiner*)

'We feel that, in some circumstances, logic is a poor thing, a thing moreover out of keeping with our nation's political temperament'. The leader repudiated any suggestion that either MacSwiney's friends or the authorities had been able to feed him surreptitiously: 'the final answer to those who doubted has been given by Alderman MacSwiney himself. His sincerity and his courage, at all events, are now vindicated and beyond all question.'[57]

MacSwiney was given a huge funeral in his native city. The authorities refused permission to allow the body to be taken to Cork via Dublin. But that did not prevent Sinn Fein from turning the occasion into a national demonstration against the British. MacSwiney was seen to be a national hero and there was little Dublin Castle could do about it. He had been arrested six times for his political activities between 1916 and 1920. MacSwiney had died in Brixton after a protracted hunger strike: 'the battle has already been fought and won' wrote the *Freeman's Journal*, on 29 October 1920; 'Terence MacSwiney comes home to his own, a conqueror whose name will live with those of Emmet, Tone and Mitchel.'

But one man's hero is another man's villain. There is evidence that there was considerable lobbying by the British to persuade the Vatican to issue a condemnation of nationalist violence and the hunger strike tactic in particular. When Desmond FitzGerald was in Rome in 1923 he learned from high Vatican officials that they had come under pressure from Britain to condemn hunger striking. There is a suggestion that Lloyd George might have intervened in the matter directly. On 12 November, de Salis reported that he had just seen the Pope, who was very perplexed by the MacSwiney issue. He told the envoy that the matter was being discussed but 'for his own part, he did not see that such proceedings could be advisable'. Efforts to get the Vatican to make a ruling on the question of hunger strikes had begun, probably, as early as September. The fact that the Vatican had not made a pronouncement indicated yet again that the Pope and Gasparri were against such a move – which was certainly supported by some cardinals in the curia.

During the same audience, Benedict is reported to have told de Salis that it 'seemed to him that in the course of the strike MacSwiney must have taken nourishment; no other supposition was possible'. While Benedict was not prepared to intervene, where the Irish bishops did not think it was appropriate, he was concerned that 'at the funeral there was too much parade. There was a certain element of farce with it all.' De Salis agreed but commented that while there was a comic opera side to the Balkans, 'there were tragic endings'.

About the same time, de Salis also talked to Gasquet. The Cardinal understood that Merry del Val's opinion of the Lord Mayor's death was 'clearly to be treated as one of suicide'.[58] It is probable that del Val was pressing for Vatican action in the matter, in keeping with his duties as Secretary of the Holy Office. There was nothing improper in that.

Cardinal de Lai also expressed himself strongly on the question of the way that the funeral had been used for political purposes. Benedict XV had expressed the same disquiet to de Salis, who was convinced that disciplinary action would be taken against Amigo and Mannix. The Superior General of the Redemptorists, Patrick Murray, had heard rumours about a possible condemnation and was approached by an Irish bishop, through members of his order, to try and do what he could to prevent it:

Just at that time I had occasion to visit the two Vatican Offices that deal with such matters, and I was informed in both that they were convinced that it was impossible in present circumstances to make such a pronouncement either in favour of or against hunger striking. However, of course it is better to do all one can to make sure that no such injury is done.[59]

Both Hagan and Curran had been active throughout the summer. The Rector had gone to Ireland for holidays and Magennis was left to document the Irish case and present it to the Vatican. The various overtures appeared to have been quite successful. No condemnation was issued. That was due, in large measure, to the determination of Gasparri and Benedict to remain detached from what might be perceived as partisan intervention in Irish affairs. The animosity between del Val and the Pope – which dated back to the time when the former was Secretary of State under Pius X – may have been another factor in preventing the publication of a statement on hunger strikes.

As a postscript to the MacSwiney death, both Amigo and Mannix were mildly reprimanded from Rome for the manner in which the funeral service was allowed to be conducted at Southwark and in the streets of London. The outcome was not very satisfactory for the British government. The Irish bishops, on the other hand, had cause to breathe a sigh of relief. It was becoming increasingly evident, however, that if the Crown forces were capable of the excesses described in the inflamed language of the October pastoral, then the IRA could be equally ruthless. On 21 November 1920 Michael Collins's hit squad, the Dublin Brigade Active Service Unit, raided eight Dublin houses and shot dead twelve British officers who were undercover agents. The Irish Executive met at Dublin Castle to review the situation, the same morning, and a decision was taken to restore internment on suspicion, extend curfew, and step up searches and road-blocks. Within the next few weeks, about 500 arrests were made. Among those held was Arthur Griffith.[60]

On the afternoon of the shooting, 21 November, troops went to Croke Park – the day of a big football match – in search of IRA men. It is not clear how the shooting started, but twelve people were killed and eleven were seriously wounded in the incident. Cardinal Logue issued a pastoral condemning both the shooting of the officers and the killings at Croke Park.

The Cardinal, referring to the IRA assassinations, was convinced that every man and woman in Ireland who retained a spark of Christian feeling, or even of the interests of humanity, 'deplores, detests, and condemns the deliberate cold-blooded murders of Sunday'. Logue stated: 'No object would excuse them; no motive could justify them; no heart, unless hardened and steeled against pity, would tolerate their cruelty.' He upheld nobility of patriotism when it pursued its objects by means that were 'sincere, honourable, just and in strict accordance with God's law'. Otherwise, it degenerated into 'blind, brutal, reckless, passion, inspired not by love of country but by Satan'. Logue also deplored and condemned the 'general indiscriminate massacre of innocent and inoffensive victims which was perpetrated by the forces of the Crown'. The Cardinal then added a rather controversial sentence before going on to describe the abuse of power by government forces: 'If a balance were struck between the deeds of the morning and those of the evening, I believe it should be given against the forces of the Crown.' That balance was generally inclined to tip against government activities in the country. But it was quite unusual for the cautious Logue to formulate his thoughts in that particular way. His statement was finely balanced. But it was written in such a way that it could be easily cited selectively in the press. There followed a number of examples of journalism at its most selective.

The treatment the pastoral received in some sections of the international press underscored the wisdom of the hierarchy's decision to set up a Publications Committee some weeks earlier. The *Osservatore Romano*, on 1 December 1920, published a short abstract of Logue's Advent pastoral – based on a telegram from the Stefani news service – and omitted the detailed condemnation of violence by the Crown forces. What appeared was the section relating to the shooting of the British officers with no reference to the killings at Croke Park. A leading article appeared in the paper based on the selectively reported pastoral from the Stefani service. The Paris correspondent of the *Corriere d'Italia* also made a similar reporting error. A correction was published on 5 December.

Both Hagan and Logue were furious at the way the *Osservatore* had handled the matter. There was considerable dissatisfaction with the way the editor, Count della Torre, conducted editorial policy towards Ireland. A formal protest was lodged by O'Doherty of Clonfert on behalf of the Standing Committee. Within an hour of its receipt, the editor was at the Irish College explaining his position. At the end of the conversation, della Torre agreed to give 'the other side a fair show in the future'.[61]

A number of the officers who had been shot on 21 November 1920 were Catholics. They were buried after a funeral service in Westminster Cathedral presided over by Cardinal Bourne. The only evidence of direct contact between Lloyd George and the Cardinal in these months is a letter in the Westminster archives from the Prime Minister:

The manner of their deaths has filled the hearts of Catholics, no less than Protestants, with horror and I feel sure that this expression of public feeling will serve to assist in putting an end to the reign of terror which is hindering the free development of the life and prosperity of Ireland.[62]

Bourne, who had many Irish priests working in his archdiocese, was no strong admirer of Sinn Fein or of any other nationalist movements seeking self-determination. He did, however, support limited devolved government within the Empire for Ireland. On 12 November 1920, just over a week before the shootings in Dublin, he gave an interview to *The*

Times in which he spoke about 'a secret, oath-bound association using assassination as its weapon' which was active in Ireland. But he also said 'We view with shame the presence of these troops [the Black and Tans] in Ireland and have a great desire for their withdrawal.' That was a theme he was to return to again in a letter to Lloyd George on 6 April 1921, when he wrote on behalf of the English and Welsh bishops:

Our Bishops have been holding their annual meeting this week, and I need not tell you that they are most gravely concerned about the condition of Ireland. They feel that the good name of England in other countries has been, and still is being, obscured by terrible happenings which it is impossible to explain or to justify. They desire me to impress upon you most earnestly that all ground should at once be removed for the definite charges which are so constantly being made of reprisals exercised by the forces of the Crown upon perfectly innocent persons. In this connexion they are convinced that much could be done towards promoting a good understanding, and the restoration of law and order, were the auxiliary troops withdrawn without delay from Ireland.

This letter reflects the degree of public disquiet felt among English and Welsh Catholics over the political situation in Ireland. It also echoed the many statements made by the Irish hierarchy.

Individual Irish bishops had repeatedly preached against, and condemned, the actions of 'physical force' nationalism. But their pronouncements had always been conditioned by wider considerations of state or institutionalised violence. No joint pastoral, however, had threatened to excommunicate those responsible for police shootings, ambushes and acts of intimidation. It must have been the topic of discussion at episcopal meetings in Maynooth – although there is no known documentary evidence of this – but it had not been utilised. The bishop who finally broke ranks in this matter was, quite surprisingly, Cohalan of Cork – a prelate who had been extremely sensitive and sympathetic to Dail Eireann. His action can be explained by the fact that the South – and the Cork area in particular – had witnessed intensive IRA activity, state repression and reprisal killings. The city had lost two Lord Mayors, one killed by police and another who died on hunger strike. There was a growing number of IRA attacks on the RIC and on British forces in the area. There followed acts of incendiarism, intimidation and vicious reprisals as the spiral of violence moved ever upwards. Cohalan was not impressed by what he considered to be 'freelance' activity by local 'roughs'. He wrote to a politician friend on 19 November:

A policeman has been shot on Tuesday: not, it is stated, by Volunteers or by members of any secret society, but, as may happen at any time, by a few roughs who had some grievance against the policeman. Then as a reprisal the police

12 The morning after: part of the centre of Cork in ruins after fires started by
some members of the British forces (*Cork Examiner*)

entered the house of the people on Wednesday night or Thursday morning and
shot five men – one indeed only a boy of 17 years. Three were shot dead and
two wounded, one it is feared fatally. I enclose the newspaper photographs of
the killed.[63]

In the weeks that followed the situation in the Cork area grew
immeasurably worse. A major engagement between the IRA and the
Auxiliaries took place at Kilmichael. On 28 November 1920 two tenders
were attacked. The British suffered eighteen casualties and the attackers
three dead and two wounded. Another major ambush was laid on 11
December at Dillon's Cross, on the north side of the city. As a lorry of
RIC and Auxiliaries drove towards the city, bombs were thrown from
behind a wall and the IRA opened fire, killing one and wounding eight
others. The attackers made good their escape. Later that evening, the
Auxiliaries returned to the area and burned the homes of 'Sinn Feiners'.
That night the centre of Cork city was set alight by British forces. The
Freeman's Journal estimated the damage done to the city at two-and-a-
half million pounds: 'Industries built up by generations of toil and
industry had gone. Hundreds were without their property, thousands
without their means of livelihood.' The respected Sinn Fein TD and

close friend of MacSwiney, Liam de Roiste, made the following entry in his diary at midnight on Sunday 12 December:

Last night in Cork was such a night of terror and destruction as we have not yet had. An orgy of destruction and ruin: the calm, frosty sky red – red as blood with the burning of the city, and the pale, cold stars looking down on the scene of desolation and frightfulness. O! GOD! O! GOD! let Thy mercy prevail . . . Hundreds, if not thousands, are thrown out of employment by this destruction.

It is in the context of such social and economic devastation that Bishop Cohalan preached in the cathedral at twelve o'clock Mass on 12 December 1920. He said the city 'had suffered as much damage at the hands of the servants of the government as Dublin suffered during the rebellion of 1916'. Cohalan has been much misunderstood for his subsequent decision to excommunicate offenders. The decree applied as much to the British forces as it did to the IRA; as it referred to anyone taking part in ambushes, kidnapping and murder. His Sunday sermon also reflects the dilemma of a nationalistic clergyman, in the *Freeman's Journal* sense of the term, who had to provide moral leadership at such a troubled time. The sermon is interesting because it argues at two levels – the moral and the practical. On two occasions, Cohalan leaves aside 'the moral aspect of the question for the moment' and asks what the country has gained politically 'by the murder of policemen'. He puts the point of some republicans who argued that areas had been delivered from British control. That was a 'narrow view' and it was also groundless: 'No, the killing of the RIC men was murder and the burning of barracks was simply the destruction of Irish property.' He acknowledged that reprisals began in the area with the shooting of Lord Mayor MacCurtain and 'now it is like a Devil's competition'. Curiously, he again leaves out 'for the moment the question of the moral aspect':

. . . the ambushers come to a place from no-one knows where, and, when the work is done, they depart, no-one knows to what destination. There is not much risk to the ambushers personally but, by this time, boys or men who take part in ambushes, must know that by their criminal acts they are exposing perhaps a whole countryside, perhaps a town or city to the danger of terrible reprisal; that when they depart and disappear in safety, they are leaving the lives and property of a number of innocent people unprotected and undefended to the fury of reprisals at the hands of the servants of the government.

But he left his congregation in no doubt about what the morality of the situation was: 'Let there be no doubt about it, these ambushes were murder and every life taken in an ambush was murder. There was danger of even becoming familiar with murders, simply considering a successful ambush as a nice exploit and the shooting of a policeman as the shooting of game or a wild animal.' In a Christmas pastoral, Cohalan reiterated his hostility to all violence. He revealed how a meeting of RIC men in the city had taken place early in 1920: a motion was defeated which stated that for every member of the force who was shot a volunteer was to be killed in reprisal. Cohalan was making the case that the RIC were caught in an invidious position. He implied that they were not all guilty of undisciplined action. The Bishop said that after the killing of every policeman 'a false theory was at once started that the policeman deserved his fate, that he had himself committed murder, that it was he who had murdered a boy in bed, and by these false theories the consciences of the people was drugged and their horror of the murder was considerably lessened'.[64] Cohalan had to endure much criticism in the wake of his excommunication decree; in reply, he once said: 'Nonsense. I desire Irish independence as sincerely as you. When you come with an army able to fight the enemy and defend the weak and unprotected, I will act as Chaplain.' Cohalan was simply echoing the position as stated by Benedict XV: the struggle for Irish independence was justified, but the methods to be used should not include shooting a policeman from behind hedges. In his diary entry for 14 December, de Roiste observed perceptively:

On casual reading the censure seems to justify the right of the English to rule in Ireland and condemn *every* action on the part of Irish people to defend themselves or assert their independence. But careful reading shows that His Lordship really does not express this view. But the censure is very ill-timed owing to the excited feelings of the people . . .

De Roiste refused to join in a public condemnation of the Bishop. He recognised the moral right of the Irish to assert their claim to freedom and to resist tyranny: 'I am not prepared to defend every particular and individual action taken for those purposes, on moral grounds, and much less on grounds of worldly prudence. As I believe His Lordship is not right in a general condemnation, so I hold some of our people are not right in general commendation of *every* act.'

De Roiste was quite sensitive in his evaluation of Cohalan having carefully read the local episcopal statements. Moreover, he referred in his diary to an interview which Cohalan gave the *Times* correspondent and which appeared in the paper on 15 November 1920. It was a response to Cardinal Bourne's statement of a few days earlier that an oath-bound society was behind the assassinations. Cohalan responded and he was alone among the bishops in doing so:

Cardinal Bourne speaks of the existence of a secret oath-bound society in Ireland as a generally admitted fact. I venture to say it is not a generally admitted fact. Many took the erroneous view that because the elected representatives declared a Republic, Ireland is a Republic. The transition to the claim to shoot members of the army of occupation was easy. Add to that from the beginning of the trouble reprisals on policemen who exceeded their duty, and you have an explanation of the murder, without supposing the existence of an oath-bound secret society.

The Bishop went on to argue for a 'cessation from crime on both sides, Government and Volunteers. (Does it not appear strange to ask Government to cease from crime?)' Cohalan was in favour of a Home Rule parliament. But that did not satisfy Michael Collins and the separatists. After the excommunication notice, Collins wrote that the Bishop's decision was a 'foolish and unpatriotic action'. On 12 January 1921, he told his friend Donal Hales in Genoa:

It is satisfactory, however, to note that very little attention is paid to his statements. Nearly all people now realise that a pronouncement from a bishop on behalf of the enemy deserves the same treatment as a similar action by anybody, whether more or less exalted. The statement has done more injury to his own reputation than it has done to the cause against which it was directed.[65]

It was somewhat one-sided to describe the pronouncement as 'an unpatriotic action' on 'behalf of the enemy'. It is quite likely that Cohalan's letter and pastoral articulated the feelings of many Cork people caught in the cycle of violence.

Cohalan's actions may also have been partially motivated by the fact that many priests in the Cork area had received anonymous death threats. The clergy were perceived by the Auxiliaries as being closely identified with the 'Sinners' and Cohalan feared for their lives. On 15 December 1920 – three days after the excommunication notice – one of the most respected priests in his diocese, a close personal friend of the Bishop, was shot dead by an Auxiliary in cold blood. Cohalan saw the murder of Canon Thomas Magner of Dunmanway as 'the latest move of what I call the devil's competition in crime which is taking place in our midst'. He felt the death of Canon Magner was a reprisal for Kilmichael; and all the deaths since the ambush 'have not brought us nearer the Republic'.[66] While many bishops had cause to reject the violent actions of the IRA, it was felt that the onus lay with the government forces, who had set very low moral standards. Moreover, Canon Magner was not the first priest to die at the hands of the British forces. There had been numerous acts of intimidation and public humiliation of priests. In Galway, Fr Griffin was taken from his house by a party of men. His body, with a bullet through the temple, was found buried in a bog some days later. The Bishop of Galway, O'Dea, had called a conference of senior clergy in his diocese on 21 November before the body of Fr Griffin was recovered. The secretary of the national conference of bishops, O'Doherty of Clonfert, also attended. In a statement afterwards, the group said: 'We cannot but hold the British Government as responsible for this outrage upon the Catholic priesthood of Ireland.'[67]

In a letter to the Chief Secretary, Bishop O'Dea of Galway resorted to very strong and direct language:

It is the belief of all in Galway that Father Griffin was shot by Government forces. The people of Ireland do not shoot their own priests. There were, at one time, Government executions without number, after some sort of trial, but a murder like this is almost, or altogether, unparalleled in Irish life.

Moreover, O'Dea was himself the recipient of an anonymous threatening letter which had a Galway postmark: 'If any member of His Majesty's forces are interfered with in Galway you will meet with Father Griffin's fate. Beware.' Another priest in his diocese, Fr Considine of Gort, also received a similar note: 'your efforts to stir up the blood-lust against the Crown forces are duly noted. You will be duly compensated, as will all the friends of the hero, Michael Collins'. The Bishop claimed that he had been even-handed in his denunciation of violence, from whatever side it had come, and his priests had followed his direction in that regard: 'I am now liable to be shot at any hour of the day or night if an event occurs over which I have no control'. He went on to outline the threat against another of his priests and the attacks on yet another and the desecration of his church. It is little wonder that both O'Dea and O'Doherty were both staunch allies of Hagan in Rome, as indeed was Cohalan.

Not everyone in Sinn Fein regarded Cohalan's action as 'unpatriotic'. The nationalist TD for North Wexford, Rogert Sweetman, had considerable doubts about the morality of IRA violence. According to a memoir in the possession of his family, he had come to regard the fight between the IRA and the RIC as a civil war — a view shared by many members of the police. Sweetman had been disheartened by the fact that his repeated efforts to persuade the Sinn Fein leadership to halt the shooting of policemen failed. Even a direct appeal to Griffith on 5 August 1920 did not meet with success. What saddened Sweetman still more was the belief that the violence was avoidable. In January 1920, he had a meeting with a sergeant of the RIC in the Ferns district of Wexford. The policeman indicated that his men had had enough of the 'Civil War' and were prepared to surrender if they could get honourable terms. Sweetman went to Dublin on 30 January 1920 and relayed the news to Eoin MacNeill. Collins is said to have turned down the proposal on the grounds that the RIC were finished and would have to surrender unconditionally. That may have been so. But Sweetman felt that the Black and Tan episode in Irish history might have been avoided if a more flexible attitude had been adopted. On 25 November 1920 he was about to announce his resignation to Griffith, when the latter was arrested. Sweetman narrowly missed the same fate when his farm in Wicklow was raided on 28 November. He had already gone into hiding. In Ferns, he consulted the local curate, his friend Fr Darcy, who urged him to see the Archbishop of Dublin. On 21 December he travelled to Drumcondra: 'The interview was no good. I found him a broken old man, jumpy and criticising everyone, and saying everything I suggested was no good'. Sweetman wanted the Archbishop to follow the example of Cohalan. But his rather pathetic portrait of Walsh goes some way to explain the lack of decisive leadership within the hierarchy in these weeks. The archdiocese was being run by the auxiliary, Edward Byrne. Sweetman 'got more good out of him'. Byrne 'considered that things would have to get worse, so that the young men would have to learn in the hard school of adversity; I think he included in this category the young priests'. The interregnum in Dublin may help explain some of the events involving the hierarchy which occurred in Rome over the succeeding months. Sweetman attended his last Dail meeting on 25 January. He had made repeated efforts to discuss his problems with de Valera, who had his own difficulties accepting the radicalisation of Irish politicians. At that session, two resolutions were passed agreeing that all British Ministers and all men in British uniforms in the streets of Dublin, on a day to be fixed, were to be shot. Sweetman resigned the following day.[68]

Despite the escalation of nationalist violence in late 1920, the British appeared to be making relatively little impact on Vatican authorities. That placed considerable pressure on de Salis. Curzon was quite scathing in his criticism of the envoy. On 10 December 1920, he minuted:

The recent despatches of Count de Salis give me the impression that he is not playing his part in justifying the continuance of his appointment. In view of the appalling events that have happened in Ireland I think that he should have spoken to the Vatican and should in future speak in much firmer tones. I think he should be told this. If we had to publish his despatches as a justification for his appointment what would be thought of us.[69]

On 31 December he was sent a sharp reminder that 'more pressing and insistent representations' were called for, adding that he could derive assistance from the recent action of the Bishop of Cork, Cohalan, who had resorted to the threat of excommunication in an effort to stop the violence.[70]

The Foreign Office hinted that there was a growing feeling against keeping a mission at the Vatican. What was wanted 'is not that the Vatican should interfere in a political struggle, but that the Church should speak out on a question of morals, which she can and should do, without having to take sides in a dispute between G.B. and Ireland'.[71] But Gasparri was evasive and refused to give any formal undertaking to the British envoy. The Secretary of State did propose that some measure ought to be taken to bring the two sides together. He wondered whether there was anything the Holy See could do to contribute to a peaceful settlement and whether the moment was opportune; some step, of course, which would be received with satisfaction by the English and without dissatisfaction by the Irish. It was true that his efforts in the case of Fiume had not been successful, but that would not deter him from trying in Ireland.[72]

In an earlier interview, Gasparri had explained again how the Holy See did not want to become directly involved in the Irish question. It was his view that the Vatican should keep as clear of current political questions as possible. He cited the question of the constitution for Yugoslavia, the Upper Silesian problem and the reconstruction of Poland. None of these 'he intended to touch'.[73] Gasparri felt that the bishops, even if they did not control the situation, would be followed by the people if a moderate solution were put forward. Gasparri, a man of vast diplomatic experience, was extremely well briefed on the Irish question. He accepted that intervention could, as far as the Irish Church was concerned, only make a bad situation worse. His prediction that the people would follow the bishops if only a moderate solution was put forward proved to be accurate. The peace efforts by Archbishop Clune and others have been brilliantly narrated by David Miller in his outstanding work on the subject. The Archbishop of Perth, Patrick Clune – whose nephew had been killed by the military while 'attempting to escape' in Dublin – was supported in his initiative by Lloyd George.[74] But the strong conservative presence in the British cabinet did not give the Prime Minister much latitude for compromise. Clune, who came to Dublin on 4 December, was also supported by Fogarty of Killaloe. The latter had narrowly escaped an assassination attempt by drunken soldiers. Fortuitously, he had travelled to Dublin via Limerick the very night the raid was carried out on his home. Some years later he explained what had happened. He received a telegram from Clune to meet him in Dublin and replied that the Archbishop should come to Ennis. When he received no reply he decided to make the journey to Dublin. In his absence, his home was raided by four Black and Tans. Fogarty believed that it was a murder attempt. After he had left, a telegram arrived from Clune saying that he was willing to go to Ennis as requested. The postal delay saved his life. From that point onwards, unknown to Fogarty, an IRA guard was placed on his home. The incident did little to endear the British to the moderate Fogarty.[75] Even the mildest of Irish bishops had been alienated by the lawlessness of the authorities.

Clune was disappointed by the failure of his peace initiative. He was outraged by what had happened to his nephew and had nearly happened to a fellow bishop. This former chaplain in the British army had seen what was happening in Ireland, read about events in Galway and the shooting of Canon Magner in Cork. He had extensive talks with a number of Irish bishops, where it was obvious that even conservative Cardinal Logue had run out of patience. In London, he had talks with Mannix, O'Brien – the Sinn Fein representative – Amigo, and Cotter of Portsmouth. In early January 1921 Clune set out for Rome. He travelled via Paris, where he met O'Kelly on 10 January 1921. O'Kelly sent a rather one-sided account of why the talks failed to Hagan, and added: 'Perth expects to be called to give an account of his work in high quarters in your neighbourhood.' He warned that 'words like republican are not quite pleasing to his ears'.[76]

Clune arrived in Rome at a time when there were rumours that a statement was being prepared at the Vatican about the Irish question. Hagan had informed O'Donnell on 25 January that suspicions about such action had become widespread and what was once 'a more or less probable deduction then, has now become a dead certainty'.[77] Clune went immediately to see Cerretti, where he learned that Merry del Val was once again the villain of the piece. Cerretti insisted that Clune should have an audience with the Pope as quickly as possible. According to Hagan, del Val was out 'to remind the Irish that there was such a thing as the fifth commandment'. The planned document was not to take the form of an open condemnation of Sinn Fein, but 'it was rather to condemn deeds of violence on all sides, but in substance, it would be taken both by friends and enemy to be a death-blow aimed at Irish aspirations'.[78]

Hagan had written to Logue on 24 January telling the Cardinal that Clune had 'ascertained beyond any shadow of doubt that a Pontifical document was ready to be issued on the subject of violence in Ireland'.[79] Clune had been a member of the Redemptorist order before becoming Archbishop. When he went for his audience with Benedict he was accompanied by Patrick Murray, who acted as interpreter. The Superior General of the Redemptorists was a practised Vatican diplomat. He wrote to Sean T. O'Kelly on 19 February 1921 describing the meeting. He emphasised that newspaper reports about the pronouncement had been exaggerated. He felt certain that the Vatican had considered the possibility but had come to no final decision. That would appear to be the most plausible explanation of the events. Del Val was making the running. His old rival, Benedict XV, supported by Gasparri, remained sceptical, as he had done on other occasions.

Clune surprised his friend Murray by the forthright way he spoke to the Pope. The Superior General of the Redemptorists wrote 'in strict confidence' to O'Kelly on 19 February 1921:

... he told the Holy Father amongst other things that such a pronouncement would be a disaster for the Church, not only in Ireland, but in every country where there were descendants of the Irish race. In fact his language was so strong that when I, as his interpreter, translated it into Italian, I had to excuse him for speaking so strongly as the matter was so grave. His reasons seemed to make a great impression on His Holiness because he asked Dr. Clune to speak also to a certain Cardinal who, I presume, had the question in hand.[80]

Murray was convinced that Clune had 'succeeded in removing the threat of condemnation'.

Even at the request of the Holy Father, Clune found it difficult to get an interview with del Val. The first time he called he was informed the Cardinal was out; the second time he was told the Cardinal was in – but engaged. It was only on the third visit that he was seen. That did precious little to cool the Archbishop's temper.

That was a lesson which would not be lost on the other side, Clune told del Val, citing 'chapter and verse'. By the time he was finished, according to Murray, who did not accompany him on that occasion, 'the cardinal in question told him he saw the whole question of Ireland in a new light'. He alerted his friends in the hierarchy. Rumours of a papal condemnation had been received by many bishops with uncharacteristic shows of hostility, as can be gauged by remarks of the moderate and influential Mulhern of Dromore. He wrote to Hagan on 9 February:

... and now when inhuman cruelty, unparalleled in any previous period of our history, takes the place of Justice, our good people look to their Common Father on earth for his blessing and sympathy. They know he is powerless to act as his predecessor did centuries ago, but they are grateful for what he can give them. You may ask yourself why I write in this way. It has often been said that if the Irish people become alienated from the faith and the priests, it will be the fault of the priests. At the present time there are distant rumblings of intrigues at Rome by persons highly placed in Church and state, for the purpose of inducing the Holy Father to interfere in the present political movement of our people for their just claims to self-government, and that the part His Holiness is asked to take is one adverse to us.

Mulhern said that he was not alone in his fear 'of dangers ahead for the warmth and loyalty of Ireland's attachment to Rome and all it stands for' should anything 'inopportune' occur at this crisis in 'our affairs'. He did not want any mists to cloud the brightness of 'our motto "*ut Christiani ita et Romani* [*sitis*]"'. But he warned: 'I need hardly say that our people would not dream of resenting any statement or action on the part of

Rome, if they knew it was spontaneous. What they cannot, and I fear will not, bear is that, in their legitimate action and movement for independence of our country, they should be thwarted by the intrigues of their hereditary foes. One can easily imagine how by false reports or misrepresentations of facts even careful and diplomatic men may be led astray.' He referred to past friction between Rome and Ireland: 'bad as things were, on occasions I refer to, they would be thousand times worse now'. 'Inopportune action' now would cause great strain:

Then the leaders were the movement, the crowd agreed with a sort of sentimental approval of what they hardly fully understood; now the leaders are led. Nearly everyone, lay and cleric, from the universities down to the meanest hovel of a school, men, women, boys, and girls are in the movement. They know what they want and are bent on having it. They work for it. They pray for it and they suffer as people have never suffered before. We are an excitable people and it is easy to imagine what would be their feelings if now in the midst of their agony with their nerves strung to the highest pitch their hopes are dashed to pieces by one power on which they rely for the greatest moral support.

That was not altogether for 'Hagan's eyes only'. Mulhern urged the Rector that if he had the opportunity he should tell his views 'to His Holiness as coming from a bishop whose people suffered most in the past [Northern diocese], and are now suffering . . .'. A translation of the letter promptly found its way to the Pope via Cerretti.

The Standing Committee of the hierarchy had met on 18 January 1921 and the question of a pronouncement and the handling of Logue's letter in the *Osservatore* had been discussed. The Cardinal, no supporter of strong nationalist rhetoric, was less than enthusiastic on that occasion to deter his more vocal colleagues. O'Doherty wrote, in his official capacity as secretary to that body, using language reminiscent of the late 1880s:

English violence and oppression our people can endure; English slanders they despise. But, we need not say, it would be utterly heartbreaking to them if Rome were to step into this quarrel on the side of the enemies of their race and faith. Such a step would result in the most serious consequences to our religion not only in Ireland but also in England, America, Australia and wherever our exiles have found a home and helped to build up the Church.

O'Doherty was sure the cry of the 1880s would be raised again: 'We will take our religion from Rome, but our politics from home.' But he warned that the bitterness would be far greater now:

We know our people, and can forecast the effects of any adverse pronouncements Irishmen would feel that as a result of threats or promises made by a great empire, Rome had become the instrument of British domination here – Rome which in time past has actively assisted in our struggle for freedom and has always sympathised with our sufferings.

The language used in the Mulhern and O'Doherty letters – both of which were read in the Vatican – may have allowed curial officials to see Hagan as a moderate for the first time. It is not surprising that some Irish bishops should have felt aggrieved. One of the most respected men on the bench, Fogarty of Killaloe, had narrowly escaped death at the hands of a group of undisciplined British troops and two priests had been killed. The Bishop of Galway, O'Dea, and a number of his priests had received threats on their life and that also applied in other dioceses. Mulhern and O'Doherty were not necessarily representative in their views, but Hagan did not draw the Vatican's attention to that fact. Both men were among his strongest episcopal supporters.

The Irish initiative was pressed home still further when an unrepentant Mannix arrived in Rome.[81] He attended a reception at the Irish College and lectured the seminarians afterwards. He said he was opposed to 'unworthy compromise'. Mannix went further than any of the Irish bishops when he denied that there was a gang of nationalist murderers in Ireland. It was only 'an infuriated and exasperated' nation. The only gang of murderers there was in Ireland was the one sent over by the British government. He quoted de Valera as saying that God owed something to Ireland and the Irish people, 'if we might say so without irreverence, and God is just and will some day stand by his own'.[82]

When Mannix met the Pope he was probably a little less florid in his language and more theologically sound in his arguments. Cerretti acted as interpreter in an audience that lasted for nearly an hour. Mannix declined the Pope's offer to intervene on his behalf with the British over allowing him to travel to Ireland. Mannix, with his sympathetic interpreter, stated how surprised he was that the Vatican had remained silent when even priests had been attacked and killed. He expressed the general feeling of regret that the Pope, who had words of sympathy for Poland and Belgium, neglected to say anything encouraging about Ireland. Most of the arguments being put forward were familiar to the Vatican authorities. Hagan had used them so often in the past. Mannix was assured that no condemnation was contemplated.

The Pope asked if the Vatican could do anything to help the situation and Mannix quickly replied that a suitable contribution to the White Cross – a voluntary relief organisation with Logue, among other prominent public figures, on the committee – accompanied by a suitably worded letter, would be very helpful. Mannix was instructed by Benedict to discuss the matter with Gasparri the following day. The

Secretary of State suggested to Mannix that he bring a draft letter to him as soon as possible. The letter was submitted immediately with the help of Hagan. 'And that's the nearest I ever got to writing an Encyclical Letter', Mannix confided to Bishop Patrick Lennon of Kildare and Leighlin in 1961.[83]

The final version which was prepared by Cerretti, appeared on 22 May. It is likely that Benedict's letter did not diverge significantly from the draft prepared by Mannix and Hagan, who were advised by the sympathetic Cerretti. The Pope stated that it was the 'deliberate counsel of the Holy See' – not only in the case of Ireland – 'to take sides with neither of the contending parties'. Benedict hoped that a lasting peace and a sincere union of hearts might take place. He called for a negotiated settlement.

If there was a basis in the letter it leaned in favour of the Irish – where a country known for her loyalty to the faith was 'subjected today to the indignity of devastation and slaughter'. But there was even-handed condemnation of the violence conducted by both sides:

For, indeed, we do not perceive how the bitter strife can profit either of the parties, when property and homes are being ruthlessly and disgracefully laid waste, when villages and farmsteads are being set aflame, when neither sacred places nor sacred persons are spared, when on both sides a war resulting in the death of unarmed people, even of women and children, is carried on.[84]

Sean T. O'Kelly was not over-enthusiastic about the letter and the contribution to the White Cross. It had stopped short of condemning 'the doings of the enemy'. While he could not call it 'wholly satisfactory', he did consider it 'most useful'. In fact, the letter was a major diplomatic achievement for Dail Eireann. The Pope had spoken for the first time directly on the Irish question. He had not condemned the nationalists. If anything, the letter leaned slightly towards the position of Hagan and other nationalists. O'Kelly was correct in his surmise that 'the British were very displeased about its publication'.[85] Curzon found the letter 'just the kind of casuistic performance that might have been expected from the Vatican'.[86] One Foreign Office minute said the Pope was executing a 'clever feat of tight-rope walking' and added: 'A Sinn Feiner will read into it that his political ambitions have His Holiness's sympathy and that HMG stands condemned by an imperial outside authority, while the English Catholics will not find it easy to discover anything objectionable.'[87]

The main objection to the letter was that 'HMG are placed in exactly the same category as the authors of arson and cold-blooded murder'. It was felt that amounted to taking sides, where Vatican policy was to steer clear of partisan statements:

The question arises whether we should make a very serious protest to the Vatican against this deliberate interference in the political affairs of this country (a definite suggestion is even made as to how the problem should be settled). It is quite clear that nothing we can ever say will alter the Vatican view that the Irish are oppressed people struggling for their freedom, and that it is useless were we to hope that the Pope will take any action aiming at the prevention of crime. Our past efforts in this respect have been ignored. But it is another matter when His Holiness comes down publicly on the side of the forces of disorder which this letter seems to me practically to amount to. I do not think we should let it pass.[88]

Cadogan also felt strongly that there was good ground for formal complaint. When the British had requested that the Pope should speak out on the question of morals 'involved in the Irish murder campaign', they were told that it was against the traditional policy of the Vatican to mix itself up in politics. The recent statement had 'put HMG and the Irish murder gang on a footing of equality'. He suggested that the strength of British feeling should be made known to the Vatican through a prominent English Catholic and that de Salis be instructed to point out 'the want of justice and logic' involved in the Pope's action, and intimate that such papal interference 'in our domestic politics is fraught with the gravest consequences'. The Irish Office was also asked to supply details on the White Cross, but that did not prove the basis for a strong diplomatic initiative. There was little that could be done except make a vigorous protest. Gasparri, in response, was authorised to offer the good offices of the Vatican to mediate between the two sides.

Archbishop Walsh did not live to read the papal letter. He died on 9 April 1921 after a long illness. No individual prelate had done more over the previous forty years to shape the direction of Church–State relations. He was a nationalist who recognised the need for bishops to keep close to successive generations of Irish leaders, and that also included the present generation of 'physical force' nationalists. Despite his failing health, he had tried, with diminishing success, to meet his pastoral responsibilities. He met the Labour Commission of Inquiry into Conditions in Ireland in early December at his palace in Drumcondra. He urged on Arthur Henderson the necessity that 'something must be done speedily to avert disaster.' A month earlier, he had intervened unsuccessfully to try to save the life of a young university student who was hanged on 1 November 1920. Although Roger Sweetman found Walsh fragile and negative in his outlook, the Archbishop had cause to feel pessimistic in mid-December 1920. He was fighting a losing battle. His health was deteriorating rapidly, as was the situation in the country generally. Had retirement been possible in those days, Walsh would probably have stepped down in favour of his auxiliary Bishop, Edward

Byrne, on whose shoulders the responsibility for running and administering the diocese had rested since he was provided Coadjutor on 19
August 1920 and ordained on 27 October 1920. He succeeded to the
archdiocese on 9 April 1921.

The new Archbishop was born in 1872. He was not as brilliant
intellectually as his predecessor, but he had studied theology in Rome
and won many prizes. He returned to Ireland in 1895 and served in the
parishes of Rush, Howth and Blackrock. In 1901 he was made Vice-
Rector of the Irish College in Rome. He was succeeded by Hagan in 1903
and he returned to Dublin to continue his work in a number of inner-city
parishes. Byrne, who had considerable experience of the workings of
the Vatican, was cast in the same diplomatic mould as Walsh. He
was far more than a dull prelate placed between two outstanding
Archbishops, William Walsh and John Charles McQuaid, who took
over in December 1940. Byrne was a close friend and supporter of Hagan.
(They were also brought closer together by the fact that they were both
Wicklow men.) He was a welcome voice among the bishops, capable of
giving leadership. The contribution of the new Archbishop of Dublin to
the bringing about of political stability in Ireland in the 1920s has yet to
be fully explored and documented. To date, it has been both
misunderstood and understated. Byrne, who did not enjoy robust
health, was never a close friend of de Valera. He was, however, to
develop a strong personal friendship with William T. Cosgrave – a man
who was to come to national prominence in the summer of 1922. De
Valera returned from the United States in December 1920. He had missed
some of the worst violence of 'the Troubles'. His absence had also put
him at a further disadvantage – he had lost many opportunities to
develop strong personal links and a good working relationship with the
hierarchy. He was aloof from many of the nationalist politicians and the
'physical force' elements. He symbolised the nationalist 'apostolic
succession' with the 1916 Rising. Details of his attempt to break back
into Irish politics await a good biographer. It was relatively easy to
regain a grasp of ecclesiastical politics and Vatican diplomacy. He had
Sean T. O'Kelly and his other close friend, John Hagan, to advise him.
Moreover, he had many clerical friends only too willing to show their
support for more moderate forms of nationalism. What must have
surprised de Valera upon his return – although I have no evidence for
this – was the dramatic change in clerical attitudes towards the British
authorities. One of the most fundamental laws of Irish hierarchical
thinking was, at all costs, to keep the Vatican out of local politics.

It is in this context that a number of nationalist initiatives are to be
understood which were misguidedly designed to solidify a good
working relationship with the Vatican. In March 1921, W. T. Cosgrave,

who was a 1916 veteran and Minister for Local Government, suggested the setting up of a Second Chamber:

The suggestion contained in it, is that there should be a sort of 'Upper House' to the Dail consisting of a Theological Board which would decide whether any enactments of the Dail were contrary to Faith and Morals or not. There is also a suggestion that a guarantee be given to the Holy Father that the Dail will not make laws contrary to the teachings of the Church, in return for which the Holy Father will be asked to recognise the Dail as a body entitled to legislate for Ireland.[89]

On 4 March 1921, de Valera wrote to Diarmuid O'Hegarty: 'tell L. MacC. that I read his theological proposal, and there is no necessity at the moment to consider it further'.[90] That somewhat impractical suggestion – given the assumptions on which Irish–Vatican relations were based – was an indication of the degree to which some politicians were prepared to go to consolidate the support of the Catholic Church for Dail Eireann. Members of the hierarchy would have been the first to shy away from acceptance of such powers, while the bishops would also have been reluctant to grant such a direct role to the Vatican in the vetting of controversial legislation. There was little need to contemplate such a gesture in view of the general feeling of sympathy many bishops shared for the political aspirations of responsible nationalists.

When an intermediary approached the Cardinal to put de Valera into contact with Lord Derby, there was little hesitation about complying. At the Standing Committee meeting on 5 April, Logue reported that he had been contacted by a Liverpool priest acting on behalf of the Earl of Derby. The latter wanted to meet de Valera. The Standing Committee felt that the proposal was hopeful and 'certain steps were taken to facilitate it'.[91] This episode has been related in detail elsewhere.[92] De Valera, who had not reached agreement with Lord Derby, prepared very carefully for the June meeting of the hierarchy. He lobbied the bishops intensively to declare their recognition of the Irish Republic. He appeared relatively confident of success and he wrote to the Publicity Department on 16 June:

I am working hard to get the bishops to give straight recognition to the Republic in their pronouncement on Tuesday. If any statement of theirs can at all be construed as recognition, you should be ready on Tuesday to see that the newspaper headlines are: – THE IRISH BISHOPS RECOGNISE THE REPUBLIC. DO NOT MOVE IN THIS MATTER UNTIL THE LAST MOMENT. A step too soon might spoil everything . . . I need not lay stress on the extreme importance of this being attended to as most important and most urgent.[93]

It is unlikely that de Valera would have given such an instruction if he had not strong grounds for thinking that the hierarchy was about to make such a pronouncement. Nothing is known about the details of preparing the draft statement for the June meeting of the hierarchy. But de Valera's directive of 16 June would indicate that he was optimistic about the outcome. He must also have been fully aware that the move to get the hierarchy to recognise the Irish Republic formally was bound to meet with stiff opposition from some bishops.[94] Minority dissent on the bench would be sufficient to jettison his plans. The draft statement was put before the Standing Committee on 20 June 1921. The contents of the document were simply 'noted'. This could signify that the contents of the draft statement were indeed controversial. It is hard to accept that, even at this stage, the draft statement would have gone as far as de Valera wanted. But a discreet formula may have been found which would have pleased the more subtle minds in Sinn Fein. On 21 June 1921, Professor Miller is quite right to suggest, there was considerable disagreement among some of the bishops over the draft statement.[95] Opposition was probably further fuelled by the appearance of de Valera at Maynooth. He had an opportunity to put his case to the hierarchy. While there is no record available of what de Valera said it is unlikely that he assuaged the fears of his episcopal critics. It might have been a far more prudent tactic to allow his position to be put by one of the senior bishops who most sympathised with Sinn Fein and had standing within the hierarchy.

Some of the bishops were incensed. According to oral tradition the Bishop of Ross, Denis Kelly, threatened to break the rule of unanimity if episcopal recognition was granted to the Republic.[96] But whatever the details, when de Valera left the room in Maynooth the hierarchy had one of its most heated debates. At the end of the day, the agreed statement issued to the press could hardly be described as a total victory for de Valera. He could not use his bold headline: THE IRISH BISHOPS RECOGNISE THE REPUBLIC. But the statement did represent a major defeat for those most critical of Sinn Fein. De Valera had the satisfaction of seeing a phrase in the statement which condemned the setting up of the government of Northern Ireland. But what must have given him the greatest comfort was the line: 'Until repression ceases, and the right of Ireland to choose her own form of government is recognised, there is no prospect that peace will reign amongst us or that the reconciliation which His Holiness so ardently desires will be accomplished.'[97] There may have been some disappointment in over-sanguine Sinn Fein circles at the outcome. But could the Irish bishops have gone any further? It is most unlikely that they could have done so and still retained an outward unity. What the events of June 1921 show conclusively is the fact that the Irish hierarchy was not a monolithic political group. More pointedly, it has not been realised to what degree many members of the hierarchy had been radicalised by the terrible events of late 1920, when members of the clergy and even the bench of bishops were the subject of threats and actual attacks, two of which resulted in the deaths of Canon Magner and Fr Griffin – indubitably the work of the British forces. It was an extreme political situation which drove the hierarchy to state that the forces of the Crown had established in Ireland 'a reign of frightfulness which, for murdering the innocent and destroying their property, has a parallel only in the horrors of Turkish atrocities, or in the outrages attributed to the Red Army of Bolshevist Russia'. If the moral balance tilted in this period, it was perceived to weigh finally in favour of Sinn Fein – and that despite the excesses of the IRA.

Chapter III

THE HIERARCHY AND THE TREATY

The events of 1920 and early 1921 had pushed most of the hierarchy – including Cardinal Logue – into a position of open hostility to British policy in Ireland. The actions of the Black and Tans and the Auxiliaries had blackened the name of Dublin Castle among some individuals who might otherwise have been well-disposed. The temper of the hierarchy was not helped by the partitioning of the island in early summer 1921, which created a new range of problems for the Church. On 22 June King George V opened the parliament of Northern Ireland in Belfast. Two separate elections had been held in May for the Six Counties and the Twenty-Six Counties under the provisions of the 1920 Government of Ireland Act. Sinn Fein candidates were returned unopposed for 128 seats in the new Southern parliament. (Nationalists did not contest the four seats allocated to Trinity College.) Sinn Fein deputies later met as the Second Dail. Partition was vigorously opposed by the bishops, who were faced with the additional problem of having to operate in a Northern Ireland state where Catholics were a permanent minority. This forced a major readjustment in the Irish Catholic Church and it ought to be the subject of a separate monograph.

On the same day as the opening of the Northern parliament, de Valera was arrested in Dublin but he was quickly released. This gesture of goodwill reflected the desires by both sides to end the violence. It is clear from at least one oral source who was active in the IRA at the time that the British were 'beginning to get our measure'.[1] A 'Truce' came into effect on 11 July 1921.[2] Irish bishops and clergy welcomed the end of the violence. But as the IRA began to emerge in full uniform from the mountains there were those who looked at the possible victory of Sinn Fein with apprehension. An interesting diary has been located which looks at these events with suspicion and hostility; Miss Helen MacLean was a Presbyterian from Ardgour, near Westport. In her 3 September entry she describes the situation in the area:

Our side keeps it [the truce] loyally, the S.F. make hay while the sun shines –
they are drilling regularly here, nightly, in two parts of the town. The
'gunmen' as they are called, have come down from the hills, and throng the
town and roadsides far and near, and very lusty and well-to-do they look but
they have lowering faces and a lazy loafing attitude as if they are just waiting
and hanging about for orders, which is exactly what they are doing.

Weeks of preliminary correspondence between Lloyd George and de
Valera kept the country in a state of high tension. Miss MacLean had
heard from the local commander of the Auxiliaries that 'the present
attitude on both sides is bluff, that they do not really want war again,
but that if the S.F. do break out, that it will be war and no mistake'. She
reported that roads had been blown up and bridges destroyed. Sinn
Fein had landed 20,000 machine-guns in two months. The British forces
had their hands tied: 'the priests, the young ones, seem to be
ringleaders, they are bitterly spoken of by their own flock'.

 While Miss MacLean waited in fear for the outcome of events, many
Irish clergymen abroad saw the Truce as the beginning of Irish
redemption. Most prominent among these was the voluble Cardinal
O'Connell of Boston. He wrote to his fellow bishops hoping that 'God in
his wisdom may bring Ireland's history of seven hundred years to an
end'. He prayed that 'God may grant to you and your colleagues to live
and see Ireland's Golden Age, and find your people even more faithful
to their Church in the sunburst of their New Freedom than even they
were in the years of their exile and expectancy'.[3] But Miss MacLean was
less hopeful and enthusiastic. She related several incidents of
intimidation. She found ominous signs on all sides:

One of the priests here preached a sermon a fortnight ago, telling his flock they
should treat the Protestants like St Patrick did the snakes in Ireland, i.e. banish
them. The D.[istrict] I.[nspector] is not to be trusted, he is an R.C. and
apparently in league with the IRA. He has been known to have said that as soon
as the truce is over he will resign his position in the RIC and take one waiting for
him in the IRA.

These entries reflect the panic of a person who was witnessing the old
political order withering away. The possibility of further violence was
remote. A negotiated settlement seemed likely and Miss MacLean was
apprehensive that the politics of her maid would now prevail. The
domestics were obviously getting 'uppity'. Whatever the outcome to
the Truce might be, it was least likely to be a case of 'the more things
change the more they remain the same'. The overwhelming majority of
people wanted peace once the cycle of violence had been finally broken.
A team of negotiators – plenipotentiaries – had begun talks with Lloyd
George in London on 11 October. Surprisingly, de Valera chose to
remain at home. Arthur Griffith, Michael Collins, Robert Barton, George

Gavan Duffy, and E. J. Duggan were sent, with Erskine Childers and John Chartres making up the secretariat. Gavan Duffy had spent the previous months in Rome as Irish envoy. He had had talks with Gasparri and an audience with the Pope. Hagan had not got on as well with Gavan Duffy as he had with O'Kelly. He had found him less than effective. But Hagan had had a very difficult year personally and he was left a little shaken by the experience. He had been investigated for 'modernism'. The entire affair was so unfounded that it could be interpreted as a spiteful act by vindictive people who had been bested by the Rector over the years. As he recovered from this episode – he was completely exonerated – he received numerous reports about the progress of the London talks. Sean T. O'Kelly sent a somewhat pessimistic account of progress in a letter on 4 November 1921:

I understand that our people, but in particular A.G. and C., have fallen as complete victims to L.G.'s machinations, as ever Wilson and Clemenceau did during the days of the Paris peace conference. I am told the history of the present conference has been a story of continued surrenders on the part of ours while they have nothing so far from the enemy but promises.[4]

On 17 November, O'Kelly wrote to Hagan that the talks were resulting in capitulation on the Irish side. He had been told what was happening in confidence but he felt that it was such 'a betrayal' that he was 'sorely tempted to blow the scheme skyhigh by publishing it'. But before moving he decided to go to Dublin to consult some of his friends about what ought to be done. While passing through London the news that he heard 'only confirmed my worst fears'. He had a long talk with de Valera 'and while he did not refute my information in any particular, he maintained that so far nothing had happened to cause him at least any anxiety. He said he personally was quite satisfied with the progress of events and that he was of the opinion that our people had handled the situation remarkably well. I told him frankly what my views were on the question of the possibility of a recommendation being made for the recognition of English sovereignty and he said his views were in accordance with mine.'[5]

On 1 December Hagan received a report from Gavan Duffy, only five days before the treaty was signed:

You will understand that I cannot say much about the conference, which has been a very interesting but a very exacting ordeal. Crisis has succeeded crisis, until now we find ourselves at the most crucial stage of all, and though we may be still a long way from a settlement, I fancy that the next move will lie rather with Dail Eireann than with us. All reports agree that the spirit of the country is hardening admirably, and I suppose one cannot expect in a few weeks to bring the enemy up to scratch after he has been for so long (until Easter Week) in practically undisputed possession. What will happen next is on the knees of the gods.[6]

De Valera rejected the settlement terms and for the next few weeks he led the opposition to ratification in the Dail. The President's identification with the anti-Treatyite position – which was characterised by a wide range of political views – turned what might have been a relatively serious situation into a major political crisis. The position of the Church was obviously likely to have a major impact on the outcome.

A special meeting of the bishops was held in Dublin on 13 December 1921 to discuss the Treaty. Although there is no direct evidence to support the view, it is probable that both political factions were engaging in intensive lobbying of the clergy and the bishops. In the circumstances, the hierarchy had little option but to take the unusual step of convening a meeting to discuss the position of the Church in relation to a Treaty which had so radically divided the country. According to one contemporary source, the Treatyites had requested the open support of the bishops. The anti-Treatyites, sensing the direction in which episcopal sympathies lay, urged the Church to take no action.[7] The meeting confined itself to a statement afterwards which 'held in highest appreciation the patriotism, ability, and honesty of purpose in which the Irish representatives have conducted the struggle for national freedom'.[8] Logue was very annoyed at this outcome. It was not decisive enough for him. The Cardinal was convinced the Church could only be on one side – pro-Treaty.

Although one bishop had expressed a reservation over the wisdom of signing the Treaty before returning to Dublin, the overwhelming majority of the hierarchy was very satisfied with the terms. Logue wrote to Hagan on 10 December: 'I don't think there is a man alive who ever expected that such favourable terms could be squeezed out of the British government in our time.' It had prevented the return of the country 'into a more intensified course of burning and bloodshed'.[9]

At the Vatican, senior officials reacted positively to the Treaty. A telegram of congratulations was prepared and was about to be sent to Logue and the King when Hagan intervened. He pointed out that the outcome was still far from definite until both parliaments had ratified the agreement and it should not be taken for granted that 'all was over'.[10] On 9 December Hagan had a long interview with the Under-Secretary for Extraordinary Ecclesiastical Affairs, Mgr Borgongini Duca. He advised that the Vatican consider carefully the right moment to send a telegram and to whom it should be sent. Hagan also prepared a memorandum for him on the implications of the Treaty. He stated that 'English occupation comes to an end, and for the first time in seven centuries and a half, since Christmas Day 1172, the city of Dublin will within one month from today be without an English soldier'. The Treaty gave Ireland 'for the first time . . . complete legislative and economic control of her own internal destinies, freedom of enterprise, freedom of ideas, freedom of policy, freedom of action etc. . . . but . . . externally, the freedom was less ample and is subject to certain galling limitations'. Hagan explained how the country had divided and the majority might rest with the separatists. He pointed out that those opposing the Treaty, like de Valera, were 'good Catholics' and not the 'semi-anarchists' and 'American gunmen' paid by 'American gold', as the 'anglophile press of Rome informed their readers'. He explained how he had sent a telegram to the speaker of the Dail stating: 'all honour to men and women of Ireland who have brought the nation so near the golden milestone'.[11]

Borgongini Duca called to see the Rector on 12 December to discuss the memorandum. It was shown, or its contents explained, to the Pope on 14 December.[12] The bishops' letter was also translated and sent to the Pope. Curran reported that the pressure continued to have the Papacy send a telegram; 'you would be surprised from whom', commented a high Vatican official. Telegrams were finally sent on 16 and 19 January.

When the Dail met in open session on 19 December, the motion for ratificaton was moved by Arthur Griffith. On 21 December O'Kelly described the debate:

I am writing this in the midst of the long-drawn out discussions on the motion to approve of the Treaty. I am listening to Miss MacSwiney who is against the acceptance of the document. She is making an able speech, one of the best made here so far but I fear twill be without avail for most members have their minds made up on one side or the other. My sizing of the situation is that approval will be carried by a majority of not more than five or six . . . All the women in the Dail are against approval but you will be sorry to hear that the majority of the young soldiers who are members of the Dail have followed the lead of Collins.[13]

The Dail went into recess for Christmas.

Bishop Fogarty, who had narrowly escaped being murdered by Crown forces during the Anglo-Irish conflict, was now one of the most actively political of the Irish bishops. While the Dail was due to reconvene on 3 January, he wrote to Hagan three days earlier giving his assessment of the political situation. There was absolutely no doubt where he stood. He was pro-Treaty:

The Irish papers must be sad reading for you these times, with our big split in full blast. I don't know what your view is. I suppose you are conversant with the facts. The great bulk of the nation want acceptance. And pay no attention to all the talk about surrendering their birthright, they know their own minds. They have no idea of surrendering any right. They mean to take the treaty and make the most of it as the shortest way to the final acquisition of all their rights. Unfortunately they are not allowed to be heard. The Dail, it is said, will reject the treaty, and then chaos, war, civil and international. De Valera has a new treaty every other day. He now wants to get over to Lloyd George with a new document to be turned down of course, and then to say the nation was insulted and then on with the war. We can only wait and pray.[14]

Gilmartin of Tuam did not feel that de Valera's alternative proposals, contained in Document Number 2, were substantial enough to risk war:

We don't think that the difference between the Treaty and external association is of a sufficiently substantial character to warrant the risk of a renewal of the war. That is the frame of mind in which most of us find ourselves. The withdrawal of soldiers, Auxiliaries, Blacks and Tans, and RIC is an unqualified pleasure. It would delight you to see our fine lads in charge.[15]

That view was echoed by the Bishop of Limerick, Denis Hallinan. He felt that Ireland was getting 'substantially what she has suffered and fought for. There were still some accidentals wanting', but those, he believed, would come in due course through the natural evolution and peaceful use of what 'we are getting'.[16] Logue told a congregation in Armagh Cathedral on 1 January that the Treaty 'seemed to give everything substantial which was necessary for the welfare and progress of the country'.[17] The Archbishop of Cashel, Harty, knew that the 'vast majority' were in favour because they realised that it contained the substance of freedom and they were determined not to reject substantial gains 'more especially when the rejection would mean a renewal of hostilities, terrorism, and turmoil'. The content of the speeches looked very much as if the bishops had agreed in favour of the Treaty at their last meeting but decided not to issue a joint statement until the Dail had voted on the issue. But that did not prevent individual bishops from making their personal views known in their own dioceses.

On 7 January the Dail ratified the Treaty by sixty-four votes to fifty-seven; O'Kelly had been accurate in his voting prediction. Hagan was one of the first people to whom de Valera wrote about the outcome. On 13 January 1922 he explained his view:

A party set out to cross a desert, to reach a certain fertile country beyond – where they intended to settle down. As they were coming to the end of their journey and about to emerge from the desert, they came upon a broad oasis. Those who were weary said: 'Why go further – let us settle down here and rest, and be content.' But the hardier spirits would not, and decided to face the further hardships and travel on. Thus they divided – sorrowfully, but without recriminations.

De Valera felt that he ought to be with the 'hardier spirits – the pioneer party'. He had no doubt in his mind that the goal of 'sovereign independence' would be reached. His aim was to use the circumstances of each situation as it arose to work towards that goal.[18] De Valera found himself on what came to be known as the 'Republican' or 'anti-Treaty' side. But he was not, as Hagan had pointed out, a 'semi-anarchist' or an 'American gunman'. He was a 'good Catholic'. De Valera was swept along by events; he was not a hardline, 'physical force' nationalist.[19]

No matter how alienated de Valera was from the hierarchy at this stage in his career, he continued to have clerical friends in high places who distinguished him from his wilder and more radical allies. Circumstances did not allow him choose his own political company. But while Hagan, Magennis and Curran might have been forgiving, the Irish bishops were not. De Valera fell from grace in their eyes. The corruption of the best was always the worst. The delicate pro-Sinn Fein consensus which de Valera had so successfully cultivated in 1921, and which culminated in the June statement, was eroded in the early months of 1922. His anti-Treaty campaign in the countryside gave rise to the use of the most inflamed rhetoric. De Valera was never totally discredited in the eyes of the hierarchy. But his political stock was fast falling after the Treaty split. It was the one sustained period in his life when he was deserted by the basic feel for politics for which he was best known. There was an air of rarified desperation in his behaviour as he strove to explain the contours of his own constitutional reflections to audiences who clearly wanted peace and lacked his passion for symbols. In retrospect, some bishops were prepared to see this period in de Valera's life as an aberration, which it was. Others, like Fogarty, found it difficult to forget.

Pope Benedict XV sent telegrams of congratulation to the Dail, Logue and the King on 16 and 19 of January; he said he was 'overjoyed with the agreement happily reached in regard to Ireland'.[20] The Pope, who had been much more pro-nationalist than contemporary Irish clerics credited, died on 22 January 1922. Hagan was never very enthusiastic about the late Pope. He had his own personal reasons for feeling so critical. Hagan had written quite unfairly to Dublin on 7 October 1921 that 'the present Pope is immersed in one hobby, that of extending and consolidating diplomatic relations. No other consideration seems to count and anything that interferes with the success of this policy is damnable and damned.' Hagan – whose judgement was not usually so one-sided – claimed that the Pope was heavily committed to mollifying England:

For the success of this policy a good understanding with England and the English ambassador is of the utmost consequence and anything endangering that understanding has to be trampled under foot, that state of mind naturally refers only to the period that has elapsed since Germany went down and England came out on top and it is going to last just as long as England maintains that position or as long as the present pontificate lasts.[21]

Hagan claimed that Benedict and the curia had been prepared to listen to the British envoy, Gasquet and others, while the Irish were kept on the periphery. Had Hagan been privy to Foreign Office despatches, he would have had cause to think otherwise. He was defective in his judgement and he misrepresented the diplomatic subtlety of Benedict and Gasparri. Hagan was inclined to see the Vatican as a political unity. It was not. He also failed, on occasions, to take account of the political rivalries between cardinals. Benedict was a sophisticated judge of Irish affairs. It was he – probably on the advice of Gasparri – who prevented the publication of certain documents relating to the violence; when he finally issued a statement, it was construed by the Foreign Office as leaning towards support for the nationalists. He also showed his goodwill by donating 200,000 lire to the White Cross. Benedict did not deserve the criticisms made by Hagan. But the Rector did not know how difficult a time de Salis was having, trying to satisfy a demanding Foreign Secretary in 1920 and 1921. If he had known, he might have changed his mind about the late Pope.

Benedict was succeeded by Damiano Achille Ratti on 5 February 1922. He took the name Pius XI. Hagan was moderately pleased with the outcome, if a little cautious. He saw the new man as a scholar who had been elected by the group least associated with outright hostility to Ireland:[22]

So far we have little to go on in forming an idea as to what line the new pontiff is likely to take in our regard. One item is ominous enough. He spent some weeks in Gasquet's house, the time he received the Hat, and naturally learned that gentleman's views on all and sundry. But against this, there is the fact that he is a clever man and a learned man, a man who has some knowledge of the outside world and of the struggles that have to be waged by small peoples. Besides there is a story which is bound to reach his ears and which will have some effect. The observation was to this effect (made in Gasquet's house) that it would be interesting indeed to have a Pope like him. He had muddled the Vatican library, he muddled the Nunciature in Warsaw and now they talk of giving him a chance of muddling the papacy. I mention that his opponents were de Lai and Del Val. To these I think should be added the whole anti-Irish crowd, Bisleti, Pompili, Van Rossum. If the new Pope has a good memory this fact should be no harm to us. In any event, I can say with a whole heart that the new Pope cannot possibly be worse than his predecessor.[23]

Pius XI had extensive diplomatic experience as an apostolic visitator and then as nuncio of Poland in 1918.[24] The reappointment of Gasparri as Secretary of State ensured continuity of papal policy towards Ireland, some aspects of which Hagan did not particularly care for very much. He had been sounded out on the possibility of the new administration in Dublin sending an Irish diplomatic representative to

Rome. Hagan reminded Byrne that this would 'involve the presence of a nuncio in your archiepiscopal See though this feature of the case was not mentioned to me'.

A number of factors had arisen in early 1922 which gave both Hagan and the hierarchy cause for concern. The Church had come under repeated pressure from Cardinal de Lai of Consistorial to change the system of appointing bishops in Ireland (see Appendix I). A nuncio would play an integral part in the proposed new system. Diplomatic relations with the Vatican strongly recommended themselves to the members of the Provisional Government and to the acting Minister of Foreign Affairs, George Gavan Duffy. He was more convinced of the need to have an Irish envoy at the Vatican than to have a nuncio resident in Dublin. But thinking in the Department of Foreign Affairs altered radically on this point when Gavan Duffy was replaced by Desmond FitzGerald in summer 1922 and the Secretary of the Department, Robert Brennan, resigned and Joseph Walshe took over about the same time.

The Department lost many of its senior 'diplomats', including Sean T. O'Kelly, Art O'Brien, Harry Boland, Sean Nunan and Leopold Kerney, who traditionally supported Hagan's position on the Vatican and Irish politics. De Valera no longer exercised any influence in this area. Hagan found himself exposed with the change in the political situation in Ireland and with the election of Pius XI.

Hagan's thinking on this matter was clearly set out in a letter to Byrne, which was probably never sent:

If we take Poland as a sample – and there are obvious reasons for doing so – the first step will be the nomination of a Visitator Apostolic, who in due course will be translated into a Nuncio at the first suitable moment. I am not so sure but that the person of the first Visitator is not already identified in Salvatore Luzio who, as you know, was formerly in Maynooth. The mention of his name reminds me to observe that if anybody has to be accepted from this city he would be the best of a bad lot by long odds.[25]

The British, Hagan was convinced, would find a nuncio in Dublin very useful, since the idea of such an appointment in London would be considered impossible:

At the same time, I imagine that John Bull would have no insurmountable objection to having in Dublin a semi-diplomatic English machine who in ordinary times might be counted on to keep the clergy in due subjection to imperialism and to make known to those concerned all the tittle-tattle which would be dished up when occasion served in this city of Rome for the purpose of creating impressions and attitudes.

Hagan proposed the recognition of a representative in Rome, without having a corresponding representative in Ireland. There were a series of precedents for such a course. Prussia was represented at the Vatican, as was Russia, without nuncios in those countries. England, of course, was yet another example. If it became necessary to produce reasons why there should not be a nuncio in Dublin, Hagan believed that 'plenty of arguments could be found in the antics of former Vatican representatives from Vivian to Persico'. This rather frank letter, which appears never to have been sent, was probably written before the Archbishop's note of 2 February had reached Rome. There was no need to send the letter when Hagan read:

a Nuncio or even a delegate here would cause us immense embarrassment. His ear would be always open to tittle-tattle of all kinds of Catholic and 'Cawtholic' cranks. He would be a centre of disaffection for all disgruntled clergy . . . The Irish College is, in my opinion, the proper mechanism for dealing with the Roman authorities. I don't know what you think, but it appears to me the less the laity have to say to ecclesiastical matters the better. Of course, I speak of normal times.[26]

There was no immediate cause for concern in February 1922. The Vatican was as anxious as the Department of Foreign Affairs and leading members of the Provisional Government to establish diplomatic relations. But the Vatican was reluctant to contemplate such a move in the troubled climate of Irish politics. Until the crisis was resolved, there was no imminent danger of a nunciature being established in Dublin.[27] On 22 March 1922, Hagan wrote to Byrne from home describing

the existence and growth of something very like a state of panic which if allowed to develop may easily lead to regrettable results or to actions that cannot be recalled. Men's minds seem to me to be raw with irritation and their nerves seem to be in a state of tension, so that they seem to be drifting into a condition in which reason and conciliation have but a poor chance of operating. Misunderstanding would seem to be the natural result to be expected from this frame of mind; whereas as far as I have any opinion it would be in the direction that the hour is one calling for wholehearted endeavour to arrive at mutual understanding on the part of all who may be in a position to exercise soothing influences and thus prevent asperities from becoming more intense.

Hagan believed that there was a moderate wing of the republican movement which ought to be cultivated by the hierarchy. He felt that it was still possible to avoid military confrontation. The Rector repeatedly stressed the fact that O'Kelly, who had visited Rome in late February, was not out for bloodshed, and that he was neither unreasonable nor irreconcilable. The latter wanted constitutional change under the leadership of de Valera, whom he considered, 'for the present at least, the best man to keep in order various unruly elements which must be expected to accompany great revolutions'. Hagan felt that 'it will be easier to control these elements from within than it would be to restrain them from without'.[28]

Curran shared Hagan's view on this matter and he, too, wrote to Dublin urging a policy of caution and conciliation. He wondered whether it was judicious for the hierarchy to interfere in politics beyond declaring for freedom of elections.[29] His view was coloured by reflecting on the probable position of the Irish Church in fifteen or thirty years' time; were the bishops to declare against the separatists, Rory O'Connor and his extremists would not listen any more than the Fenians had done in the last century. While a declaration would certainly influence many, it would not bring about unity, and the fight would go on as in Parnell's time:

Even Dr Fogarty and those who think like him, admit that the republic or separation will come in 20 or 30 years' time. Why should the Catholic bishops of the next generation and the church of Ireland for all future time, be under the incubus of an episcopal anti-separation pronouncement, because of the seemingly critical position of the moment. Nothing is more humiliating to read than the pseudo-history of the O'Donovan Rossas, the Davitts, the T. P. O'Connors – ever harping on the policy of Troy, of Cullen, of McCabe, etc. Yet such will be our fate forever if the bishops persist in condemning . . . every forward movement of Irish nationality. Separation and independence *will* come. It's just and inevitable. Let us remember the countless generations of the future, not that of the moment. The politicians are responsible for the present mess, not the bishops.

Both Hagan and Curran were very well briefed on the intricacies of republican politics. Both were in regular contact with Sean T. O'Kelly, whom they linked with de Valera in the moderate wing of the anti-Treatyites. O'Kelly had warned the Rector that the split in the IRA had resulted in the emergence of a newly-formed hard-line high command, determined neither to allow elections nor to accept the Treaty. Neither Cathal Brugha nor Harry Boland had been put on the executive and the militants were spoiling for a fight, irrespective of what the politicians might do or achieve. They would defend the republic with arms, according to O'Kelly.

Hagan distinguished between the moderates and the radicals among the anti-Treatyites. Byrne and at least one other bishop – Mulhern of Dromore – had not written off de Valera completely as an intransigent. The Rector encouraged the Archbishop to use his good offices to try to bring both sides together. But the most pessimistic among the hierarchy regarded war as virtually certain. Fogarty of Killaloe wrote on 11 April:

We are in for the military coup d'etat with D. Val. proclaimed Dictator at proper time. There is some effort being made in Dublin for peace. But the 'Dictator' of the future wants no peace but his own . . . Meanwhile we can only trust in God.

De Valera is losing every day and intimidation is now his last resource . . . I have lost all confidence by him.[30]

Bishop O'Donnell, a measured voice among the hierarchy, told Hagan that he had recently received a letter from another Irish prelate – who usually 'weighed' his words but on that occasion 'language is used which I would not transfer to this paper. The violence is cut and dried and seems to be all on one side.'[31]

Logue was not unrepresentative in his views when he warned Byrne, on 5 April, against the idea of a conference, which the Archbishop had raised by letter with the Cardinal:

I have no confidence in a conference with the de Valera party. They would talk and wrangle for days about their shadowy republic and their obligations to it. Judging by their past, I believe if an agreement were come to, these people would not keep it.

The Cardinal did not think that it would be possible to keep de Valera and his party from 'wriggling out of any agreement reached'. Unlike Byrne, Logue did not distinguish between moderates and intransigents. He considered that the political situation was going 'from bad to worse'.[32]

He wanted the bishops to instruct their people, direct them, warn them, 'against wrong-doing and point out what is for their good, spiritual and temporal'. This done 'boldly', he thought, would have 'effect'. The people ought to be warned solemnly 'not to let what they have won be filched away from them and not to be led into grievous courses'. The last general meeting of bishops called was a 'mere fiasco' because the bishops did not speak out boldly.[33] The Cardinal called a special general meeting of the bishops for Low Week and asked O'Donnell and Fogarty to 'block' something out; and that Byrne would act with them as a committee to try and prepare a formal declaration.

The opportunities for resolving the differences between the Provisional Government and the anti-Treaty forces were dwindling rapidly. On 14 April, 1922, republicans led by Rory O'Connor occupied the Four Courts. De Valera could exert little influence over these men. The growing militancy of the republicans had been accompanied by acts of violence in which a number of people lost their lives. In Mullingar, a government soldier and an 'irregular' were shot dead in an armed confrontation on 27 April and the following day eight Protestants were killed in West Cork in what the *Freeman's Journal* described as 'sectarian assassinations'.[34] That newspaper – one of the oldest in the country – had been the subject of an attack on 30 March 1922, when 'republicans' smashed up the printing machinery with sledge-hammers and then sprinkled petrol over the case room and set it on fire. Such an attack, which was reminiscent of the behaviour of Mussolini and his Blackshirts, was a serious assault on freedom of expression in the country.[35] There were also other incidents throughout the country where government ministers were shouted down at public meetings and shots were fired. The Labour movement organised a general one-day strike on 23 April.[36] It was a major success.

Archbishop Byrne was not very optimistic about the possibility of bringing the rival groups around the conference table. But he was convinced that he should at least try. Byrne was a very close friend of W. T. Cosgrave, and it is probable that moves for conciliation may also have been encouraged from that quarter. But both Cosgrave and Byrne had colleagues who had long since given up any hope of getting through to the anti-Treatyites. As long as the republicans were not a monolithic force, there was a slender hope that de Valera, O'Kelly and Harry Boland could help avoid violence and possible civil war. As the hierarchy prepared to hold a special meeting, Byrne, with the cooperation of the Lord Mayor of Dublin, convened a conference at the Mansion House in mid-April. Among those who attended were Michael Collins, Arthur Griffith and de Valera. The conference quickly ran into serious difficulties. It had to be adjourned three times.

Owing to his involvement in the Mansion House talks Byrne missed part of the special meeting of the hierarchy at Maynooth on 26 April. It was an important session with a crowded agenda. A committee of bishops (Dublin, Cashel, the Coadjutor of Armagh, Killaloe, Dromore and Clonfert) was set up to request a copy of the 'report of the constitution of the Free State' and having examined its contents they were to report back to the bishops.[37]

Another problem which raised its head was the appointment of army chaplains. The military authorities had made the request. The Archbishop of Dublin and the Bishop of Killaloe, both with large camps in their diocese, were asked to discuss the matter. They reported to the June meeting where it was decided that the local bishops should make the appointments and it was the feeling of the bishops that the anti-Treatyites should not get official chaplains.[38]

In December, when the bishops had last met at a special meeting, both sides had approached members of the hierarchy to win support. It is doubtful if the anti-Treatyites lobbied the bishops in April, so changed was the political mood in the country. But the Provisional Government was in contact.[39] The pastoral which was issued was supportive of their position.

The bishops stated on 26 April 1922 that, like the 'great bulk of the nation', the 'best and wisest' course for Ireland to take was to accept and work the treaty making 'the most of the freedom it undoubtedly brings us – freedom for the first time in 700 years'. The pastoral declared that final acceptance would be determined by the outcome of the elections. The statement repudiated claims that any army, 'or part of it, can, without any authority from the nation as a whole, declare itself independent of all civil authority'. There was no doubt, despite 'speculative views' on the subject, that the supreme authority in the country was the Provisional Government and the Dail acting in unison. Anyone who took up arms against it, added the statement, were 'parricides and not patriots'. The 'use of the revolver' and the murder of the 'free soul of Ireland' had to cease.[40]

The *Freeman's Journal*, in a banner headline, stated: 'Catholic hierarchy unsparingly denounce militarism'. The Mansion House Conference held a final session and dissolved without finding any basis for further discussion.[41] On 1 May 1922 Byrne wrote to Hagan that his attempt to ensure that 'pro- and anti-treatyites might at least keep their hands off each other' had ended in failure.[42]

Apart from the friendship between some members of the hierarchy and leading pro-Treatyite politicians, the *ad hoc* episcopal committee to examine the Constitution brought some bishops and ministers into a close working relationship. In fact, the cabinet had first taken the initiative when, on 10 April 1922, it decided to consult the bishops on the wording of Article 10, concerning free primary education.[43] It may well have been that the initial contact encouraged the hierarchy to request the government to provide a copy of the draft document for study.[44] The tone of the pastoral letter and the courtesy over the drafting of the Constitution laid the foundations for a good working relationship. The Archbishop of Dublin remained very close to men like Cosgrave. But he was not totally without respect for some of the more prominent anti-Treatyite politicians. As was pointed out earlier, the Catholic hierarchy was not a monolithic political force.

As the country prepared for an election, a final effort was made to restore the political unity which characterised the Sinn Fein movement prior to the Treaty. Michael Collins and Eamon de Valera signed an electoral pact on 20 May designed to retain the political balance of the old Dail. The compromise broke down. On election day, 16 June, the new Constitution was published in the morning press. The anti-Treatyites were very much opposed to the document. The election confirmed the majority support for the terms of the Treaty. Arthur Griffith and the pro-Treaty group won fifty-eight out of 128 seats, while other party groupings got seventy seats; of these, the Labour party won seventeen, Farmers seven, Independents ten, while thirty-six seats went to anti-Treatyites.

But if Griffith and his political associates had fought the election on the question of acceptance or rejection of the Treaty, there was strong criticism from Collins and others over the final format of the Constitution. Curran was on holiday in Dublin at the time, and he reported the news to Hagan in Rome:

The pro-Treaty people are crest-fallen over the much-booned constitution. Collins has spoken very strongly against it but I suppose he will support it in public. He told Sean T. there would be trouble on his side over it and he is reported . . . to have said: 'the king is smeared all over it'. Gavan Duffy prepared me for it and said the mischief was due to the bad tactics of the treaty people who at the Sinn Fein convention insisted on it being sent to the English cabinet before it was sent to the Irish people . . . I suppose he forgets his own brave talk of 'relegating the king into exterior darkness'. The outlook is threatening.[45]

The Provisional Government felt compelled to take some action to prevent the political situation from deteriorating further. The intransigence of the Four Courts garrison and their political supporters placed considerable strain on Anglo-Irish relations. Members of the Provisional Government, according to Cosgrave, were 'generally of the opinion that the British negotiators had taken their political lives also in their hands' when they signed the Treaty on 6 December 1921.[46] It is certainly true that those Irish politicians who supported the treaty claimed – and believed – it was unpopular in England. But it is also true that such claims might have been exaggerated. The Treaty was seen as a success for Lloyd George. Had he pressed Ulster against her will, he would have lost the support of certain Conservatives; while once trouble emerged in Ireland itself, the treaty became more generally discredited in England. The climate of political uncertainty continued into the early summer of 1922. There was considerable fear in Merrion Street that there could be a radical change in British policy towards Ireland at any time. On 22 June, Sir Henry Wilson, the Chief of the Imperial General Staff from 1918 to 1922 and a 'diehard' MP who had acted as military adviser to the Northern Ireland government, was shot dead at his doorstep in London by Irish gunmen. The murder placed even greater pressure on the Provisional Government to act against the militant anti-Treatyites. The shelling of the Four Courts began on 28 June 1922.

Curran, back in Dublin from Rome, felt that he was 'among a strange people'.[47] The tension within the Provisional Government was reflected in Gavan Duffy's resignation from the Foreign Ministry. About twenty years later, Gavan Duffy was to sum up the political atmosphere in pre-Civil War Ireland:

National public opinion generally took a childlike view of politics; it saw the country sharply rent by the Treaty into two fields of thought, the one pure white and the other a murky black, but the initial difficulty for many good men was to determine which was which; once you felt that you had discovered which really was the field of white, you enrolled as a White and proceeded to champion your side through thick and thin . . . if you were not whole-heartedly with the White or the Black, you were generally put down as a 'Tadhg an da Thaobh' or a factionist.[48]

Curran has left a vivid account of the opening rounds of the Civil War. He was awakened

by machine gun, bomb and rifle fire from the [Four] Courts and it continues off and on during the day . . . and at present [afternoon] the sniping is widespread around Parnell Sq. and Courts. I expect that day by day it will extend all through the town. A man was shot dead beside Paddy Dunne (secretary to archbishop) this morning as they were going down Parnell Sq. The shot was fired at a small group of British soldiers, armed, passing down the square. All, including soldiers, decamped, but Paddy returned and was able to give the man absolution before he died. We are in for a very hot time, but so far the people are very calm. They may be more alarmed as the sniping increases and food runs short or becomes unprocurable.[49]

Curran expected the fighting would last for a long time. He also feared a 'possible reoccupation by the British'. He detected that 'people are queerly indifferent in the mass' to the essence of the conflict. Curran was convinced that if they get the chance 'they would clear out five-sixths of the people on both sides and replace them by independent pro-treaty people of the type of the lord mayor (of Dublin) and Labour'.[50] Another prominent clergyman, J. F. D'Alton, was convinced that 'all the fine enthusiasm that marked the struggle of a year ago has evaporated'. Politicians were 'playing England's game' and a full scale civil war looked likely.[51] On 10 July 1922 Curran wrote pessimistically to Hagan: '. . . we are in for the dreary years that followed the Kilkenny Confederation. The two parties hate each other as they never hated the English . . . the virtue of charity has simply cleared out of the country and until it, and a little of the old tact returns, we are hopeless'.[52] He said that de Valera was 'broken-hearted'. All hopes of establishing a republican party had been smashed while the politicians had been blamed for 'the intransigence and vandalism' of O'Connor. De Valera was hated 'by the pro-Treaty people as no other man is hated, except Childers and Collins on the other side'.[53]

De Valera had disappointed many people by his response on the morning of the shelling of the Fourt Courts. He immediately issued a statement describing the garrison under attack as the 'best and bravest of our nation'. He depicted the Provisional Government as acting under British pressure: '. . . at the bidding of the English, Irishmen are today shooting down, on the streets of our capital, brother Irishmen, old comrades-in-arms, companions in the recent struggle for Ireland's independence and its embodiment – the Republic'.[54] It is quite difficult to imagine the actual confusion and indecisiveness which followed the shelling. Many prominent anti-Treatyites, who were not in the military wing, knew what side they were *not* on. Some of the republican politicians did not consider civil war, even then, inevitable.[55]

De Valera had been ignored by the military leadership of the IRA. Yet he quickly rejoined his old unit, the Third Dublin Battalion, as a private. He remained on the periphery of military planning and strategy throughout the Civil War. He had relatively little influence over the military men on either side who kept hostilities going. De Valera was in Fermoy barracks, on 9 August 1922, when he heard of the death of his close friend, Harry Boland. That night, the anti-Treatyite forces abandoned the barracks. The war appeared to him both pointless and futile. Many years later he confided to a leading Irish diplomat that he was convinced at that point the war should have ended.[56] According to both Col. Dan Bryan and Professor Williams, de Valera had made a determined effort to convince the anti-Treatyite leadership that he should return to Dublin and try to enter the Dail without taking the oath. He was convinced that that action would have beneficial political consequences. But he was prevented from doing so by Liam Lynch in particular. Precisely what de Valera was doing during the Civil War will only be revealed by further research.

On 12 August, Arthur Griffith, the President of the Provisional Government, died of a heart attack.[57] Ten days later, Michael Collins was shot dead in an ambush. William T. Cosgrave was not the most obvious choice among the range of politicians likely to succeed Griffith. But he was the wisest. A very close friend of Archbishop Byrne, Cosgrave had served as a member of Dublin Corporation, had fought in the 1916 Rising and been sentenced to death. He had been jailed in Frongoch, Wales. On his release he resumed his active role in nationalist politics and served as Minister for Local Government in the First Dail. Cosgrave became President 'at the most disheartening moment of recent Irish history'. He inherited a country that was in a state of civil war. He presided over an Executive Council in which sat at least two people who felt that they should have his position. Cosgrave asserted himself gradually and guided the government and the country on the path of moderation and constitutional politics.[58]

In August Hagan arrived in Ireland, intent on trying to succeed where Archbishop Byrne and the Mansion House Conference had failed. The Rector made contact with Sean T. O'Kelly, who was in jail, and through him – with the cooperation of Mulcahy – he wrote to Liam Mellowes and Rory O'Connor in Mountjoy. Tom Barry and Oscar

13 Clergy lead the funeral procession of Michael Collins, Cork, 1922

Traynor, who were imprisoned with O'Kelly in Kilmainham, appeared willing to go and see the imprisoned republican leaders in Mountjoy.[59] They were willing to try to persuade the others to halt the violence. Fogarty of Killaloe and Mulhern of Dromore were suggested as intermediaries. Mulcahy was accommodating but sceptical: 'I have been in close association with those who are responsible for this campaign, and I have not been able to trace any gleam of intention, other than to continue that campaign . . .'.[60] The peace moves collapsed.[61] Hagan, as a last resort, tried to see de Valera. But the latter wrote to him, through a Miss Ryan: 'I am afraid nothing will be gained by seeing us at the moment.' That was an admission of his political impotence. Before his return to Rome, Hagan had learned that de Valera, O'Kelly and the moderates were in no position to exercise any influence over the intransigents. Liam Lynch and Rory O'Connor were not prepared to negotiate.

The bishops were scheduled to meet in October. One of the more nationalistic on the bench, O'Doherty of Clonfert, who had sung 'A Nation once again' at a party hosted by O'Kelly in Rome in 1920, wrote to Hagan using the most unrestrained language: 'Things are not very hopeful here. De Valera has allowed himself to be hoisted into the "presidency" on the remaining bayonets of Rory O'Connor's squad. It is not a very dignified or comfortable position now. The republic is out now for victory, or extermination, and the women are screaming or fasting.'[62] O'Doherty was referring to the fact that the anti-Treatyite side had set up an 'Emergency Government' on 17 October 1922 with de Valera as President.

The tone of O'Doherty's letter indicates the degree of irritation felt even by his strongest admirers on the bench of bishops. The decision to allow himself become the symbol of authority in a rival government reflected the 'policy of drift' which so characterised de Valera's behaviour during the Civil War. There is some evidence to suggest that de Valera, after the succession of military defeats throughout the summer of 1922, seriously considered the possibility of attempting to enter the Dail when it met on 9 September *without taking the oath*. He canvassed support for the idea and was moderately successful in attracting some followers. He also opposed the idea of setting up a 'republican government'. What prevented him from taking the courageous step of entering the Dail is a problem which remains outside the scope of this study. But the opposition from the militarists was extremely strong. They were afraid of being betrayed by the diplomats and politicians among them. De Valera temporised and finally found himself being 'hoisted into the presidency.' He had again shown a lack of decisiveness. De Valera was identified by this move with the military republican wing. Hence the bitterness of his erstwhile sympathiser, O'Doherty. There was, as a result, a receptivity on the bench of bishops to any overture from the constitutional authorities which might be considered helpful to put an end to the violence and rebellion.

The Provisional Government made a formal approach to the hierarchy following a meeting of the Executive Council on 4 October. The Ministers had discussed 'the low moral standard prevailing throughout the country'.[63] A strong statement was considered desirable and it is assumed that every effort was made to achieve that end. It is doubtful if the hierarchy required much convincing. On 22 October 1922 the bishops stated that the militant anti-Treatyites had 'wrecked Ireland from end to end'. The pastoral condemned the campaign of destruction which had resulted in murder and assassination. The minds of young people were 'being poisoned by false principles, and their young lives utterly spoiled by early association with cruelty, robbery, falsehood and crime'. They had tried to browbeat the bishops and the clergy:

And, in spite of all this sin and crime, they claim to be good Catholics, and demand at the hands of the Church her most sacred privileges, like the Sacraments, reserved for worthy members alone . . . All those who, in contravention of this teaching, participate in such crimes, are guilty of the gravest sins, and may not be absolved in Confession, nor admitted to Holy Communion, if they purpose to persevere in such evil courses . . . It is said that there are some priests who approve of this Irregular insurrection. If there be any such, they are false to their sacred office, and are guilty of the gravest scandal, and will not be allowed to retain the faculties they hold from us. Furthermore we, each for his own diocese, hereby forbid under pain of suspension, ipso facto, reserved to the Ordinary, any priest to advocate or encourage the revolt, publicly or privately.[64]

De Valera was deeply upset by the pastoral, which he regarded as 'most unfortunate'. 'Never was charity of judgement so necessary, and aparently so disastrously absent', he wrote to Mannix on 6 November 1922. 'Ireland and the Church will, I fear, suffer in consequence.'[65]

The government introduced the severest measures to deal with the anti-Treatyite forces, including the right to try before a military tribunal as a capital offence those found in possession of arms and ammunition. The first to die under the new measures were four Dublin youths found in possession of arms. The action provoked acrimonious exchanges in the Dail, on 17 November 1922, as the Labour party leader, Tom Johnson, expressed his shock and revulsion at the action of the courts. Kevin O'Higgins, the Minister for Justice, replied that the action was not vindictive but a deterrent. He said the life and honour of the nation was worth 'the lives of many individuals' and the government had decided, after grave deliberations, that when it was necessary to take the lives of many individuals 'the lives of many individuals will be taken'.[66]

Erskine Childers had been arrested on 10 November 1922, in possession of a small pistol which had been given to him by Michael Collins.[67] Among the many prominent anti-Treatyite politicians, de Valera and Childers were the two who provoked most resentment in government circles. Childers, in particular, symbolised 'republican' intransigence. He was executed on 24 November 1922. His death shocked and outraged leading members of the hierarchy, as did the general policy of executions.

'No event of recent years has saddened me in the same way as the execution of Erskine Childers', O'Donnell wrote to Hagan:

Since I heard of it I think of little else. I knew him some years ago and derived much friendly assistance from him during the Irish Convention [1917]. I think I was the first to suggest that his services would be sought at that time. So, much as I disliked intervening in any way, when I saw a few days ago that he was in jeopardy, I wrote to the law adviser suggesting that he should be spared. Plainly I had nothing for my pains. All the executions are most deplorable especially that of poor Childers. I said mass for him to-day . . . Up to then the Irish government seemed to me to have done well on the whole and then, I can judge, wisdom left them. I trust it may soon return . . . Our Cardinal and the Archbishop of Dublin are against the executions.[68]

Byrne was one of the most vigorous opponents among the hierarchy of the policy of executions. He made his views known to Cosgrave by letter which has not come to light in the course of this research; but Hagan wrote to congratulate him over his intervention in the case of Childers:

I knew poor Childers, and I knew his wife and one of their children, God help us! I am wondering if it is a case of *quis vult Deus perdere*? Your action in writing to have him spared does honour to you and him; and I am glad indeed to know that even one voice was raised on the side of mercy. Unfortunately deeds like this are bound to awaken deadly echoes, and only one endowed with the gift of prophecy can venture to foretell where it is going to stop. But perhaps I had better rest satisfied with saying this much. If I went on I should perhaps say things I might regret later on.[69]

The first of the 'deadly echoes', spoken about by Hagan was the murder of Deputy Sean Hales by gunmen, on 7 December, as the veteran Cork guerrilla leader and nationalist organiser was on his way to the Dail; it was part of a vicious republican reprisal policy. The killing provoked a savage response from the government. The following morning, on 8 December, four imprisoned republican leaders, including Rory O'Connor and Liam Mellowes, were executed without trial, as a 'reprisal', according to an official communiqué.[70]

The Calced Carmelite Superior General, who was a personal friend of the executed Mellowes, wrote from America on hearing the news, in a vein not usually associated with heads of religious orders, but nonetheless illustrative of the revulsion evoked by the shooting:

I received the news of the shooting of four amongst which was dear friend Liam. That has given me a turn I am almost afraid to contemplate. I know those fellows [Free Staters] were contemptible curs, but it never occurred to me they were such vampires. Drunk with this sudden greatness their one idea is to revel in human blood. However, for the present I must keep quiet until we meet.[71]

Sean MacBride, who was in jail for his anti-Free State activities, recalled how he heard the news from the priest in the sacristy early on the morning of the 8th. He was so shocked and furious that four of the most prominent republicans were dead that he walked with the chaplain quite unselfconsciously through the main gate of Mountjoy and was some distance outside the prison before he realised that he was free. He then had to double back and knock at the gate for re-admission.

The Archbishop of Dublin, according to one source, had spent a number of hours on the eve of the execution with Cosgrave trying unsuccessfully to persuade him to have the cabinet reverse the decision.[72] His efforts failed, despite Cosgrave's personal sympathy for the Archbishop's point of view. Byrne was deeply shocked and outraged when he read in the papers that the action had been taken as a 'reprisal' and he drafted a very stern reprimand to Cosgrave on 10 December:

It was with something like dismay that I saw by the Army Communications to the newspapers on Friday that the four men were executed as 'reprisals' for the death of General Hales. Now, the policy of reprisals seems to me to be not only unwise but entirely unjustifiable from the moral point of view. That one man should be punished for another's crime seems to me to be absolutely unjust. Moreover, such a policy is bound to alienate many friends of the Government, and it requires all the sympathy it can get.[73]

He hoped that the road to clemency was not closed. People were entitled to a fair trial 'without the appearance of heat or haste'. He did not write to embarrass the government but he thought it was 'only fair to the position I hold to put you in possession of my honest views'.

Cosgrave was personally deeply concerned by the withering criticism of his episcopal friends. According to Professor T. Desmond Williams, Cosgrave 'regretted, more perhaps than some of them, the harsher aspects of the Civil War, including, for example, the precipitate execution of Rory O'Connor and his three comrades'. So important was the adverse ecclesiastical opinion considered that Byrne was invited to a meeting with ministers to discuss the matter. He was accompanied by his secretary, Bishop Dunne. The meeting lasted about half an hour and, according to Bishop Dunne, the intervention was effective in moderating government policy.[74] The executions continued, but no other prisoner was shot 'as a reprisal'.

Hagan had returned to Rome in late October to learn that the pastoral letter, condemning the anti-Treatyites, had provoked widespread opposition in the United States, Australia, New Zealand and Britain. The Vatican had received a huge correspondence voicing disapproval of the recent action of the Irish bishops. The Rector also received a large mailbag on this matter: 'Many letters reach me, containing statements to the effect that the executions would never have been possible had the bishops not given their official corporate sanction by the October pastoral.'

Hagan added that 'great stress is laid on the silence observed with regard to the execution of Mellowes and his companions . . . but I think in all justice it is a pity that there was not some public expression of what I believe to be the Episcopal mind on the Mellowes incident'. The Rector may well have been reflecting disquiet shared by some members of the clergy – as he indicated – but he was also putting his own point of view. It would have been extremely difficult for the hierarchy to take a public position on the executions of the four men on 8 December without running the risk of strengthening the resolve of the anti-Treatyites to continue the hopeless fight with further loss of lives.

There is evidence that Byrne, in particular, had gone out of his way to use his authority to modify the Provisional Government's policy in that area. It was both impractical and imprudent to suggest that an episcopal statement ought to have been made. The hierarchy would have had to have called a special meeting – it was not scheduled to meet again until April 1923 – to issue a statement. The Standing Committee would, perhaps, have been in a position to draft and publish a statement. But that would have been quite awkward in view of the fact that episcopal unanimity on this matter would have been extremely difficult to achieve.

The execution policy was quite a distinct issue from the manner in which Rory O'Connor and the other three men had been shot. Byrne was not only opposed to those executions; he also had considerable doubts about the political wisdom of the policy generally. Apart from O'Donnell and, possibly, Mulhern of Dromore, it is doubtful – and this is speculation – whether the Archbishop of Dublin would have got much support for his broader objections from the bench of bishops. But as the local ordinary – in the archdiocese – of Dublin he had the obligation to deal with the matter as he saw fit. He did so diplomatically and firmly.

It is a moot point whether the policy of executions helped shorten the Civil War or increased the bitterness and prolonged the violence at a time when the anti-Treatyite forces were practically beaten in the field. Byrne had felt that the policy was 'bound to alienate many friends of the government, and it requires all the sympathy it can get'.

A contemporary source, Mr Alexis Fitzgerald, regards the harsh policy as 'necessary, but it was a horrible, horrible thing to have to do'. He recalled being told by Paddy Ruttledge that it was the execution policy which ended the Civil War, 'because then we realised that we were faced with people as terrible as ourselves'.[75] In a letter to the author, Mr Liam Cosgrave wrote:

Regarding the Executions no civilised Government likes to have to do these things, but a Government's first duty is to Govern by vindicating and asserting the will of the people. The Irregulars opposed the will of the people by every means and the Government after having shown considerable restraint eventually enforced the law. The Government considered the Executions shortened the Civil War and saved more innocent persons being killed by the Irregulars. My father accepted responsibility for the actions of his Government.[76]

In retrospect, it is relatively easy to agree with the leaders of the hierarchy that the policy of executions was neither necessary nor morally justifiable. But the men in government who faced having to make such a terrible decision were not certain that the State could withstand the threat from the anti-Treatyites. More mature and experienced politicians might have acted otherwise. It is clear, however, that if Byrne had not intervened with Cosgrave the policy of executions might have been used with less discrimination. It is very doubtful if such a draconian policy – and in particular the execution of Childers and the 'reprisal' shooting of the four leaders in Mountjoy – helped shorten the Civil War.[77] The term 'reprisal' has universally repugnant overtones. But, as has been argued in Chapter II, the highly respectable *Freeman's Journal* had repeatedly and courageously taken the British administration to task during the most violent period of 1920 for bringing the law into disrepute by carrying out a policy of 'reprisals'. The fact that an Irish Government could use such a discredited term, as a justification for executions, equated their actions in the popular mind with those of the Black and Tans under Hamar Greenwood. The Catholic bishops were deeply perturbed by the establishment of such a moral precedent. But some less than others.

Chapter IV

THE VATICAN AND THE CIVIL WAR

Hagan returned to Rome in mid-autumn 1922 disappointed with the failure of his recent peace overtures in Dublin and dejected by the general political deterioration in the country. He was highly critical of the government and remained broadly sympathetic with de Valera and the political wing of the anti-Treatyite camp. He was not long back in the Italian capital when he began to hear of 'alarming' diplomatic developments which had taken place in his absence. It made excellent sense to take advantage of Hagan's prolonged stay abroad to harness forces in the Vatican. Curran was of like mind with the Rector but he was not nearly as imposing a character. This chapter examines the efforts of the Vatican to 'do something' for Ireland and the determination of the hierarchy to frustrate the initiative for reasons rooted in recent history. Hagan heard from an 'impressive' source that a condemnation had been prepared in the Vatican relating to the situation in Ireland. Hagan described the 'impending crisis' as 'distinctly menacing'. Byrne obviously also shared that point of view. In such a delicate political situation any Vatican intervention could only have a negative local impact. It was a source of added irritation for Byrne to learn – as ordinary of the Dublin archdiocese – that 'the mischief is that Armagh is pressing for a fulmination'.[1]

Hagan found himself in a rather weak position. It was all very well for him to assert at the Vatican that 'a majority of the Irish bishops would not be in favour of the Holy See mixing itself up in the present imbroglio', but as long as Armagh was 'knocking at the door' his word was not likely to carry great weight:

The whole situation is peculiar, and it is not easily handled either here or at home as Armagh is acting behind the backs of his colleagues; and if he acts behind their backs in the matter of Vatican intervention he may easily be driven by force of circumstances into doing something similar in the matter of a delegate; I know that he is opposed to any such project; but his vanity and his eagerness to score may lead him into such a course which he otherwise would not dream of.

On the same day that Hagan wrote to Byrne, 13 November, he included a memorandum outlining the situation in the frankest of terms. He also wrote to O'Donnell, now Bishop of Attalia and Coadjutor of Armagh, advising him that he had drafted the document. For obvious reasons, he could not risk sending it to *Ara Coeli*, the home of the Cardinal of Armagh. Hagan had talked over the matter of a possible Vatican condemnation when he was in Dublin with Byrne and the latter had 'very emphatically expressed the opinion' that such intervention was 'inadvisable' since it 'could do no possible good and might easily be the cause of very great harm'. That was also the view of other members of the hierarchy, according to Hagan. Policy on the question of a nunciature for Dublin was quite clear. The Rector was to follow the instructions given to him after the October meeting of the hierarchy, which presumably directed him to discourage the idea should it arise. He had learned that Logue was both anxious for a condemnation and also for the sending of an apostolic visitator. So definite was that prospect that the 'name of Luzio is a matter of gossip in interested circles'.

Hagan suggested that Byrne write a personal letter either to himself or to the Pope outlining the likely damage a condemnation could do to the position of the Catholic Church in Ireland. He also suggested that the episcopal Standing Committee might be persuaded to write along the same lines to Vatican authorities.

Quite unfairly to the Vatican authorities, Hagan felt it was pointless even to 'dwell on the harm that would be done by arousing Orange bigotry in the North'. In Rome nobody 'cares one pin how Northern or even Southern Catholics are affected or are likely to be affected by a policy in which the Empire is interested'. He suggested, somewhat scathingly, that it might be hinted that such a move could lead to a falling off in the Peter's Pence collection.[2] Byrne immediately wrote to Logue on the matters raised by Hagan in his letter and memorandum. He received a stern reply from the Cardinal on 22 November, indirectly confirming most of what Hagan had set out in his memorandum. Logue was opposed to the idea of a resident nuncio but there was 'another kind of delegate to which I would not object, would rather welcome: that is if the Pope sent some trustworth [*sic*] person, in a temporary way to report on the conditions of Ireland'. Logue said that the Vatican authorities had a 'very hazy notion of the state of Ireland'. Gasparri had told Logue that they had only 'scraps from the news agencies in the Italian papers'. The matter was very urgent because, in his view, the Vatican was being 'flooded with de Valera's propaganda'. While the Cardinal was certain that it was so intemperate that 'it betrays itself', he nevertheless added, 'in mud slinging some will stick'.[3]

Logue admitted that he had written to Gasparri encouraging a fulmination from Rome:

The authority of the Bishops is impeached, vilified and condemned, and it is the part of the Holy See to support and maintain the authority of the Bishops. I know that this was done frequently by the late Popes when any of the Italian Bishops were opposed. I wrote that to Cardinal Gasparri some short time since. It might have little effect on the bad people in this country and America, but they can scarcely be going more to the devil than they are going at present. But every real Catholic would listen to the voice of the Holy Father, and yield obedience to his authority.[4]

Byrne had also taken up the suggestion by Hagan that a letter should be sent to Gasparri opposing the idea of a nunciature in the present circumstances. When he proposed the idea to Logue, the Cardinal replied icily:

I don't see how I could write, in cold blood, to Cardinal Gasparri against a project which seems to have no better foundation than the speculation and chit-chat of Rome. I have had two or three letters lately on matters of much less importance from Cardinal Gasparri; and not even a hint of this project. I think in the present crippled state of the finances of the Holy See, it is not likely, except it became absolutely necessary.[5]

That was an implied criticism of the Rector's judgement.

But Hagan felt his instructions were clear enough to send a letter on 13 November – the day he wrote to Byrne – to the Under-Secretary of Extraordinary Ecclesiastical Affairs, Mgr Borgongini Duca. He impressed upon him the need for the Vatican to take a course involving 'as little intervention as possible . . . in Irish political or semi-political affairs'. He urged 'a neutral and procrastinating attitude . . . at the present dark hour.' In giving that advice, he felt he was voicing the views of the great majority of the Irish bishops when he offered the carefully considered opinion that 'any action, even a negative one, on the part of the Holy See, may easily lead to developments and complications gravely prejudicial to the interests of religion for many a year to come.'[6]

Byrne wrote the requested letter. In the note the Archbishop said that there was some local tale, following visits by republicans to the Vatican, of sending a papal delegate to Ireland to investigate complaints. He considered such a move inadvisable, as the Holy See could then be seen to be acting under the influence of those who had flouted religion in Ireland. The sending of a delegate would also exacerbate the religious tension in the North, and might give rise to the suspicion that the delegate was under British influence. The real reason why such people wanted a delegate, wrote the Archbishop, was to show that the Irish hierarchy did not enjoy the confidence of the Papacy. Those who had shown disrespect for the Irish bishops would have scant respect for the Holy See or its representative.[7] The note was exactly the clarification Hagan had requested. It was promptly translated into Italian and sent to the Vatican.

However, the Rector saw Pius XI before the arrival of the Dublin note and found the Pope very perplexed about the situation in Ireland as a result of the volume of telegrams coming from America on the Irish question. He gave no hint about either the existence of a letter of condemnation or an apostolic visitation. Bishop Cotter of Portsmouth had also visited both Gasparri and Pius XI. The Secretary of State had spoken to him about a contemplated letter. But the Bishop got the impression that neither the Pope nor Gasparri were anxious about the scheme. They wanted 'to find any excuse for not sending anything of the kind'.[8] Another nationalist sympathiser, Amigo of Southwark, also discussed the Irish situation with the Pope. Pius XI told him that the idea of writing a letter had been abandoned.[9]

On 21 December, Hagan had a long conversation with Mgr Borgongini Duca and mentioned the Byrne letter which the Rector had sent over to him. Borgongini Duca assured the Rector that there was nothing in the rumour; and Hagan quickly asked whether he was free to write that to the Archbishop. The latter became embarrassed and said finally that 'no step had been taken, and that if people took every rumour for gospel that he could not help it'. Hagan came away convinced that there was something to the whole affair but 'the chances are that your letter has upset their calculations and has probably postponed the evil day'.[10] But Hagan was warned by one of his reliable contacts at the Vatican that, while it was true that the contemplated letter had been scrapped, that should not 'be regarded as final'.[11] He had some satisfaction in knowing that Logue's manoeuvres were known to his fellow bishops, 'and with this knowledge in their minds they will not be too hard on me if they find me slow in putting forward any statement on their behalf until I am very certain of my ground. It would be simply ruinous to make representations purporting to be the mind of the bishops, while all the time the chief one among them was giving expression to the opposite.'[12]

The constant stream of correspondence from anti-Treatyite sympathisers in the United States, Australia, New Zealand, Britain and Ireland was a source of continuous concern to the Vatican. Although I have not seen the letters, it is certain that the volume must have increased following the executions in November and December. Apart from the predictable political attacks on the Free State government, responsible people must have written making many of the same arguments to the Pope that O'Donnell and Byrne had made to Cosgrave over the executions of Childers and also the four men on 8 December. There were also personalities among the Irish community in Rome who would have expressed the strongest reservations. There was an additional factor, which was a source of widespread grievance, among the anti-Treatyite group: they were, as a result of the October pastoral, denied the sacraments by many priests and prison chaplains. A decision was taken to appeal to the Pope.

Two men, Dr Conn Murphy and Professor Arthur Clery, travelled to Rome with a document in French of over eighty pages setting out their case against the Irish hierarchy.[13] Although I have been unable to see this document, Curran commented that 'it had all the usual drawbacks of a paper amended by too many cooks'.[14]

The two men passed through London on their way to Rome, and they visited Amigo at Southwark. He urged both men to confine themselves to securing the removal of penalties, and to avoid attacking the hierarchy. Amigo wrote to Hagan on 10 December that Cleary and Murphy struck him as 'excellent men, desirous of peace'. He advised Hagan that the Vice-Rector, Curran, should arrange all audiences.[15] The two men arrived in Rome and were well received by Hagan. The delegation was treated very seriously by the Vatican authorities. They saw the Pope and they also spoke to Gasparri. Curran felt that 'they certainly fought their corner very well and courageously, despite the difficulties'.[16] The delegation could feel quite pleased with their mission. Logue returned from the episcopal Standing Committee meeting, in early January, to discover a large packet containing the appeal from 'the two gentlemen in Rome' waiting for him. (The matter had been briefly touched upon at the meeting.) A source of further annoyance for Logue was that the press had got to know about the document and had been telephoning *Ara Coeli* repeatedly for reaction. It has not been possible to see the letter from Gasparri, but a clue to its contents can be found in a letter from Logue to Byrne on 21 January 1923. He rejected any idea that the bishops had had anything to do with 'pacts, and first and second Dail and elections'.

The only charge that could be brought against the bishops was 'that we lamented the state of the country, which was bad then and worse since, warned the people against crime, which was our duty, appealed for justice and exhorted the people to obey the present government and, if they wished, work for a republic by constitutional means, which we had every right to do'. The most serious charge was that 'we deprived the republicans of sacraments', which Logue stated was not true: 'We made no reserved case; but merely stated that those who persisted in committing crimes which we enumerated were not fit for sacraments which is the plain doctrine of the Church. Impenitent sinners are not fit for sacraments.'

Logue wrote that he and Bishop O'Donnell would draw up a short reply which would omit the longer discussion about Dails, pacts and elections, which were not *ad rem* to the bishops.[17]

At the Standing Committee meeting on 10 April 1923 an outline was given of the reply that had been made by Gasparri. But this was far from being the end of the matter.[18] The question of administration of the sacraments to republicans remained a contentious issue, as did the use of excommunication. A more flexible and charitable approach by some of the clergy might have caused less bitterness.

The Civil War, in the early months of 1923, had turned into a struggle between the superior Free State forces and the splintered republican forces. When Fogarty wrote to Hagan on 10 January 1923, he described the situation in the countryside in rather colourful and partisan language: 'The irregulars as far as the rank and file are concerned are fast breaking up. Now they are dwindling into a mere assassination club, with a few clumps of desperados scattered through the country. The rank and file are most anxious for peace, but their leaders are holding out for some trial of their own, which they are hardly to get. We may have some troubled months ahead of us, but the worst is over in my opinion.'[19]

The hierarchy continued to have some difficulties with a minority of the clergy who were either simply not pro-government or else were confirmed supporters of the anti-Treatyites. In more normal circumstances, each bishop would have preferred to deal with the cases occurring in his own diocese. That had happened in 1919 at a time when pressure was being put on the hierarchy by Dublin Castle to curb the nationalist activities of some clergymen. But in October 1922, as stated before, the assembled bishops gave a stern warning to the clergy who were reportedly involved with the 'irregulars':

It is said that there are some priests who approve of this Irregular insurrection. If there be any such, they are false to their sacred office, and are guilty of the gravest scandal, and will not be allowed to retain the faculties they hold from us. Furthermore, we each for his own diocese, hereby forbid under pain of suspension, ipso facto, reserved to the Ordinary, any priest to advocate or encourage this revolt, publicly or privately.

The actual number of priests thought to be supporting the 'irregulars' was not very large; some were members of religious orders, and it was from that quarter that the anti-Treatyites drew most of their clerical support. That was a very sensitive matter for the bishops concerned.

Very little work has been done in this area to date. Certain religious orders had a reputation for supporting the anti-Treatyite forces, but they were usually as divided as Irish society on the matter. During the Anglo-Irish war and the Civil War the Cistercian monastery in Mount Melleray was noted for the support men 'on the run' received. But that community, too, was divided badly by politics. While serious work remains to be done on this topic, it should be noted that the administration of the sacraments to men on the run did not automatically make the clergy involved political sympathisers with the republicans.

One incident, in particular, shocked many clergymen. Fr Patrick Browne of Maynooth, who was later to become President of University College Galway and brother-in-law of Mr Sean MacEntee, was arrested in a raid on a house in Dublin. He was in the company of a number of noted anti-Treaty supporters, including Mary MacSwiney, who was the sister of the Lord Mayor of Cork referred to earlier, and Mrs Tom Clarke, widow of the executed 1916 leader. According to one Dublin priest, a number of 'extremely seditious documents' were found in the house.[20] Browne called himself Fr Perry, and, according to the same priest, who was not at all sympathetic, 'he gave the officers a considerable amount of very unpriestly abuse'.[21] Browne refused to sign an undertaking normally required of all suspected anti-Treatyites before being released. One of Hagan's informants felt that Browne had 'disgraced' all priests. It is probable that most clergy would have been quite unsympathetic to Browne. In Maynooth, the authorities were very perturbed by the incident, which had put the name of the college in the papers.[22]

In Rome, Hagan continued to keep in close contact with his old circle of nationalist 'diplomatic' contacts – many of whom, like Sean T. O'Kelly, Art O'Brien in London and Donal Hales in Genoa, were anti-Treaty. The Rector was very much in political sympathy with Eamon de Valera. That made his position in Rome very difficult. He was at variance with the hierarchy over politics and he was hostile to the Free State. In a letter to Art O'Brien, on 13 February 1923, Hagan advised against having a full-time 'diplomat' in Rome but urged the setting up of a propaganda office. The Rector claimed that Count O'Byrne, who succeeded Gavan Duffy in the city, 'proved a dreadful failure', and no doubt 'he had conveyed my views to his chiefs, who probably decided that without the active support of this establishment little can be accomplished in this city'.[23] The Free State was forced to find a means of circumventing the Irish College, or at least to lessen government dependence upon it. FitzGerald enlisted the skills of the Marquis

MacSwiney, who had been living in Rome for over two years and, through frequent visits to the city earlier in his career, seemed to know his way about, or was certainly very good at giving that impression.[24] Hagan dismissed him rather harshly as a charlatan.

Rumours about the establishment of diplomatic relations began afresh at the end of January 1923. Hagan believed that a report in the *New York Herald* speaking of the possibility of Vatican–Irish diplomatic relations 'was inspired'.[25] He 'knew that the government is most anxious to have at least one foreign representative', so as to save face. But at the Vatican, he thought that there 'seems to be nothing doing'. On 6 February, he thought it looked as if 'our Vatican friends are keeping quiet' and so far as he could gather 'their anxiety is to keep their fingers out of the Irish stew'. But one could never tell 'when they will get busy again'.[26] But the situation had changed a few weeks later. Hagan heard 'most disturbing' rumours to the effect that 'Luzio has been told to proceed to Ireland on a mission, the ostensible object of which is to try and bring the warring leaders together with a view to bring about peace'.[27] There was no doubt about the truth of the reports. On 7 March the *Freeman's Journal* wired claiming that the *Daily Mail* had reported that a papal legate was to be appointed for Ireland but that Cardinal Logue had said he had received no information.[28] Hagan replied that he knew nothing of the matter. He then took the wire with him to an audience with the Pope: 'It so happened that I was down to see Achille [Pope Pius XI] at 12.00 and I brought the wire with me, to produce in case he mentioned the matter. He did indeed ask what was the news from Ireland and what were the signs; to which I replied that they seemed less optimistic than some weeks ago. He then indulged in some reflection on the situation, and wound up by saying "*pensiamo a far qualcosa per l'Irlanda*", but he stopped short there and at once turned to something else.'[29]

Hagan declined to show the wire then since he could always say that he 'knew nothing about what was being done officially'. In Rome, the news of the delegation was 'public property' at that stage. Hagan was most interested to learn that Cardinal Logue had heard nothing of the plan, 'though I am wondering whether his ignorance is of the same specific nature as mine'.[30] He also suspected that Gasquet and company had known all about the mission for some weeks and he asserted that the two men who had 'most influence' on the Pope were Merry del Val and Gasquet. That was most improbable. Yet according to Hagan, Gasquet was really only the mouthpiece for his secretary, Philip Langdon, 'who makes the balls which his master fires'.[31] Langdon 'laughs at the idea of a peace mission', and 'chuckles at the idea of a delegate'.

The secretive way in which the entire mission was organised led

Hagan to believe that there was some other aim in view besides trying to restore peace:

and this suspicion is strengthened by the surmise which is being made by people in the curia to the effect that the real object in sending him is to ascertain whether there would be anything like strong opposition among clergy or laity to the appointment of a delegate apostolic. Should this surmise be true, and I am afraid it is, the whole result will depend largely on the attitude of the body of the bishops and I am sorry to have to think that he will find some, if not many, of them ready to be induced to declare in favour of the step.[32]

This elaborate scheme to get a permanent Vatican delegate in Ireland was explained in greater detail by Hagan on 8 March when he wrote to Dublin that there was no doubt how the mission was meant to end: 'Both Achille and his secretary are bent on this', his source had told him.[33] And they were 'warmly' backed up or urged on by Luzio himself for reasons of a more or less personal nature. It seems that 'his name was down for Washington' a year and a half before and that he was put off on 'the excuse that he was destined for the Irish Nunciature'.[34] The Vatican were so keen on the scheme that they did not 'want to hear of opposition from any quarter'. According to Luzio, 'he reminded Achille of the opposition . . . which he knew their lordships would make'.[35] But it did not make the slightest difference: Hagan had also learned 'in the most secret way' that 'a pile of documents have been handed to Luzio for his guidance, together with a letter which he is to publish or not according to his discretion. I also hear that he has instructions to see de Valera soon after his arrival . . . he is also to stay a month during which he is to ascertain how the idea of a delegation would be received and is to report thereon before any further step is taken'.[36] Luzio had been provided with copious funds which he was to spend entertaining the prominent men of both parties: 'it will be a choice time for the CID men', quipped Hagan.[37] He felt also that the 'Gasquet crowd' were quite jubilant, ready to condemn the Irish for showing no respect to the emissary of 'Achille' once the mission had failed, as inevitably it would. But if Hagan was upset, the Vice-Rector, Curran, was quite beside himself over the proposed mission. The latter's strong feelings on the matter were revealed in a letter to Bishop O'Donnell. On 14 March 1923 he wrote to the Coadjutor of Armagh that while the Luzio trip was obviously a peace mission, nobody was deceived 'whatever the nominal reason of the mission, whatever the secondary objects of the mission may be, its real object is to pave the way for an apostolic delegate'.[38] He felt that the timing was particularly clever, as the Free State 'want some recognition, or something they can call recognition, and I am firmly persuaded that they have been angling for it'. Curran regarded the situation as even more complex:

The Cardinal wants the republicans condemned by the Holy See; the republicans want the bishops condemned for their censures; the British want some ecclesiastical weapon in Ireland to replace the Irish bishops since the Conscription crisis – for, as Colonel Repington phrased it, 'the puppets no longer respond to the wire pulling'; and lastly the Holy See won't be happy till it gets it. Apparently the Secretariat of State thinks that neither the Cardinal nor the republicans can object to an impartial first-hand investigation of facts in view of their respective appeals for intervention. Of course, in the end nobody will be satisfied except Downing St and Rome, and the next generation of Irishmen, lay and ecclesiastical, will not be praying for the churchmen and republicans who called in, or caused to come in, the outsider.

Curran's reputation for bluntness was evident in this document. He wrote:

An apos. Delegate in Dublin will simply be an unaccredited Nuncio to the Court of St James, or rather to Downing St. politicians and Westminster ecclesiastics. Protestant opinion won't allow even a Protestant Government to receive a delegate much less a nuncio – but it is the easiest thing in the world, especially with our *laissez faire* policy – to establish one in Dublin, and through it and the British Legation in Rome to keep the Irish bishops and people in check. The Legation conveys the complaints against Irish ecclesiastics to the Vatican and the Vatican communicates its restraining and dampening counsels through the Irish Delegate. So simple and effective in view of the opportunities for log-rolling that the necessities of the two great empires, spiritual and temporal, increasingly demand of one another.

He felt, however, that the mission might do some good if it afforded the opportunity to the Irish hierarchy to point out the 'iniquity of English influence in curia, of the boycotting, ignoring or penalisation of the Irish Church and its work'. He added that the 'sympathy of the curia is sickening'. It was like the 'penitence of an Englishman for his grandfather's sins towards Ireland – it never covers the present'.[39]

Meanwhile, Hagan mistakenly believed that the combined efforts of British ecclesiastics and the Foreign Office were largely responsible for the mission. Yet Gasquet appeared to be as surprised as the Free State when the mission was announced. The Cardinal told Marquis MacSwiney, who called on him, that he had known nothing of the mission: 'Without the slightest hesitation, the Cardinal declared that he had never heard of anything more stupid than this story of Monsignor Luzio's mission, and exclaimed that they would like to know *who* had advised them (meaning by that the Vatican) to send a mission to Ireland under the present circumstances. He added that the only two Cardinals (he did not mention their names) who had talked to him about the affairs disapproved of it as much as he himself, and also wondered who was responsible for this colossal blunder.'[40] Hagan blamed Gasquet and company and they, in turn, hinted that the Irish College might be responsible.

Contrary to what Hagan might have believed, Foreign Office files reveal a certain bewilderment among senior officials over the mission. On 12 March 1923, Theo Russell, who had replaced the Count de Salis, reported to Curzon that the mission arose out of the joint letter of the Irish bishops prohibiting 'access to the sacraments to anyone taking part in the republican campaign of murder and arson'.[41] He felt that the Vatican was attempting to mollify aggrieved feeling among many Irish Catholics resident in the United States, Australia and New Zealand. Although recently appointed to the post, Russell had come very close to understanding the real reason for the proposed trip. He saw Gasparri on 17 March and, contrary to instructions, raised the question of the Luzio mission. The Foreign Office concluded that 'no action on our part is called for'.[42]

The Secretary of State, Gasparri, had on file an urgent request from Logue – the Irish Cardinal – to send an apostolic visitator in order to lend weight to the moral authority of the bishops against the 'anti-Treatyites' who had succeeded in winning so much sympathy among the Irish abroad. The two most influential members of the Irish hierarchy, however, did not agree on this matter. Where Logue saw the apostolic visitator as having a narrowly defined mission, Byrne doubted the wisdom of such a policy, on the grounds that the members of the Irish hierarchy were the best judges of the situation in their own country. The mission might only make a bad situation worse. The competence of an envoy could not be depended upon.

Gasparri was quite well aware of the conflicting positions within the Irish hierarchy on this question from Hagan's able championing of 'decentralisation'. But Pope Pius XI, with his experience as a nuncio in Poland, was well disposed to the idea of sending a peace mission to Ireland where the image of Catholic fighting Catholic seemed such an absurdity. Gasparri was not so convinced about the wisdom of sending the mission. Then an episode occurred which overrode all hesitations and objections to the initiative.

The Superior General of the Calced Carmelites, Peter Magennis, had been outraged by the shooting of his close friend, Liam Mellowes, 'as a reprisal'. He was repulsed by the subsequent behaviour of the Government towards the anti-Treatyites, in particular by the continued policy of executions. Magennis's political views were well known in Rome and he did not miss an opportunity to inform the relevant Vatican authorities of his feelings. Unlike his close friend Hagan, he favoured the idea of a mission. Some anti-Treatyite politicians also favoured the same course of action. But de Valera was not among them. He remained convinced that Hagan was accurate in his overall assessment. Magennis made repeated efforts to see the Pope during the early months of 1923. But he was not granted an audience, presumably because he wished to discuss politics rather than matters that related directly to the running of his order. Senior Vatican officials, with whom he was in regular contact, would have made Pius XI aware of Magennis's position. In exasperation, on one occasion while he was attending a papal audience in his capacity as Superior General of his order, he retired abruptly from the company, taking the large sum of money with him which was to have been handed over to the Vatican on that occasion. His exit was noted – as was Magennis's intention – by the Pope.

Instead of going directly to the Friary, he dismissed his carriage just outside the Vatican and spent the day visiting the sick and catching up on many corporal works of mercy. He spent a leisurely day in the city and returned after supper to his house, where he found three cardinals, all of whom had been there since early morning, impatiently waiting for him. They had been sent by the Pope to find out what was amiss. Magennis did not hesitate to tell his captive audience exactly what was on his mind concerning Ireland. As a result, he may also have had an opportunity to discuss the matter privately with the Pope, who was personally well disposed to the idea of a mission all the time.[43]

The rather forceful presentation by Magennis of the case for a Vatican mission to Ireland helped to sweep aside further consideration of the difficulties which Gasparri and the Secretariat of State were aware of concerning the Irish Church. The decision was taken by the Pope to send Luzio. That was his way of 'doing something for Ireland'. In many ways, Luzio was a suitable choice for the mission. Theo Russell reported that he was 'highly thought of in Rome and I hear favourable reports of him from an English source'. He had the advantage of 'knowing de Valera personally'. It appeared, reported Russell, that they 'studied together, played billiards together and were on intimate terms in former days'.[44] That was not correct. Luzio had been a professor of canon law at Maynooth. De Valera also taught mathematics there – but not at the same time. That piece of misinformation was relayed to Dublin from London.[45] The Irish government regarded the mission with considerable suspicion. A peace initiative was uncalled for at a time when the 'irregulars' were on the point of capitulation. But a Vatican envoy who was reported to be friendly to de Valera was completely outside the bounds of usefulness.

Luzio, who was a regent of the Apostolic Penitentiary, arrived in Dublin on 19 March 1923. He was accompanied by a secretary, a young Irish priest who had remained on in Rome after ordination; the latter was completely out of touch with political events in Ireland. Both men took up residence in the Shelbourne Hotel. The apostolic visitor, who was in a much more sensitive position than he himself realised, made two serious tactical blunders of a most elementary diplomatic nature from which his mission never quite recovered. He did not visit the local ordinary, Byrne, in whose archdiocese he had taken up residence.[46] Luzio was certainly aware of the hostility of the Archbishop to his presence in Ireland. But that was not a reason to deny him minimal courtesy. Not unnaturally, since Logue had sought such a mission, he immediately went to Armagh where he unwittingly destroyed his goodwill by making one foolhardy suggestion. When he saw Logue on 21 March, he suggested to the octogenarian Cardinal that they both go on a mission to the rebels. Logue had not asked for a 'peace' mission to Ireland. He was anxious to have papal support for the moral teaching of the hierarchy. The Cardinal at no stage believed that it was possible to talk to the anti-Treatyite forces. He had even tried to discourage Byrne from hosting the Mansion House Conference. Tim Healy, the Irish Governor General, recorded how the Cardinal 'sent him away with a flea in his ear'.[47] Lionel Curtis of the Colonial Office commented that Luzio had to 'divest himself of all idea that the cardinal would stoop to go running round with him after the rebels'. Logue told Luzio that if he could bring back surrender terms from the rebels to Armagh, he would look at them. At one meeting, Luzio had lost the support of his single most important contact in the Irish hierarchy. At that point, he might as well have gone back to Rome.[48]

The bishops boycotted Luzio almost completely. Their treatment of the papal envoy stood in marked contrast to the hospitality shown to his immediate predecessor Persico in the 1880s. Luzio was very much out of his political and diplomatic depth. He found it extremely difficult to understand why his former friends were acting in such a cold manner towards him. He spent a few days at Maynooth visiting the college where he had previously taught canon law. He also met some bishops at Armagh during an Education Committee meeting. O'Donnell was courteous towards a man he had known quite well.[49] Without episcopal assistance, Luzio was left to flounder. He was even deserted by Logue, who had inititiated the mission.

The Government was also quite frigid towards his presence. That left the ill-fated envoy little option but to rely heavily on republican contacts. That only reinforced the somewhat one-sided and mistaken Free State view that the man was 'pro-de Valera'. With Sean T. in prison, Cait O'Kelly was a constant visitor to the Shelbourne Hotel. Luzio also had contact with the republican go-between, Tommy Mullins, who was later secretary of the Fianna Fail party. On 13 April 1923 O'Kelly's wife wrote to Hagan that 'l'Espagnol et l'Italien have met without settling the

Irish question so far'. She believed that Luzio was 'most anxious to see peace reign here and then the sacraments will cease to be a state monopoly'.[50]

According to Mrs O'Kelly, Luzio had said he felt a free election would settle the entire affair:

He is very accessible and very nice and sympathetic in manner to our side, and no doubt to the other too, tho' they say that he is a republican envoy. But that is because he attempts to be fair-minded. Someone put the idea of a complicated plebiscite before him with a 1, 2, 3.
for you [written in margin]
1. Is the F.S. a final settlement?
2. ,, ,, ,, accepted under duress?
3. ,, ,, ,, accepted at all with or without duress?
He was very enthusiastic about it. He lives and prays for all who talk of peace and gives them a great welcome. Miss MacS. likes him. De Valera likes him but could not see much further tho' naturally he is not given to bash his peace moves. We all like him, but perhaps as A.C. says he is more sympathetic than helpful – so far . . . We feel very much in the grips of the most ruthless, unscrupulous and indelicate band. But yet we'll probably muddle through . . .[51]

Cait O'Kelly was a perceptive commentator. She realised that Luzio was sympathetic but in no sense partisan. De Valera, who also had a number of meetings with him, felt that he had come at 'a bad time for us'. He did not regard Luzio as 'pro-republican'. But he was sympathetic. Yet de Valera argued that he was also somewhat domineering in his attitude: 'The peace-maker has always an almost irresistible temptation to try to effect his object by bringing pressure on the weaker side to give in. I am afraid our visitor succumbed to it when he should have stood rigidly for impartial justice.'[52] De Valera mitigated his view slightly: 'however, his task was almost superhuman and it is easy to criticise'. De Valera had some difficulty persuading 'some of our people' from petitioning for a permanent delegation: 'I had some difficulty in pointing out to them that it is easier for a powerful Empire to secure friends than it is for a struggling small nation. I know that these are your views on this matter.'[53] It is of considerable interest to see how respectful de Valera was of Hagan's view in this matter.

The government continued throughout the visit to regard Luzio with studied disinterest. Cosgrave met him on 11 April 1923 but as a 'purely courtesy visit' in a 'personal, unofficial way'. The President had heard that Luzio was on a purely ecclesiastical mission 'with which, of course, the government was not involved'. No credentials had been presented.[54] At the time, it might have helped Cosgrave if he had realised that Luzio was not 'pro-republican'. That was something that Russell only found out on 1 May, when he wrote to Curzon that a telegram from Dublin to Gasparri on the ending of the Civil War showed that Luzio 'who had been frequently credited with republican sympathies, was genuinely relieved by the virtual capitulation of his so-called friends'.[55] As Russell had been responsible for sending inaccurate information to London, he must take some responsibility for the mistaken attitude of the Irish government towards the envoy. In other circumstances, the government could have used Luzio in domestic Irish politics and, at the same time, secured diplomatic relations with the Vatican.

Without any real assistance from either the hierarchy or the government, Luzio inevitably fell prey to the designs of the anti-Treatyite politicians.

On 14 April, Luzio announced in the press that he was willing to intervene in the interests of peace, if it was apparent that such action on his part was desired by the people. He obviously had no opportunity to raise this matter with Cosgrave, who regarded his visit as purely for ecclesiastical purposes. The public offer to mediate had angered the government because it had first been made to a Sinn Fein delegation on 10 April. As a result, a series of resolutions were passed by public bodies throughout the country urging Luzio to intervene.[56]

A memorandum put up to the Executive Council argued most trenchantly against Luzio and his activities. The 'plan of campaign' was to send Sinn Fein representatives 'on the Q.T.' to the various county councils and local bodies who would then call a special meeting to request intervention by the delegates. That was exactly what was happening:

Should the Monsignor lend himself to this very obvious manoeuvre at this late stage in the day it will be tantamount to an act of gross discourtesy to the Irish government in so much as he had refused to recognise the lawful government of the land to which he had come as envoy from perhaps the greatest world power, and had endeavoured to engage whilst in that country, on a line of policy in direct conflict with the policy of the de jure and de facto government.

The memorandum also went on to mention that the October pastoral had laid down, in the strictest terms, that persons guilty of certain crimes would not be admitted to the sacraments. Priests who approved of the 'saddest of revolts' were declared to be false to their sacred office and guilty of grievous scandal, and they were forbidden, under pain of suspension, to advance such doctrine publicly or privately: 'This being the solemn, deliberate and unanimous ruling of the Highest Christian Authority in Ireland, the alleged activities of Mgr Luzio appear all the more extraordinary and, considering them in conjunction with the reported grant of Benediction of the Holy Father to one who comes under the Bishops' interdict, one would have to draw the conclusion that the Roman authorities were in direct conflict with the grave and considered opinion of the Irish Church.'[57]

The *Freeman's Journal*, in an obviously inspired editorial, criticised the envoy for not producing any credentials. Under the curt heading, 'Monsignor Luzio' it challenged the view that the envoy had 'a mission to the government'. It described the statement that the envoy had a mission to the government as 'quite unfounded'. Were Luzio to change the nature of his mission, it would require letters from the Secretary of State to the government and he did not have any: 'Apparently it is thought in some quarters that under shelter of the Monsignor's robe the rebels who have been making war upon the Irish people and their government can be set up as a political party to be placated by agreements and compromises made over the people's heads and behind the people's backs. We do not for a moment countenance any such proceeding.'

The editorial concluded that his 'representative capacity has ceased', and any effort to convert the mission into a political initiative was 'bound to fail' because essentially there was 'nothing to arbitrate about between the Irish people and their assailants'. The authority of the Free State could not be 'impugned from any quarter'. Those in arms could have peace any day by simply returning to their homes but they need not expect 'to be set up again as a disturbing political power in Ireland by any agency whatsoever'.[58]

As far as the government was concerned, Luzio had arrived at the worst possible time. It was quite apparent that the war was nearing an end, and Logue told Hagan on 24 April:

I think we are near the end of the strife here. A great part of the irregulars' forces and nearly all the leaders are either killed or in prison. The misery is that so many young lives on both sides have been sacrificed. I doubt whether there will be any cordial agreement between the parties; and it is likely that small parties of the so-called republicans who were living by loot will hold out in places till they are caught. The peacemakers are appealing to Mgr. Luzio to act as an intermediary; but this does not seem to be pleasing to the government if one can judge by the rather rough way in which the 'Freeman' has questioned his credentials. I think it was a mistake to imagine that he could carry out an inquiry privately and, as if by stealth, it cannot be done in the present world of newspapers.[59]

Logue was quite well informed. But the day before he had written to Hagan, 23 April, the *Freeman's Journal* had published a letter from Logue together with a copy of the credentials which Luzio had taken to *Ara Coeli* when he first arrived. They had been signed on 9 March 1923, in Rome, by Gasparri. The letter was addressed to Logue and stated that

Luzio had come to learn at first-hand what was going on *viva voce* from the bishops and to 'cooperate as far as he possibly could in the pacification of minds in the interests of a much desired and definite settlement in your country'. In the second harsh editorial on this topic, the paper complained that the first time the Irish government had seen the Gasparri letter was in the newspapers a month after the arrival of Luzio. The idea of sending Luzio in that way was unfair to the Free State and 'fraught with danger to the good relations between Ireland and the Holy See'. The editorial concluded: 'We submit that there is nothing un-Catholic in claiming that the established representative government of the Irish people is entitled to be treated with the same courtesy, and that its rights are entitled to meet with the same respect, as would be shown to the government and its rights of any other country, Catholic or non-Catholic.'[60]

Logue's rather unusual behaviour in relation to Luzio was explained by Lionel Curtis at the Colonial Office in a rather charitable fashion. He said that the Cardinal had published the credentials to 'cover Mgr Luzio's retreat'.[61] But why did Logue wait so long? He could, at the very least, have sent a copy of Gasparri's letter covering the mission to Cosgrave. But when the credentials were finally published, the government had already sent the assistant secretary of the Department of External Affairs, Sean Murphy, to Rome with a formal note demanding the recall of Luzio.[62] About 24 April Tim Healy, the Governor General, was in London where he had talks with Lionel Curtis and James McMahon. Healy told Curtis that a definite request had been made by the Free State, with the support of the Irish bishops, for the withdrawal of Mgr Luzio, 'as he is now regarded as being definitely in sympathy with the rebel cause'. The bishops, according to Healy, were 'absolutely solid on the side of the Free State against the Vatican'.[63] On 25 April Murphy reported from Rome to the Executive Council that 'Mgr Luzio was being re-called from Ireland immediately'.[64]

When Luzio finally realised the controversy over his 'missing' credentials, he attempted to get an interview with Cosgrave. The Minister of External Affairs, FitzGerald, wrote him a curt reply to his note, enquiring whether Luzio requested an official or an unofficial interview. The latter was sought, to which FitzGerald replied that he had been instructed by the Executive Council to say that the President could not see his way to granting an unofficial interview to Luzio.[65]

Luzio's diplomatic failures were both tragic and bizarre. On one occasion he was being brought to meet Liam Lynch, the Chief of Staff of the IRA, when the area was suddenly surrounded by Free State troops and the poor envoy retreated ignominiously through the hedgerows.[66] At a meeting to honour the musician Professor Esposito on 16 April,

Luzio told the Italian consul in Dublin that he considered his mission a complete failure. He explained that he had been blocked by senior clergy who feared Vatican censure. He had been caught between the hammer and the anvil (*'cacciato in un ginepraio, come disse lui'*), between the clergy who feared Rome and a government that resented interference in their internal affairs. All the time, the consul reported to Rome, Luzio protested that the motive of his mission was the pacification of souls purely from a Christian and humanitarian point of view.[67]

But the Free State was quite upset by the diplomatic pantomime. Murphy of External Affairs had been quite successful in his Vatican mission. He was joined at the end of April by his minister, FitzGerald. On 30 April, Murphy and his interpreter, MacSwiney, went to see Mgr Pizzardo, the secretary to Gasparri. They expressed the cabinet's gratitude to the Vatican for acting so promptly in having Luzio recalled (the Monsignore was still in Ireland). This had 'put the relations of the Holy See with Ireland on such a friendly basis that no hitch could in future occur between them'. The same evening, the Minister met Gasparri and, to FitzGerald's surprise, much of the conversation focused on Dr Conn Murphy, who had been a 'republican' envoy to Rome, and who had been recently arrested in Dublin. The Minister brought documentation to prove that Murphy's home was a distribution centre for 'irregulars'' despatches. The Cardinal stressed that a telegram sent to the Archbishop of Dublin, who had taken up the case with Cosgrave, was in no sense an order from the Vatican. The question of intervening to secure the release of Murphy was left entirely to the discretion of the Archbishop. The telegram was occasioned by the large number of wires sent from Ireland and America – all stating that Murphy's imprisonment was due to his visit to Rome as a 'republican' emissary. FitzGerald denied the allegation and said that his government never stood in the way of peaceful initiatives to the Holy Father by the 'irregulars'. With the arrival of Luzio many people could only conclude, countered the Minister, that the Holy See believed all the reports received from Ireland and the USA against the bishops and the established government.[68]

The Cardinal seemed to be a little put out by the whole affair. It was understood in Rome, he said, that elections were to be held in May and Luzio's trip was regarded by the Holy See as a means of 'aiding the government to convince the people' that the result of the poll ought to decide the controversy finally. The contentious question of hunger striking was raised by Gasparri. FitzGerald stated that there were 10,000 prisoners in the Free State and the government could not allow such pressure to be used as a means of securing premature release. The Marquis added that the Vatican had not intervened in the Terence

MacSwiney case. It would be ill-advised to do so at that moment. At that point, Gasparri volunteered the information that Lloyd George had made strong representations to have MacSwiney condemned and the Pope had not taken any action, much to the displeasure of the British. When leaving, FitzGerald said he was pleased to find the Holy See well disposed to the Free State. He was confident that 'similar painful incidents' would not occur in the future.[69]

On 1 May, the Irish delegation visited the Vatican library. They saw the British minister, Theo Russell, in the evening. The latter mentioned that he had never come into contact with the Irish College but he hoped 'that in the new order of things, amicable relations might be established'. On 3 May, in view of the impending change in the method of selecting bishops in Ireland, the Marquis, at the Minister's request, interviewed the Brazilian and Portuguese representatives for the purpose of finding out what system was in operation in their respective countries. The bishops were selected by the nuncio without direct reference to either the local clergy or the government. Before recommending his choice in Rome, the nuncio found out unofficially whether the individual was *persona grata* with the government, but he did not have to find out the wishes of the local clergy. That was precisely the method which the Irish hierarchy most disliked.

On 4 May the delegation had an audience with the Pope who spoke for half an hour saying that Ireland was ever-present in his thoughts. During his stay in Poland he often thought of the similarity between the history of the two peoples. He asked the Minister to convey his blessing to the President and Ministers of the government. Later they met Cardinal Van Rossum, head of Propaganda, who showed 'an intimate knowledge of Irish affairs'. He was pleased at the strong position of the new government.

On 5 May Murphy's report of the Rome mission was before the Executive Council and the Ministers were satisfied that they had managed to have the envoy recalled. A letter of thanks was sent to the Pope and to Marquis MacSwiney, who had acted as guide and contact man for Murphy in Rome.[70] Luzio left Ireland in May, 'glad to get away from the cold of our climate and from the heat of our policies'.[71]

On 24 May 1923, following the death of Liam Lynch and his replacement by Frank Aiken, the order was given to cease fire and dump arms. De Valera wrote to Hagan dejectedly that 'peace "by understanding" would be by far the best in the national interest – but our opponents want a "triumph"'.[72] Logue, from a different political perspective, confirmed that view: 'We have comparative quiet here now. There is no real peace by consent. De Valera is keeping up his republican claim as stubbornly as ever; but the republican leaders and most of the rank and file are in prison; so it is a peace of exhaustion on one side.'[73] He feared that armed gangs would continue looting and robbing and that isolated outrages would increase. In fact, the aged primate had been correct in stating that what emerged was a 'peace of exhaustion'. People had had enough. As de Valera confided: 'as far as public opinion goes the people would probably vote just now *against both* sides'.[74]

In Rome, Theo Russell reported that when Gasparri heard news of peace 'he seemed happy'.[75] Hagan saw the Pope, for the first time after a period of two months. The Pope did not mention Luzio at all: 'He asked as usual how things were going in Ireland and apparently has had reason to change his mind about the possibility of all being settled there in five minutes. His tone now is that all will come right "col tempo".'[76]

Luzio had become something of an embarrassment to the Vatican and he seems to have been kept out of sight for quite a while. 'All I know for certain', reported Hagan, 'is that Gasparri is very mad and that Langdon has been fulminating against the missioner in a most ferocious way.' The trip was a diplomatic fiasco. He also learned that Luzio was disgruntled and was feeling dissatisfied with everybody. Mgr Tizi had reported to Hagan that he had overheard a conversation in which a friend of Luzio's was telling how the visitor 'was glad he escaped with a whole skin and that he was much surprised to find coldness and want of welcome among the very people whom he regarded as his warmest friends [a reference to the bishops]'. He was not quite sure how much the Pope actually knew of the affair. There was the general impression that 'he knows what Gasparri wants him to know', since it was felt that everything of a displeasing or awkward nature 'was carefully hidden from sight and never reaches his ears'. Hagan knew nothing of the details of the Irish government mission to the Vatican. Hagan, the main architect of Luzio's diplomatic downfall, and his episcopal backers took no satisfaction in the humiliation of the well-intentioned envoy. In May, Hagan had told his friend Byrne: 'The one good result of the fiasco will I hope be the indefinite postponement of all ideas about establishing a permanent delegation and should this be the case we may, I think, consider the mission as anything at all but a failure. Indeed, it was the only possible way of knocking the notion on the head.'

In a letter to Mannix, Hagan explained the reaction in Rome to the mission:

The Luzio episode was as unfortunate as it was ill-advised and by one of the curious twists which sometimes occur in Irish life, the very man who was sent to help the Free State was turned down by them and the very people he was sent to crush took him to their bosom. I hear that he has been very bitter against most of the F.S. ministers since his return, especially against O'Higgins and

Fitzgerald – and that he has formed a higher idea of the republicans as a body and individually than of their opponents.

But I gather that the Secretary of State is very severe on the bishops for the amount of cold shoulder they exhibited to Luzio; and my own experience would go to show that His Holiness is sick and tired of Ireland and does not want to hear the word mentioned. He has made no reference to the country the last three or four times I have been speaking to him; and this I take to be a sign that he has adopted Cardinal Gasparri's view, who apparently is the power behind the throne in all matters of foreign policy.

As far as I am concerned I have done my best to keep their fingers out of the Irish stew; but one has always to remember that the policy of the Cardinal Secretary is steadily set in the direction of diplomatic triumphs, and that in order to achieve these they must do nothing to offend England and must do much to show that he wishes to placate the country.[77]

The nunciature idea had been postponed rather than defeated. Although Pius XI was considerably upset by the recent developments in Ireland, he had had direct contact in May with senior Free State officials. FitzGerald had created a favourable impression. While Cosgrave did not particularly trust the Marquis MacSwiney, the latter remained in Rome as an unofficial Free State representative.

Cosgrave liked the idea of establishing diplomatic relations with the Vatican. But he was acutely aware of the opposition to such an idea among the bishops and particularly from his personal friend, Byrne of Dublin. The government could only achieve that goal by risking the alienation of the hierarchy. Luzio was in a position to produce convincing evidence of that fact. It was a lesson that had been learned at quite a cost to the reputation of the Holy See. Luzio had gone to Ireland to bring about peace with the help of the bishops and found that he 'had to deal with 26 Popes'.[78]

Chapter V

CUMANN NA nGAEDHEAL AND
THE QUEST FOR LEGITIMACY

The relationship between the hierarchy and the government – despite the strains imposed upon it by the Civil War – had emerged stronger for having experienced the political crisis together. The sharp differences between Byrne and Cosgrave over the policy of executions were of a temporary nature. De Valera, who might have been expected to moderate republican action, failed completely to discipline the 'gunmen' on the Anti-Treaty side. The country had undergone a costly and bloody civil war which was to muddy the waters of Irish politics for generations. Many Irish bishops felt great bitterness towards de Valera, in particular, because they believed that he had not acted with the clarity of judgement demanded in the circumstances. Although it was realised that de Valera had not as much latitude as he might have liked, the political leader of the opposition to the Treaty had sunk very low in the esteem of the overwhelming majority of the hierarchy. The bishops unhesitatingly acknowledged in private the debt the new state owed to William T. Cosgrave for having helped preserve the rule of law and fragile democratic institutions. There was no enthusiasm in that quarter for a change of government.

In early 1924 there were very few higher clergymen who would have predicted that, within a matter of years, de Valera would become President of the Executive Council. Apparent unfounded optimism gave Hagan confidence enough to write to O'Donnell, in January 1924: '. . . and who was to know that in a year or two the Church's best friends in Ireland may not be the present Republicans . . . but stranger things have happened'. He felt that there could be little good holding aloof from 'people who happen to be opposed to one's own policy at the present hour'. Even though a group was 'really wrong', he felt it was prudent to remember 'how many are the surprises to which Irish public life is exposed . . .' and they had not to go 'back far to find examples of the united becoming dissevered and the sundered coming together'.[1]

Hagan, who had recently received his sternest rebuke from the hierarchy for his political activities, was outlining an open approach to Irish politics to his close friend, who was soon to become Cardinal Archbishop of Armagh.[2] But in 1923, Logue was not open to such a strategy. He was not even aware that Hagan – of whom he disapproved – had made such a suggestion.

Byrne of Dublin – despite his disapproval of Hagan's more imprudent political contacts – continued his moderate policy towards the anti-Treatyite groups. In the summer of 1923, a general election returned Cosgrave to power. His Cumann na nGaedheal party won sixty-three seats while Sinn Fein got forty-four.[3] De Valera was in jail, together with thousands of others active in the Civil War, and he was to remain there until July 1924. Although he had been arrested on 15 August – less than two weeks before the election – he was easily returned for his Clare constituency. De Valera was in no position – even if he had wished – to challenge the abstentionist policy of Sinn Fein. Relations between the anti-Treatyites and the Catholic Church remained very strained following the role of the bishops during the Civil War.

Very few members of Sinn Fein, if any, were aware of Byrne's petition against the policy of executions, just as the rank and file remained oblivious to the attempts made by the Archbishop of Dublin to modify the government's attitude to hunger strikers.[4] In early October 1923, there were under 8,000 prisoners refusing food. As a result of a series of petitions from prominent Catholics who were sympathetic to the jailed 'republicans', Byrne wrote to Cosgrave urging him to get the government to take a more lenient view.

Cosgrave – who had been most receptive to the representations of the Archbishop over the policy of executions – proved less accommodating on this occasion. He may have been inclined to put Byrne's representations to the Executive Council quite forcefully. But Cosgrave was obliged to write on 28 October 1923 that his government 'could not give way on it'. Byrne – who remained a close personal friend of Cosgrave – had written that he considered that it would be a 'downright calamity for the country if any of these hunger strikers were allowed to die'. He opposed the policy, on humanitarian grounds, and because the leaders of the hunger strikes had 'declared that the reign of violence is over, that they will work now to spread their views only by the constitutional way of educating the public'. That meant that their claim to constitutionalism seemed strong before the world. No government could afford to allow thousands of men to die causing a 'revulsion of feeling that would shake the foundations' of the Free State:

What you have to weigh in the balance is this, whether the release of the people would be a greater danger to the state than allowing them to die on hunger strike. I distinctly incline to the view that the latter course would be fraught with far more danger to the state. You must remember this, that there are numbers of moderate people, supporters of the Free State, who would receive a great shock and whose good feeling towards the [government] would be distinctly affected.[5]

Byrne's line of argument was rejected with surprising vehemence by the government; the Ministers were so convinced of the correctness of the policy that each one would prefer 'to leave public life altogether than to yield'. Cosgrave also argued that the hunger strike was breaking down. On 21 October, there were '7,000 more or less' involved and some 6,400 a week later. The day Cosgrave wrote to Byrne, about 425 more had come off the strike. The President also told the Archbishop that he was not convinced that 'there had been a change of heart as well as label in this matter of armed versus constitutional agitation'. Documents being found by the security forces revealed not just opposition to the government but hostility to the existence of the Free State itself. There were arms dumps in the country and drilling was still going on.[6]

It was a measure of the maturity of relations between Church and State that Cosgrave and Byrne could disagree so directly on an issue of major political importance and yet remain close personal friends. That friendship was of considerable support to Cosgrave throughout the 1920s, as he faced the difficult task of trying to overcome the legacy of the Civil War, which had injected so much bitterness into Irish politics.

As Professor T. Desmond Williams has pointed out, Cosgrave 'knew good advice when it was offered – though it may not always have been given to him. He was calm where some of his colleagues were dogmatic and passionate.' Nowhere was his expertise more noticeable than in his handling of Church–State relations. He had to avoid extremism of a confessional and a secular kind. The most influential Protestants in Southern Ireland were given a role in the Free State through the establishment of the Senate. This was as imaginative and liberal a move as it was politically adroit. Cosgrave was fortunate to be able to steer successfully a middle course – although there was little pressure from the Catholic hierarchy as a body to do otherwise. Cosgrave was not a flamboyant politician:

There were men who were more brilliant, others more academically favoured than Cosgrave in the cabinet of those first ten years; there were none with more practical experience. He was probably, when it came to handling men, the ablest of them all. The team he picked for the organisation of the new Civil Service would be regarded as the most outstanding single contribution of the President. Without Gregg, Brennan, Coogan, Merrick and McElligott the Civil Service could easily have become both corrupt and inefficient.[7]

14   William T. Cosgrave, President of the Executive Council, visits the mother
house of the African missions, Cork, 1928 (*Cork Examiner*)

It may not be without significance that Professor Williams did not
include Joseph Walshe in that list. He was unquestionably one of the
most influential of the senior civil servants in the area of Church–State
relations and Free State policy towards the Vatican. As acting secretary
of the Department of External Affairs from September 1922, he was
directly responsible for shaping the future of Irish foreign policy. He
must take credit for helping establish a department, with the most
limited resources, which more than competed with the more advan-
taged and better favoured departments in the earliest days of the Free
State. A devout Catholic, Walshe took a particular interest in Church–
State relations. As a former Jesuit scholastic who had taught for a
number of years in Clongowes College, he had many powerful clerical
friends. One of his former students, John Charles McQuaid, was to
become Archbishop of Dublin in 1940. Another former student, the
noted Celtic scholar and jurist, Daniel Binchy, became Irish envoy to
Berlin in 1929. Walshe was a good linguist, knowing French, German,
Italian and Dutch. He possessed some rare qualities which made him a
rather powerful figure in the public service, with his influence
extending beyond the Department of External Affairs, which he ruled

in rather autocratic fashion. He was secretive and mistrustful. Walshe also had a reputation for deviousness. He had the highest regard for his own intellectual capacity and capability, yet he was not the equal of the younger men who came into the Department in the late 1920s and 1930s. But he must take credit for recruiting them and building up his department in the early years of the Free State when some backbenchers wanted it abolished. Walshe was a self-trained diplomat who valued secrecy highly. He was inclined to interpret his role rather narrowly, looking askance at such 'plebeian' areas as trade and commerce, which had to be 'tolerated'. Such mundane activities simply took the department, and Walshe himself, away from the 'real world' of top-level meetings, confidential memoranda, and long conversations with the most intelligent and most senior people in politics. He resented having to 'sell spuds'. Walshe, therefore, saw himself as exercising much more power than he ever actually enjoyed under either Cosgrave or de Valera. It was in the area of Church and State that Walshe was most self-opinionated. By temperament, clerical background and list of friends he could claim expertise in that area. His approach was also coloured by a belief in world conspiracies; and that was to reach a high point in the year 1930, when fear of left-wing republicanism was rife. He also expected the Catholic hierarchy to take a highly political stance in support of the Free State – a position which the hierarchy resisted no matter how attractive the short-term benefits.[8] The implications of Walshe's approach to Church–State relations were most acutely felt in 1929 when efforts were made by the government to establish diplomatic relations with the Vatican. Part of Walshe's thinking, as will be seen later in this chapter, was to forge a closer bond between the Free State and the Catholic hierarchy, over which the government could exercise some influence through the Vatican.

Although Cosgrave appeared anxious to establish diplomatic relations with the Vatican from the very outset, he did not see the move in terms of disciplining a hierarchy and clergy who were wayward in their political views. The President of the Executive Council and other Free State Ministers built up a good working relationship with the hierarchy.

When O'Donnell became Cardinal Archbishop of Armagh in 1924, the hierarchy had in this former supporter of the Irish Parliamentary Party a leader of considerable quality and decisiveness. The tension that had existed between Dublin and Armagh when Logue was Cardinal evaporated completely. The two most powerful figures in the Irish Catholic Church were at one in their determination to keep the clergy out of partisan politics. (They were to play a far less visible political role in the post-Civil War society.) Cosgrave and his fellow ministers had substantial contact with the hierarchy in the 1920s, particularly on questions of education, divorce, contraception, public house closing hours and censorship. The politicians most involved in discussions with the hierarchy were the Ministers for Justice and Education, while Cosgrave and Byrne also corresponded and met frequently.

In 1923, a film censor with wide-ranging powers was appointed. The Intoxicating Liquor Act, the following year, reduced public house opening hours while, in 1927, measures were taken to reduce the number of public houses. In 1929, the Censorship of Publications Board was set up consisting of one Protestant, three Catholic laymen and one Catholic priest, with power to prohibit the sale and distribution of 'indecent or obscene' books. The publishing, selling or distribution of literature advocating birth-control was also deemed an offence under the Act.[9]

Divorce provides one of the better examples of how Church–State relations functioned in the early days of the Free State. Before 1922, divorce was obtained by private bill in parliament. But soon after independence, three private divorce bills were introduced. In this regard, the Dail now took the place of parliament.[10]

The Attorney General, Hugh Kennedy, pressed for a decision from the Executive Council as to whether legislation would be promoted to set up the necessary procedure. It seemed to him that while the religious and sacramental aspect of the matter were outside the purview of the government, 'the bond, in so far as it can be regarded as resulting from a legal contract, might be considered from that point of view, with reservations in favour of a controlling voice by churches which did not regard the merely legal and contractual aspect of the matter'.[11] Cosgrave sought the advice of Archbishop Byrne, who said cautiously that it was a matter for the bishops as a whole. He did offer his personal point of view: 'That under no circumstances could the Church give any sanction to divorce. That the Church regards Matrimony as a Sacrament only, and claims sole jurisdiction in regard to it. That they could not even sanction divorce for non-catholics for the reason that all persons who had been baptised are members of the Church and under its jurisdiction.' Byrne agreed to have the matter brought before the next meeting of the bishops on receipt of a memorandum from the government.[12]

As anticipated, the October meeting of the bishops at Maynooth adopted a resolution similar in substance to the Byrne formulation: 'Hitherto, in obedience to the divine law, no divorce with right to remarry has ever been granted in this country. The Bishops of Ireland have to say that it would be altogether unworthy of an Irish legislative body to sanction the concession of such divorce, no matter who the petitioners may be.'[13] That did nothing to relieve the legislative dilemma facing the government. In March 1924, Byrne sent Cosgrave a memorandum outlining the Catholic position. 'I must confess that in the beginning', wrote Cosgrave to a bishop, 'I was a child so far as my information and knowledge of the subject was concerned'. He had direct and indirect contact with Byrne, 'from which I learned that His Holiness had jurisdiction over all baptised persons'.[14]

The outcome of the various discussions was that Standing Orders were suspended to prevent a bill being introduced in the Dail.[15] But when the routine amendment was challenged in the Senate, on 11 June 1925, the distinguished poet W. B. Yeats opposed the government; and from men of less enduring reputation such as William Magennis: 'You cannot be a good Catholic if you would allow divorce even between Protestants'.[16] The chairman of the Senate, the distinguished Lord Glenavy, ruled that the motion was unconstitutional. There the matter rested until 1937.

The Catholic hierarchy and the clergy were never a monolithic political force and that was reflected in a letter to Hagan from Michael Browne of Maynooth on 23 July 1924. He wrote of 'a spirit of deep brooding quietness over all this land – broken only by the denunciation of dancing'. Browne, who was a supporter of de Valera, felt that the people were 'obviously sitting tight for a change and wondering when it will come'. He detected a 'deep discontent through the country and the disorganisation of the government party'. Despite being quite partisan in politics, credence ought to be given to his views, particularly in relation to the hierarchy and clergy:

There is trouble brewing – deep and dark – over the divorce question; the bishops may yet assist in the unseating of their canonised government . . . I met the President [de Valera] recently; he is very, very busy gathering up the skeins. He looks forward very eagerly to the return of the young priests as a preliminary step on the road to victory.[17]

One of the most dramatic examples of the political divergence within the hierarchy came at the consecration of the new Bishop of Clonfert, John Dignan. He is reported to have said at his ordination: 'I predict that the Republican Party is certain to be returned to power in a short time. Prepare for that day and do your best for its quick approach, while in the meantime you obey the law of the Free State and subordinate your politics to the national interest.'[18]

An *Irish Independent* reporter who was in Loughrea for the ordination told Sean T. O'Kelly that the Archbishop of Tuam had remarked, on hearing Dignan's republican prophecy: 'after that I am finished consecrating bishops'.[19] Browne was even better placed to get episcopal reaction. The statement caused a mild sensation, according to Browne:

Dignan has caused more heart searching and burning. The Bishop of Ardagh declared he does not know what to do with an irregular curate when one of his own bench publicly professes the same policy. At the general meeting, Dr

Dignan created a strong impression of determination and fearlessness. Among the clergy it is generally thought that the Vatican with shrewd foresight will now appoint only republican bishops! Some joke.[20]

Dignan later explained his position to Hagan. He wrote:

I am not a politician – all I claim is that I am an Irishman – but I felt that the 'other side' was badly treated and in all honesty and fair play, I felt bound to say a word on its behalf. I knew I would be pitied and blamed and praised and that many would 'assume' scandal from my remarks. I am so built, however, that when the occasion arises, I say what I think it right to say and heed not what squeamish or interested persons may say or think of me. I said many things that were not published. I meant every word I said, published or unpublished, and I see no reason why I should change or withdraw a single word of my 'pronouncement'.[21]

Dignan was, in his own words, a blunt, outspoken man. He was in no sense as explicit a supporter of de Valera as were both Browne and Hagan. But all three men were disaffected from Cumann na nGaedheal. From Maynooth, Browne wrote at the end of 1924: 'What with public houses and Boundary Commissions and League of Nations and trips to the continent to avoid Mr Tobin . . . WE ARE NOT FINDING THE BED OF ROSES AS PER INVOICE.'[22] The Maynooth professor was inclined to exaggerate, perhaps, the nature of the swing away from the government towards de Valera. But among the clergy, particularly the newly ordained men coming out of the Irish Colleges in Rome, Paris and Salamanca, there was great sympathy for de Valera.[23] While such a view must remain tentative until more comprehensive research has been done into the matter, it is probable that by 1924 de Valera had good cause to feel optimistic about the 'return of the younger priests as a preliminary step on the road to victory'. De Valera had been released in July 1924 after a year in jail. Hagan had maintained contact with his family throughout that time and had tried to help them in their straitened economic circumstances. He visited Mrs Sinead de Valera, for example, in 1926 but he did not meet de Valera on that occasion. He received a letter from Mrs de Valera:

Both Dev and I are extremely grateful not only for your generous present but for the very thoughtful way it was given. But at present we have no anxiety about financial affairs and it would be selfishness and covetousness on our part to personally accept such a gift. Many, many thanks. You have been kindness itself to us all along. Dev was very disappointed when he found he had missed you . . . I was so glad to see you look better than you did last year. As the Irish phrase says – 'may you be seven times better next year'. With warmest thanks and prayers for your happiness and welfare.[24]

Hagan had continued to support the view that de Valera would some day come to power, but that looked very unlikely in 1925. Although he often advanced that idea in a manner that placed the self-interest of the Catholic Church at the centre of his reasoning, he personally wanted de Valera to replace Cosgrave. At times of major crisis, he kept the lines of communication open to people like Sean T. O'Kelly, de Valera and other leading anti-Treatyites. He exerted whatever influence he could from the ending of the civil war to try to persuade de Valera to give up his policy of abstentionism from the Dail. In October 1923, he had written to Mannix: 'I am unable to state anything definite with regard to the republican policy in the immediate future. On the whole I should be inclined to wish to see them enter the Dail even at the price of taking the oath; but any information I have on the subject would lead me to conclude that such is far from their intention.'[25] In 1925, Mannix led an Australian pilgrimage to Rome. The two men took time to discuss the matter and Hagan got the impression that Mannix 'would not be disposed to balk at it, in the circumstances, provided there was no danger of a split'. He relayed this to de Valera, adding that there was the possibility of a split 'arising sooner or later, even if the present policy of non-entry was maintained; it was simply a question of weighing which was the lesser'.[26] Hagan also involved Magennis in the discussions based on a document which he had prepared: 'and even Fr Magennis, uncompromising man that he is, went so far as to state that while he would not go in for recommending the swallowing of the oath, he would not have a word to say against this being done, provided it was decided on with unanimity'.

Hagan stressed to de Valera the danger of a split or disintegration if the present policy was continued for an indefinite period. There was also no possibility of securing control of the army, or even of obtaining a parliamentary majority without either abolishing or swallowing the oath. The Rector sent the document, which provided both a theological and historical explanation of how to enter the Dail,[27] with Mannix, who arrived in Dublin in late summer 1925. He was met at Dun Laoghaire by de Valera and Count Plunkett. Hagan also arrived some time later that year and a number of discussions were held on this topic. Both the Rector and Mannix threw their weight behind the idea of 'a new departure'. De Valera had come under pressure from a number of other sources, including men like Gerry Boland, Sean Lemass, and Sean T. O'Kelly.[28] The Hagan memorandum was an 'authoritative document' prepared by a prominent, trustworthy ecclesiastic and supported by an archbishop. De Valera was not easily convinced.

Sean T. O'Kelly, who had spent most of 1925 in New York, returned to Dublin at the time that both Mannix and Hagan were in the country. He lent his weight to the Hagan proposal. It would appear that de Valera

agreed to try to get Sinn Fein TDs to drop the abstention policy. Back in
New York again, O'Kelly was informed of developments by his wife,
Cait. He wrote to Hagan: 'Yesterday I received a letter from Cait, from
which I gathered that the suggestion agreed upon between the Chief and
myself has not proved acceptable to the majority. I gather that before
placing the matter before the Ard Fheis it was discussed at meetings of
the TDs. There, I take it, the opposition was so strong that our friend
found it advisable not to go to the limits in pressing it. I am presuming
that this is what happened.'[29]

In December, Professor Michael Browne, who had proved to be a
reliable observer of earlier events, wrote to Hagan:

Things have developed a great deal along the lines you marked out last summer,
the process could have been much faster and it was fortunate that the boundary
crisis came to give it an impetus. There have been acrimonious discussions of
which you have heard and there is a good deal of soreness left in some quarters.
But the air has been cleared and it has become evident that the people that
count are on the forward side and that those who keep their principles nursed
in swaddling bands will not pull any weight if it comes to a trial. The feeling is
growing especially among the young and impatient that it would be desirable if
a trial of strength came quickly; and even some old and thoughtful ones believe
that it would be better to show these people the real state of their weakness and
thereby reduce them to proper discipline before a crisis should arise which
would give them an opportunity for a real and dangerous split.[30]

De Valera travelled to Rome, accompanied by Sean MacBride (who
acted as his interpreter), in early 1926. He had been ill for a number of
months and had been advised to take a rest. But he obviously planned a
working holiday in Rome. De Valera travelled on a forged passport.[31]
The visit to the College was kept secret. When an Italian employee at the
College pointed out to the Rector that he had seen de Valera coming out
of the Rector's rooms, Hagan replied that he must have been mistaken. It
was somebody who looked very like him.[32] But the employee was not
mistaken. In Hagan's rooms, a small group which included MacBride, de
Valera, and probably Magennis, argued about political strategy. The
group – with the exception of MacBride – favoured risking a split in
order to get into the Dail, even if that meant having to found a new
party. The idea appealed to Hagan in particular.

When the Sinn Fein Ard Fheis met on 10 March 1926 in Dublin, de
Valera proposed a motion that, with the removal of the admission oath
to the Dail, it would be a matter of policy, not principle, whether the
deputies attended. An amendment was tabled by Fr O'Flanagan,
opposing de Valera, and carried by 223 votes to 218. The following day,
de Valera resigned as President of Sinn Fein. His new party, Fianna Fail,
was launched on 16 May in Dublin. After fighting two elections in 1927,

he led his party into the Dail on 12 August. De Valera vigorously denied that either he or any member of his party had taken an oath. They had simply 'signed their names in the book'.[33]

The entry of Fianna Fail into the Dail was a source of considerable relief to high clergymen like Cardinal O'Donnell.[34] It was also a vindication of Hagan and his analysis of Irish politics since the Civil War. He had helped de Valera evolve towards the acceptance of the need for a 'new departure' in Irish politics. There was now a constitutional alternative to Cumann na nGaedheal, even if some of the Fianna Fail backbenchers were inclined to a 'slightly constitutional' position, as they maintained a rather ambivalent attitude towards the IRA and the use of violence in relation to Northern Ireland.

While de Valera must take credit for carrying the most politically significant section of Sinn Fein with him into Fianna Fail and then into the Dail, Cosgrave made it possible for entry into Leinster House to take place without too much bruising of republican consciences. This was an episode in Irish history which reflected the statesman-like qualities of both political opponents. It is probable that Cosgrave had difficulty persuading some Cumann na nGaedheal ministers of the wisdom of the gesture.[35]

De Valera's change of political direction was not welcomed universally by either high churchmen or politicians. Hagan was nearly as controversial a character in episcopal circles as was de Valera. His political activities relating to the founding of Fianna Fail were probably not very well known to the bishops. Even if the Cardinal was aware of what was going on – which probably was the case – O'Donnell would not want to have any official knowledge of the discussions for obvious reasons. De Valera was disliked intensely by some bishops – particularly by the powerful Bishop of Killaloe, Fogarty.

O'Kelly had been told by the Archbishop of Cashel, John Harty, that 'very strong efforts had been made to get the bishops to denounce us [Fianna Fail] but we would not stand for it'.[36] This judgement has not been supported from other sources. It is improbable that a condemnation proposal from the government came formally before the bishops in 1927. But there may have been unofficial soundings made to determine whether such a condemnation would have been possible. There was at least one senior civil servant who, in 1927, was most unhappy with the detached political role of some leading members of the hierarchy. Joseph Walshe of the Department of External Affairs was quite resentful of the somewhat aloof approach that O'Donnell and the bishops collectively took to politics.

Following the murder of the Vice-President and Minister of Justice and External Affairs, Kevin O'Higgins,[37] by IRA gunmen in July 1927,

Archbishop Byrne issued a pastoral describing the deed 'as murder stark and hideous. Let us not fear to call it by its name.'[38] Yet despite the unequivocal denunciation of the murder and the warnings to young men not to become involved in secret societies, Walshe took grave exception to the content of the pastoral, which 'merely denounces the act as if Kevin O'Higgins were an ordinary citizen struck down in private vengeance'. In a memorandum, Walshe criticised the Archbishop because he had almost narrowed down 'his denunciation to describing it as a crime against Catholic piety . . . [when it was] a moral offence against God of the very gravest kind because it was a crime against the existence of the state, against the natural law, and against the highest order imposed by God on human society'. The Archbishop had left people believing that 'there is no difference between murdering a man set up by the people as one of their rulers and murdering a private citizen'.

Walshe was convinced that the Catholic Church was partially responsible for the fact that there were still many people who regarded themselves as being 'outside the state', making no distinction between the party in power and the state itself:

This deplorable attitude is due no doubt to many causes amongst them the almost entire absence of ceremonial surrounding the elect assembly, the poor salaries of Ministers preventing them from exerting a permeating social influence, and the lack of a proper national outlook in the press. But the primary and most widespread cause is the lack of support from the Church.[39]

Walshe argued that had the doctrine of obedience to the state – independent of party – been preached from all the pulpits from the beginning of the state's existence and taught in the schools 'no Catholic would have dared to write and speak, as so many of them have done, in direct defiance of the interests of the State as the Supreme social organism of the whole people'. Church support was doubly needed in the Free State because of the 'false theories by political leaders of the de Valera type'. Walshe – who was to serve under the 'de Valera type' from 1932 – had a somewhat inflated view of the power of the Catholic Church in Irish politics. He was also arguing very much in favour of a politically compromised Church; at least, that is what is implied in the memorandum – Cumann na nGaedheal at prayer.

There were two ways that the government could exercise direct influence over the Catholic Church. Although Walshe was careful not to be so explicit in his memorandum, he singled out the appointment of bishops and diplomatic relations with the Vatican for special note. The Secretary of the Department of External Affairs pointed out that the Vatican had been careful to appoint bishops who were favourable to the new regime in the newly created states of Poland and Czechoslovakia. That point was highly significant. The system of appointing Irish bishops had been changed in 1925, giving the Vatican more direct control over the process; it was unlikely that – under the new system – 'mistakes' like Dignan of Clonfert would occur in the future.[40] (See Appendix I.)

Walshe concluded his memorandum with the recommendation that definite steps should be taken to keep the Vatican in touch with the situation in Ireland and to have definite directions issued from Rome to the clergy:

For this purpose a Minister should be appointed to the Vatican and a Papal Nuncio sent to Dublin. We have too many enemies at Rome – Irish and others – to allow our interests to look after themselves any longer. Apart from the early effects on our internal situation a Minister in Rome can do untold good by gradually securing the good will of the Irish Clergy throughout the world for the State, and incidentally by obtaining the sympathy of high ecclesiastics of all nationalities. This is the best and cheapest form of propaganda at our disposal and is well worth looking for.[41]

The reference to 'too many enemies at Rome' was obviously directed against Hagan and Magennis. Despite the warnings from O'Donnell, Hagan had not repented his political ways. When Cosgrave travelled to Bobbio in 1923 for the thirteenth centenary of St Columbanus, the Rector did not attend.[42] There was also another incident – which I am not at liberty to reveal – which brought Hagan into direct contact with Cosgrave, to the great astonishment of the President and acute embarrassment of the Rector.[43] The government was very much aware that another voice in Rome was needed besides that of the Rector of the Irish College.[44] Since the files of the Department of Foreign Affairs are not open, it is not possible to determine what influence the memorandum had on government policy. But it is probable that it was quite important. Walshe had the facility to reflect the feelings of ministers in his presentations. His memorandum probably accorded very closely with the political attitudes of the better informed ministers, although Cosgrave may not have been moved to accept fully his criticisms of the Church and of Byrne in particular.

It was rare – but not unknown – for the Cumann na nGaedheal government to request the hierarchy to issue a pastoral condemning the activities of secret societies who had as their objective the overthrow of the state. That happened in 1922. It was to happen again in 1929. It also occurred two years later (see Chapter VI). But in 1927 the available evidence does not present a clear picture. Feelings obviously ran high in government circles. It is likely that political representations were made by individual politicians – not the government – to individual bishops to act in the wake of the O'Higgins murder. O'Kelly, who had occasion to speak to the Archbishop of Tuam, Gilmartin, got the impression that the hierarchy had been put under some political pressure to act.[45]

The Catholic Church suffered a severe reverse at the end of 1927 when O'Donnell, who had been both sensitive and decisive in his leadership, died suddenly in Armagh. He had, as Coadjutor of Armagh and Archbishop since 1924, pursued a very conciliatory policy towards de Valera while retaining excellent relations with the government. Following the death of Logue, he had closed the political gap between Dublin and Armagh. At the same time, he provided an even-handed approach to Irish politics – an approach which did not suit Walshe of External Affairs. O'Donnell has to be given credit for not putting any obstacles in the way of Hagan, who made no secret of his determination to bring de Valera back into constitutional politics. Michael Browne of Maynooth, who was never short of an acerbic comment, was deeply moved by the death of the Cardinal: 'Strange how from polite indifference he came to occupy a very special place in the esteem and – if we still have such – the affection of our rather cynical body. He has left the bench very much poorer for his absence.'[46]

In Rome, the vacancy at Armagh gave some cause for concern as it was rumoured that Britain was trying to influence the Vatican's choice of successor.[47] While some republican wishful thinkers felt that Mannix stood some chance, the alleged pro-British 'candidate' was the Irish Superior General of the Redemptorists, Patrick Murray. Some thought that because Cardinal Bourne stayed in his house in Rome, the English ecclesiastic was favourable to his candidature; while that may have been true, there was no reason to believe that Murray would have been a pliable Archbishop of Armagh. Murray, when he heard the rumours regarding his name in Rome, wrote immediately to Hagan and urged him to make it known that he had no desire to leave his present post.[48]

The Bishop of Down and Connor, Joseph MacRory, succeeded to Armagh in 1928. He was a man of many fine qualities, but he could not compare with his predecessor, who still awaits a biographer. O'Donnell, together with Walsh of Dublin, had provided leadership of calibre and distinction for the Irish church. The former had set a standard which was extremely difficult for the new Archbishop of Armagh to follow without appearing to compare unfavourably with the many public achievements of O'Donnell.

MacRory shared many policy ideas with his predecessor. The Northerner was vigorously opposed to the idea of establishing a nunciature in Dublin. That was one issue which continued to produce vociferous support from the bench of bishops. The Walshe memorandum – the contents of which were unlikely to have escaped the notice of some members of the hierarchy close to Cumann na nGaedheal – was one of many signals that the government wanted to exchange diplomatic relations with the Vatican as part of a general drive to broaden the Irish diplomatic network in Europe. Cerretti, the longtime friend of Irish nationalists, had been appointed papal nuncio to Paris. His secretary, Mgr Valeri, came to Dublin in October 1926. Professor Michael Browne wrote to Hagan: 'It was hardly a visit of sight-seeing as he would then have certainly called on some of us here [in Maynooth] whom he knew in his lowlier days.'[49] A further opportunity for the government to discuss the possibility of opening diplomatic relations with the Vatican occurred in summer 1927, soon after Walshe had written his strong memorandum. Cardinal Van Rossum presided at the Maynooth synod. Although no definite links can be made – in the absence of official documentation – it is unlikely that either Walshe or the government would have allowed such an opportunity to slip to press for an exchange of envoys. There was little need for any government official to stress the point that the Irish had 'too many enemies at Rome'. Van Rossum knew Hagan of old. The Cardinal would not have been broken-hearted to see the Rector's position undermined as much as possible. Walshe would not have been sorry to see the 'republican' Irish College reduced in stature. One of the ways to undercut the College – and the hierarchy's dependence upon that channel of communications with the Vatican – was to exchange envoys.

Cosgrave's reasons for supporting this move remained quite political. Therefore, it is necessary to distinguish between the desire to set up relations with the Vatican and the general expansion that the minuscule diplomatic service was to undergo in 1929 under the rather forceful and dynamic Patrick McGilligan as Minister of External Affairs. The Vatican had been one of the earliest priorities of Walshe, and McGilligan's predecessor, Desmond FitzGerald.[50]

The government remained extremely worried about the persistent and dangerous armed opposition that continued to exist throughout the late 1920s to the very existence of the Free State. The problem was growing, and so alarmed had the government become at one point that the hierarchy was asked to issue a statement condemning the activities of subversives. The matter was brought before the Standing Committee and the episcopal conference. The bishops declined to issue the statement.[51] This may have appeared curious to Cosgrave, who believed the very existence of the state was threatened by such groups as the IRA, which appeared to be undergoing a renaissance in 1929. The presence of a nuncio in Dublin could prove to be a potent sign that the legitimacy of the Free State was recognised by no less an authority than

15 Cosgrave and family in the 1920s: on the right, young Liam, a future Taoiseach of Ireland (*Cork Examiner*)

the Papacy. There was also the calculation that the government – which had been coming under increasing political pressure – could derive an increase in popularity from the ceremonies marking the arrival of the nuncio. The hundredth anniversary of Catholic Emancipation was to be celebrated in 1929. The arrival of a nuncio to coincide with the planned festivities could accentuate the political benefit to be derived from the establishment of diplomatic relations with the Vatican. Finally, the presence of a nuncio in Dublin would – as Walshe had hinted in his 1927 memorandum – place the government in a much stronger position to influence episcopal appointments and generally bring pressure – when required – on the hierarchy through the Vatican. The Vatican would no longer be informed about affairs in Ireland by Hagan, who had shown himself to be a critic of the government.

But there were also dangers in the strategy. The reaction of the hierarchy – if past performance was anything to go on – would be overwhelmingly hostile to the idea. There may have been a number of bishops who supported the idea of a nunciature, but Byrne of Dublin was still very much opposed. The government was also handing Fianna Fail a ready-made issue with which to demonstrate that de Valera, and not Cosgrave, was more sensitive to the wishes of the hierarchy in this

16 Cardinal Van Rossum, Prefect of the Congregation of Propaganda, arriving for the Jubilee celebrations of the arch-confraternity in Limerick, 1928 (*Cork Examiner*)

crucial area. After all, the appointment of a nuncio would require a major readjustment, both in the psychological and the real sense, in Irish–Vatican ecclesiastical relations. Fianna Fail was a growing political threat to Cosgrave and his badly organised party.

In March, McGilligan had told L.S. Amery, the Dominions Secretary, that his government had been 'somewhat perturbed by the recrudescence of trouble from Mr de Valera and his followers', and he thought 'that it would strengthen the government's position if it were made clear, in some public way that the existing regime in the Free State is recognised by the Pope'.[52]

There appeared to be some disagreement between Walshe and McGilligan as to whether it was more important to have a nuncio in Dublin or an Irish Minister at the Vatican. Walshe considered that it was more important to have a nuncio in Dublin because 'of the influence which they hoped a Papal representative would be able to exercise on the Irish hierarchy'.[53] That difference of emphasis was also indicative of an even more fundamental difference between Walshe and McGilligan. The Minister did not have a very high opinion of Walshe. Before the

17 Eucharistic procession in Cork, 1931 (*Cork Examiner*)

negotiations were over with the Vatican, Walshe had dropped even lower in his esteem.

The early contact with the British indicated just how important the government considered Foreign Office support for the Irish diplomatic initiative. The British were anxious not to put any obstacles in the way, but there was the fear expressed at the Foreign Office that 'if our representatives at the Vatican were to take the initiative' in the matter, the Cardinal Secretary of State might raise the question of a papal nuncio for London.[54] That consideration hampered full British cooperation for the Irish initiative. But the British Minister to the Vatican was very supportive of Walshe, despite his awareness of the delicacy of the matter and the potential embarrassment which might be caused if he was responsible for any unguarded remarks likely to give the wrong impression to Gasparri. The British did not want an apostolic delegate at the Court of St James. That was a matter of policy.

Aware of the opposition from the hierarchy, McGilligan was advised not to discuss the matter with the bishops until negotiations were completed: 'The Minister is convinced that his method of approach without previous consultation with the heads of the clergy in Ireland has proved to be the best, and he believes that any intimation even at this stage to the clergy might result in the nullifying of all his efforts. He considers that the correct and wisest procedure is that which he has already discussed with the President, namely, that the President should tell the Archbishop of the *fait accompli* within twenty-four hours of publication.'[55]

McGilligan was in a dilemma. Telling the hierarchy was akin to alerting a ready-made and powerful opposition with connections at the Vatican. But to think that the initiative could be kept secret from the bishops and the Irish College was quite foolhardy. The *fait accompli* approach was ill-advised. Throughout the negotiations, the government had to curtail contact with the hierarchy and while it did not have to cope with episcopal delegations, it had to face episcopal opposition in Rome. The idea that the Vatican would negotiate 'behind the backs' of the Irish bishops was also quite unthinkable. Walshe certainly showed himself to be very amateurish in hoping to wrap the negotiations up and then inform the Archbishop 'within twenty-four hours of publication'. Gasparri was too experienced to allow the Vatican be compromised in any way.

The British Minister at the Vatican, H. G. Chilton, was instructed to get in touch with Gasparri and he told him on 12 April that if the appointment of a Minister from the Free State to the Holy See commended itself to the Vatican, His Majesty's government would be in favour of it. In reply, Gasparri said he would report the matter to the Pope. He made no mention of a reciprocal appointment in Dublin.[56] Chilton had been warned not to be drawn into a conversation on nuncios lest it might lead to a suggestion concerning London.[57]

Walshe travelled to Rome a few days later and discussed matters with Chilton. He was joined by McGilligan on 17 April and, accompanied by the British Minister, they had an audience with the Pope the following day. It was purely an informal meeting and diplomatic issues were not raised. The group met Gasparri immediately afterwards. McGilligan pressed his case, also raising the question of a nuncio for Dublin. The *aide-mémoire* presented to the Cardinal stated that the Free State government contemplated sending a representative to the Vatican and 'hoped to have the great happiness of welcoming at the same time at Dublin a representative to the Holy Father'.

However, the Vatican insisted on more formal procedures. Chilton reported to the Foreign Office: 'I think McGilligan is a little piqued that the Pope, as he thinks, does not consider him of sufficient importance to carry on negotiations and that His Holiness requires a direct request from the head of the Irish Free State. McGilligan apparently thinks he is as big a man as Cosgrave.'[58] Chilton had to explain that it was only reasonable for the Vatican to insist upon such a procedure. But McGilligan was impatient for results and the Vatican was not a place where decisions were taken at great speed.

But Chilton did his best to hurry up procedures. He had received an assurance from Walshe that there was no danger of a nuncio interfering in Northern politics, and if he did so 'they would immediately take steps to put a stop to it'.[59] Chilton was instructed to present an official note 'at the instance of His Majesty's Principal Secretary of State for Foreign Affairs' asking whether the Pope would agree in principle to the establishment of diplomatic relations between the Holy See and the Free State government. In reply, the Secretary of State said the Pope was particularly glad in principle to establish relations 'because it would be gratifying to His Britannic Majesty'. The official note was sent on 3 May.[60]

Chilton had been very helpful to the Irish delegation. He had extended them every courtesy. His diplomatic expertise was placed at the disposal of Walshe and McGilligan, who needed all the help that they could get. Neither man was very experienced in dealing with an institution which had centuries of practice in the art of diplomacy. McGilligan and Walshe were convinced that the matter had been resolved. It was not 'unduly optimistic to hope that the nuncio's ceremonial arrival should be timed as a grand climax to the Emancipation celebrations'. Walshe believed that the political consequences of such an entry would be 'far-reaching'.[61] A public announcement was to be made in Dublin on 11 May 1929. Walshe stayed on in Rome to tidy up remaining affairs, while, at the end of April, McGilligan returned to Dublin. In early May, Chilton was writing in exasperation to the Foreign Office:

I wish Walshe had gone away with his chief. Though he is quite amenable and ready to do what we want, he is terribly fussy and is in and out of the Chancery all day. I have pointed out to him that the Vatican never hurries and that he must have patience. The whole business would have been settled by now if the Irishman had stayed at home.[62]

On 5 May Gasparri notified the Irish bishops of the proposed reception of a Free State Minister to the Vatican. But, of course, they had been aware of the initiative from the very outset. Hagan, who had been extremely ill, had passed on relevant information to Sean T. O'Kelly in March. About the same time, the Foreign Office had picked up similar rumours from Irish clerical circles in Rome, and the name of Sir Thomas Esmonde had been mentioned.[63] O'Kelly doubted that such an appointment could be made, when he first heard it, because of lack of funds.[64] But by 8 May, he was convinced that the appointment would be made, if Cosgrave could find a suitable person for the job of Minister.[65] The President appeared to have some difficulty making a decision. Professor J. M. O'Sullivan – whose uncle had been Bishop of Kerry – was willing to leave his post as Minister for Education to go to

Rome. The original plan to make a public announcement on 11 May had to be postponed. Walshe wrote to the Executive Council that he had explained the staffing difficulty to Gasparri and that there was general agreement 'without a moment's hesitation' that the 'first appointment might be from the Department and merely provisional'. The envoy would not spend more than four weeks in Rome after arriving and would probably not need to spend more than a further eight weeks until a permanent representative was found: 'The diplomatic corps has only recently begun to develop seriously and it is only beginning to adapt itself as a body to the habits of residence and stability in office common to diplomats at secular courts.'[66] Walshe had himself in mind to fill the post temporarily. On his way back from Rome, he met H. F. Batterbee of the Dominions Office in London on 17 May, who minuted: 'Mr Walshe, whose health I was sorry to learn still gave some cause for anxiety, told me that it was proposed that he himself should go to Rome at least for a time, and that we should very shortly receive an official despatch from the Free State government to that effect.'[67]

When Walshe arrived back in Dublin he found that McGilligan was very anxious to have the nuncio arrive, if possible, on 23 June, the anniversary of Catholic Emancipation. The idea of sending a temporary representative did not particularly appeal to the Minister. Neither would such an *ad hoc* arrangement have suited the Vatican – even if Gasparri had indicated his understanding in the matter. Walshe was under considerable pressure to get the Vatican to deliver a nuncio *on time*. He phoned the Dominions Office on 31 May urging 'extreme expedition'. But the British were in a delicate diplomatic situation. If they exhibited enthusiasm for the idea of a nuncio in Dublin, Gasparri could easily suggest that what was good for Ireland might be equally advantageous to the British. They wanted to avoid being seen to rush the Vatican. Chilton had cautioned Walshe about undue haste. But both Walshe and the Minister felt that it was possible to get the Vatican to comply. Even if it was not a sensitive ecclesiastical matter, it is doubtful if Gasparri would have allowed the Vatican to be used for such overt political purposes as a dramatic entry to end the celebrations. McGilligan told the Dail on 5 June 1929 that Ireland and the Vatican were to exchange envoys. Probably on the advice of Walshe, he quite unwisely said that it was hoped the nuncio would make his solemn entry into state at the appropriate climax to the celebrations. Such optimism was without foundation.

McGilligan said the announcement would give satisfaction 'not only to the Irish people here in this country, but also the millions of our race all over the world'. He said the whole of Irish history had 'received its dominating characteristics from our adhesion to the principles of the

Catholic religion', and 'this present stage of our history' had been 'pre-determined in all its details by our fidelity to the Church of Rome'. It was the feeling of the government that 'the attachment to the things of the spirit which has been the outstanding characteristic of our people in the days of persecution' should continue to be 'the chief characteristic of the organised Irish State'. The speech, which was almost certainly written by Walshe, would not have pleased Wolfe Tone and adherents of the secular traditions of the United Irishmen of 1798. But Tone's followers were not really conscious of that dimension of his thought.

In the course of the debate which followed, O'Kelly's friendship with both Hagan and Curran showed in the type of questions he was able to pose the Minister. His speech might almost have been written by Hagan. In fact, the Rector of the Irish College was in Dublin at that time and might indeed have given O'Kelly some help with his script. Speaking as a member of the party that represented 'the big element of Catholicity', he asked a series of questions which were much more embarrassing to the government than was realised in the Dail at the time.

Had any bishops or any priests been consulted by the Minister about the new diplomatic initiative? Had proper account been taken of English influence over the Vatican? Had it been made clear that the nuncio would have nothing to do with the Court of St James?[68] The answer to the first of the questions was emphatically 'no' and O'Kelly knew just how acutely embarrassing such suggestions were to Cosgrave – a personal friend of the Archbishop. The Dail exchanges did little damage to Fianna Fail's standing in high clerical circles.

The government was hard pressed for time. The idea of a short-term appointment was abandoned – if it was ever seriously contemplated by anyone other than Walshe – and Charles Bewley, an Oxford-educated convert to Catholicism and a prominent member of the Irish Bar, was selected to be first Irish envoy to the Vatican.[69] Bewley would have preferred Berlin, which was being filled along with Paris at the same time. Cosgrave sent the brilliant legal scholar Dr Daniel Binchy to Germany where he became envoy at the age of twenty-nine – the youngest ever appointed in the history of the service.

Because of the tight deadline, Walshe and Bewley had set out for Rome before McGilligan had spoken in the Dail. They had talks in the Dominions Office. There, British officials repeated the advice already given that it would be a mistake to try to rush the Pope through telegrams to Mr Chilton.[70] Bewley, who later grew to dislike Walshe as intensely as the Secretary of the Department of External Affairs loathed him, has left a rather unflattering account of the meeting, which cannot be relied upon very heavily by the historian. According to this account, when Walshe told Bewley that he wanted to introduce him to British officials in London, the future Irish Minister to the Vatican replied 'whatever for?' That ought to have been sufficient to have had him sent on the next boat back to Dublin. But Walshe is quoted as replying: 'You must always remember that the Minister's policy is to collaborate as closely as possible with the British.' That, said Bewley, was the first indication of the policy of the Minister, since 'no instructions of any kind' had been given to him before leaving Dublin.

Bewley wrote many years later, after he had left the diplomatic service, that in his simplicity he had not realised that Ministers sometimes 'shrink from formulating their policy even to themselves and leave the task of explaining it to others in the hand of their permanent official', who had 'no responsibility except that of interpreting the desires of their superiors'. Bewley portrayed Walshe in a most unflattering light. His picture of the Dominions Office meeting was neither fair nor accurate. He cited one remark of Walshe's, when driving away from the meeting, as indicating the Secretary's subservience to British officials: 'It's very important to be on good terms with the English officials. They can be of great use to us. Whenever I have difficulties of any kind, I only need write them a couple of lines, and they give me their advice. I don't know what we'd do without them.'[71] What Bewley did not record in his memoir was that Walshe was under very great pressure at the time. McGilligan had announced in the Dail that the nuncio would arrive in Dublin in time for the Catholic Emancipation celebrations. Officials in London had just told Walshe that there was little they could do to bring that about. McGilligan faced public embarrassment over this and he knew that Fianna Fail would not be slow to exploit his dilemma. In doing so, de Valera and his front-benchers would be speaking on behalf of the Irish bishops.

In the course of the Dominions Office interview, Walshe was told that the British envoy to the Vatican, Chilton, had been informed by Gasparri on 6 June that 'he had no idea whom he was going to send to Dublin'.[72] Chilton had emphasised how anxious the Irish government was to receive a Vatican representative by 24 June, but Gasparri had replied that it was completely out of the question. He did give a promise to hurry the matter up. Walshe left London depressed but still convinced that an envoy could be sent in time.

When Gasparri told the British envoy, on 6 June, that he had no idea whom he would send to Ireland, it is possible that he had a few names in mind but had not made a final decision. Paschal Robinson, who was ultimately picked for the job, was still very busy discussing his report on the Maltese crisis; that Church–State conflict had placed consider-able strain on relations between London and the Vatican,[73] and had made it even more difficult for the British to be as active as Walshe would have liked in the Irish nuncio negotiations. Robinson reported to Pius XI on 2 June. Walshe and Bewley arrived about a week later, 'where it was considered best that Mr Bewley should remain *incognito* until the formal agreement was received'.[74] If that meant the latter should not be taken formally to the Vatican, then Walshe was acting according to the dictates of protocol. But if it was also intended that Bewley's presence in Rome should be kept a secret, there was little chance of success. The Irish community in the city kept itself very well briefed on all local developments. Both men might as well have been trying to conceal their movements in an Irish village; the arrival of Bewley was *an event*, and an unwelcome one to some.

Not long after arriving in Rome, Walshe had begun to realise that the opposition of the Irish bishops to the appointment of a nunciature was the real stumbling-block to immediate success. In fact, it seems that there was absolutely no communication between the government and the hierarchy on the question. Repeated requests, in dispatches, failed to evoke any helpful information on the episcopal opposition. By then the disadvantage of trying to keep the bishops in the dark on this matter was quite apparent. But it was too late to reverse the decision.

There was, of course, another aspect which was bound to upset the Vatican a little. Why, Gasparri might reasonably have speculated, was there such a rush to secure an appointment? It was bad enough from his point of view to be aware of the hierarchy's opposition to the nunciature; but there was also the prospect of placing the envoy in a situation where he might be seen to be favouring one particular party in domestic Irish politics. If Gasparri was not fully aware of the latter calculation, it was at least a standard test to be applied before any decision was made in a similar case. Walshe set about his task under the brief given him by McGilligan:

Your instructions to me on leaving for Rome were (1) that I should do everything possible to better the then existing situation with regard to the Papal Representative in Dublin, i.e. to secure that the Chargé d'Affaires should be replaced by a nuncio, and in general to secure that the Papal representation should be definitely determined in the most satisfactory manner at the earliest possible moment – and (2) that I should help Mr Bewley out of his early difficulties with my acquired knowledge of the situation here.[75]

His 'acquired knowledge' was rather basic, but he certainly knew more about diplomacy than Bewley. Walshe first went to see Alec Randall; he had been present when Borgongini Duca gave the verbal assurance in April about the Chargé d'Affaires arriving in time for the end of the Emancipation celebrations. On 10 June, Walshe went on to see Mgr Pizzardo, the new principal Assistant Secretary of State, and was received after a long delay with 'his usual affability and kindness and he listened most attentively while I set out quite frankly all the difficulties which would arise if the very definite promise to send a diplomatic envoy immediately at the end of the celebrations were not kept'. He made it clear that the Cardinal was not completely in touch with the situation and had spoken without his papers. But he did suggest that the nuncio from Belgium, Hungary or Czechoslovakia might be granted leave of absence from his post and accredited for a period of two or three months to the Irish government until the final occupant of the post should be appointed – of course, also as a full nuncio. He promised to lay the proposal before the Cardinal and the Pope and would be in a position to give an answer by 12 June. Walshe undertook to write a *pro-memoria* document for Gasparri, in which he stated that the Irish government were not in control of the Emancipation celebrations. They were, therefore, not in a position to consider any proposals concerning a special delegate sent for the purpose of purely participating in the celebrations. Such proposals ought to be directed to the Irish hierarchy. It was not possible for the government to give a state reception to a non-diplomatic envoy. In fact, the arrival of a special envoy was only likely to cause confusion in view of the fact that the public was expecting a full envoy. 'It should also be borne in mind', warned Walshe, 'that the general good effect of the ultimate state reception of the diplomatic envoy would, in such circumstances, be considerably lessened.' He urged that it would be better to defer sending an envoy unless he had 'a definite diplomatic character, i.e. a nuncio or inter-nuncio'. But it was of great urgency 'in order to calm the minds of our people' that a definite announcement should be made as soon as possible and Walshe accommodatingly ended that the announcement could take the following form: 'The Holy Father, owing to the extreme urgency of the work connected with the Lateran Treaty has not been able to give to the Dublin appointment all the consideration he would have desired to give it and he has accordingly found it necessary to omit the intermediary step of sending a Chargé d'Affaires to Dublin at the end of the Emancipation celebrations. He will send a Nuncio in the early days of August'.[76] When Walshe returned to the Vatican he was 'dumbfounded' to discover 'a distressed' Pizzardo informing him that they had decided to send a bishop or archbishop to the celebrations bearing a letter to the government. It took Walshe 'fully two minutes to realise the full meaning' of the 'complete change of front'. Pizzardo then urged him to go to see the Cardinal as he was powerless in the matter. They both went down to Gasparri's rooms and Pizzardo went in, only to disappear after a few minutes through another door. Walshe was ushered in by the Secretary of State himself. 'To be faithful to the truth' wrote Walshe, 'I must say that he was very difficult to deal with and his manners presented a very sharp contrast with those of his two subordinates.'[77] He complained later that both the Pope and Gasparri subjected the Irish to 'rather cavalier treatment'.

Gasparri repeated 'rather emphatically' the decision taken by his department, but Walshe urged reconsideration on the grounds that 'he did not seem to appreciate the definite manner in which the promise had been given by Mgr. Borgongini Duca on his behalf, nor the additional fact that my Minister had formally announced in the Chamber' what he believed to be the Holy Father's intention. But the Secretary of State 'took no trouble to get out of the promise'. He simply said that when the Free State government 'had a little more experience they would find no difficulty in recalling their statements. It was an everyday affair in the life of Governments well-established.'

Walshe then had to 'retreat definitely to the line' of direction given in the McGilligan telegram of 10 June that 'no envoy at all should be sent until His Holiness could find a suitable person to send in a definite diplomatic character provided that could be done within two months'. He was then told that he should return on the following Thursday, the 13th, for final proposals. Walshe then managed to get to see Borgongini Duca for half an hour and present him with the *pro-memoria* document intended for Gasparri. He emphasised the danger of the Irish bishops thinking that the government had interfered in their sphere, if the negotiation conducted by the government resulted – even indirectly – in the sending of a *legato a latere* without a special invitation from the bishops:

As a last argument I urged while adding that it was only as a Catholic I spoke – that anybody with less standing than a Cardinal would not be a proper person to send for the purely ecclesiastical purposes of the celebrations. Mgr. Borgongini Duca asked me not to go to the Cardinal that day. He would take the responsibility of advising the Holy Father and the Cardinal against the Envoy going 9-10ths to the bishops and 1-10th to the government and if at all possible would persuade them to send a full Envoy on Mgr. Pizzardo's line, at once.[78]

On 15 June, he saw Mgr Ottaviani, the new second Assistant Secretary of State. The latter also agreed with Borgongini Duca and Pizzardo but Ottaviani was convinced the Pope and Gasparri had made up their minds. Gasparri saw Walshe immediately afterwards and said that the proposed legate, an Archbishop Pisani, would be a 'simple bearer of a letter from the Pope to the bishops of Ireland' and would take no prominent part. He would have nothing whatever to do with state affairs. The bishops had already been informed. The Vatican would send a diplomatic envoy *'dans un avenir prochain'* which, on being pressed by Walshe he interpreted as meaning about September. Walshe then told him that his government would no longer be satisfied with a Chargé d'Affaires but wanted a nuncio. Gasparri countered by saying that the appointment would not be at a low diplomatic level but he could not guarantee a full nunciature. 'I could not possibly request a promise in writing', wrote Walshe.

McGilligan was then left with the task of amending his public announcement. Walshe, however, put his position a little more bluntly in a personal letter to his Minister. He knew McGilligan would be disappointed but explained that he had found himself 'up against a stone wall in the Cardinal's determination to send one to see how the land lay before sending the final representative'.[79] Walshe was piqued at Gasparri's lack of concern over the degree of embarrassment caused by the Vatican's change of mind: 'he would have pawned off on us a very curious melange of *legato a latere* and "diplomat" who would be such only to the extent of carrying a message to the Government or a message on the subsequent appointment to be made public by him'.[80]

He stressed that Pisani, the man who would travel to Dublin for the celebrations, had no political function. He was not likely to be selected as nuncio in Dublin, 'which everybody here regards as a very difficult post'. Pisani, reported Walshe, was 'said to be on the shelf, having made some mistakes in the course of a mission to India a few years ago'. But he was certainly being sent to get the attitude of the bishops on 'the new departure'. A few days later, on 20 June, Walshe reported rumours that Pisani was in fact being considered as nuncio and he urged McGilligan privately to take the following course of action:

As he is going to stay two or three weeks, I am sure we would take him for a run in the Park and show him the house which we intend giving to the Papal Representative provided he is a Nuncio, not an Internuncio – as of course nobody but a Nuncio would be allowed to have a residence so near the King's representative. Archbishop Pisani loves good fare and a nice house. If he comes back with information favourable to the Vatican's prejudices he will get a plenary indulgence for his faux pas in India and we may have to take him. Monsignor Paschal Robinson who settled the Maltese affair is spoken of, but, as you know, I told the Vatican Authorities during my last visit to Rome that an Italian would be more likely to be received with universal favour than an Irishman or an American.[81]

Walshe was on a collision course with Hagan, Rector of the Irish College, on the nationality question. The latter considered that if they could not put off the evil day then an Irishman would be the best choice as Italians were more likely to be flattered by the British. (Fogarty of Killaloe was mentioned.)

Walshe had been very badly put out by the treatment meted out to him by Gasparri. He found that in Rome 'the old idea of Ireland being a holy but somewhat savage island is not yet dead'.[82]

Gasparri was, according to Walshe, 'near the end of his useful years' and would soon be replaced by either Cardinal Cerretti or Mgr Pacelli, nuncio in Berlin.[83] Walshe suggested that if Gasparri tried to get out of his commitment of an envoy by September 'we could go as far as threatening a withdrawal of Bewley if it came to a real crisis. A very mild threat would do. I do not for a moment believe it will be necessary.'[84]

What Walshe missed most acutely during his negotiations was the 'fullest information about the bishops' attitude'. It was a necessary background: 'all the religious orders here know more than we do and the Vatican people have their lines of communication'. In fact, Walshe was very badly briefed and had made some rudimentary diplomatic errors on his second visit to the Vatican in 1929. As Hagan had long since realised, the man who really counted in the Vatican was Gasparri and no final decision on a diplomatic question could be taken without his formal approval. Walshe, through inexperience, had been misled. But his attitude to the Irish houses in Rome had also caused more annoyance than need have been the case.

For all his inexperience, Bewley was aware that the behaviour of both Walshe and himself was a cause of 'scandal' to some influential members of the Irish clerical colony in the city, which was 'out of all proportion to our small population'.[85] Bewley felt that some of the Irish 'could not fail to interpret my promptness in visiting the British as a political demonstration'. He had been warned by the Irish diplomat Con Curran, the brother of the Vice-Rector of the Irish College, 'that any preference given to the British would be strongly resented by the Irish clergy'. He told this to Walshe who remarked: 'Curran thinks he knows our job better than we do.' They then paid a formal visit and dined with the British ambassador to the Quirinal.

It must be stressed here that this account may also be infected by a certain amount of retrospection and 'wisdom-after-the-event'. Bewley spent quite a lot of time in Rome during the early years of the Second World War and may have been told of his initial impact by Curran's successor, Mgr Denis McDaid.

But whether Bewley's autobiographical account was based on beginner's intuition or hindsight, he was quite correct in his opinion. Curran, acting on behalf of Hagan, who was on holiday in Ireland at the time, learned that Bewley had been dining with the British diplomats without ever calling to any of the Irish houses in Rome. He was being chaperoned by Canice O'Gorman, the Augustinian who had run foul of Hagan earlier in the decade. 'I think it little less than treason and think of Second Peter 11.22', wrote Curran to his Rector in disgust.[86] The verse in question reads: 'For them the proverb has proved true: "The dog returns to its own vomit" and "the sow after a wash rolls in the mud again".' Curran considered Bewley's close relationship with the British in Rome to be a very bad start. It was 'the very rejection of Irish ecclesiastical policy in Rome since Cardinal Cullen's time. He was in wrong hands and would make a mess of his mission.'[87]

Curran saw his good friend Cerretti, and briefed him on the latest developments. He also gave him a copy of the *Irish Independent* containing the 5 June Dail debate, with McGilligan's announcement that a nuncio could be sent by 24 June. He also wrote to Dublin outlining the position and he suggested that Sean T. O'Kelly 'ought to expose the above treason of the envoy as well as the previous one of his chief (*circa* 16–17 April)'.[88]

On 16 June Walshe and Bewley visited the Irish College. Walshe reported:

After about ten minutes wait, Fr. Curran appeared. Bewley told him that he had been in Rome some days but had only just received his agreement. Fr. Curran made no reference during an hour's conversation to Bewley's post, to the Irish Free State, to the Vatican, in fact, to nothing except to the weather and the new college building (through which he conducted us). He did not offer us either a drink or a cigarette (though that is usual at any hour); he did not ask Bewley for his address, or even hint that another visit to the college would give any pleasure; he was about as insulting and uncivil as he could be without being aggressively rude.[89]

According to Bewley, Walshe remarked afterwards: 'Did you notice that he treated us as tourists, that he made no reference to my position or yours?' 'It would have been hard not to notice', Bewley replied. 'Outrageous', fumed Walshe.[90]

Walshe concluded his report that Curran had not concealed his hostility to the very existence of 'our state' while in Rome 'and is apparently praying for the coming of de Valera to power with all the disasters that would involve'.[91] If Curran could be converted to the Free State 'so much the better' and if not – 'the major interests of the state require his transfer (together with his Rector) and I believe the Vatican will not make very serious difficulties about it'.

Walshe was correct in assuming that Curran was definitely hostile to the Free State mission to the Vatican. But so much of the overt hostility might have been avoided if the diplomatic conventions established by Sean T. O'Kelly and others earlier in the decade had been observed. There was little point in alienating, at a personal level, one of the main spokesmen for the hierarchy in Rome if such a situation could be avoided. Walshe also called upon Fr Magennis, 'an unconvertible Republican but not a hostile intriguer of the Curran ilk'. Curran had been most annoyed because the first person the two men had contacted was the Augustinian Canice O'Gorman, who gave a dinner for Walshe and Bewley to which most of the influential Irish ecclesiastics in the city were invited. At the meal Walshe was told by Prior Michael Browne – later Cardinal Browne – that the Vatican was delighted to send a nuncio to Dublin: 'He believes that their intention is to keep a general control of the Ecclesiastical side of Great Britain from Dublin without, of course, attempting to have any political contact with London.' That was a view shared by Hagan and Curran, who had once described a nuncio in Dublin as an unofficial envoy to the Court of St James.

From what could be learned at the Vatican, it was said that a letter had been drawn up to be presented at the Emancipation ceremonies by a delegate 'who was to make it clear that he had no diplomatic mission'.[92] It seemed that the Holy See had asked the Irish bishops for their views on the question of a nuncio. The response was less than enthusiastic. They were annoyed in the Vatican at McGilligan's announcement in the Dail, details of which Curran had given to Cerretti, 'dotting I's and crossing T's'.[93] By that he probably meant that he had given a realistic appraisal of Irish episcopal opposition to the idea.

In Rome, Walshe had been frustrated in his efforts to secure for Ireland a nuncio whose arrival would coincide with the ending of the Catholic Emancipation celebrations. But he was not even sure that Bewley would be received by 24 June. Ottaviani told him on 18 June that the feast of the Roman Martyrs on 27 June was the earliest date possible. Walshe argued that having been disappointed in their first objective – a nuncio for the celebrations – it was an occasion 'for exceptional treatment'. Ottaviani retorted that the Holy Father, who had the highest esteem for Ireland, was bestowing a great favour on them in receiving their envoy so soon. Usually it took place at least a month after his agreement. There followed a not unfamiliar diplomatic roundabout for Walshe. Ottaviani told him that Pizzardo would raise the matter with the Holy Father to see if the Irish could be accommodated. On 19 June, Walshe 'phoned Ottaviani only to be told that he was out and was not likely to be back'. The following morning he 'phoned to be informed that he was with the Holy Father.' A further call found that Ottaviani had left a message with the usher to say that Pizzardo would be in touch with him by phone with a definite message that afternoon. Walshe phoned Pizzardo and was told to come with Bewley the following morning to meet the Cardinal. He pressed Pizzardo to tell him if the date would be Monday the 24th at the latest. He answered 'Monday or Tuesday, perhaps before'.

Walshe and Bewley saw Gasparri on 21 June. He was in very good humour and was complimentary to Ireland. The Cardinal read Bewley's address and was very pleased with the words *'réouverture de relations diplomatiques'*. He interrupted his reading of the text to stress the importance of the Irish in the American church, *'très, très, grande'*. He told Bewley *'félicitations, félicitations, vous faites de l'histoire'*, but gave no final word on the date when he could present his credentials. He told them to return to see Pizzardo the following day for the final word. The meeting took place and Pizzardo told them *'Peut-être mardi, mais certainement pas plus tard que jeudi* [the 27th]'. At that point all the three could do was laugh. Walshe correctly speculated as to the reason for such a chain of apparent indecision: 'Perhaps there was pressure from some Irish source urging that we should not be allowed to gain any political advantage from the Emancipation Celebrations. No other explanation that I can conceive explains the rather curious way in which we have been treated.'[94] Walshe concluded his report on 22 June to McGilligan with the observation:

'Forse', perhaps, is the most frequently used word in the Vatican vocabulary. I think we should not allow ourselves to be in the least degree discouraged by its frequent use in regard to matters of serious importance to us. On the contrary, we should draw the conclusion that our interests have been disgracefully neglected at this most vital world centre, and determine to teach them the whole truth with patience and perseverance until the *'forse'* is entirely eliminated from their attitude towards us.

As Walshe waited in Rome most of Ireland celebrated the centenary of Catholic Emancipation amid scenes of national devotion and piety: FAITH OF OUR FATHERS TRIUMPHANT, THE NATION'S ACT OF THANKSGIVING, ran the headline of the *Irish Independent* as some half-a-million Irish people attended an open-air Mass in the Phoenix Park. 'It was pious, it was grand, it was Irish', commented the papal envoy, Luigi Pisani, on 25 June in the *Independent*, which had a circulation for that special issue of 240,000. Two days later, Charles Bewley presented his credentials to the Pope. In an address, probably written by Walshe, he told the Pope:

For is there, indeed, any nation in the world whose history can show greater devotion to the cause of Christianity, or is there any other nation whose whole history has been so determined in all its phases by its attachment to the Catholic Faith and to the Holy See.

In his last dispatch from Rome, a disappointed Walshe had warned that it would be necessary to keep up the pressure for the appointment of a nuncio. By the end of summer, his forebodings had proven correct. The months of July and August had passed without any news of a nuncio. Sometime in early September, while McGilligan was attending the

Assembly of the League of Nations, Walshe wrote to him urging that he should go to Rome again in an effort to expedite the matter:

What about Rome. I feel that you should slip down there. That nuncio is not becoming more incarnate and a few days in Rome, a visit to the Pope, Gasparri and Pizzardo would settle the question. Bewley's desire is to my mind not strong enough to make him take the necessary action. So much depends on the way things are done. Your visit would make the Vatican realise that you attach considerable importance to the early completion of the agreement to exchange legations. The President told Dr. O'Gorman in confidence a few days ago that he did not believe the nuncio would ever come and to my mind this particular view won't allow him to take a single step to ensure his coming. He is too much absorbed by the local episcopal view and he does not mind being beaten by Hagan's intrigues. The very least assurance you would obtain would be that the nuncio will be appointed by a certain date. That would do us for the moment if the date were fairly soon.[95]

The President, W. T. Cosgrave, who was a close friend of Byrne, did not seem to have much enthusiasm to push the issue, given the Archbishop's strong personal objections to the scheme.

Bewley was being hard pressed by his department to bring the entire affair to a successful conclusion but that proved much more difficult than anticipated. The Irish hierarchy, through Hagan and Curran, had kept the Vatican well supplied with the negative views of the Irish bishops towards the idea of a nunciature. Mgr Pizzardo told him that he was aware of some opposition and had seen some reference to it in a daily paper, the name of which he could not remember. He said the delay was useful to enable the bishops to get accustomed to the idea and added, '*c'est de la psychologie*'. Bewley wanted instructions from Dublin on 'exactly what to say as to the attitude of the government if an Apostolic Delegate were to be forced on them contrary to their desire and to the undertaking given in June'.[96]

But there was no immediate development and McGilligan became more and more impatient with the temporising of the Vatican. His own personal position does not appear to have been very strongly backed up by his cabinet colleagues, since Cosgrave was not personally inclined to push the issue too much and thus risk alienating the bishops.

In exasperation, McGilligan tried to put pressure on the British to exert influence on the Vatican. In a conversation with the British Attorney General, McGilligan said that the possible obstructive attitude of Irish Free State delegates to future Dominion legislation might be modified if 'active steps were taken [by the British] to induce the Holy See to send a Papal Nuncio to Dublin'.[97]

This proposal 'appears to be sheer blackmail' read one Foreign Office minute. A memorandum, drawn up by H. F. Batterbee, outlined the

Dominions Office position which favoured an initiative – but the Foreign Office were totally opposed and Orme Sargent minuted that the desire for a nuncio was the direct outcome 'of a struggle between Cosgrave and de Valera's party. The latter at present can count on the tacit, if not open, support of the hierarchy and the clergy in Ireland.' It was the object of Cosgrave's government to enlist the assistance of the Vatican in order to put an end to this 'dangerous alliance and to secure for the existing administration the valuable support of the church'. There was the widespread view that the Cosgrave government was only provisional and that a nuncio could obviate that feeling.[98]

But the dispute was purely internal, continued the memorandum, and if Britain intervened, it could be accused by both the Vatican and the Irish hierarchy of involving itself in matters which did not directly concern them and thus risk British prestige. At the Foreign Office it was felt that no precipitate steps should be taken particularly in view of the strained relation over the Maltese question which was only then being repaired. No action was recommended.

The sending of a nuncio was still in the balance in October. Randall wrote to the Foreign Office that he had learned from Bewley that, although the Irish hierarchy was not united on the matter, the opposition was organised and well supplied with arguments, one of them being that a nuncio would make for less satisfactory relations with Northern Ireland.[99] A final effort to stop the appointment came in November when the Bishops of Kerry and Raphoe spoke vigorously to Pizzardo and were emphatic in their contention that the contemplated step 'was likely to prove a source of regret'.[100] But at this point Hagan believed it would be an achievement if the nuncio idea was deferred until after the conferring of a red hat on Ireland and 'much will have been accomplished'.[101] Hagan was told by Cerretti that Paschal Robinson was being appointed as nuncio; and, on 27 November, he learned that 'the thing is done' for definite. Hagan saw his selection as a sort of compromise 'or better still a manoeuvre to disarm opposition by making it appear that the Holy See is anxious to show deference' to local feeling by 'appointing one of themselves'. The best thing that could be said in that connection was that Robinson was 'better than the best Italian they could send'. Cerretti, Hagan thought, had more to do with the affair than he was prepared to admit since he was the first approached by the Free State in that regard, when he was nuncio in Paris:

The whole thing is clear in the extreme. On the one hand, they can and will say that they have honoured all Ireland by conferring the Red Hat on the Primate; and on the other they will point out that they are settling an Irishman as their representative in the capital of the Free State. It is worth adding that this is not the first time a similar expedient has been tried. Some thirty years ago when

18 & 19 Receiving the papal nuncio, Paschal Robinson, January 1930. Above, Joseph Walshe, Secretary of the Department of External Affairs stands beside the nuncio outside the Shelbourne Hotel, Dublin. Below, the nuncio poses for photographs after presenting his credentials to the Governor General, James McNeill (left) with the Minister for External Affairs, Patrick McGilligan (standing) and W.T. Cosgrave (*Cork Examiner*)

they wanted to establish relations with Bavaria, the people there insisted on a native, and Frühwirt was sent. He was the first, and of course, the last, of the natives to be chosen . . . Where the future is so uncertain, it is hard to make forecasts. God has saved our people and carried them safe out of many tempests. We can only pray that his hand will continue to be stretched out over us in the future as in the past.[102]

There was one other factor which may have helped delay the sending of a nuncio to Dublin. During the period of negotiations with the Vatican, which had begun in March 1929 and ended in June, the question of who was to be made Cardinal in Ireland had also to be decided. Cosgrave favoured Byrne and Bewley let this be known in Rome. But, according to Bewley, the personality of the Archbishop was 'not considered suitable for the hat'. Byrne – who never enjoyed very good health – was believed to have made a poor impression at a papal audience; he was not fluent enough in Italian to translate Pius XI's address to a group of pilgrims. In June, Gasparri hinted that the 'red hat' would be going to MacRory of Armagh. The envoy seemed surprised to learn that the Secretary of State knew that Armagh was not in the Free State. That reflected badly on Bewley and his preparedness to serve as a diplomat. The final decision to make MacRory Cardinal was known in November.

Paschal Robinson was given a most lavish reception when he arrived in Dublin in January 1930. He was welcomed at Dun Laoghaire by Byrne – a man who had done so much to discourage the appointment – and members of the government. He was then taken by carriage to the centre through streets crowded with well-wishers. This was a moment of major importance for a new state.[103] Robinson – whose arrival was greeted with some apprehension by certain members of the hierarchy – quickly established a reputation as a solid, balanced, experienced diplomat. He was both liked and respected by politicians and ecclesiastics alike. His presence helped indirectly the smooth running of Church–State relations. The Vatican also received the most incisive reports from Ireland, which made it unlikely that misunderstandings could arise between Rome and Ireland either on the secular or the sacred plane for as long as Robinson was nuncio to Dublin. His presence in Ireland, until his death after the war, was a major stabilising influence in the area of Church and State. Such a small and relatively unimportant country was fortunate to have in residence so practised a diplomat, who was very highly thought of at the Vatican.

Chapter VI

COSGRAVE, DE VALERA AND
THE CONFESSIONAL CHALLENGE

John Hagan, the Rector of the Irish College, died in Rome in March 1930. He was never very widely known in Ireland, except among the more important Sinn Fein leaders and the hierarchy. It is quite paradoxical that the ecclesiastic who had done most in his generation to influence the direction of Catholic Church policy towards nationalism and the politics of Church and State has not been mentioned by the two most outstanding works on Church and State.[1] Hagan had helped shape ecclesiastical political policy throughout his lifetime – particularly in the years 1919–23. He had encouraged the bishops to remain close to the Irish people and had always encouraged a policy of conciliation. Byrne and O'Donnell were both receptive to his line of argument. The Mansion House talks in 1922 (see Chapter III) had been inspired by him. He had helped dissuade the Vatican from becoming involved in Irish politics.

If he had a major fault, it was his repeated inability to understand that many different forces were at work in the Vatican. He was far too inclined to see the British behind every move. That tendency, which became more pronounced in 1922 and 1923, is partially explained by the somewhat hostile approach to him personally exhibited by certain powerful personalities at the Vatican. He was often in trouble with Cardinal Logue. The investigation of the Rector for modernism left him rather embittered. Hagan was much more political and perceptive than some members of the Irish hierarchy. He became quite close to de Valera and the moderate anti-Treatyite politicians. Hagan has to share a lot of the credit for helping bring de Valera and Fianna Fail into the Dail. While many of the hierarchy had lost all confidence in de Valera, Hagan remained close to his family, helped them financially and then helped stimulate discussion on the need to found a new party and enter the Dail.

Hagan knew de Valera to be a devout Catholic and a politician who was likely to set a good Christian example, should he ever come into

government. The Rector always thought that was possible. It became a
reality two years after his death. Hagan had also imbued many of his
students with his own political ideals. He had never got on well with
Cosgrave and some of the Cumann na nGaedheal ministers. The
executions policy during the Civil War had soured relations perman-
ently. In a qualified sense – and this will only be substantiated by
further research – many of the young priests from Rome, Salamanca
and Paris were pro-de Valera. Those trained at Maynooth and the other
Irish seminaries are more difficult to categorise. But with Michael
Browne on the staff, it is certain that the occasional political comment
escaped in his lectures which might have orientated young men towards
support for Fianna Fail.

There is always the danger of exaggerating the impact of setting up a
nunciature on Church–State relations. But certainly the move did not
enhance the popularity of Cosgrave and his government in the eyes of
the bishops. The appointment of the adroit Paschal Robinson probably
lessened the impact of the blow to the hierarchy. De Valera and Fianna
Fail were quite capable of taking full advantage of the cooling of
relations to demonstrate that they were a viable alternative to Cumann
na nGaedheal.

In the late 1920s, some leading members of Fianna Fail had been
working very hard to ensure that good relations existed between the
party and the clergy and bishops. Sean T. O'Kelly was very active in the
Catholic Truth Society, and on close terms with many of the bishops.
Under de Valera's guidance, the party was fast leaving behind its extra-
parliamentary image. He was helped in this by the growing discomfort
which Cosgrave experienced trying to preserve the pluralism of the
Irish political tradition:

The Irish tradition is a mixed one; it has been influenced by ingredients
deriving from Protestantism and Catholicism, republicanism and monarchism;
its society was rural, and is rapidly becoming industrial. Its constitutions have
been avowedly based on American and French precedents; its conventions and
its laws derive largely from Britain. Ireland has an affectionate memory for the
past, symbolised in particular by the movement for the revival of Irish, yet at
the same time everyone either speaks or wishes to speak English. It was
Cosgrave's achievement that, right at the very beginning he understood the
mixed nature of Irish society, and appreciated the role played in its evolution by
Irishmen of different racial origins and possessing varied religious and
intellectual convictions. To set the ship in motion, it was necessary to achieve
reconciliation.[2]

Thus, Professor Williams summarises the basis on which the devout
Catholic Cosgrave tried to establish the political institutions of the Free

State. By the early 1930s, he had begun to discover that there were forces at work which were not quite so liberal in outlook. The dilemma in which Cosgrave found himself can best be illustrated by referring to the discussions a government minister had with one of the bishops on the question of contraception and its availability in the Free State. The Bishop of Ossory, Collier, met the Minister for Justice, J. Fitzgerald Kenney, in late 1929. As a member of the Standing Committee of bishops, he expressed the concern of the hierarchy that the law governing the sale of contraceptives was quite inadequate.[3] The Minister, who was accompanied by the Secretary of the Department, pointed out the difficulty of introducing legislation just at that particular time.

The government had lost much Protestant support over the Immoral Literature Bill and 'they considered another dose would be dangerous'. Collier deduced that the objection to taking up the question of legislation came not from choice but from the weak position of the government 'and the inference was plain that were the government in a safe position there would be no hesitation'. The Minister admitted the strength of the case, but argued that Protestants strongly objected to have what they called 'Catholic Morality' forced upon them by law. The bishop countered: 'to the obvious objection that this is a Catholic state and has a right to what is called "Catholic Morality", the Minister, and especially the Secretary, enlarged upon the instability of the government at present, of the danger of alienating more Protestant support, and said the Government would not be justified in running risks which would result in a grave upheaval in the country, at least for a few more years. The Minister promised to prevent the dissemination of contraceptive literature through the post and he welcomed all help in the matter, especially reports of chemists who might be spreading such literature by post or hand.' There the matter rested. It remained an unresolved issue until de Valera introduced his legislation some years later.

In 1930 Cosgrave also had a rather serious problem on his hands arising from the income taxing of clergy. This matter was first aired in the Dail by J. T. Wolfe, a non-Catholic TD who was no friend of the Revenue Commissioners. On 4 June 1930, he complained that he had followed two of the biggest employers in his constituency 'to their last resting place as a direct result of what is now known as income tax treatment'.[4] In point of fact, the Revenue Commissioners were entirely independent of the Department of Finance. This removed Customs and Excise, as well as income tax, from the pressure of politics. Moreover, the chairman of the commission was 'a hard, ruthless, fearless, competent but utterly unimaginative person' called William O'Brien. On several occasions, for example, he was utterly remorseless in assessing ecclesiastics for income tax beyond what they had actually returned.[5]

Wolfe was aware of the popular concern that this had caused among the clergy and he raised it in the Dail:

I have been attending the sittings of the Special Commissioners courts for close on 40 years. In the old days I never saw a priest or other clergyman there. Nowadays if you attend a sitting of the Special Commissioners, it is not an infrequent sight to see a queue of priests going in whose explanations would not be accepted by the inspectors of taxes . . . As a non-Catholic, I dislike drawing attention to this, but whatever was said about the old officials they were not priest hunters.[6]

Wolfe was given to exaggeration, but he would have had a lot of support for his views in the presbyteries throughout the country. Some clergymen obviously had considerable difficulty making accurate returns. There was a problem in determining what constituted a priest's income. In the Senate, the Minister for Finance, Ernest Blythe, made a statement on the problem which was very revealing of the de facto situation:

In dealing with clergymen I may say it is an instruction that is given to the Revenue Commissioners and acted upon by them that when a clergyman makes a return, if the return appears to be, on the face of it, made by a man who understood the nature of the return, it is accepted without question. There is no policy of saying, 'This should have been £25 more', or anything like that. As I pointed out before, you have occasionally amongst the clergy and other people the idea that income is what is left over after all expenses have been paid. Occasionally, you would have a clergyman returning a form setting out his income as £25 or £30 a year. When a form like that is sent in it is challenged, but when any sum is returned in a form which indicates that a clergyman understands what sort of return he was expected to make it was not challenged.[7]

According to W. T. Cosgrave, some clergymen were making annual income returns as low as £100. P. J. Little of Fianna Fail had even raised the case of an unnamed bishop who had been in dispute with the commissioners. Matters came to a head, when the 'remorseless' William O'Brien pursued the case of one priest to the point of prosecution. It was only as a result of a behind-the-scene intervention by the government that the prosecution was dropped.

Privately Cosgrave pointed out that priests had to face many calls on their charity, and their actual income was substantially below what they received. Under the existing law, the Revenue Commissioners would not be prepared to accept many of the allowances which clergy were claiming. Cosgrave told Archbishop Byrne to make sure his clergy returned an account which was not 'improbable and ridiculous'. It was agreed that all should return a figure of about £300 as a maximum, at which point only would they begin to become liable. A precedent was established on that basis. But William O'Brien found it 'distasteful'.[8]

Cosgrave had acted very generously in the matter. As a result, a very favourable outcome for the clergy was assured despite the disquiet of the Revenue Commissioners. But it is unlikely that Cumann na nGaedheal secured any votes out of the episode. The activities of the Revenue Commissioners, although independent of the government, might not have been interpreted unpolitically by clergymen who were being investigated. In popular eyes, the Revenue Commissioners were not independent of government. But it would be wrong to make too much of this episode. A clash over the possible prosecution of a priest might have developed into tension between Church and State. It did not. But, politically, that episode did not help the flagging image of Cumann na nGaedheal in clerical circles.[9]

Cosgrave had not shown himself insensitive to the large areas of criminal law amendment which were so much a genuine concern of the hierarchy.[10] His government appeared unwilling, for political reasons, to contemplate the introduction of legislation which might alienate the Protestant community still further from the governing party and from the Free State.

However, the views of the hierarchy were accommodated in at least two areas: The Vocational Educational Act and the Legitimacy Act of 1930. The first piece of legislation provided for the expansion of technical education. The schools were controlled by local authorities. The Minister for Education, John Marcus O'Sullivan, is believed to have given the bishops a written assurance that the vocational education system would not develop so as to interfere with the denominationally-run secondary school system.[11]

The Legitimacy Act was a source of initial embarrassment to the government. The Fianna Fail front-bencher, P. J. Little, introduced a Private Members Bill which forced a defensive Minister for Justice to admit that his department had had the matter under review for some time. He had seen a deputation of bishops on the matter and had agreed to introduce a bill. When the bill was introduced, its content was strongly influenced by canon law. It provided that 'children born illegitimate should be legitimised if their parents subsequently married.'[12]

Cosgrave set up a Committee on the Criminal Law Amendment Acts (1880–5) and Juvenile Prostitution, which reported in 1931. In that way, Cosgrave parried clerical pressure to have legislation introduced immediately and provided the government with what was hoped would be a factual foundation on which to base future draft legislation.

The pressure on the government grew when the Committee on the Criminal Law Amendment Acts (1880–5) and Juvenile Prostitution reported in 1931:

The testimony of all the witnesses, clerical, lay and official, is striking in its unanimity that degeneration in the standard of social conduct has taken place in recent years. It is attributed primarily to the loss of parental control and responsibility during a period of general upheaval, which have not been recovered since the revival of settled conditions.[13]

The committee felt that the unsettled moral state of the country was also due to the introduction of 'new phases of popular amusement', carried on in the Saorstat in the absence of supervision or legal restraint, which 'are the occasions of many abuses baneful in their effect upon the community generally, and are the cause of the ruin of hundreds of young girls, of whom many are found in the streets of London, Liverpool and other cities and towns in England'.

Dance halls, picture houses of sorts, and the opportunities afforded by the misuse of motor cars for luring girls, were the chief causes 'alleged for the present loosening of morals'. The Commissioner of the Gardai, Eoin O'Duffy, said that dance gatherings in many districts were turned into 'orgies of dissipation, which in the present state of legislation the police are powerless to prevent'. Fr John Flanagan, the parish priest of Fairview, Dublin, submitted a memorandum, which was endorsed by Archbishop Byrne, in which he stated that the 'conduct that in other countries is confined to brothels is to be seen without let or hindrance on our public roads'. Another parish priest, Canon Lee of Bruff, County Limerick, referred to dance halls as 'schools of scandal'. Canon Lee referred to a 'sinister feature of these dances, namely, that they were attended by strangers who travelled from distances in motor cars and were accustomed to take the country girls they met there for "night drives"'. Another Limerick priest, Fr Fitzpatrick, of St Michael's parish, described public indecency as 'rampant in defiance of priests and police'. He knew of girls being drugged or doped in dance halls and he was also witness to misbehaviour in a cinema. The use of motor cars for purposes of misconduct was 'notorious'. The result was an increasing number of 'forced' marriages, 'even of girls under 18 years'.

Illegitimacy was a growing problem, according to the report. There had been a drop to 1,520 in 1922 but since 1926 the figures showed a rapid increase:

Year	Illegitimate Births
1926	1,716
1927	1,758
1928	1,788
1929	1,853

Allowing for the large numbers of girls going to England, the official statistics in Dublin were a wide understatement of the problem. One Limerick priest told the committee that in his city less than twenty-five per cent of illegitimate births were registered. Perhaps the most telling paragraph in the report, revealing a prevailing Irish attitude to the problem, was 'the objectionable fact' that unmarried mothers of first-born children 'cannot be maintained apart from the other [county home] inmates *(the decent poor and sick)*'.

The general 'smell of moral decay' was also evident in the area of homosexuality, or 'gross indecency between male persons' as the report phrased it. That form of 'depravity' was 'spreading with malign vigour'. The committee also had evidence of 'girls who began to lead immoral lives at 16' which they attributed not to economic or social factors but to the fact that the girl of 16 'is often mentally and emotionally unstable; she has not finished growing and developing, and though she may be excited and her passions awakened, yet she cannot really appreciate the nature and result of the act to which she consents'. There was another factor stressed by the evidence pointing to differences between English and Irish social conditions:

Generally speaking, Irish girls of 16 to 18 years of age, by nature, habit and training, possess less knowledge and experience of the moral and physical dangers to which they are sexually exposed. They are less capable of protecting themselves against such dangers than are girls at the same period of life in England, for these are mostly brought up from childhood accustomed to live in gregarious surroundings, which, it may be said, instil in them instincts of 'canniness' and self discipline that the conditions of Irish agricultural life do not foster.

The committee recommended, a point made by the Commissioner of the Gardai, that whipping should be added to the term of imprisonment as an extra deterrent for such crimes as intercourse with minors.

The findings of the report, which was presented on 20 August 1931, were not received in the Department of Justice with enthusiasm; they should 'be taken with reserve', was the response. Their recommendations were 'invariably to increase penalties, create offences, and remove existing safeguards for persons charged'. Moreover, it was felt that the clergy who gave evidence may have been too enthusiastic and colourful in their presentations:

Unless these statements [relating cases of brothel conduct on Dublin streets and the drugging of girls in dance halls] are exaggerated (as they may easily have been owing to the anxiety of the reverend gentlemen concerned to present a strong case to the committee) the obvious conclusion to be drawn is that the ordinary feelings of decency and the influence of religion have failed in this country and that the only remedy is by way of police action. It is clearly undesirable that such a view of conditions in the Saorstat should be given wide circulation.[14]

Nor was it. There was very little that Cosgrave could do at this stage anyway. Cumann na nGaedheal had to prepare for an election which had to take place at the latest by the autumn of 1932. In the summer of 1931, there was all the more reason to follow the political logic used by the Minister for Justice, Fitzgerald Kenney, when speaking to Bishop Collier in 1929. The government, for a combination of philosophical and self-interested political reasons, did not want to pursue legislative reform in the Criminal Law Amendment area just at that time.

Before the Criminal Law Amendment Committee had actually reported, a relatively minor incident involving the appointment of a librarian in Mayo diverted attention away from the issues which had occupied the centre-stage position. The Letitia Dunbar-Harrison case was important in much the same way as the issue of taxation of the clergy. In both cases, there were many other issues under the surface of which Cosgrave and his ministers were very much aware. Cosgrave had managed, through direct intervention, in the taxation episode to contain the possible conflict by resolving the matter at the highest level. But the Mayo library case proved much more difficult to resolve for two main reasons: it was not confined to the Dublin archdiocese and government handling of the problem was quite uncertain and hesitant in the initial stages.

The woman appointed to the post of librarian for Mayo was Protestant and an honours graduate in languages from Trinity College. The local library committee refused to give formal approval to the appointment and was supported in its stance by the county council. The government stood over the decision of the Local Appointments Commission, disbanded the council and attempted to sit out the storm of protest which involved a clergy-supported boycott of the libraries in the area.[15]

But local feelings ran very high. Chancellor Hegarty of Killala said that if the 'people of Mayo cannot have a Carnegie Library without a Protestant Librarian being made director of the literature distributed to their children, they will do without a Carnegie library. They have made bigger sacrifices in the past'.[16] Dunbar-Harrison was deemed not to be suitable by the local clergy and people for a series of bizarre reasons. A Christian Brother, M. S. Kelly, believed 'her mental constitution was the constitution of Trinity College'.[17] Mgr D'Alton of Tuam told the local library committee that they were not appointing a 'washerwoman or a mechanic, but an educated girl who ought to know what books to put into the hands of the Catholic boys and girls of this county which was at least 99 per cent Catholic'. He stressed the difference between the two churches on birth control and the recent Lambeth Conference decision: 'Supposing there were books attacking these fundamental truths of Catholicity, is it safe to entrust a girl who is not a Catholic, and is not in sympathy with Catholic views, with their handling?', he asked.[18]

On the county council, three Fianna Fail men voted against the appointment of Dunbar-Harrison – not on religious grounds, but because she was not fluent in Irish.[19] One might have expected that the rival candidate for the Mayo post, Miss Ellen Burke, was a native speaker. Unknown to de Valera, she had done particularly badly in the Irish part of her interview. It is certain that Miss Dunbar-Harrison, who was a prize-winning honours graduate in French and Spanish from Trinity College Dublin, had the greater facility to learn Irish.

De Valera delivered a speech in Irishtown, County Mayo on the issue. It is in that political context that his remarks have to be understood and interpreted. Fianna Fail were not sure when a general election was to take place. But they knew that it had to be soon. There was the strong possibility that Cosgrave could go to the country at very short notice.

The leader of Fianna Fail told his audience that he never stood for the idea of an Appointments Commission on the basis that the 'concentration of all power in Dublin was a mistake'. He played on local feeling when he added that he believed that the same amount of intelligence was to be found in the country. The post could as easily be filled from among local people as by a Dubliner. He then addressed himself to the main reason why Fianna Fail opposed the appointment of Miss Dunbar-Harrison – Mayo was a Gaeltacht area and a knowledge of Irish was essential.[20] De Valera then went on to deliver an address for which he was to earn the reputation, in other circumstances, of being a debating adversary likened to trying to pick up 'quicksilver with a fork':

Another question had arisen, apart altogether from question of qualifications in Irish and that was whether the lady appointed, holding religious views contrary to those of the majority of the people, should hold the position. The whole question hinged on the duties of the librarian. The Catholic position, as far as education was concerned, was that in the past they had not availed themselves of education, because it was not of the kind that Catholics needed.

If it was insisted that this was to be a denominational question they would have to face it as such, and provide for the minority the same facilities as they provided for themselves. If it was necessary that the appointment should be regarded as an educational position it would be better to keep it so. But they would have out of public funds to provide others not of their Faith with the same facilities, and give fair play to the minority.

If the functions were simply the functions of an attendant in the library, who handed out books asked for, having behind her a committee responsible for the selection of those books, then the religious views of the librarian would not matter very much . . . If instead of her duties being passive they were active the position was an entirely different one.

De Valera said that Fianna Fail held that every person in the country, no matter what his religious belief, was entitled to a fair share of the public appointments.

If in this case it is made a denominational post, in all justice they must provide similar facilities for those who don't agree with them. This is not being done in the Six Counties, but they did not propose to follow in their footsteps and ignore the rights of minorities here.

The meeting at Irishtown went away feeling that de Valera supported the local opposition to the appointment of Dunbar-Harrison. But the reasons on which he based his opposition were not so clear. What weight did he personally give to the various arguments presented? It was one of the most consciously Socratic speeches that he was ever to deliver. Fianna Fail did not lose any votes as a result of his 'deftness'. But the 'republican' dimension of the Fianna Fail ideology, tracing apostolic succession back to the United Irishmen in 1798, did not enjoy a major philosophical advance. Politically, his speech had been a success. It was very much a pre-election address.[21]

What the Dunbar-Harrison case emphasised was the complete absence of bipartisanship in Irish politics – even in matters of Church and State – where both Cosgrave and de Valera shared so many ideas in common. The government did not trust the opposition sufficiently to reveal issues of major importance to the state. As a result, the opposition had no reason to feel constrained; every issue could be politicised, as indeed was the Dunbar-Harrison case.

The governing party faced the prospect of a local row with obvious national political implications that could expose Cumann na nGaedheal's 'poor' legislative performance and provoke an unprecedented confrontation between Church and State. There were many issues beneath the political surface which revealed the potentially difficult nature of government relations with the Catholic Church in the early 1930s. Cosgrave feared that the Dunbar-Harrison case might act as a catalyst. There followed a period of intensive discussion with churchmen, never witnessed before in the history of the state. It was serious enough to have an entire county in revolt against the government over the library question. But an article in the February issue of the *Catholic Bulletin* – an anti-Cosgrave journal pulsating with confessional prejudices – opened up another dimension to Church–State relations of a potentially inflammable nature. A study of Trinity College medical school, entitled 'A call for Catholic Action', maintained the high standard of bigotry which singled out practically every issue. But they had hit on a central issue which had exercised the minds of many Irish Catholic bishops since the Lambeth Conference had, on 15

August 1930, given conditional approval to the use of contraceptives in special cases. That opened up a new area of conflict between the Protestant and Catholic Churches. It also made an issue out of the appointment of Trinity College Dublin medical graduates as dispensary doctors. The *Catholic Bulletin*'s Molua put the problem starkly:

Is the School of Medicine, Trinity College, Dublin, a safe place for the training of doctors who are to practise, even to practise with the prestige a civil appointment, among the Catholic people of Ireland, poor or rich? Can any distinction be made, as regards this issue of safety, between the Protestant graduate and the Catholic graduate coming out of that Protestant School and University? Is not the title of Catholic, assumed and used by such a Catholic Medical Graduate of Trinity College, Dublin, simply an added danger for the morality of our Catholic population, rich and poor? Is it not the case, as regards every local medical appointment all over Ireland, that the Civil Appointments Boards feel themselves obliged, now and hereafter, to be deaf, dumb and blind as regards the medical tenets that are certain to prevail in the School of Medicine within Trinity College, Dublin? Are not these tenets manifest from the published proceedings and debates at Leinster House, and at Lambeth Palace, within the past three years? Finally, what about Catholic Action? Is it a mere name, a vague phrase? Or does it point to a clear, urgent, specific Catholic obligation?²²

Soon after the article appeared, a minister (possibly John Marcus O'Sullivan) had an interview with Archbishop Harty of Cashel, who was a friend of Sean T. O'Kelly. He was assured that the bishops would not pronounce on the question of librarians. Harty, Fogarty of Killaloe and a third unnamed bishop would prevent any such decision being taken. Fogarty had already 'spoken very strongly that we were only carrying out the law' at an episcopal Standing Committee meeting. He did not pay much attention to criticisms of the government by the *Catholic Bulletin*, and thought 'we ought to know enough about politics not to mind them'.

But when the Minister drew attention to the offending article on doctors, the Archbishop remarked, according to a government report: 'Oh, there your [*sic*] are on serious ground. If a Protestant Doctor was appointed in my area, I would have to come out and denounce you, and there isn't a bishop would say a word in your favour.' The Minister felt that meant the 'wiping out of Trinity Medical School, which meant Trinity University and that it would appear that the Bishops wanting to do this wanted to do it by means of us, without taking any steps to let us know why they wanted us to do it'.

Harty quoted the Maynooth statutes of 1927 – paragraph 256 – which stated that: 'The Parish Priest will see to it that the Faithful, especially Midwives, Doctors and Surgeons should learn the proper method of administering Baptism to provide for cases of necessity.'[23] He also quoted paragraph 256, which referred to abortion: 'The Parish and other priests are bound to prevent that horrible crime by which through the means of surgical instruments or other means the child is killed in the womb.' The article added that the clergy would take all means in their power to ensure that 'only doctors and surgeons shall be appointed to public positions who have gone through their studies in schools where Catholic principles with regard to these matters are recognised'. Harty appeared to support the government on the Mayo question. He also strongly approved of the principle underlying the method of appointment: 'Stick to the Local Appointments Commissioners', he told the Minister, and then gave instances of bribery over medical appointments in South Tipperary during his father's life in public affairs. The Minister had occasion to report to Cosgrave with mixed feelings. Mayo was an acute embarrassment. The President had panicked. But there was no danger of a national Church–State conflict on the issue. However, the library 'crux' had opened up yet another area where real conflict was probable.

Before the Harty meeting, Cosgrave had sent Sir Joseph Glynn to the West armed with a memorandum setting out the government position. He also hoped to set up a meeting between the President and the Archbishop. But Gilmartin was on holiday until 1 March and Glynn had to settle for talks with the Vicar General, Mgr Walsh. He handed over the memorandum, and in the course of conversation suggested that if the Archbishop were to claim that the appointment of a librarian was on the same plane as the appointment of a teacher, 'it would create an entirely new situation', and the President was prepared to take up such an overture from the hierarchy 'sympathetically with the Government'.

Cosgrave had told Glynn that he was prepared to discuss the question at that level with the hierarchy – that the library question was educational – but that 'many difficulties had to be overcome such as the rights of minorities, the question of machinery, and assuming that an agreement was come to with Their Lordships on the main question, how such agreement might be carried into effect.' Glynn also suggested that the young lady could be given promotion. Everything hinged on the resolution of the question of principle. That would be made all the more difficult if settlement talks followed condemnation of the government in Lenten pastorals.[24]

While Gilmartin was still on holiday, Cosgrave inadvisedly contacted Bishop Keane of Limerick, the secretary to the Standing Committee, looking for a meeting. The latter was quick to interpret the request as a move to have the Mayo crisis discussed at the subsequent bishops' meeting (possibly the Standing Committee at the end of March). But the

Bishop told Cosgrave sharply that 'such meetings never deal with and have no power to deal with the administrative acts in his diocese of any individual bishop'. On the agenda, 'such matters never find a place'.[25]

What in fact had prompted Cosgrave to seek a meeting was that, despite the overtures on his behalf from Glynn, Gilmartin's Lenten pastoral had made specific mention of the library issue: 'Not to speak of those who are alien to our Faith, it is not every Catholic who is fit to have charge of a public library for Catholic readers. Such an onerous position should be assigned to an educated Catholic who would be as remarkable for his loyalty to his religion as for his literary and intellectual attainments.'[26]

Cosgrave, ever respectful of clerical opinion, had good reason to pin his hopes for a successful resolution of the crises on the Keane meeting.[27] A meeting between Cosgrave, O'Sullivan and Gilmartin on 25 February had not gone very well. Sir Joseph Glynn met Gilmartin the following day and while the Archbishop realised 'the difficulties which faced the government on this [Mayo] and kindred questions . . . it was inevitable in a "neutral state" that the Church might put forward a claim to which the Government of the State would be unable to accede'.

Glynn responded that that 'left the government in a very uncertain position, as they might be attacked at any point, and that our people would only see that the bishops had made a complaint, and would not recognise the difficulties in which the Government was placed either by the Treaty or by the Constitution'.

In response to information on the library issue, Glynn helpfully proposed the idea of abolishing the existing library system and replacing it by a centralised national repository of books which could be dispensed to parochial libraries at the request of the local priest or rector. The Archbishop considered the idea 'an admirable solution'. Some members on the Executive Council might not have been in agreement.

But the real sticking point had moved away from the library question to the more contentious matter of the appointment of doctors. The Maynooth Statutes were interpreted as meaning by Gilmartin that in the event of a 'doctor appointed in areas where no Catholic doctor was available', they 'should have taken out a course in the National University of Ireland'. A simple solution to the problem would be to direct selection boards to ask each candidate for such a medical appointment if he was prepared to accept in his practice the Catholic teaching in regard to contraception and craniotomy.[28]

But as a permanent way out of the related problems under discussion, Gilmartin urged the idea of signing a concordat with the Vatican and he cited the cases of Italy and Czechoslovakia; it was 'a matter for the government as to whether they would not take similar steps in this country'. He advised Glynn to get in touch with Michael Browne of Maynooth if he wanted to learn more about the proposition.[29]

The following day, 27 February, Gilmartin sent on translations of Statutes 256 and 257 which had already been supplied earlier in the month by the Archbishop of Cashel. He also continued to push the idea of a concordat – a policy which would have found very little favour among many of the more influential bishops:

'Concordat' is a big historic word and might suggest to some minds the idea of some interference in such matters as payment of the clergy and appointment of bishops – both to be absolutely avoided, excluded in any discussion on the lines referred to for obvious reasons. What occurs to me is that the Government would intimate in some way their willingness and anxiety to have an understanding with the Ecclesiastical authorities in all questions in which there might be a clash between the discipline of the Catholic Church to the laws of the state or article of the Constitution.[30]

Cosgrave wrote to Gilmartin on 2 March, indicating that as a result of the meeting 'we are faced with a problem arising from an apparent conflict between the discipline of the Catholic Church and the constitutional position of the State'. He appreciated the efforts of the Archbishop 'to prevent a situation arising in which the good relations happily existing between the Church and the Government may be endangered'. The idea that an understanding 'could be effected by a Concordat . . . is an idea which has not been before the Government and would require the fullest consideration by them'.[31] Gilmartin was convinced that the Mayo 'crux' could not be solved without moving the librarian[32] and he told Cosgrave on 4 March that if three terms were met the matter could be quickly resolved:

1. The Mayo County Co. to be elected next June and allowed to function as there is due then a general election of county councils for Ireland.
2. The recognition by the government that a librarianship is an educational position and that a place be found elsewhere for Miss Dunbar-Harrison.
3. Until Miss Dunbar-Harrison leaves the people cannot use the library in principle.[33]

The terms, as outlined by Gilmartin, were in substance what Sir Joseph Glynn had partially put forward somewhat tentatively in discussions as a basis for a solution. But it is clear in Glynn's meeting with Mgr Walsh on 8 February that there was not unanimity in government on how best to proceed. Cosgrave may have intimated that he was prepared to go further for the sake of Church–State harmony than some of his Executive Council colleagues were determined to go. He may have felt the conflict 'between the discipline of the Catholic Church and the constitutional position of the State' more acutely than many of his colleagues. A cabinet split on the matter may provide the explanation for the rather curiously unfinished 'NOTES BY PRESIDENT' and 'NOTES BY MR FITZGERALD' found in the departmental files. The texts are as follows:

Notes by President

Bishops make the claim that the office of Librarian should be the same as teachers

A. That claim must be admitted.

B. I am not prepared to dispute it.

C. Its implementation can not be carried out by me.

A. Office of Librarian – that it should be filled in the same manner as teacher of a National school. I am not prepared to oppose their claim in public and in consequence I am prepared to retire from public life. That the final determination of this question be that which is authoritatively laid down as church doctrine then.

A. If the Bishops claim that the office of Librarian should be filled in the same manner as that of teacher of a National school, I am not prepared to oppose this claim in public and in consequence I am prepared to retire from public life.

A. Then this is a new claim.

B. If the final authority in the matter supports this claim then the matter has to be reconsidered in that light and if it was pushed to a final conclusion it should be left open to us as what to do.

Notes by Mr Fitzgerald

If the Bishops claim that Librarians must be appointed as National teachers are appointed that is a completely new claim and raises a new situation.

In no circumstances am I prepared to embark on a course at variance with the declared instructions of the Church

As far as I have considered this matter)

I have considered this matter and)

I do not see how this decision could be translated into administrative action. Put into the position of being unable to function in complete harmony with the authority of the Church my only course is to resign my responsibility for government.[34]

The Minister for Finance, Ernest Blythe – the only Northern Protestant ever to serve in a Dublin cabinet – would not have been too pleased at such reasoning and would certainly have taken a tough line.

It is difficult to say definitely whether Cosgrave was serious about leaving public life at that time. It is certain that he considered the option. However, it is also possible that he used the threat of withdrawal as a bargaining counter with the bishops – some of whom would have been among his staunchest supporters – and as a means of achieving cabinet support for his policies. There is the further consideration that, faced with a general election, some of Cosgrave's rivals in the Executive Council might not have been displeased to see him quit and thus make way for 'new blood'. However long Cosgrave's agonising about retiring to the seclusion of Dun Laoghaire might have lasted, it is evident that some of his nine cabinet colleagues stiffened his resolve to take a firm line on the question of medical appointments and other issues. McGilligan's strategy was that the best method of defence was attack.

Whatever the reason, by 11 March 1931 Cosgrave's tone had changed and his policy had toughened considerably. The original uncertainty which had resulted in frenetic letter-writing and rounds of talks had given way to businesslike crispness indicating that fears of a collective episcopal condemnation were superseded by an executive decision not to give way. Gilmartin was isolated.[35] The President's letter to the Archbishop was firm and direct in its rejection of his three-point programme for settlement. He told the Archbishop that to discriminate against any citizen on the basis of religion 'would be to repudiate some of the fundamental principles on which this state is founded'.

That the librarianship question as a whole could be solved as an educational position 'was open to considerable doubt'. The hierarchy had not made such a claim. Cosgrave pointed out that obviously general legislation for the country – not particular legislation for a part of it – would be to recognise the law, and the Minister had no option but to take effective steps for its reinforcement.[36]

Cosgrave next set about clearing the air with Cardinal McRory. A government memorandum – which may have been drawn up by John Marcus O'Sullivan – on the Maynooth Decree 257, concluded that 'as it stands it is unconstitutional and unworkable'; after consultation with the government it 'would have been more reasonable and practicable'. The Constitution did not give the government the power to reject every Protestant doctor who applied for a public post, or every doctor who graduated from Trinity or any non-National University of Ireland institution. In that context Decree 257 was 'unworkable'. Protestant doctors would occasionally be appointed to dispensaries. Even if those doctors held 'lax views on craniotomy and contraceptives' it was unlikely that they would act upon them in the Free State. They would be more careful to avoid giving offence to the Catholic conscience than a Catholic doctor would be. And that for obvious reasons. The memorandum stated that the government was prepared to meet the wishes of the bishops making the sale of contraceptives illegal.

In general, the memorandum recommended that the bishops ought to lay their grievances before the government before attacking it publicly. It was embarrassing for the government 'to learn the bishops' views for the first time through a condemnatory pastoral letter, or a chance conversation between the bishop and a minister. The government feels it has a grievance here.'

The memorandum also intimated that in the recent Church–State tension the bishops may have been misinformed: 'They may not see that their demands are impracticable; that they are asking what the government cannot grant, or cannot grant in that way. Frank and friendly co-operation between Church and State will smooth away much misunderstanding, and make peaceful government easier. The bishops will find the government most accommodating, willing, and even anxious to meet their lordship's [sic] wishes as far as it is possible'.[37]

But when Cosgrave took pen in hand to write to Cardinal MacRory he was far from conciliatory. On 28 March 1931 he laid out government policy in a number of sensitive areas: he troubled His Eminence with 'matters which have recently given rise to considerable anxiety in the minds of my colleagues and myself because of their possible reaction upon State institutions' and upon 'the happy relations which exist between the Church and State in this country'. Any appearance of public disagreement between individual ecclesiastical authorities and the state was always deplorable, he said. In a country so overwhelmingly Catholic as Ireland it could have very serious and far-reaching results. That danger was augmented 'by the unfortunate fact' that there existed here a considerable body of opinion which either openly or by implication refused to accept and recognise 'state institutions' and were only too glad of any pretext for attacking them:

We feel confident that Your Eminence and their Lordships and bishops appreciate the effective limits to the powers of government which exist in relation to certain matters if some of the fundamental principles on which our state is founded are not to be repudiated. Such repudiation, direct or indirect, by an Irish government would, we are convinced, entail consequences very detrimental to the country's welfare.

Of the matters which seemed most likely to lead to danger, Cosgrave singled out the appointment of dispensary doctors:

The system of appointment of medical officers now in operation was devised to prevent grave abuses which were, unfortunately, far from uncommon in the past. It has been recently conveyed to us that if a non-Catholic doctor, or indeed a doctor not qualified in the National University is appointed as a dispensary doctor, some of the bishops may feel it to be their duty to denounce the appointment.

Cosgrave believed that a denunciation of that kind 'would be regarded and represented as a denunciation, by implication at least, of the government under whose agency the appointment was made'. The President then went on to point out that Statutes 256 and 257 of the Maynooth synod (1927) had been adduced 'in support of the contention that action of this nature is a duty incumbent on the bishops'. Cosgrave did not wish to interpret the statutes in question, but he was concerned with the principle and the public reaction to any course of action based on that principle. He firmly rejected the idea that it would be possible to discriminate by way of religious test against non-Catholics as such or graduates of Trinity or Queen's, Belfast. It was even open to doubt whether 'a demand for information as to the religious belief of a candidate would be sustainable'. This rejection was rooted in the 'fundamental principle upon which the state is based'. The same principle was also operative 'in regard to the position of country librarians, which had been acute in one portion of the country'.

Cosgrave pressed his advantage by raising the possibility of attention being brought to dispensations of marriages, on grounds of non-consummation, granted by the church 'of which the civil authorities receive no notification'. There was also the possibility of attention being drawn to the difficulties arising out of a marriage which was recognised as valid by the civil and not by ecclesiastical law:

That these and other difficulties exist is not open to question. That in the present circumstances, they are capable of a solution which could be regarded as satisfying, at once, the requirements of the church and the state is, I fear, open to grave doubt. Any failure following an attempt to solve these problems would only add to the difficulty, and if it came to public knowledge, might prove a source of unrest, if not a scandal.

Those considerations made the government all the more fearful of the danger 'that incidents, which with the good-will that exists, might be avoided, may be precipitated if the attention of the public is unduly focused on these questions in an unauthorised way'. What Cosgrave was hinting at here was that popular Catholic pressure for confessional legislation could provoke a counter-reaction from the other denominations, leaving the above-mentioned issues exposed and the government virtually powerless to regularise the law in that regard in a manner exclusively favourable to Catholics.

The President wanted the hierarchy to look to the 'attitude of certain periodicals which, by their titles, lead the general public to believe that they are authorised exponents of Catholic doctrine'. Their comments on government policy and on government departments were 'often inaccurate' and at times 'so intemperate as to be violently abusive' and that had done considerable damage not just to the governing party but to the state as a whole, 'and have resulted in weakening the respect for authority'. The weakening of the authority of civil government derived from the confusion, in the absence of a directive from the hierarchy, caused by newspapers and journals speaking groundlessly to pious Catholics.[38]

In response, Cardinal MacRory wrote on 10 April 1931 that he would be in Dublin the following Monday for a meeting with the President. Although there is no account of the discussions it is quite clear that matters were resolved in favour of the government. Cosgrave was, therefore, in a stronger position to deal with the outstanding Mayo issue.

On 15 April Cosgrave and O'Sullivan had a meeting with Gilmartin on Mayo 'and to some extent the general questions connected therewith'. From the outset, it was clear that the Archbishop was on the defensive. He stressed, on several occasions, that owing to its peculiar history regarding proselytism Mayo constituted an exception. The changing of appointment procedures was no longer negotiable. There was some room for manoeuvre on the timing of the holding of county council elections in Mayo. In response to a request from Gilmartin to have Dunbar-Harrison transferred, Cosgrave indicated that 'if it were possible to do so, the government at a suitable time, would see whether a position could be found'.[39]

The government did not display unseemly haste in soothing ruffled feelings in the West. In the fullness of time, Dunbar-Harrison was promoted to a post in the Department of Defence in January 1932.[40] The outcome was, according to the acerbic correspondent of *Round Table* 'fair to the lady, soothing to the Mayo bigots and good for the government'.[41] It was certainly not good for the government in Mayo, as the subsequent election was to show.

The Dunbar-Harrison case did not result in a crisis between Church and State. But there was every possibility that it might have done so, but for the restraint and good sense shown by bishops and politicians. The hierarchy were not anxious to elevate the conflict to a national level. It was a matter for the local Metropolitan, Gilmartin of Tuam. But the Dunbar-Harrison case focused clerical and political attention on a wider area of public appointments which involved dispensary doctors. Cosgrave, who had not handled the case well initially, soon regained the initiative and used the opportunity to press home a number of points which counselled the hierarchy to leave well alone. With the Criminal Law Amendment Committee still sitting in March 1931, there was no reason to make an issue out of such matters.

The security question was now the most important question facing Cosgrave and his government. So exercised were they by the reorganisation of the IRA, and the growth of 'republican' violence in the countryside, that the hierarchy had been approached to make a statement condemning what was happening in 1929. The matter went before the Standing Committee of the hierarchy and then was put in front of the national conference. But, on that occasion, the hierarchy had refused to comply with government wishes.[42]

By the summer of 1931, Cosgrave had become very alarmed about the deteriorating political situation, with the recrudescence of IRA violence. Joseph Walshe, the Secretary of the Department of External Affairs, had alerted Cardinal MacRory about the situation in early August. Cosgrave wrote indicating that he knew the Cardinal was 'fully alive to its gravity'.

The President said he had refrained 'as long as possible from adding to the many anxieties of your exalted position until the facts made it imperative that the head of the church in this country should be given the fullest information about a situation which threatens the whole fabric of both church and state'. It was imperative that their meeting 'should not give rise to conjecture of any kind' and while he would like to travel to Greenan (where the Cardinal was on holiday) for talks, 'every exit of mine from Dublin is duly chronicled'. He suggested his own house as a secret venue on 18 August.[43]

Cosgrave had very good cause to be worried. The police had compiled an extensive dossier on the growth of a conspiracy against the state. There are no details of what was discussed at the meeting between Cosgrave and MacRory – or indeed, whether the meeting ever took place – but the President was in contact with all the bishops a month later. It is virtually certain that Cosgrave also discussed this matter with Byrne of Dublin. So serious did the President consider the situation that he got the approval of the Cardinal to circulate memoranda on subversion and conspiracy in the country to all the bishops. In a letter to the Archbishop of Dublin, Cosgrave described the threat from subversion as 'a situation without parallel' which endangered the 'foundations of all authority'.[44] In his note to MacRory, Cosgrave was even more explicit:

We are confronted with a completely new situation. Doctrines are being taught and practised which were never before countenanced amongst us and I feel that the influence of the Church alone will be able to prevail in the struggle against them. Only through the powerful influence of the Church will innocent youths be prevented from being led into a criminal conspiracy, escape from which is impossible because it involves the certainty of vengeance and the grave danger of death. The Church alone, in my view, can affect the consciences of parents and others in regard to the dangers to which our young people are exposed through Communistic and subversive teachings. The Church, moreover, can bring powerful influence to bear on those who through inadvertence or otherwise have in the past, by unreasonable or uninformed criticism of State institutions and State servants as apart from political leaders, parties or programmes, contributed in some degree towards preparing the ground for the spread of the doctrines mentioned.[45]

There is no opportunity here to evaluate the evidence supporting the idea of a conspiracy which had created 'a situation without parallel' in Ireland, but Cosgrave seemed convinced that the militant republican movement had been infiltrated by communism.[46] There were a number of senior civil servants, in the Departments of Justice and External Affairs, who believed this to be the case. This may well have turned into a 'red scare' for deliberate political purposes. But when Cosgrave wrote to each member of the hierarchy – an unprecedented step – he was genuinely convinced that the very life of the state was now threatened. It is quite understandable that he should have felt like that. He had lived through the Civil War, an 'army mutiny' in 1924 and the murder of his Vice-President in 1927. By the late 1920s, there were the most disturbing signs that the IRA had regrouped and become much more dangerous because of the radical socialist philosophy professed by the new leaders.

All this has to be seen in the context of a Cumann na nGaedheal leadership, which had begun to feel that there was a real possibility of the governing party losing to Fianna Fail.[47] The 'slightly constitutional' nature of Fianna Fail was emphasised when – at the height of private discussions between bishops and the government on the question of the conspiracy – a prominent member of Fianna Fail, Frank Aiken, unilaterally proposed that the government should host round-table discussions with the republican group Saor Eire.[48] The government considered that that group, in particular, was at the very heart of the conspiracy.

De Valera was sorely tried by what was going on. He had been shown a copy of the Department of Justice 'red book' – the documents circulated by the government to all the bishops – by *one* of the bishops. That underlines the central argument of this book that the Irish hierarchy was not a political monolith. Fianna Fail were aware that the hierarchy was being encouraged to issue a pastoral condemning Saor Eire and the IRA. It was imperative that his party should not be blighted in any way by the document which de Valera realised would be published after the October meeting of the hierarchy. He immediately wrote to the Cardinal requesting a meeting, as he was 'anxious that certain important considerations be submitted' to him before the bishops' October meeting. The fact that MacRory actually agreed to meet him was a sign of changed times and minuted on the de Valera letter was: 'I had a long talk with him at Maynooth'.[49] The 'important considerations' discussed most certainly referred to the 'threat to the state' and the forthcoming pastoral or the question of subversion.

MacRory's minute indicated that the conversation between the Cardinal and de Valera had been productive and amicable. Whether the leader of Fianna Fail saw other members of the hierarchy on that occasion is not supported by archival material. Neither is it clear what was the precise date of the meeting. It is probable that de Valera met the Cardinal on 16 October. It is also likely that he met other bishops informally. His stock had risen significantly in that quarter since his arrival in the Dail in 1927. Some of his bitterest critics on the bench had died in the 1920s and been replaced by more politically open-minded prelates. But as long as Fogarty of Killaloe was a member of the hierarchy, de Valera had a strong and unforgiving critic.

De Valera could not have been pleased by the intervention in the Dail from his close friend and colleague, Mr Frank Aiken, on 16 October – two days before the pastoral was due to be published – suggesting all-party discussions with Saor Eire.[50] Not content with that unhelpful statement, he wrote directly to the Cardinal the day after the pastoral had been published repeating his proposal. He hoped that the Cardinal would not be put off by advisers 'who would say that it would be undignified for you as head of the Church in Ireland to sit in conference with representatives of the IRA and Saor Eire'. The idea was not merely 'undignified' for MacRory and Cosgrave; it was quite unthinkable. Aiken warned:

. . . the excommunication of members of the IRA creates such a danger to the future of the Church and to the people that I am impelled, as an Irishman who wants to see the Church stand as a bulwark to the faith and rights and liberties of the people, to appeal to you not to be content with condemnation of the results of evils but to take active and fatherly steps to deal with the root cause . . . Immediate action on your part is all important.[51]

On 18 October 1931 the joint pastoral was read in every church. It spoke of the 'growing evidence of a campaign of Revolution and Communism, which, if allowed to run its course unchecked, must end in the ruin of Ireland'. Saor Eire was condemned by name as a 'frankly Communistic' organisation trying to 'impose upon the Catholic soil of Ireland the same materialistic regime, with its fanatical hatred of God, as now dominates Russia and threatens to dominate Spain'. The ranks of communist revolution were 'no place for an Irish boy of Catholic instincts: one stands for Christ, the other for Anti-Christ. Neither can you, and for the same reason, be an auxiliary of Communism.' If Saor Eire was successful, Ireland would witness 'the ruin of all that is dear to us in History,

Religion and Country'. It also meant the overthrow of 'Christian civilisation . . . class warfare, the abolition of private property and the destruction of family life'.[52] The pastoral was very firm but it did not meet the high standards of condemnation required by some in the government service.

Charles Bewley, the envoy to the Vatican, was in Dublin for discussions in the Department of External Affairs. He was told by an irate Walshe that 'we hoped the bishops would come out strong but they have no courage. The only hope is that the nuncio will make them see reason.' Any such move would have been most impolitic for Robinson and the nuncio would never have seriously contemplated so undiplomatic and contentious an initiative. Walshe explained that he had spent three hours with the nuncio the day before, explaining the crisis without result. Bewley was instructed that when he lunched with the nuncio he should impress upon him 'that the Communists are really a danger to Ireland. Perhaps he'll come out against them.' Although this source is not the most reliable, the behaviour is consistent with Walshe's reaction to the episcopal pronouncement following the death of Kevin O'Higgins. It, too, was considered not strong enough. The Secretary of External Affairs consistently expected the Catholic Church to do the bidding of the government. Moreover, he also seemed to operate on a false assumption that clerical initiatives would produce magical political results. The power of the hierarchy in Irish society was overestimated consistently by senior figures like Walshe.

According to Bewley, he had no intention of carrying out the mission entrusted to him by his superior. But at the lunch Robinson, a highly polished and practised diplomat, pre-empted any discussion on the matter by remarking rather casually: 'Sean MacBride was here with me yesterday. A nice fellow.' That name had turned up repeatedly in Department of Justice memoranda as the 'principal travelling organiser of the IRA, in July, 1931'. Bewley asked: 'Your Excellency didn't find him a dangerous communist?' 'No, I didn't notice it.' When Bewley told Walshe that he did not think the nuncio would enter the domestic political controversy, the Secretary made a despairing gesture.[53] Walshe showed remarkably little insight into the sensitivity of the nuncio's position in Ireland. Any approach by him to the bishops − except on instruction from the Pope − was liable to meet with a rebuff. A statement made by Robinson on the 'red scare' would not only be a breach of protocol but also an implied insult to the hierarchy. Given the controversy surrounding his coming to Dublin, Robinson was in no position to anger the bishops. Walshe's demand was entirely impracticable.[54]

The government introduced the Constitutional (Amendment No. 17)

Bill, which established a military tribunal to replace the normal jury trial system, and all the revolutionary groups were proscribed.

Tom Johnson, the former leader of the Labour party, did not trust Cumann na nGaedheal's sense of justice, and he wrote to R. J. P. Mortished at the International Labour Organisation Office in Geneva:

. . . and in the times that may come if Europe goes smash, or if unemployment extends and prices rise at home, I dont trust them to refrain from using the new powers against normal civil agitation. Neither the present government nor their successors can be trusted with those powers. The introduction and the passage of the bill was accompanied by an anti-communist, anti-Russian rampage-attacks on the church − anti-God, look at Spain, our beloved faith in danger, etc., etc. . . .

In fact, Johnson saw a positive side in the Saor Eire–IRA 'link-up'. He mentioned that one 'republican' leader was planning to use key social issues to agitate for school meals and free books:

. . . quite in line with the Bolshevik tactic. I don't think he has any great success outside the IRA followers but the IRA appears to have been captured by the communist wing. As the Russian communists are not anarchists and do not rely upon assassination as a useful method, this change would lead away from the secret army of the republic notion and the fanatical 'partitionism' of the past. The new tactic might be more dangerous to the established order but it would be healthier albeit wasteful and costly and probably futile into the bargain.[55]

Cosgrave dissolved the Dail on 29 January 1932. At the Mansion House in Dublin the same night he spoke of 'the conspiracy solemnly condemned by the hierarchy'. He was tough and uncompromising and laid the main stress on law and order issues, while the Lord Mayor of Dublin, Alfie Byrne, urged the citizens to leave

no stone unturned in securing that the fires of communism − which were still smouldering − would be surely extinguished and that the disciples of paganism would never again find either Dublin city or any part of Ireland an easy prey to their anti-God preaching.

It was difficult to see where exactly 'the fires of communism' were smouldering in Ireland. But that did not prevent Cumann na nGaedheal from launching a wall-poster and newspaper advertisement campaign with that theme: de Valera was shown playing cards with Cumann na nGaedheal and a loutish criminal type with a cap and eye-mask with Saor Eire and IRA written on him. In another, an unsuspecting Cumann na nGaedhealer does not see de Valera slipping the joker under the table to his shady partner. Yet another even more explicit poster entitled 'his master's voice' showed de Valera being prodded along by the same criminal type with a gun in his back but his face betraying complicity. Another showed the 'shadow of the gunman' stalking the countryside while another had the red flag being superimposed on the tricolour and warned against communism taking over.

A series of Cumann na nGaedheal advertisements in the national and local papers were equally shrill in their denunciations of Fianna Fail. The *Cork Examiner* carried a series of front-page 'ads' with banner headlines like 'Sanity or Suicide . . . a vote for Fianna Fail is a vote for national suicide'. On polling day, the line was bold and direct:

THE GUNMEN AND COMMUNISTS ARE VOTING FOR FIANNA FAIL TODAY

The flaws in the Cumann na nGaedheal campaign were mercilessly exposed by Alfred O'Rahilly of University College Cork, a man of impeccable Catholic credentials. O'Rahilly declared, in the *Irish Press*, that he would not vote for Cumann na nGaedheal because he had been repulsed by 'Cosgrave's new fangled synod', and his 'attempts to intimidate us by issuing impertinent lenten pastorals'. He rejected the inference that 'Catholics can only vote for him.' That amounted to an usurpation of Catholic religion at the hustings. He said that Fianna Fail were being wrongly depicted as bad Catholics advocating socialism and wanting to bring in state control and state inference in every aspect of private enterprise.

In another article, published just before polling day, O'Rahilly stated positively that he was voting for Fianna Fail. Cumann na nGaedheal propaganda, he said, consisted of vile caricatures, unjustified abuse and hysterical misrepresentation. He had sought in vain for rational argument amid the reeking mess of unchristian vilification. The news that aeroplanes were about to drop leaflets saying the gunmen were going to vote for Fianna Fail had as little impact on him as the British saying in the 1880s that the Fenians were going to vote for Parnell: 'The people who fancy that the Coercion Act has stamped out or is going to stamp out certain ideas and organisations are living in a fool's paradise. They have a very superficial knowledge of Irish life and history.'

He attacked the publishing of a pamphlet containing Cosgrave's speech at the state banquet to welcome the papal nuncio in January 1930, as part of the election campaign. That, he said, was not only a flagrant breach of diplomatic courtesy, it was also 'a disgraceful attempt to pin an unpopular programme to the sacred vestments of the Pope's representative'.

O'Rahilly was a good barometer of informed Catholic opinion in Ireland. He made a very pertinent point when he attacked the false equations: good Catholics vote for Cumann na nGaedheal, and those who would not were either misguided or untrue to their religion. Nobody could say that O'Rahilly was a disinterested Catholic, and he was voting for Fianna Fail. That did not augur well for Cumann na nGaedheal.

Fianna Fail emerged with seventy-two seats. Cumann na nGaedheal were pushed into second place with fifty-seven, Labour were reduced from thirteen to seven, Farmers got three and others thirteen. Fianna Fail had captured forty-four per cent of the vote – a major improvement on the thirty-five per cent won in the second 1927 election. And what of Mayo – the county where Miss Dunbar-Harrison had been appointed librarian? Fianna Fail took five of the nine seats.[56]

Chapter VII

DE VALERA, FIANNA FAIL AND
THE CATHOLIC CHURCH

A few weeks before the general election, McGilligan and the Irish High Commissioner in London, John Dulanty, visited King George at Sandringham to receive the Great Seal of the Saorstat. The King enquired about the health of the President, expressed admiration for the fine way he had fought through such difficult times and said he hoped that there might be no doubt about the return of the present government. 'Whilst an Opposition was a necessary part of any Parliament', the King thought 'it a pity that the Fianna Fail party should be led by somebody who was, as far as he could discover, not an Irishman at all'. Two ministers had described the possible outcome as 'one of touch and go'. 'But', said the King, 'what are we to do if Mr de Valera is returned?' He did not wait for a reply but went on to say that whilst 'shooting would be no good' he would not be surprised if 'a trade boycott were attempted'.[1]

In March, Fianna Fail, led by 'somebody who was not an Irishman at all', according to the King, occupied the government benches at Leinster House. Many members of Cumann na nGaedheal were less concerned about de Valera's 'racial' purity than they were about the revolutionary reputation enjoyed by a man who, according to his critics, combined metaphysical meanderings with the 'art of the possible'. Yet to extreme republicans, despite the tactical electoral alliance with Fianna Fail, de Valera was a traitor and a reactionary. The IRA paper, *An Phoblacht*, gave cause for concern when it borrowed a worrying historical parallel: 'Cosgrave's rule is as dead as the Tsar's and Kerensky is in power.'[2] Those sentiments echoed the fears behind the Cumann na nGaedheal 'shadow of a gunman' electoral strategy.

Many members of Fianna Fail were quite convinced that Cosgrave would not permit them to take power. A newly elected deputy to the Dail, James Dillon – a man never lost for a colourful turn of phrase – recalled how some Fianna Fail men came to Leinster House with the

pockets of their trenchcoats bulging while he also stated that an elderly
republican was seen assembling a machine-gun in a telephone box.[3]
That account may have been a good story to dine out on, but it was
hardly an accurate reflection of the atmosphere in Leinster House that
day. Cosgrave effected a peaceful transfer of power. Perhaps further
research will reveal that the transfer was not quite as automatic as may
have been thought by some historians. That will only reflect to the credit
of Cosgrave and some of his ministers who relinquished the authoritar-
ian temptation.

The smoothness of the transfer of power may well have been helped
by a stunned incredulity with which Cumann na nGaedheal ex-
ministers looked across at the government benches. Some may have been
forgiven for believing that Fianna Fail could not field a strong Executive
Council. The same sentiments may have been shared by pragmatists like
Sean Lemass, who regarded Fianna Fail after their entry into the Dail in
1927 as 'a raw lot'.[4] But opposition had given them an opportunity to
have some of the rough edges knocked off their parliamentary
performance.

De Valera was President and Minister of External Affairs. Sean T.
O'Kelly was made Vice-President and Minister for Local Government.
Sean MacEntee took Finance while Sean Lemass was made Minister for
Industry and Commerce. Lemass was only thirty-two and, according to
the hostile correspondent of *Round Table*, 'the coming man of the Fianna
Fail Party'. Had he lived, John Hagan could not have hoped for a better
outcome. The party that he had helped to create was in office. Some of
the men who had shown themselves to be such loyal Catholics held the
highest posts in government.

Although there was no major hostility among the bishops as a body
against de Valera, the hierarchy could not have been too pleased at some
of the antics of Fianna Fail ministers in their early days in office. Where
Cumann na nGaedheal ministers had found no difficulty wearing 'court'
dress on formal occasions, Fianna Fail showed great hostility to donning
the 'top hat and tails'. For a time at least, soft hats and ordinary suits
were the order of the day. *Dublin Opinion*, a satirical magazine, asked at
the time how one would know a government minister attending a state
reception. The answer: he was the one wearing the bicycle clips.

The failure of Fianna Fail ministers to conform to the dictates of
protocol caused particular problems for Joseph Walshe. The Secretary
of the Department of External Affairs had, like other senior civil
servants, survived the transfer of power. The likely victory of Fianna
Fail had caused understandable apprehension in the upper echelons of
the civil service – many heads of department were seen to be close to
Cumann na nGaedheal ministers with whom they had worked for nearly

a decade. De Valera let it be known that there would be no victimisation. The Secretary of the Department of Finance, James McElligott – who had been a member of the 1916 GPO garrison – advised his colleagues that they should reduce social contact with former ministers to facilitate the transfer to Fianna Fail. While most secretaries applied McElligott's advice prudently, Walshe ended relationships abruptly. Former Cumann na nGaedheal ministers resented his lack of sensitivity and basic good manners. There is some evidence to suggest that Walshe did not mourn the passing of Cumann na nGaedheal, and, in particular, the passing of Patrick McGilligan as Minister of External Affairs. In the ministers' eyes, Walshe had not distinguished himself over the nuncio affair. It is possible that he would have been replaced by the second in command, Sean Murphy, had McGilligan returned as Minister after the election. There is also some evidence – although not very strong – to suggest that Walshe contributed substantially to the Cumann na nGaedheal strategy for the 1932 election. He may have influenced Cosgrave to fight on an anti-communist platform and to go to the country *before* the Eucharistic Congress.

Walshe very quickly made his peace with de Valera when he came to office. He had known Sean T. O'Kelly and future members of Fianna Fail well in 1919. Walshe was one of the more 'political' and strongly anti-de Valera of the senior civil servants. But he immediately adjusted himself to the new dispensation. Walshe was nothing if not adaptable. He very quickly established himself under de Valera. He was influential but not as important as he appeared in his own eyes. Both men had quite a lot in common. They were conservative, given to secrecy and supportive of 'closed' government. Walshe, who was never a particularly popular figure either in his department or in the civil service generally, did little to improve his image when he began to attend the same daily Mass as de Valera at a convent on Fitzwilliam Square. The coincidence of religious devotion with that of the President of the Executive Council was interpreted in the most uncharitable light by the more secular spirits inside the civil service.[5]

Conor Cruise O'Brien recalls that when he joined the Department of Foreign Affairs in the 1940s there was a rumour that Walshe had gone to de Valera after he had come to power and offered to help get rid of the Governor General.[6] De Valera later appointed an unknown former Fianna Fail backbencher, Donal Buckley, to that post. The latter was a 1916 veteran and an Irish language enthusiast. He accepted a small part of the salary and was 'installed in an unpretentious suburban "villa" with Irish-speaking civil guards in attendance'. In short, according to one commentator not known for his charity to de Valera, Buckley fulfilled 'all Mr de Valera's requirements and reduces the position of

Governor General to that of a Gaelic rubber stamp for affixing to Acts of the Oireachtas'.[7]

The former incumbent, James McNeill, had been treated rather harshly by the new government. On one occasion an English colliery band was hired to play the national anthem during the Dublin Horse Show in honour of the Governor General after the government had refused to allow the army band to do so.[8] The incident occurred on 24 August. On another occasion two ministers walked out of a function at the French Legation. The incident was the subject of unfavourable comment in Rome. Bewley recalled how while the diplomatic corps was waiting for its weekly audience with Gasparri, the Belgian ambassador remarked to a colleague 'in an undertone possibly intended for my ears, *mais ce sont des paysans'.*[9]

Walshe complied readily with de Valera in his wish to bring a number of 'republican' envoys who had served abroad with Sinn Fein in 1919 and later remained with the anti-Treatyite side back into the Department. Sean T. O'Kelly was a minister in the new Fianna Fail administration. Robert Brennan, who could have become the Acting Secretary of the Department in 1922, was reinstated along with Sean Nunan, Leo Kerney and Art O'Brien. Most of those reinstated made the adjustment to the world of professional diplomacy with relative ease. But Walshe was to discover in the 1930s that there were problem cases. There is one episode, possibly apocryphal, where de Valera was reportedly told by one of the diplomats while visiting the Paris Legation in the 1930s that he could not have the staff car that afternoon 'because his sister needed it to do the shopping'. But that was the least of Walshe's problems.

Within a few months of assuming office, de Valera and his ministers had to face a major diplomatic test. The latter months of the Cosgrave government had been given over, in part, to preparations for the Eucharistic Congress, a major Catholic event which was held in different capitals every three years. Dublin was chosen as the venue for 1932; and Cosgrave had put a tremendous amount of effort into ensuring that the Congress would be an occasion to remember. He may even have switched the general election to ensure that the Congress would not be an occasion for unseemly politicking. Nevertheless, that may not be the full reason why he went to the country in February and not September 1932, after he had enjoyed the prestige of welcoming and playing host to so many leading churchmen from all over the world. Cosgrave left de Valera with an enviable task – Cumann na nGaedheal had planned the occasion while Fianna Fail reaped the political benefit. The first weeks of June were almost completely given over to the preparations. On 5 June a retreat for women in the Dublin diocese began, and on 12 June

20 Popular piety: one of the many shrines built by households throughout the country for the Congress (*Cork Examiner*)

there was general communion for women throughout Ireland followed a week later by general communion for men.[10] Bunting and flags were hung out in every street in readiness for the arrival of the Cardinal legate on 20 June. G. K. Chesterton, who visited the city, found the walls filled with graffiti such as "Long Live St. Patrick", as hoping that he might recover from his recent indisposition' and "God Bless Christ the King", and I knew I was staring at one of the staggering paradoxes of Christianity'.[11]

The papal envoy to the Congress, Cardinal Lauri, had very mixed first impressions of the Irish government, as he told Bewley some time later: 'When our steamer entered the harbour of Dublin we saw the Nuncio with the diplomatic corps, the bishops and an enormous crowd. We wondered if it was possible, that the government was not present. Then a group of men in dark coats and soft hats whom we had taken for detectives came up to us. They were the Ministers.'[12] The Fianna Fail aversion to formal dress had not been communicated to the legate beforehand. But behind the scenes, there had been some protocol difficulties between the Department of External Affairs and the Archbishop of Dublin. There had been a certain insensitivity shown over who was to receive the papal legate as he landed. On 9 June 1932,

21   The last word: The Lord Mayor of Dublin, Alfie Byrne, greeting some of the
Irish bishops at Dun Laoghaire while awaiting the arrival of the Cardinal legate
(*Cork Examiner*)

22 & 23 A contrast in styles: above, Cosgrave and the Cumann na nGaedheal front bench dressed for the formal occasion. Below, de Valera and his more casually dressed ministers. When Cardinal Lauri first met members of the government at the boat he mistook the ministers for Special Branch men. (*Cork Examiner*)

Byrne wrote to MacRory: 'I may say that I have had considerable trouble with the President'. He explained that External Affairs had suggested to him, as sponsor of the Congress and the legate's host, that he accompany the legate. But that was 'superseded by the extraordinary proposal that the President alone should accompany him.'[13] The matter was resolved by reverting to the original suggestion of External Affairs. It is possible that the first decision had been changed when it was realised that there might be a problem over protocol and precedence between Armagh and Dublin. There was no lasting ill-feeling between Byrne and de Valera over the slight misunderstanding. But poor relations between the President and MacRory were to pose a problem in the future.

Lauri was given a welcome to Dublin previously reserved only for royalty: 'No Emperor or King ever received a welcome more sincere or more heartfelt than Ireland gave yesterday to the Prince of the Church who has come to participate in the Eucharistic Congress', announced the editorial of the *Irish Independent*. It was the proudest day in 'one of the greatest weeks in our history'. The Congress was to be 'the greatest of all the congresses that have yet been held'.[14]

The series of public events were quite spectacular. Over 14,000 attended a garden party at Blackrock College on 21 June; in the evening the legate attended a state banquet at which he was formally welcomed by government ministers clutching soft hats. The diplomatic success of the occasion was marred by the fact that no formal invitation had been issued to the Governor General to attend the function. Despite that source of friction, the public ceremonies passed off with great displays of popular devotion, culminating in an open-air Mass, in the Phoenix Park, which over a million attended. This was followed by a procession through the city to O'Connell Bridge, where 500,000 people attended Benediction.[15] All the ceremonies were carried out under the watchful eye of the chief marshal, Garda Commissioner Eoin O'Duffy, who was later proudly to tell a bemused General Franco that that was his biggest command.

The Eucharistic Congress was a major diplomatic, social and political success for de Valera. All the months of Cumann na nGaedheal planning had paid off handsomely for Fianna Fail. Few political leaders could ever have hoped for a better flying start. Irish Catholicism was made into a world showpiece. De Valera got the credit. Moreover, the final planning of the event brought both the government and the hierarchy into the closest contact. That showed not just the goodwill of de Valera himself towards the Catholic Church, but also that his ministers could work cordially and efficiently inside their new departments; in the complex, multi-level planning of the Eucharistic Congress celebrations, bishops,

24 & 25 In command: above, Joseph Walshe, Secretary of the Department of External Affairs, leaving Government Buildings, Dublin with (from right): Cardinal Lauri, de Valera, and Sean T. O'Kelly. Below, O'Kelly, de Valera and Walshe entering the Pro-Cathedral for the opening of the Congress
(*Cork Examiner*)

26 & 27 All roads lead to the Phoenix Park: above, a traffic jam in Dublin;
below, all aboard the tram for the 'Park' (*Cork Examiner*)

28 & 29 Faces in the crowd: above, relaxing in the summer sunshine before the
Mass in the Phoenix Park. Below, the Lord Mayor, Alfie Byrne, and members
of the Dail and Senate renounce the Devil and renew their baptismal vows (*Cork
Examiner*)

clergy and Fianna Fail politicians were working as an efficient team. The Congress had enabled both bishops and ministers to overcome their initial awkwardness towards each other. While there was a small percentage of men on both sides who never forgave nor forgot the Civil War, the majority worked most cordially together.

MacRory took umbrage at the President in 1932 – after de Valera had come to power – and that conflict of personality was to be a source of major concern in 1937 during negotiations on certain articles of the draft Constitution. The exact cause or date of the falling out is difficult to ascertain. But MacRory was not on speaking terms with de Valera at the St Patrick Centenary Celebrations, held in Slane in 1932. Both de Valera and the Cardinal gave addresses in the church grounds. Neither men spoke to the other. They went their separate ways afterwards. The parish priest of Athboy, Fr James P. Kelly, attended the service as a boy. His father was a local Fianna Fall TD. He recalls: 'I was told by priests in later years that Dev was not invited to the parish house in Slane for a meal with the Cardinal. The priests in Navan, led by Fr. Kilmartin, brought Dev for a meal to the Navan Parochial House.'[16] It would be wrong to over-stress the importance of the personality difference between MacRory and de Valera. That does not seem to have affected, in any substantial way, the day-to-day contact between hierarchy and the government. De Valera was never very close to Byrne or the other archbishops – with the possible exception of Harty of Cashel. But he did not lack episcopal support. The Irish hierarchy was unusual in that it operated *as a body*. It was rarely possible for personality differences to develop to the point where Church and State were brought into open conflict.

One of the people who most inconspicuously contributed to the smooth running of Church–State relations, was the deft, practical and personable Paschal Robinson. Soon after his arrival in Dublin – the city of his birth – in 1930, he quickly established a wide network of lay and ecclesiastical friends. The nunciature in the Phoenix Park was soon a popular port of call for many of the city's down-and-outs, where they were sure to be given a half-a-crown, which was by no means an inconsiderable sum in the 1930s. There were, however, often less impecunious callers on Robinson. William T. Cosgrave visited at least once a week, while, on Sundays, he often left his two sons at the residence while he attended a local race meeting. Robinson, in turn, was a regular guest in the Cosgrave home where he used to celebrate Mass in their private oratory. But de Valera kept his relationship with the nuncio on a more formal basis. A former secretary of Robinson once described him as 'a bit stiff'.[17]

Robinson quickly overcame the hostility of the bishops towards the

30 & 31 Greeting the nuncio; above, with Mayor of Waterford, 1930. Below, a special salute of welcome from the confraternity in Limerick (*Cork Examiner*)

idea of having a nuncio in Dublin. There were at least two intransigent members of the hierarchy who continued to send their communications with the Vatican through the old channels. The various congregations usually returned the correspondence unopened suggesting that it be directed through the nunciature. But that was a minor problem. Robinson sedulously avoided what might be construed as any overt interference in the domestic affairs of the Irish Church. He never attended meetings of the hierarchy at Maynooth, but he did receive a copy of the minutes. Cardinal William Conway began the practice in the 1960s of inviting the nuncio to the *opening* of national episcopal meetings. But this is very much *pro forma*; on the first occasion when it occurred, one bishop said to another on the way out, 'and nobody is fooling anybody'.

Robinson was a highly experienced and successful diplomat. His presence, contrary to the initial fears shared by many members of the hierarchy, proved to be a decided asset to both Church and State. As highly connected and respected a figure as Robinson was of considerable assistance to the clergy to get routine business conducted at the Vatican. Moreover, the claim that the Secretariat of State was often the unwitting victim of British pressure – if it was ever true – was less likely because of Robinson. He filed accurate, analytical reports which helped assuage some Vatican fears about de Valera.[18] Furthermore, in the event of a possible confrontation between Church and State emerging, Robinson was in a strong position to take pre-emptive action. There was a very good example of this in 1937 over the religious clause of the Constitution.

Apart from the pro-Catholic ideology of Fianna Fail, there was another reason why Church–State confrontation was unlikely even in the political atmosphere of the 1930s. De Valera and other prominent members of Fianna Fail were very well connected in clerical circles – at all levels – through either friendship or marriage. De Valera had many friends in religious orders. He knew some Jesuits, Dominicans, and Carmelites such as Peter Magennis (who had ceased being Superior General of his order and had returned to Dublin, where he died in 1937). He used to spend a week at Mount Melleray every year where he was friendly with the Cistercian monk, Ailbe Luddy. He used also to visit his close friend the parish priest of Clogheen in County Tipperary, Fr Tom Power, who lived not far from the monastery. On the same trip, de Valera often visited his friends at Rockwell, where he had taught for a time.

De Valera was probably most friendly with the Holy Ghost Fathers at Blackrock, where he had been educated. John Charles McQuaid, a former President of Blackrock, was a close friend of the family. At

32 All Cashel turns out to welcome the nuncio, 1930 (*Cork Examiner*)

Maynooth, he was friendly with Michael Browne, who became Bishop of Galway in 1937. He also knew quite well the clerical brothers-in-law of his Minister for Finance, Sean MacEntee: Patrick Browne, a Maynooth professor who later became President of University College Galway, and the critic of the bishop of the same name. Two of his other brothers were

33 Receiving the freedom of Waterford: the nuncio and Bishop Bernard Hackett with the reflection of a delighted young onlooker in the carriage lamp (*Cork Examiner*)

also priests, one of whom, Michael, was a member of the Dominican order and who later became a cardinal. Sean T. O'Kelly's brother-in-law was also a priest, while Frank Gallagher – de Valera's press officer and then editor of the *Irish Press* – had a brother who was a Jesuit priest.

In the familial sense, politicians and the clergy did not stand in two hostile camps, as might have been the case on the Continent in some political traditions. There were ties of friendship and blood which seldom allowed major misunderstandings to lie just below the surface and explode at a time of crisis. There was a certain intimacy about Irish society where clerical and political institutions were interlocked. As a result, Irish society was characterised by an inability to find out officially what was going on in the spheres of Church and State; it was also a society where unofficially even the most confidential of material could not be kept secret.

It is little wonder that de Valera and his ministerial colleagues were quite assertive in their handling of Church–State affairs from the time they came into office. They possessed inside clerical information which enabled the Executive Council to act decisively. A good example of de Valera's self-confidence in this regard was his early opposition to the Knights of Columbanus – an opposition shared by some of his ministerial colleagues such as Sean MacEntee.[19] There is every reason to believe that his stance on this matter was not hostilely received by members of the hierarchy.

The President never liked that organisation, which had been set up in Belfast in 1915. They moved their headquarters to Dublin in 1922. The nature of de Valera's opposition to the Knights is not quite clear, but it has been possible to discover from oral and written sources that he did not want any member of the Fianna Fail party associated with them. It should not be assumed that the Irish hierarchy automatically approved of that organisation. De Valera repeated his opposition to his ministers being members of the Knights on more than one occasion. At a meeting of the Fianna Fail Parliamentary Party on 28 June 1933, Deputy M.J. Kennedy proposed: 'that membership of the Fianna Fail party and the Knights of Columbanus are incompatible and that the party requests members of the executive and party to resign immediately from the latter'.[20] The reason for, and the timing of, this motion is not quite clear. But it was not brought forward without the approval of de Valera. After a lengthy discussion, the motion was passed.

In May 1933 de Valera paid a visit to Rome amid rumours in the Italian capital that 'he was a dangerous revolutionary and Bolshevist, and that the Pope would refuse to receive him'. His arrival in Italy was preceded by a rather frantic exchange of telegrams between Bewley and External Affairs asking the Irish envoy 'whether it would be necessary for him [de Valera] to wear a top hat on his way to his audience with the Pope, or whether it would excite unfavourable comment if he went bareheaded to the Vatican'.

Bewley felt that de Valera, like any other head of government who possessed no diplomatic or military status, should wear evening dress and a top hat. He informed the department of this but added that if 'there were urgent reasons against doing so, the Vatican authorities would show themselves indulgent'. He also pointed out in the telegram that Mahatma Gandhi had recently visited Rome, but had not been received by the Pope: popular rumour had circulated 'the ridiculous story' that he had refused to go to the Vatican without his goat and spinning-wheel. The story was 'obviously pure invention' but Bewley feared that the Roman populace, 'whose sense of humour was as highly developed as it was scurrilous,' might seize the occasion to 'make unsuitable comparisons'. External Affairs sent a 'curt communication' that the President would 'wear a top hat'.

De Valera submitted to the exigencies of the protocol, and as Bewley added waspishly, he wore his top hat 'whenever no photographers were about'. He was received by the Pope, the Cardinal Secretary of State, Pacelli, the King of Italy and Mussolini.[21] The Holy See conferred on him the Grand Cross of the Order of Pius.

During the 1933 Holy Year, O'Kelly went on pilgrimage to Rome, where he had a private audience with Pius XI, who remembembered their last encounter eleven years earlier, when the Pope had told him that the Treaty was a 'magnificent settlement'. After he had stopped O'Kelly from retelling him what a wonderful job Ireland was doing for the missions, the conversation turned to communism. The Pope expressed his concern over the spread of the ideology and over the intention of President Roosevelt to give official recognition to Russia. If that happened, the spread of communism all over the world would be the result, he said.

Asked whether there was any communism in Ireland, O'Kelly replied that there was some in Dublin, to which the Pope said that such a state of affairs was disgraceful. He was even more disconcerted to learn that there had been communist candidates in local government elections and that one unofficial one had been elected. He was disappointed to hear that there had only been a thirty-per-cent turn-out. O'Kelly explained that the man who had been elected, presumably James Larkin, was a very good friend of the working class and that people appreciated what he had done. 'But,' said the Pope, 'if he is a communist the fact that he had done these things is no reason why he should be elected to the municipal council. That is entirely wrong. Catholic men should be on the platforms. They should be everywhere preaching and telling the people that it is their solemn duty to keep the communists out of office. I must see to it that that state of affairs is changed in Ireland.'[22]

O'Kelly had been in Geneva before travelling to Rome, attending the League of Nations, where a medical report with a controversial clause on contraception was being discussed. The Vatican had requested de Valera to join with the other Catholic delegates in opposing that measure and he had agreed, sending O'Kelly in his place because of domestic political commitments. The Report of the Health Organisation of the League of Nations on Maternal Welfare (C.H. 1060), dated October 1931, contained under the heading 'Abortion and Contraception' the following passage:

Apart from the practice of contraception for personal or economic reasons, it may be necessary to avoid pregnancy on account of the mother's own health and in such cases it is preferable to avoid pregnancy occurring at all rather than to interrupt it. But it is not sufficient merely to tell a married woman suffering from tuberculosis or heart disease or nephritis that she should not again become pregnant. It is necessary to explain exactly what steps she and her husband should take to prevent this happening. If the private doctor is not prepared to do this, information can be given most appropriately at the health centre.[23]

On 28 September 1933, Sean T. O'Kelly told delegates there were certain strong objections to the passage, even as amended. In deference to the objections from the Catholic delegates the clause 'due account being taken of the individual's religious beliefs and moral principles, as well as of national legislation' had been added to the original passage. O'Kelly considered the revised text still contrary to the doctrine of the Catholic Church:

The practice of contraception for any purpose was abhorrent to the people of many countries, including Ireland. The association of such recommendations with measures taken for maternal welfare would be calculated to bring health centres into disrepute in the minds of the faithful and to nullify the efforts made by the Governments in the sphere of public health. Moreover, the advocacy of this practice was inconsistent with the legislation of several countries; the government of the Irish Free State had constantly received very strong protests from medical and other organisations against the inclusion of the passage in the question in a League of Nations document.

O'Kelly complained that contributions made to the funds of the League by governments which shared the point of view of the Irish Free State should not be devoted to an investigation into the use of contraceptives, or to the publication of documents dealing with moral and medical aspects which might give rise to the most acute controversy and cause offence to member states. The Irish lobbied hard, together with the Italians and the Belgians. Largely as a result of O'Kelly's intervention, the Assembly invited the Health Committee 'to reconsider further the paragraphs in question in the light of the observations put by the delegates, the circulation of the document in question [C.H. 1060] being this time suspended indefinitely'.

A few days later, on 4 October 1933, O'Kelly delivered a speech to the Cercle Catholique in Geneva, where the Irish Vice-President said he was pleased to hear Chancellor Dollfuss say, at the League, that Austria was engaged in providing herself with an economic and political constitution answering to her needs and inspired essentially by the principles set forth by the Pope for the solution of social problems. That was all the more pleasing because such declarations of adherence 'to Catholic principles are too seldom heard nowadays from heads of states, great or small, at all events from the same or equally important platforms'. But there was one other government, however, that was

inspired in its very administrative action by Catholic principles and Catholic doctrine, and that government is the one to which I have the honour to belong – the government of the Irish Free State. That government is now engaged in endeavouring to do for its people what Chancellor Dollfuss announced his government is trying to do for Austria. In the development of its programme of economic and political reform its work is founded on the same Catholic principles.

The social encyclical of Pius XI had had a profound effect throughout the world but, he added, 'in no country was this inspiring pronouncement read and studied with greater eagerness and interest than in Ireland'. He went on to outline the various schemes being pursued by the government to ensure that society was structured according to the principles of the encyclicals. They wanted to ensure that 'the remuneration paid to the wage-earner shall be sufficient to support him and his family in reasonable and frugal comfort'. What the Irish government was attempting was 'Catholic Action in practice'.[24]

The speech was hardly an exhaustive statement of the philosophy on which Fianna Fail were attempting to restructure Irish society. But it demonstrated, at least, the image of Ireland that the government wanted to convey abroad at the time. In the context of Irish unity, such sentiments were unlikely to have proved helpful. But in the 1930s, Southern politicians rarely thought beyond their immediate, domestic political context. It would have been hard for them to do otherwise. Indeed, de Valera had inherited all the problems that Cosgrave had faced so resolutely in relation to the Criminal Law Amendment Acts. It was one of the most pressing issues facing the President when he came to power in 1932. The Eucharistic Congress had acted as a welcome distraction.

De Valera was in a very strong position to address the issues immediately. Indeed, had Cosgrave been thinking in exclusively political and opportunistic terms before the elections, he would have introduced a number of Criminal Law Amendments in the hope that he would pick up waning clerical support for Cumann na nGaedheal – even if he had to risk alienating some of his Protestant followers. The new Minister for Justice, James Geoghegan, addressed the problem immediately. Fianna Fail were in a much stronger position to push through legislation following de Valera's second general election victory within a year. He now governed without the support of the Labour Party.[25]

On 27 October 1932, each member of the Executive Council had been sent a copy of the report and the Department of Justice memorandum discussed in the previous chapter. The evidence at this point is not very clear. But it would appear that an all-party committee was set up, under the chairmanship of Geoghegan, to make recommendations. The proceedings and personnel were regarded 'as strictly confidential'. In December, the Minister met a deputation from the bishops, who were concerned about a number of questions which had been raised by the report:

(a) the sale of 'mechanical contraceptives' and drugs used for similar or kindred purposes;
(b) the lack of public control over dance halls, especially in provincial areas;
(c) the amendment of the law so as to raise the 'age of consent' in certain sexual cases;
(d) abuse of motor cars;
(e) certain conduct in public highways.

The episcopal delegation pointed to the anomaly in the law which prohibited the publicising of contraceptives for sale, while 'permitting the sale of apparatus of this kind in the state'. The Minister said he recognised the great importance of the problems raised by the use of contraceptives and by the abuse of dance halls, and would favour legislation designed to deal in a suitable and effective way with these problems. He would like to see a bill go through which would bring the law into accord with the best Catholic practice and teaching on these subjects. But it had to be understood that the legislation had to be practical and workable. Many otherwise desirable provisions might have to be omitted because of the difficulty of giving effect to them. The bishops stated that a distinction had to be drawn between mechanical apparatus and drugs which might be used for either an innocent purpose or a criminal purpose. They stated that the importation, sale, or keeping for sale of mechanical apparatus should be prohibited. The hierarchy did not think it practicable to prohibit or attempt to interfere with the mere possession of apparatus by citizens. The Minister responded that he would be very glad to receive the recommendations of the general body of the bishops and 'would attach great weight to them'.[26]

The heads for a bill were prepared by autumn 1933.[27] But the terms proved to be controversial, particularly Head 16, which read:

There should be a general prohibition against the sale or distribution and importation for sale or distribution of contraceptive appliances. Qualified medical practitioners should have power to prescribe and to supply such appliances to their patients. The quantities required by such practitioners would be imported under licence granted by the Minister for Local Government and Public Health. Registers of supplies received and prescribed would be required to be kept by doctors and should contain full particulars of the persons to whom such appliances were supplied. The registers would be open to inspection by any Medical Inspector duly authorised by the Minister for Local Government and Public Health.

There was obviously a division of opinion within the Executive Council. Those who argued in favour of a more restrictive formula were ultimately successful. That position coincided with the thinking of the hierarchy. The Criminal Law Amendment Bill, banning the importation and sale of contraceptives became law in 1935. This helped resolve the perceived weakness in legislation where, under the Censorship Act of 1929, it was *only* illegal to advocate the *use* of contraceptives.[28]

De Valera may have won some latitude on the Criminal Law Amendment Act by promising to introduce separate legislation to deal with the problem of dance halls. This matter greatly exercised the minds of many bishops in the 1930s. Concern for the moral welfare of Irish youth was not without foundation if the illegitimacy figures in the 1931 report were accurate.[29]

At a meeting with the Minister for Justice, in December 1932, a delegation of bishops regarded the amendment of the law covering dance halls as 'very urgent'. A private episcopal sub-committee, in a report, deplored the dance hall system as incapable of proper control; halls were 'pitfalls for the young and innocent' and centres of 'scandal'. It was proposed that ownership might be vested in the clergy or people of the parish. Young girls should not be admitted unless accompanied by parents. A civic guard should be at the entrance at all times. Dancing was to end at 11.00 p.m. It is unlikely that the hierarchy would have taken the report in its entirety and presented each proposal to the government. But it is quite certain that there was considerable discussion between Church and State on the question.[30] The Dance Hall Act of 1935 originated as Head 15 of the Criminal Law Amendment Bill.

Many of the points raised by the hierarchy were accommodated in that paragraph: licensing, suitability of premises, parking of motor cars, age of admission, police supervision and hours proposed for dancing. This measure cannot be brushed aside as lightly as some contemporaries might wish; what was at stake was much more than episcopal obsession with sex and courting. The 1931 report had revealed a serious illegitimacy problem in Ireland. Part of the reason for that was *traceable* to problems of the supervision and the running of dance halls. The bishops had lobbied hard for the 1935 measure and de Valera had complied, not because of episcopal pressure but because he, too, must have been convinced of the necessity for the law. A possible political *quid pro quo* could be episcopal support for a new Constitution. De Valera was thinking very much ahead.

For the purposes of a study of Church and State, it is not possible – no matter how intrinsically interesting – to pay attention to all aspects of the formulation of the new Constitution. But some general details and remarks are unavoidable.

Preliminary work had already begun in this area as early as summer 1934, when an informal committee was set up to 'consider and make recommendations as to what articles of the constitution should be immune from amendment by the ordinary process of legislation, on the grounds that they are fundamental from the point of view of safeguarding the rights of individuals, of parliament, or of the executive'.

On 30 April, the following year – after the Criminal Law Amendment and Dance Hall Acts were passed – de Valera instructed the legal adviser of the Department of External Affairs, John Hearne, to draw up heads for a new Constitution.[31] In mid-1936 de Valera set up an *ad hoc* 'editorial' committee made up of Maurice Moynihan and Michael McDunphy of the President's Department, John Hearne of External Affairs, the main architect of the de Valera-inspired draft, and P. P. O'Donoghue, legal assistant in the Attorney General's Office. This group was instructed by the President not to make amendments of substance or principle to the text but simply to polish the language, cut out duplication and avoid ambiguity. The draft was to avoid the use of stilted English and read easily. Similar instructions were issued to the committee drafting the Irish version, which was not to be a literal translation. This was an absorbing task for the two committees, which reported directly to de Valera. Moynihan, who served on both committees, regarded the task as virtually a full-time job. The working language was English. Drafts were prepared in English and then translated into Irish which, paradoxically, became the official text in the event of a dispute.

But who was most responsible for contributing to the formulation of the new document over the two-year period? The central figure in the process was unquestionably John Hearne – an able and knowledgeable civil servant who had once been a student for the priesthood. He had the task of drafting articles and coordinating the submissions from sources outside the government. Some members of the staff at Maynooth were consulted. The Jesuits in Dublin were very directly involved.

The founder of Catholic Action in Ireland and the scourge of Freemasonry, Fr Edward Cahill, sent de Valera a submission in September 1936 outlining the Catholic principles on which a Constitution ought to be based.[32]

The President found it 'useful as indicating the principles which should inspire all governmental activity so as to make it conform with Catholic teaching'. But he pointed out the difficulty of trying to embody the ideas into a new Constitution: 'I can see that some of the principles might be set forth in a preamble, but I fear there is not much that can be incorporated into the body of the Constitution, i.e., made Articles of it. If you could find time to put into the form of draft articles, with perhaps a draft preamble, what you think should be formally written into the Constitution, it will be very helpful. I could then arrange, when I had seen your draft, to have a chat with you about it.'[33]

The request for assistance was taken very seriously by the Jesuit Province. Cahill was merely one interested party. He was not considered to be in the front line of Jesuit academicians. A committee 'of the best heads we have in matters of this kind' was set up, combining the skills of philosophers, theologians and an historian. They were Frs P. Bartley, J. McErlean, J. Canavan, Edward Coyne and Edward Cahill.[34] Unfortunately it has not been possible to locate the joint Jesuit submission which went to de Valera in late October 1936.

Cahill presented a personal draft on 13 November. He explained how he had 'been delayed unavoidably much longer than he foresaw'.[35] In fact, the reason why he had not been more prompt was that he had had to submit his work to two members of the committee, who suggested substantial changes. It is possible that the official biographers of de Valera have failed to distinguish between the committee draft and the one submitted by Cahill. Both may have been attributed to the latter.[36] The draft Cahill article on religion read:

(i) The Holy Roman Catholic Church, which is now and has been for centuries the Church of the vast majority of the Irish people and whose defence generation after generation has suffered and endured, that it might hand down unimpaired its treasures of Faith and Morals, occupies in the social life and organisation of the Irish

Nation an unique and (altogether special and) [the words in the brackets were crossed out], which is recognised as a fact by this Constitution and shall be as such duly recognised by the State.

(ii) The Holy Roman Catholic Church is governed by its own code of Canon Law, which in so far as it concerns Catholics is hereby recognised as of binding force and shall be so recognised by our courts.

(iii) Diplomatic relations, recognition of the Holy See both as a temporal and a spiritual power, concordat.[37]

The article went on to state that 'freedom of conscience, the free profession and the practice of religion and the formation and assembling of religious associations' were all permitted by the Constitution, 'subject to the essential requirements of public order and morality proper to a Christian State'. The final Cahill formulation was much more refined. It drew heavily on the Polish and Austrian Constitutions, and the Austrian concordat of 1934. Despite the cuts made by Canavan, Cahill must have sent de Valera his own unexpurgated original. Only in that way could de Valera have been aware of the 'special position' phrase in the Cahill draft which was to be of such importance later on. Cahill also sent a draft preamble.[38]

Although the main Jesuit submission has not been located, it is probable that it had much more influence on de Valera than the 'minority report' from Cahill. However, Cahill may have been indirectly influential in providing de Valera with the formula which helped him over the impasse with Article 44 on religion some months later. He may also have been responsible for the original suggestion to use a preamble with the new Constitution.

De Valera also had assistance in the early months of 1937 from John Charles McQuaid:

. . . in February, [the latter] sent him 'an interesting and useful criticism of the French constitution of 1814 by Pius VII'. He also sent paragraphs relating to private property and to free competition, based on a close analysis of the Papal encyclical Rerum Novarum of Leo XIII, and Quadragesimo Anno of Pius XI. He gave de Valera two books, Manuel Sociale [*sic*] by Rev. A. Vermeersch, a Belgian Jesuit, published in 1909, and Code Sociale [*sic*] Esquisse d'une Synthese Sociale Catholique, issued by the Union International [*sic*] d'Etudes Sociales in Paris in 1934.[39]

The Constitution began to take shape in February. De Valera was more directly involved in the final stages. He worked on the text of the draft in his Blackrock home at weekends. McQuaid was on hand to give advice. But it is doubtful if the Holy Ghost Father was ever made privy to the contents of the entire document. Up to the time the copy was taken to Cahills, the printers, he was on hand to counsel.[40] There is, however, a mistaken belief that McQuaid practically wrote sections of the finished document. Given de Valera's emphasis on procedure, it is much more probable that McQuaid was a privileged adviser who indirectly helped shape the various articles by laying down the principles on which they were to be based. The hard work was then done by John Hearne. This is a possible explanation for what happened subsequently over the religious clause.

Twelve copies of the draft Constitution were completed on 15 March. The following day de Valera gave the first set of proofs to McQuaid for comment. They did *not* include the religious clause.[41] What McQuaid saw was the draft Constitution, which was circulated to Ministers and heads of departments that same day. But nine galley proofs had been pulled on 9 March and sent to the President. A limited number of people saw the draft, as a departmental minute indicates: 'the attached preliminary draft of the file was circulated privately by the President. The first draft to be circulated generally to the Departments was that of 16th March.' The name on the privately circulated copy on file was 'Walshe', presumably the Secretary of External Affairs. Besides Walshe, the document would have been seen by Moynihan, McDunphy, Hearne and O'Donoghue, who were working on the editorial committee. The Attorney General and a select number of ministers would have had to see a copy.[42]

The outcome of the preliminary reaction from a private showing of the draft Constitution, was that the article on religion was deleted, leaving blank pages. When the second proofs arrived on 15 March, no substitute formula had been submitted.[43] The contentious draft article was ultramontane in tone and was referred to by the limited number of people who saw it as 'the one, true church' formula.[44] Why does the official biography miss the fact that there was a draft religious article? It is probable that de Valera was deliberately vague in his reminiscence on this matter. The biography suggests that he had received proofs – minus the religious clause – on 15 March. There is no mention of the fact that he had received a full set of galley proofs on 9 March. Yet the copy on file shows that the advance galleys were bound.

It is very difficult to explain why so astute a man as de Valera could allow the draft religious clause to appear as it did. He had enlisted the advice of a number of very knowledgeable clerical friends to contribute indirectly to the drafting of what he thought would be a relatively straightforward article. But to his personal embarrassment, he found that their combined efforts – as drafted by Hearne – were not acceptable on political grounds. The Irish version of the official biography points to de Valera's personal dilemma: 'How could he reconcile his duty to proclaim his belief in the one, true Church while avoiding doing wrong to the minorities?'[45]

The article as it was originally drafted satisfied de Valera's religious position as a private citizen. It was equally obvious that some influential members of his Executive Council, such as Sean MacEntee, would not find the formula acceptable. That must have been abundantly clear in the limited sampling of opinion that he was able to take between 9 and 15 April. It would be impossible to maintain a strong anti-partitionist stance and uphold the 'establishment' of the Catholic Church in the Free State.

Were the draft article to fall into the hands of the opposition, or become public in any way, de Valera would immediately be responsible for splitting Irish public opinion along confessional and republican lines. Cosgrave would have an opportunity to point out the 'dubious republican credentials' of the leader of Fianna Fail. But what was to be the solution to his dilemma? He played for time. Very few people were told of or shown the draft article. Sean MacEntee, when shown a copy, said that he had never seen it before. That gave de Valera an opportunity to resolve his own crisis of conscience while he took soundings from other sections of the religious community in Ireland.

The last person de Valera would have wanted to see the rejected draft article on religion was the man who had done most to inspire it. The theology on which the article was based, as far as McQuaid was concerned, was not negotiable. The problem that de Valera faced was that he was not preparing a Constitution for a monolithically religious country. The Northern dimension only accentuated the problem. As a consequence, McQuaid, like most ministers and heads of department, received a copy of the Constitution with the religious article missing, and an explanation that there were some difficulties over the drafting of the missing section.

Acceptance of the Constitution by the electorate proved also to be a major consideration for de Valera and his Executive Council. The Cumann na nGaedheal party would automatically oppose the idea of introducing a new Constitution. A split on the religious clause would further strengthen the possibility that some members of the hierarchy would actively oppose the document if the religious clause was not based on the 'one, true church' idea. The least of de Valera's problems was to win support from his colleagues. There is no comprehensive record of the internal Executive Council discussions on this matter. But it is probable that de Valera stressed the dangers of a clerical backlash for a government faced with the prospect of having to go to the polls again, in the most inclement political climate, by 1938 at the latest. The outcome of the deliberations was, according to one of the participants,

Sean MacEntee, that the Executive Council gave de Valera a mandate to
negotiate on the basis that the outcome would not result in the
establishment of any single Church.[46]

In the latter part of March 1937, de Valera worked out alternative
formulae. In the first week of April, he was confident enough to test the
response of certain prominent ecclesiastics to his draft proposals. On 3
April 1937, de Valera went to see the papal nuncio, Paschal Robinson.
One of the formulae was a modified version of the original rejected draft
article. It might have been based on the Cahill draft. By this time, de
Valera had made up his mind to reject such a formulation.[47] But he was
no clearer on what he wanted to replace the 'one, true church' idea.
Robinson was not in a position to intervene – only to listen.

But when the President said that he was going to consult the
Archbishop of Dublin, the nuncio suggested that de Valera might also
like to meet the Cardinal, who would be in Dublin the following day.
While relations between de Valera and MacRory had never been very
cordial, he nevertheless accepted the idea. On 5 April both men met at
the nunciature. But the outcome of the meeting only magnified de
Valera's dilemma. The Cardinal had produced his own draft formula at
the informal talks, which read:

The state reflecting the religious convictions of 93 pc of its citizens
acknowledges the Catholic religion to be the religion established by Our Divine
Lord Jesus Christ; while guaranteeing at the same time to all its citizens the
fullest liberty to practice their religion in public and in private, with due regard
however for public order and morality.[48]

This echoed the rejected 'one, true church' formula. It was now being
put forward by the head of the Catholic Church in Ireland. But how
representative was the Cardinal of general episcopal feeling? The matter
would be of the gravest political consequence if Archbishop Byrne
accepted the same line of argument as Armagh. The chances of Byrne
and MacRory agreeing on this issue, however, were unlikely. It is
probable that Byrne had been kept briefed by Walshe on the
developments regarding the Constitution. The arrival of de Valera at
Drumcondra is unlikely to have been the very first he had heard about
the new Constitution. To de Valera's relief, Byrne was as accommodating as MacRory was intransigent. The knowledge that the Cardinal
thought differently might have made Byrne all the more emphatic in his
contrary point of view. The Archbishop was so impressed by the
wording of the preamble that he felt it unnecessary to make any
particular mention of the status of the Catholic Church in the general
article on religion. De Valera derived great 'encouragement' from the
meeting.[49] In the early 1950s, Maurice Moynihan took a minute of a

conversation he had on the subject with the Taoiseach which supports the account in the official biography: 'Byrne sympathetic, agrees with de Valera's view'.[50] The danger of unified episcopal opposition to the constitution on the basis of the religious clause had receded. But it had not vanished. De Valera had to fashion a formula which would be a compromise for Byrne and MacRory; it had to be strong enough to neutralise even private criticism from the Cardinal. Shortly after the Byrne visit, de Valera settled upon the phrase 'recognises the special position' to overcome his personal and his political dilemma. It was a phrase he may have borrowed from a Cahill draft.[51] That decision was taken finally around 9 or 10 April.

The way out of the dilemma was to be purely descriptive in the formulation. But he was no nearer to a final wording. He had, however, satisfactorily resolved the most difficult aspect of the problem. It was a question of testing the reaction of the other religious denominations to the idea. He anticipated some difficulty. Maurice Moynihan, the Secretary of the Department of the President, was sent with an outline to the Church of Ireland Archbishop of Dublin, George Allan Fitzgerald Gregg, while de Valera visited Dr Irwin of the Presbyterians. When Moynihan met Gregg, he was asked the searching question about what legal weight the words '*recognises* the special position' had in the article. He reported back to de Valera, who went to see Gregg on 12 April. The latter's diary entry reads: 'Mr de V calls and speaks three quarters of an hr. in regard to religious clauses of the new constitution.'[52] But the Archbishop seemed reassured by de Valera's explanation that the phrase was simply descriptive and did not carry with it any legal rights.

The conversation with Gregg proved as helpful and encouraging as his meeting with Byrne. Once de Valera had decided *in principle* to draft a purely descriptive article, he was then forced to ensure that the titles used to describe the various Churches would not also become a matter of contention. Gregg, during the talk with the President, took down a volume from his shelf of the Council of Trent decrees. There, he read the phrase Holy, Catholic, Apostolic and Roman Church. The idea immediately appealed to de Valera: when listing the various Churches he would give them the titles which they themselves used. But what of a contentious phrase like Church of Ireland? MacRory tried very hard to have it excluded from the final draft. He wrote to de Valera urging that that title should 'not be allowed to remain in the draft of the Constitution of the I.F.S. [Irish Free State]'. On 29 May 1937, de Valera had replied 'at this stage I am afraid it will be very difficult, if not impossible, to make any change regarding the matter to which you refer. I will, however, give the whole question further careful consideration.' He did not change his mind.[53]

At that point de Valera was writing from a position of political strength. But in the middle of April, when the article was finally drafted, he still feared the possibility of some opposition from Cardinal MacRory. He had, at least, prevented united episcopal opposition to the still highly contentious article, which read in part:

The state recognises the special position of the Holy Catholic Apostolic and Roman Church as the guardian of the faith professed by the great majority of the citizens.

The state also recognises the Church of Ireland, the Presbyterian Church, in Ireland, the Methodist Church in Ireland, the Religious Society of Friends in Ireland, as well as the Jewish Congregations and the other religious denominations existing in Ireland at the date of the coming into operation of this Constitution.[54]

What de Valera had tried to do was produce a formula which attempted to reconcile his own conservative feelings on the question with what was politically acceptable to his colleagues and ultimately to the electorate. But it has not been fully realised just how difficult it was to get a consensus on the matter. The clash between MacRory and de Valera at the nunciature resulted in the Cardinal taking the matter personally to Rome. So serious did de Valera consider the situation in mid-April that he sent Walshe to the Vatican in an effort to put the government point of view. In the absence of documentation from the Department of Foreign Affairs, there are two historical fragments which are at variance over how Walshe was received by the Secretary of State, Pacelli. The authoritative Irish version of de Valera's official biography relates, unfortunately without citing a source, that the latter had *an-fhailte* (warm welcome) for the draft article.[55] It is to be assumed that that was based on a reminiscence of de Valera.

But in the 1950s Maurice Moynihan made a minute of a conversation which he had with de Valera, which read '[Pacelli's] attitude doubtful'. That was taken to mean that the Secretary of State was anxious to remain aloof from the controversy. Pope Pius XI was also very cautious in his meeting with Walshe. The Pope neither praised nor criticised the article, according to the Irish biography, while a minute by Moynihan read that the Pope 'neither approved nor disapproved'.[56]

Very little is known about the Cardinal's discussions at the Vatican. The Rector of the Irish College, Michael Curran, where no doubt MacRory stayed, was an old friend and admirer of de Valera. He had long been a political supporter of 'the Chief', and had hidden him after his escape from Lincoln jail in the gate-lodge of the Archbishop's palace (see Chapter II). The Rector was also from the Dublin archdiocese and a close friend of Byrne. While there is no evidence available, it is unlikely that Curran was unaware of the difference between Armagh and Dublin on the religious clause.[57]

Moreover, the Cardinal was not aware of the wording of the draft article. He did not find that out until it was published on 1 May 1937. But he was operating on the basis that if he could get some support at the Vatican for his point of view, it would place Byrne in a very awkward position. The Standing Committee of the hierarchy might, on the basis of a firm recommendation from Rome, have to communicate its view to de Valera no matter how unpalatable that might have been to some bishops. In Rome, Bill Macaulay, the Irish envoy to the Vatican, spent a considerable amount of time entertaining the Cardinal with good whiskey in an effort to persuade MacRory to drop his opposition to the principle on which de Valera had drawn up the religious clause.[58] If the early 1920s were anything to go by, then it is probable that prominent Irish religious in Rome were also enlisted by de Valera to put the countervailing point of view to the Cardinal and the relevant authorities at the Vatican.

The only indication as to how MacRory felt he fared in Rome can be found on a piece of nunciature notepaper containing his rejected religious formula and a hand-written minute: 'de V. would not accept this and the question went on to Rome. The Holy Father at first agreed with me but eventually in view of the Six Counties etc., allowed the form that stands in the F.S. constitution.'[59] The assertion that the Pope initially agreed with MacRory could only be explained if the Cardinal had gone to the Vatican and seen Pius XI before the pontiff was properly briefed on the complexities of the matter. The Pope's initial, personal response may have been supportive. But when the Secretary of State had an opportunity to study the portfolio and the reports coming from Robinson in Dublin it was clear that the Vatican ran the risk of being sucked into a Church–State controversy in Ireland where the two most influential prelates in the country were on opposite sides. It is little wonder that when Walshe came to meet Pacelli, the latter remained noncommittal. The Pope also adopted the same stance. But it is interesting that, as part of the government's submission to the Vatican, they may have relied rather heavily on the 'Six County' question to discourage the lobby for a stronger assertion of Catholic Church rights in the Constitution. That surmise is based on the reference in the MacRory minute.

It is quite unlikely that MacRory was ever in a strong enough position to bring the Vatican directly into Irish politics. Once the danger from the Vatican had been set to one side – although that did not end the opposition from MacRory – de Valera could concentrate on winning Executive Council approval for the draft Constitution and the 'missing' religious clause in particular.

De Valera had circulated the first draft on 16 March for comments to the various government departments. A few days later, all had responded except Industry and Commerce, of which Lemass was Minister; his department did not send a single line of comment, as the empty folder on file demonstrates. Finance was at the opposite extreme. James J. McElligott worked extremely hard to set down detailed comments.

The observations furnished, he wrote, were not exhaustive 'as only a short period has been allowed to examine a long and complicated document of which some of the articles are not yet in final form, and some, viz., those relating to religion, church and State have not yet been furnished'.[60]

The critical tone of his memorandum can best be captured by the comments on draft Articles 1–3:

These Articles, dealing with the Nation as distinct from the State, (a distinction which many political scientists would not admit) seem rather to vitiate the Constitution, by stating at the outset what will be described, and with some justice, as a fiction, and one which will give offence to neighbouring countries with whom we are constantly protesting our desire to live on terms of friendship.

Having been at such pains to expel fictions from the existing constitution and to bring theory into line with practice, it seems inconsistent now to impose an even greater fiction. Further, from the point of view of international law, it is not clear whether we are on safe ground in claiming sovereignty and jurisdiction over land recognised internationally, *de jure* and *de facto*, as belonging to another country . . .

From the practical point of view, apart from the fear of consequences, these articles will not contribute anything to effecting the unity of Ireland, but rather the reverse . . .[61]

The Finance submission to the 'second revise' of 10 April was even stronger although it noted that some satisfactory revisions had been made:

But the claim to territory which does not belong to Saorstat Eireann still subsists in articles three and four and therefore the general criticism contained in our previous observations on this part of the draft constitution still stand. It gives a permanent place in the constitution to a claim to 'Hibernia Irredenta'. The parallel with Italy's historical attitude to the Adriatic seaboard beyond its recognised territory is striking, and in that case it is likely to have lasting ill effects on our political relations with our neighbours.[62]

McElligott also noted in his second memo: 'We are still without the article dealing with religion, church and state. It is most important that as much time as possible should be available for consideration of its terms'. The 'second revise' Constitution was circulated on 10 April and, as has been noted already, Finance was the only department to comment on the missing article on religion. It was not until 23 April that the ministries received a circular 'including draft articles of the constitution, articles 42, 43, 44 on private property, religious and directive principles of social policy'.[63] The first section of Article 43 on religion was still not included. 'It is noted that this section is in blank', minuted McElligott in his submission to the President.[64]

The section of the clause on religion which had surfaced at such a late stage was the extensive section 2 relating to freedom of conscience and non-endowment of religion (see Appendix II). McElligott raised a very important point when he noted that, under the terms of the religious clause, 'it may no doubt be considered whether the state would not have to provide for full divorce (with the right to remarry) for those who see no objection to it on religious grounds'. As it stood in the draft Constitution, there was a prohibition on divorce (see draft Article 40, which became Article 41). That ended the anomalous situation which had existed in the country since the establishment of the Free State (see Chapter V). On 24 April, McDunphy circulated the departments:

Herein copies of a further revise of the constitution dated [no date given] . . . He [de Valera] is anxious that the text should be sent for final printing tonight, and he would like, therefore, to receive from you not later than 4 p.m. today observation of any matters of vital importance to which you consider his attention should be drawn.[65]

It seems that neither the preamble nor the first section of Article 43 (on religion) were seen even then by the departments; they had a matter of hours to comment before the document went to the printers.

The final text, which came back from the printers late on 26 April, was complete and did include the missing sections for the very *first time*. The preamble was not proofed until 23 April and twelve sets were reproofed on 24 April. If the text was not complete until the 26th, that only left the Executive Council meeting of 27 April to discuss the final draft complete with Article 43 on religion.[66]

In fact, the Executive Council met on 16 and 23 March – the days on which the first draft was circulated and comments had been submitted. Meetings were held regularly in April: on the 2nd, 6th, 9th, 13th, 14th, 16th, 20th, 23rd, 27th and 30th. The duration of some of these meetings was unusually long and would indicate that the Constitution was the subject of protracted discussions. But whenever the draft article was raised – even if it was only in late April – there were some members of the Executive Council who were not pleased with the wording. Gerry Boland, the then Minister for Lands and Fisheries, explained in an interview in 1968 that he told de Valera:

then it would be the equivalent to the expulsion from our history of great Irishmen like Tone, Emmet, Russell, McCracken and even Parnell, Childers and many more. None of these men would live in Ireland under such a sectarian

Constitution, and I would not live under it either. I would take my wife and children and put myself out of it. It seems to me that this is bowing down before all of those who were against the republicans all the time, and still are.[67]

That is a particularly weak source. Besides, Boland was not a senior Cabinet Minister. His resignation would not have rocked the government. But another source, Mr Sean MacEntee, corroborates in a reminiscence the substance of the Boland stance. MacEntee was Minister of Finance, under whom McElligott worked directly. There is little doubt that as head of the Department, MacEntee had to discuss the points raised in the Finance memoranda at the Executive Council. He said that he was 'of the same mind' as Boland. But as a politician he was very much alive to the difficulties which the government faced at the hustings. He told the author:

Now, look here is what has to be remembered in relation to the Constitution. The purpose of the Constitution was to get rid of the Oath and the Irish Free State Constitution. And we had to go a long way . . . I mean, how many people, including Dev, had to subordinate whatever private views they may have had in relation to these questions, particularly the question of the Church, to the fact that we had got to get a majority of the people. And we felt, and it was true, that we wouldn't get it if we gave the bishops any chance to attack us.[68]

Asked if the Constitution had made the Catholic Church a *primus inter pares*, MacEntee replied 'yes, but more *pares* than *primus*'.

There was nothing unreasonable about that line of argument. The Spanish Civil War was in its second year. The Irish public – through such organisations as the Irish Christian Front – had been subjected to a continued barrage of stories concerning the dangers of communism and the advances of secularism. The late spring of 1937 was not an ideal political climate in which to introduce a new Constitution for discussion. Fianna Fail faced a very stiff political task on the basis of their record since 1932. The Economic War had not made de Valera very popular with sections of the farming community. The last thing that men like MacEntee wanted in 1937 was to have to fight their political opponents and the Catholic bishops as well. The party could not have survived. On grounds of sheer pragmatism, de Valera gained acceptance for his religious clause.

It is doubtful if some of the more critical members of de Valera's Executive Council did not also realise that the draft Constitution contained other articles which were specifically Roman Catholic in inspiration. Article 41 on the Family, Article 42 on Education, Article 43 on Private Property, Article 44 on Religion and Article 45 on Directive Principles of Social Policy all owed their inspiration to Catholic morality and teaching. Such considerations raised a much wider debate about the nature of Irish society. But to have begun such a dialogue, in the context of 1937, could only have resulted in political defeat for the government.

When the draft Constitution was finally debated in the Dail, the main opposition party, Fine Gael, did not argue that it was not secular enough. The arguments seemed to be much more firmly pitched at the level that it was not confessional enough.

After a long discussion on 27 April at the Executive Council, the 'final instruction for printing was given to . . . Cahills at 4.40 p.m. today. Supplies will be delivered tomorrow, 29 instant.'[69] The President ordered a run of 1,200 copies and they were dispatched the day they were received to each member of the hierarchy, judiciary, Dail, Irish clergy and prominent figures abroad, etc., so that they would reach those in Ireland at least the following day, the 30th, when the press was scheduled to carry the text with editorial comment.

De Valera could not have hoped for a more favourable international response to the publication of the document. Vatican approval was all-important to consolidate the clerical vote and that came in an *Osservatore Romano* article quoted in the *Irish Press*: 'It differs from other constitutions, because it is inspired by respect for the faith of the people, the dignity of the person, the sanctity of the family, of private property, and of social democracy. These principles are applied in a unique religious spirit, which animates the whole constitution.'[70]

The *Osservatore* article was used to considerable advantage to win public support for the Constitution. It was taken as official papal approval. While that was not, strictly speaking, correct, it is clear that the Constitution had made a favourable impression on Pacelli, who was to become Pope on 2 March 1939.

Cardinal MacRory responded courteously to de Valera's letter on 9 May when he returned from confirmations. The Cardinal did not have an opportunity to read it but, in his travels, he heard it discussed by priests 'and in every instance the comments were favourable'. But he reserved his personal opinion.[71] After one further effort to change the 'Church of Ireland' wording he was resigned to acceptance. Later, he described the Constitution as: 'a great Christian document . . . a splendid charter – a broad and solid foundation on which to build up a nation that will be, at once, reverent and dutiful to God and just to all men'.

Archbishop Byrne was very pleased with the Constitution: 'I have noticed that the Holy Catholic Apostolic and Roman Church still retains its special position', he commented to de Valera wryly. The Secretary of the Department of External Affairs, Joseph Walshe, had delivered the document personally to Drumcondra. The government had good cause to be thankful to Byrne. The other Churches were also pleased, as was exemplified in a letter from the Irish Rabbinate Committee, which 'noted with the greatest satisfaction and due appreciation that the Jewish congregations are included in the clause giving equal recognition to the religious bodies in Eire, and they respectfully tender congratulations on the production of such a fair and just document'.[72] That was a fitting tribute from a religious community which was not receiving either fair or just treatment at the time in some Western European countries.

The final vote on the draft Constitution took place in the Dail on 15 June. A dissolution was announced immediately and de Valera announced that a referendum and general election would be held on the same day, 1 July. The marriage of the two events worked very strongly to the electoral advantage of Fianna Fail, who did not have to campaign exclusively on their economic record or the achievement of their social policies. De Valera turned the campaigns into a vote of confidence in 'Irishness'. His Constitution had been framed by Irishmen for Irishmen, unlike, he claimed, the 1922 Constitution. It was rooted in Christianity for a 'conservative people', and he rejected any criticism that it was 'derogatory to women'.

In the end, 56.5 per cent voted for the Constitution, while only 45.2 per cent voted for Fianna Fail. De Valera had won three consecutive elections for Fianna Fail and he was able to repeat his success the following year. The content of de Valera's election speeches revealed the ideas of a religiously conservative, profoundly Catholic political leader. His ideals and ideology were enshrined in his Constitution. John Hagan, the Rector of the Irish College, who had died in 1930, had many years earlier accurately analysed the political philosophy and potential of the Taoiseach. There were few bishops who would have agreed with him at the time. None would have agreed after the Civil War in 1923. But in 1937, both the Vatican and the Irish hierarchy had cause to look with favour on de Valera as one of the leading Catholic statesmen and democrats in a Europe that was fast descending into authoritarianism.

CONCLUSION

No God for Ireland! he cried. We have had too much God in Ireland.
Away with God.

Blasphemer! Devil! screamed Dante, starting to her feet and almost spitting in
his face . . . At the door Dante turned round violently and shouted down the
room, her cheeks flushed and quivering with rage: Devil out of hell! We won!
We crushed him to death! Fiend! Mr Casey . . . suddenly bowed his head on his
hands with a sob of pain. Poor Parnell! he cried loudly. My dead king![1]

The political crisis provoked by the Irish Parliamentary Party's
rejection of 'the Chief' in 1890 has helped give rise to the myth —
articulated by Mr Casey — that 'the priests and the priests' pawns broke
Parnell's heart'. W.B. Yeats implicitly supported what Professor Joseph
Lee has termed this 'emotionally satisfying myth'[2] with the lines

> The Bishops and the Party
> That tragic story made . . .[3]

But this was not a perception of the role of the church in Irish politics
confined to novelists and poets. The confrontation in the Joyce
household captures the vituperative atmosphere which prevailed
between the two sides. The Parnellites might well have been incensed
by such lines as the following from a pastoral letter of the Bishop of
Meath, Thomas Nulty:

Parnellism strikes at the very root and saps the very foundations of Catholic
faith . . . Parnellism, like paganism, impedes, obstructs and cripples the
efficiency and blights the fruitfulness of the preaching of the gospel and of the
diffusion of the divine knowledge without which our people cannot be saved
. . . The dying Parnellite himself will hardly dare to face the justice of his
creator till he has been prepared and anointed by us for the last awful struggle.[4]

Feelings ran high in many parts of the country, particularly during the
election of 1892, as one incident reported by the Bishop of Cork,
O'Callaghan, will indicate:

The engrossing subject of conversation everywhere is Parnell and politics and people are busily taking sides. In Cork there is much division. The mob is for Parnell and priests were insulted and hooted lately in the street. This was the result of money and drink given to them for the purpose. The country and country towns have taken the opposite side and so have all the priests except one and he has lately retraced his steps and made a humble apology . . . The crowd of his [*Parnell's*] followers is the Fenian society which hitherto was opposed to him but is now his main support and this is perhaps the greatest point of danger. The Irish Party destroyed the power of Fenianism in the past and remnants of it only remained. If it can be revived through Parnell's influence, it would be the source of innumerable evils. You will have heard before this reaches you that a shot was fired at Dr Healy of Clonfert from which you may imagine what we are to expect. An attack was made on me in Cork. Fortunately, the man in going at me slipped and fell at my feet receiving a wound on his forehead.[5]

Walsh was not slow to realise that the Parnell crisis, coming rapidly in the wake of the Vatican rescript on the Plan of Campaign, had created a major crisis of authority for the Irish Church. The pastoral problems created by the waywardness of Mr Casey were self-evident to the Archbishop of Dublin, who knew just how precarious the pastoral situation was for the bishops. The insensitivity of the Vatican on the land question had compounded the difficulties of the hierarchy. It was for that reason Walsh wrote to Kirby in Rome:

We are still in the midst of our difficulties here – the prospects of an amicable solution being now apparently further off than ever. It would be well if Your Grace would tell any persons who presume to offer you advice about the details of Irish affairs, that they had better keep to matters of which they are capable of forming an opinion. *Above all, let them look at home.* We here mean to strain every nerve to keep our people safe from such a fate as that which has befallen the Catholics of Rome and Italy.[6]

If the Parnell crisis and the papal rescript had helped give rise to the myth that

> The Bishops and the Party
> That tragic story made . . .

it also helped establish an internal Church myth that when it came to Irish politics the judgement of the Vatican was not to be trusted because it was too much influenced by Britain. Two generations of bishops and leading members of the higher clergy accepted that interpretation of Vatican politics, irrespective of the change of Popes. The trauma of the late 1880s was still felt in 1920. It was as if Leo XIII was still Pope. Such rigidity led to some unnecessary misunderstandings between Ireland and Rome.

What differentiated Walsh and other leading members of the Irish hierarchy from many of their continental counterparts was a pastoral concern which eventually brought prelates and politicians closer together. Walsh was not prepared to accept that political elites in Irish society would inevitably be alienated from the Catholic Church. He saw himself as a conciliator towards Mr Casey and those like him. Of course, the bishops were protecting the institutional Church. But many also had diverse political ideas and the lack of unanimity on the bench of bishops did not always serve the sectional interests of the Catholic Church.

Walsh helped the Church overcome the political difficulties of the 1890s. Mr Casey was still a member. But with the flagging of the Home Rule Movement and the 'success' of the 1916 Rising, the bishops again faced a crisis of authority, particularly with the advent of 'physical force' nationalism. This crisis was of longer duration, and it was potentially more serious than the challenge that faced the Church in the late 1880s and 1890s. What was to happen to the consensus? Many Irish nationalist leaders, such as de Valera, Cosgrave and Collins, did not view the Church as a monolith. They knew of the political and personality clashes on the bench of bishops. The island was too small to conceal many secrets between political and ecclesiastical institutions. In this regard, the role played by Hagan and Curran in Rome was of major political importance. Both clerics were well disposed toward de Valera, O'Kelly and other moderate republican politicians.

Indeed, episcopal statements and actions often provoked moments of crisis between bishops and nationalists in the 1919–21 period. But the church was multifaceted. There were the pastorals which condemned the use of physical force. (The Cohalan excommunication letter was the strongest.) But it must be remembered that not all members of Sinn Fein supported the acts of violence which the Bishop of Cork – and other bishops – consistently condemned. Moreover, the actions of Hagan and the hierarchy in Rome were well known to a small circle of nationalist leaders. As the war progressed, many bishops inclined to the view that, if there was a moral balance between the British and the nationalists, it tipped finally in favour of Sinn Fein. This process culminated in the hope of de Valera in mid-1921 that the bishops would publicly support the idea of an Irish republic. That was not as outlandish or pious a hope as it might have appeared to some of his political colleagues at the time. The manoeuvre only helped accentuate the political divisions within the hierarchy and forced a situation where a declaration was not issued, on the grounds that it could have led to an unprecedented public breach in the unity of episcopal ranks. Indirectly, de Valera got what he wanted in the episcopal statement which followed the meeting. The consensus between Church and State was preserved.

But even at moments of major crisis in the 1919–21 period between bishops and nationalists, the hierarchy knew that there was little danger of activists being lost to Catholicism. There were few – if any – 'renegade Catholics' among the leaders of Sinn Fein. On the contrary, O'Kelly, de Valera, Cosgrave, Collins, etc. were all devout, pious members of the Catholic Church. They were Catholics as their fathers were and their fathers before them and their fathers before them again when they gave up their lives rather than sell the faith. There was a distinctly Catholic hue to the political philosophy of the Sinn Fein leadership. Irish nationalism and Catholicism were symbiotically linked. As Owen Chadwick states: 'The Irish and the Belgians expressed in their Roman Catholicism not only their religious faith but their cultural and political difference from Protestant Britain and Holland.'[7] The Polish example could also be added here. There was a regard, particularly among the secondary leadership of Sinn Fein, for the republicanism of Wolfe Tone and nineteenth-century secular nationalists. But it remained subordinate to the dominant current of Catholic nationalism, which managed, paradoxically, to incorporate the separatism of Tone without espousing his secular radicalism.

One major conclusion of this work is that efforts to keep the Vatican out of Irish politics were rooted in an episcopal determination to prevent the papacy from threatening the consensus between Church and State. Historical experience had taught the Irish bishops that a combination of inexperience, ignorance about the local political situation, and the achievement of international policy objectives rendered the Vatican unsuited to intervene in secular Irish affairs. The hierarchy had kept very close to political developments and had managed to prevent a rupture between Catholicism and the nationalist movement. Hagan played a central role in this process. He was in a position to interpret episcopal divisions and fears. As a clergyman on the left wing of the hierarchy, he may, on occasions, have exaggerated the 'British' origins of a pending papal condemnation to stiffen episcopal opposition to such a move. The Irish College in Rome was at the centre of both ecclesiastical and nationalist politics. Hagan found it difficult to distinguish his role as agent of the bishops from that of political activist. But he did have a sense that the country was going through a crucial historical phase where it was necessary for the Church both to give leadership and to maintain an influence over a new generation of political leaders likely to form the nucleus of the first government in an independent Ireland. In that sense, he served the interests of the Church with his accurate political analysis. Moreover, he also ensured that his analysis was translated into political action.

The Treaty healed the political divisions on the bench of bishops. All agreed that it was a settlement more generous than anything they had hoped for. Logue was most emphatic about this. Did the episcopal position significantly sway public opinion in favour of the pro-Treatyites? It is very doubtful. There were many Catholics who voted in favour without taking any advice from their bishops. The stance of the hierarchy reflected the growing consensus in the country that a return to the violence of the year 1920 was not a viable political option, whatever reservations there might be about the small print of the agreement. Byrne of Dublin explored the possibility of bringing about a reconciliation between de Valera and Griffith in the Mansion House conference. He recognised that there was a moderate anti-Treatyite wing or, more accurately stated, a political wing led by people like de Valera, O'Kelly and Harry Boland. Hagan also recognised the existence of 'moderate republicans' and argued that the Church should take account of that when framing policy. He was aware of the confusions and divisions on the republican side at the outbreak of civil war. The Rector knew that de Valera was a reluctant soldier, as were many others in the summer of 1922. Many wanted to see an end to the Civil War as quickly as possible. De Valera, in particular, wanted to see an end to the fighting after the evacuation of Fermoy barracks in August 1922. In the autumn the hierarchy required little official prompting to issue a pastoral condemning the anti-Treatyites, using language which had been previously reserved for the actions of Auxiliaries and Black and Tans. Did the pastoral unwittingly help prolong the Civil War? There followed the policy of executions which reunited the dispirited republicans and brought down private episcopal condemnations on the head of the government. Throughout those testing months, Hagan was in touch with prominent republicans who valued his interventions on their behalf; while one section of the Church denied republicans the sacraments, sometimes in a harsh and unnecessarily vindictive fashion, another group of clergymen was sensitive to their spiritual needs.

The bridge that Walsh tried to maintain between the Church and radical politics was sustained by Hagan and others who were decidedly out of sympathy with the anti-Treatyites' use of violence; but they were highly critical of the actions of the government, particularly the use of a policy of executions. The republican leadership was not alienated from the Church; they did not feel that they had been deserted by *all* the clergy. Moreover, men like de Valera were never whole-heartedly in support of the campaign of violence. Hagan accepted that it was only force of circumstances which placed men like Sean T. O'Kelly within the ranks of militant republicans. They would have been much more content to lead political opposition to the Treaty.

In the months that followed the Civil War, Byrne attempted to influence Cosgrave into adopting a more lenient policy towards political prisoners, thousands of whom had gone on hunger strike. But government ministers were prepared to resign rather than adopt a policy of early release. That did little to defuse the legacy of bitterness and hatred which characterised Irish society in the wake of the Civil War. Besides the Archbishop of Dublin, O'Donnell, who was made Cardinal in 1924, was critical of the government's handling of policy towards republican prisoners. He, too, felt there was greater need for political magnanimity. (Some of the clergy might also have been less legalistic.) He also felt that de Valera and his followers should be quickly reintegrated into constitutional politics. Hagan and Mannix must share some responsibility for influencing de Valera and bringing about the break with abstentionist Sinn Fein. The Rector of the Irish College provided historical and theological justification for entering the Dail. In a vague sense, it can be argued that the decision to found Fianna Fail was probably taken in the Irish College.

A task of the Church in the post-1923 period was to help rebuild the political consensus fragmented by the Civil War. Hagan was, as stated above, one of the first clergymen to recognise that de Valera was not beyond political redemption. Once the latter had opted for constitutional politics and founded Fianna Fail it was only a question of time before the damage done by the Civil War to de Valera's reputation – and the reputation of many of his close political associates like Lemass, Aiken, MacEntee and O'Kelly – would be repaired.

By the late 1920s de Valera was slowly accepted by many bishops as a possible alternative to Cosgrave and his government, which had not done enough in certain areas of legislation to satisfy the hierarchy. The decision to set up diplomatic relations with the Vatican was a major source of annoyance to many bishops. De Valera and Fianna Fail had an opportunity in the Dail to embarrass Cosgrave, in particular, by putting the clerical arguments against diplomatic relations, which were strongly supported by his personal friend Archbishop Byrne. De Valera was a staunch Catholic nationalist who usually had the political skill to anticipate Church–State difficulties and introduce a workable solution which preserved the consensus between Church and State. He did this in the area of Criminal Law Amendment and dance halls. He came closest to a major Church–State crisis over the wording of the religious clause in his Constitution. The article was a compromise which satisfied all the other churches much more than it did the leader of the Catholic Church, MacRory. Quite unusually, the Cardinal encouraged the Vatican to intervene directly in Irish politics, contrary to Irish–Vatican ecclesiastical tradition. But he failed in that task and the 'flawed' article remained unaltered in the final version of the Constitution. In focusing on this article, it was not intended to neglect to point out that the entire document was heavily influenced by the teachings of one Church.

Finally, it can be said that the values and culture of the major political parties in the 1920s and 1930s reflected the dominant Catholic ethos. Yet both Cosgrave and de Valera displayed more sensitivity towards other religious denominations in the state than may have been hitherto recognised. When de Valera, in particular, had a problem in this regard, the danger came from some members of the lower clergy and the *laity*. There was a constant political need to be vigilant against what the inveterate republican Peadar O'Donnell has colourfully described as 'a yahoo-ridden church'.

The Evolution of the Episcopal Appointments System in Ireland, a List of Bishops and a Note on the Standing Committee, 1918–40

The system for appointing Catholic bishops in nineteenth-century Ireland is discussed at length in a brilliant article by Professor John H. Whyte.[1] In summer 1829, new regulations regarding the appointment of Irish bishops were promulgated, which attempted to balance the interests of lower clergy and bishops in the selection process:

The new regulations substituted precision for the confusion hitherto prevalent. Every step in the process of selection was now carefully laid down. The first stage was for the vicar general of the vacant diocese (or the bishop, when a coadjutor was being appointed) to call a meeting of the canons and parish priests. At the meeting each priest wrote, secretly, on a piece of paper the name of the person he considered most suited for the office. The papers were then scrutinized, and the names were announced of the three candidates who had received the most votes. The next stage was for the bishops of the province to meet and discuss the merits of the three names recommended (or *terna*), and they then forwarded the names to Rome together with their own comments. They were not authorized to suggest further candidates themselves.[2]

This consultative system sometimes resulted in conflict and 'electioneering'. Cardinal Paul Cullen (1803–78) exercised considerable influence over the selection of bishops as Archbishop of Armagh (1850–2) and Archbishop of Dublin (1852–78). One of the most outstanding accounts of a case where he was responsible for overturning the *Terna* can be found in the unpublished diary of Fr John O'Sullivan, who was the parish priest of Kenmare (1839–74). The latter was placed first on the *Terna* in the 1850s for the diocese of Kerry. But he was blocked by Cullen, who wrote to Propaganda: 'Father O'Sullivan, having been a parish priest for a long time, will not be disposed to put into effect the reforms prescribed by the Synod [of Thurles, 1850] with regard to the administration of the sacraments.'[3]

The appointment of a cardinal and/or an archbishop – particularly of Dublin and Armagh – was often attended by suggestions that the British

were interfering in Irish ecclesiastical affairs. In the case of William
Walsh it is quite clear that pressure was exerted by British authorities
not to have him appointed to Dublin. London played a role in
preventing him being made a cardinal. A persistent assumption of high
ecclesiastical politics in nineteenth-century Ireland, and held not
unreasonably by Walsh, was that the Vatican was too anxious to
accommodate British representations concerning the Irish Church. Any
change in the system of episcopal appointments which might involve
centralisation was interpreted as the extension, through Rome, of
British interests over the Irish Church.

In the early twentieth century the Irish hierarchy had come under
considerable pressure from Rome to adapt the local system of episcopal
appointments to conform with the practice elsewhere. The Prefect of
the Consistorial Congregation, Cardinal de Lai, wrote two letters to the
Irish bishops on 13 December 1909 and 14 February 1910. Both were
noted at the 21 June 1910 meeting.

At the October meeting, in the same year, it was decided that the
provisions in a decree, issued by Rome on 30 March 1910, concerning
the secrecy to be observed at the election of bishops did not apply to
Ireland.[4]

The weaknesses of the Irish system, as far as Rome was concerned,
were underlined after the diocese of Cork fell vacant in 1914. Daniel
Cohalan was appointed finally, but not before the diocese had been very
badly divided over support for another priest for the post.

The practice of the *Terna* continued for a number of years after the
publication of the revised Code of Canon Law in 1917. The rumoured
appointment of a papal nuncio to Ireland, which was a constant topic of
clerical gossip in the early 1920s, was interpreted as being related to the
Vatican's desire to make significant changes in the government of the
Irish Church. The matter of episcopal appointments was finally
discussed at length at a general meeting of the bishops in June 1925. A
new procedure was adopted, whereby bishops can consult with the
archbishop, the bishops, the canons (members of Cathedral chapters)
and parish priests in order to draw up a list of suitable names, at
intervals of roughly three years. The list is sent to Rome. There is no
obligation to choose from that list. Since the arrival of the papal nuncio
in 1930, the Vatican receives guidance from that quarter also. The role of
the nuncio is much more central in the appointment of a cardinal or
archbishops. In the case of Dublin, the nuncio circulates nearly 1,500
members of clergy and laity with a document requesting their guidance
in relation to an appointment.

In the case of Armagh and Dublin, unofficial soundings are usually
made in government circles by the nuncio to determine the acceptabil-
ity of a likely appointee. But this does not always happen. I have found

only two instances in the period covered where there was direct political involvement in a high ecclesiastical appointment. The evidence in the case of W. T. Cosgrave trying to secure the 'red hat' for Byrne of Dublin in 1929 is not conclusive. But in the case of John Charles McQuaid's appointment to Dublin in 1940, there is absolutely no doubt that Eamon de Valera exercised as much influence as he was capable of exerting through the nuncio and through the Irish envoy to the Vatican, when it was discovered that Dr McQuaid's name met with some resistance from Montini, who was then Secretary of State.

The case of an appointment to Armagh is complicated by the fact that that the archbishopric – residence in the twentieth century of the 'red hat' – is situated in the state of Northern Ireland, while the archdiocese straddles the border. It remains a matter of speculation whether the Vatican raises the appointment with London.

LIST OF BISHOPS

Province of Tuam

In the diocese of Achonry Patrick Morrisroe was Bishop from 1911 to 1946. In Clonfert Thomas O'Doherty was in office from 1919 until 1923; John Dignan took over in 1924, after he was translated to Galway. Dignan died in 1953. He was one of de Valera's closest friends on the bench. In Elphin Bernard Coyne was Bishop from 1913 until 1926, when Edward Doorly took over. Thomas O'Dea was Bishop of Galway from 1909 until 1923, when Thomas O'Doherty was translated from Clonfert. In 1936 Michael Browne became Bishop. In Killala James Naughton was Bishop from 1911 for thirty-nine years until his death in 1950.

Between 1918 and 1940 – the period of this study – Achorny and Killala did not change bishops. In the province of Tuam there were two new bishops appointed in the post-Civil War period.

Province of Dublin

In the diocese of Ferns William Codd was Bishop from 1917 until 1938. Patrick Foley was Bishop of Kildare and Leighlin from 1896 until 1926. He was succeeded by Matthew Cullen in 1927 and nine years later Thomas Keogh took over. In Ossory, Abraham Brownrigg became Bishop in 1884. Patrick Collier succeeded him in 1928.

Province of Armagh

Joseph Hoare was Bishop of Ardagh and Clonmacnois from 1895 until 1927, when he was replaced by James Joseph MacNamee. In Clogher, Patrick MacKenna was Bishop from 1909 to 1942. Charles McHugh was

Bishop of Derry from 1907 until 1926, when Bernard O'Keane took over.
He died in 1939. In Down and Connor, Joseph MacRory was Bishop
until his move to Armagh. He was replaced in 1928 by Daniel Mageean.
Edward Mulhern was Bishop of Dromore from 1916 until 1943. Patrick
Finegan was Bishop of Kilmore from 1910 until 1937, when Patrick
Lyons took over. Laurence Gaughran was Bishop of Meath from 1906
until 1928, and Thomas Mulvany for fifteen years. Patrick O'Donnell
was Bishop of Raphoe from 1888 until 1922, when he was translated to
Armagh as Coadjutor. He was replaced by Joseph MacHuly. In the
province of Armagh, there were five changes of bishops in the post-
Civil War period; there were also three changes of archbishops.

Province of Cashel

Charles O'Sullivan was Bishop of Kerry for ten years. He was replaced in
1927 by Michael O'Brien. Daniel Cohalan was Bishop of Cork from 1916
until 1952. In Cloyne, Robert Browne was Bishop from 1894 until 1931.
He was replaced by James Roche, who was translated from Ross. In
Killaloe Michael Fogarty was Bishop from 1904 until 1955. In Limerick
there were a number of changes: Denis Hallinan became Bishop of
Limerick in 1918. He was replaced by David Keane in 1923, who reigned
until 1945. In Ross, Denis Kelly was Bishop from 1897 until 1924. He was
succeeded by James Roche in 1926, and when the latter was translated
to Cloyne in 1931 Patrick Casey took over. In Waterford and Lismore
Bernard Hackett was Bishop from 1916 until 1932, when Jeremiah
Kinane was appointed.

ARCHBISHOP
Tuam
Thomas Gilmartin, 10 July 1918–14 October 1939 (trans. Clonfert)
Dublin
William Walsh, 2 August 1885–9 April 1921
Edward Byrne, 9 April 1921–9 February 1940 (Coadjutor 19 August
    1920)
John Charles McQuaid, 6 November 1940–4 January 1972

Cashel
John Harty, provided 4 December 1913, consecrated 18 January 1914,
    died 11 September 1946

CARDINAL
Armagh
Michael Logue, 3 December 1887–19 November 1924

Patrick O'Donnell, 19 November 1924–22 October 1927
Joseph MacRory, 22 June 1928–13 October 1945

A NOTE ON THE STANDING COMMITTEE[5]

Full meetings of the Irish Catholic hierarchy took place during the period of this study twice yearly, usually in June and October.[6] In the turbulent political years of 1921 and 1922, special meetings of the hierarchy were held on 13 December 1921 and 26 April 1922. These regular meetings of the Irish bishops as a conference were an unusual feature in European Catholic Church life. The practice dated back to the eighteenth century.

During this period the Standing Committee of the hierarchy met four times each year: (i) On the third Tuesday in January at 12 noon in University College Dublin; (ii) On the Tuesday in the Second Week after Easter Sunday at 12 noon in University College Dublin; (iii) On the Monday preceding the June meeting of the Episcopal Conference in Maynooth College at 12 noon; (iv) On the Monday preceding the October meeting of the Episcopal Conference in Maynooth College, at 12 noon. If 1 January fell on a Tuesday the meeting of the Standing Committee was held on the fourth Tuesday of January.

The Standing Committee was empowered to deal with any urgent matter arising between general meetings of the Conference by a resolution of the June 1887 general meeting. In October 1890 at the general meeting, it was decided that the Standing Committee could be asked to consider any matter which an individual bishop considered urgent and involving interests wider than diocesan scope. The Chairman would consider such a request and, if necessary, consult with the other archbishops. If a meeting was called in response to such a request, the bishop making the request would be invited to attend the meeting. There is no evidence that any meeting was held as a result of this resolution, but since the four meetings were held almost at three-monthly intervals it was hardly necessary to call another special meeting. The January 1922 meeting was brought forward to December 1921, as a special meeting of the whole Episcopal Conference was called for December 1921 to discuss the Treaty proposals.

The membership of the Standing Committee consisted of the four archbishops ex officio (Armagh presiding, Dublin, Cashel and Tuam), the Secretary of the Conference and the second secretary (he later became the Financial Secretary, and that rule has changed), also ex officio, plus one bishop from each of the four ecclesiastical provinces. The membership in 1918 was three archbishops, the Bishop of Cloyne as Secretary, the Bishop of Ross as second Secretary and the Bishops of

Raphoe, Galway and Kildare and Leighlin. (Their names were: Cardinal Logue, Armagh; Dr William Walsh, Dublin; Dr Harty, Cashel; Tuam was missing, presumably vacant at this period; Dr O'Donnell, Raphoe; Dr Foley, Kildare and Leighlin; Dr O'Dea, Galway; Dr Browne, Cloyne and Dr Kelly, Ross.)

Over the years there were meetings at which one or other of the archbishops were absent, due to a vacancy in the See or due to ill health. In October 1918, the Bishop of Killaloe is listed as a member (this probably means that he was a member earlier, since the provinces each had one bishop in addition to the Archbishop). At the January 1923 meeting the Bishop of Clonfert had taken over from the Bishop of Ross as second Secretary.

In October 1923 the second Secretary had become the Bishop-Elect of Galway – he had been transferred from Clonfert. In January 1924 the bishop from the Tuam Province on the Standing Committee was the Bishop of Achonry, in succession to the Bishop of Galway, who had died the previous year.

In 1922 the Bishop of Raphoe (Dr O'Donnell) was appointed Coadjutor Archbishop of Armagh and he continued to attend meetings of the Standing Committee as the bishop from the Armagh province. The first meeting at which he attended as Coadjutor is April 1922. He succeeded Cardinal Logue in early 1925 as he was Chairman for the meeting of April 1925. He also signed the minutes of the January meeting.

In October 1925 the Bishop of Down and Connor attended as the Armagh province representative. In January 1928 the Bishop of Ferns had succeeded the Bishop of Kildare as Dublin province representative. In January 1929 the Bishop of Cloyne had ceased to be Secretary, with the Bishop of Galway taking over and the Bishop of Limerick becoming second Secretary. At the same meeting the Bishop of Clogher had succeeded the Bishop of Down and Connor as the Armagh province representative (he had attended the previous meeting in October 1928 'by request').

In October 1937 the Bishop of Limerick had taken over from the Bishop of Galway as first Secretary and the Bishop of Waterford as second Secretary. In October 1938, the Bishop of Ossory had taken over from the Bishop of Ferns as the representative from the Dublin province.

It was commonly believed, according to a number of episcopal sources, that all major decisions were taken by the Standing Committee and then discussed and agreed to by the conference of bishops. Real power, these same sources argued, resided with the Standing Committee. That remained the situation until the early 1970s, and there have been major developments since then, with greater importance being attached to the establishment of working committees. The younger bishops feel that they are no longer spectators, as some of the earlier generations of bishops might have considered themselves to be. In the context of this study, Hagan and Curran in Rome were well supported within the Standing Committee – although they were not without their critics in that body. Nevertheless, despite the fact that Logue was a cardinal and Archbishop of Armagh, he was probably far less influential within the Church as he advanced in years.

The appointment of a papal nuncio to Ireland in 1930 did little to change the operations of the national conference of bishops. It is usual for the nuncio to celebrate Mass on the evening before the meetings begin, dine with the bishops, and then depart for home. The nuncio was never encouraged to play an active part in proceedings. There is one recent exception to that practice.

The Wording of the Draft Religious Clause, 1937
Press Reaction to the New Constitution

(a) THE WORDING OF THE DRAFT RELIGIOUS CLAUSE 1937

1 The state acknowledges the right of Almighty God to public worship in that way which He has shown to be His Will.

2 Accordingly, the state shall hold in honour the name of God and shall consider it a duty to favour and protect religion and shall not enact any measure that may impair its credit.

3 The state acknowledges that the true religion is that established by Our Divine Lord Jesus Christ Himself, which he committed to his Church to protect and propagate, as the guardian and interpreter of true morality. It acknowledges, moreover, that the Church of Christ is the Catholic Church.

4 The state recognises the Church of Christ as a perfect society, having within itself full competence and sovereign authority, in respect of the spiritual good of man.

5 (i)   Whatever may be ranked under the civil and political order is rightly subject to the supreme authority of the perfect society, the state, whose function it is to procure the temporal well-being, moral and material, of society.

(ii)   The state pledges itself, therefore, in virtue of this sovereign authority conferred on it by God within its temporal sphere to enforce respect, by its just laws, for the inalienable rights of the citizen and the family, and to preserve, as best it can, conditions of right social and moral well-being.

(iii)   In cases where the jurisdiction of Church and state requires to be harmoniously coordinated, the state may come to a special agreement with the Church and other religious bodies upon particular matters, civil, political and religious.

6 The state guarantees to its citizens freedom of religious conviction and liberty to practise their religion in private and in public, having due regard however to right order and morality.

7 The state pledges itself not to impose any disabilities on the ground of religious conviction that would be contrary to natural rights and social justice.

8 Every religious association, recognised by the state, shall have the right to manage its own affairs, own, acquire and administer property, movable and immovable and maintain institutions for religious and charitable purposes.

9 The property of a religious denomination shall not be diverted save for necessary works of public utility and on payment of just compensation.

10 Legislation providing state aid for schools shall contain no discrimination against schools under the management of a particular religious denomination.

(b) PRESS REACTION TO THE NEW CONSTITUTION

The *Irish Independent* printed an editorial with the title 'Document No. 3': 'the mountain has been in Labour and has brought forth a mouse. Mr de Valera's followers will be sadder and wiser today when they have searched in vain in his new Constitution, or Document No. 3, for any signs that the promised millennium is at hand . . . Apart from certain amendments which seem called for, he will naturally have the whole-hearted support of the Opposition in enacting this document, for it is one of his finest tributes to his predecessors.' (1 May 1937). The *Irish Times* focused on the Commonwealth link: 'Mr de Valera has kept at least one promise to the people of the Free State: he has drafted his new constitution as if Great Britain were a million miles away . . . What will be the situation now, in default of some previous arrangements between Dublin and London? . . . To these questions Bunreacht na hEireann gives no answer. It merely suggests that Eire is neither fish, flesh, nor even a good red herring. It does not tell us whether we are in the Commonwealth or out of it. Can it be that Mr de Valera does not know?' (1 May 1937); on 3 May, the same paper attacked the Constitutional claims to Northern Ireland: 'Whether we like it or not, the six counties of Northern Ireland are, in their own eyes and in the eyes of the world, a separate entity. It is the duty of every patriotic Irishman to work for reunion, but it is folly to assume reunion, and the height of folly to postpone the day of its real achievement by slights which cannot fail to be resented across the border.' That was exactly how it was taken in the North. In Britain the *Daily Telegraph* (1 May) called it a 'dream constitution'. 'To make the challenge to Ulster Sentiment more explicit and more dangerous, the constitution claims religious sanctions, forbids divorce, and assigns a special position to the Church of Rome . . . It is part of the tragedy of Ireland that the man who has stirred Irish national feeling as no Irishman since Parnell should have supposed that his mere feat could work a miracle, and that the parade of democratic terminology could alter the fact that any Irishman who accepts the Constitution now granted to him with a Sinaitic gesture would be placing himself under an autocrat's heel'. The *Sunday Times* (2 May) felt the Constitution would simply 'perpetuate the division between Dublin and Belfast'. *The Standard* (7 May) thought that there was need for improvement, 'but on one point at least we shall be all agreed: due honour has been done to the religious aspects of Irish life . . . We note, by the way, that the draft constitution not merely prohibits divorce, but refuses to acknowledge a divorce granted in another country'. The *Irish Catholic* (6 May) saw the Constitution as 'a noble document in harmony with papal teachings'. The same edition carried a statement from An Rioghacht rejoicing 'in the noble Preamble' and noting that 'provision is made for the Vocational groups so insistently urged by the present Holy Father, as the basis of stable order in Society . . .'. The *Independent* commissioned a series of articles from prominent academics and members of the legal profession. The former Attorney General, John A. Costello, contributed a long article on 6 May which brought an editorial response from the *Irish Press*, entitled 'More carping criticism', the following day. On the 8th, James G. Douglas contributed an article. The day before, Professor A. Berriedale Keith argued that 'the right of neutrality' was questionable. A judge of the Supreme Court set up by the First Dail, Diarmuid O Cruadhlaoich, attacked the territorial claims of the Constitution on 5 May, while the Hon. Frank Pakenham sounded a very positive note on the 13th. The series was concluded by a number of articles from Alfred O'Rahilly, on the 11th, 14th and 15th. See also Alfred O'Rahilly, *Thoughts on the Constitution* (Dublin, 1938). O'Rahilly in the *Independent* launched a surprising attack on the religious clause of the Constitution: 'The state, we are told, "recognises the special position" of the Catholic Church. It does nothing of the kind. This is made quite clear by the reason given, namely, that the Catholic Faith is "professed by the great majority of the citizens". In other words, the State — small thanks to it — acknowledges the ascertained statistical fact that over ninety per cent of the people are Catholics. Why this should be put into the Constitution is quite beyond my comprehension.' But that was precisely the point which Cardinal MacRory had made in his formula. He wanted such a statistical declaration included. And O'Rahilly was attacking de Valera unwittingly for implicitly complying with the wishes of the Cardinal. O'Rahilly went on to make the point that the impression was conveyed that 'the Constitution embodies a declaration that the Catholic Church is the true Church founded by

Christ. No such declaration is contained in the document. We have nothing but a piece of neutral scientific statistics expressed in fervent phraseology. I am strongly of the opinion that it ought to be expunged.' In criticising de Valera, O'Rahilly may have helped draw the Cardinal's attention to the fact that some of his views had been accommodated in the final article. What O'Rahilly failed to realise was that 'a piece of neutral scientific statistics expressed in fervent phraseology' was exactly what de Valera had set out to achieve.

Twenty years later, when de Valera visited Pius XII at Castel Gandolfo on 4 October 1957, the Pontiff told him: 'Your Constitution is intended to be an instrument of "Prudence, Justice and Charity" at the service of a community, which has never, through its long Christian history, had any doubt about the eternal, as well as the temporal implications of that common good, which it professes to seek through the conjoined prayer, toil and oftentimes heroic sacrifice of its children . . . Grounded on the bedrock of the natural law those fundamental human prerogatives which your constitution undertakes to assure to every citizen of Ireland, within the limits of order and morality, could find no ampler, no safer guarantee against the godless forces of subversion, the spirit of faction and violence, than mutual trust between the authorities of Church and State, independent each in its own sphere, but as it were allied for the common welfare in accordance with the principles of Catholic faith and doctrine.' (SPO S9715B)

NOTES

PREFACE

1 Patrick J. Corish (ed.), *A History of Irish Catholicism*; of relevance to the present work are his 'Political Problems 1860–1878', *A History of Irish Catholicism*, vol. 5, nos. 2 and 3 (Dublin, 1967), pp. 1–58, and 'Gallicanism at Maynooth: Archbishop Cullen and the Royal Visitation of 1853' in Art Cosgrove and Donal McCartney (eds.), *Studies in Irish History presented to R. Dudley Edwards* (Dublin, 1979), pp. 176–89.

2 Emmet Larkin, 'Church, State and Nation in Modern Ireland', in his collected articles and essays, James Walsh and Larry McCaffrey (eds.), *The Historical Dimensions of Irish Catholicism* (New York, 1976); pp. 1244–70 are particularly relevant. It is an excellent, original contribution to Irish Church–State relations bridging the period discussed in this book and earlier decades. See also the following monographs by Larkin: *The Making of the Roman Catholic Church in Ireland, 1850–1860* (Chapel Hill, 1980); *The Roman Catholic Church and the Creation of the Modern Irish State, 1878–1886* (Dublin, 1975); *The Roman Catholic Church and the Plan of Campaign in Ireland* (Cork, 1978); and *The Roman Catholic Church in Ireland and the Fall of Parnell* (Chapel Hill, 1979).

3 David W. Miller, *Church, State and Nation in Ireland 1898–1921* (Dublin, 1973).

4 John H. Whyte, *Church and State in Modern Ireland 1923–1979* (Dublin, 1980); *Catholics in Western Democracies* (Dublin, 1981), and 'The Appointment of Catholic Bishops in Nineteenth-Century Ireland', *Catholic Historical Review*, 48 (April 1962), pp. 12–32.

5 Among the major books on nineteenth century Ireland I should mention the pioneering work of Edward R. Norman, *The Catholic Church and Ireland in the age of Rebellion 1859–1873* (London, 1965). Two more recent works should be noted: Sean J. Connolly, *Priests and People in Pre-Famine Ireland 1780–1845* (Dublin, 1982) and James O'Shea, *Priest, Politics and Society in post-famine Ireland: a study of County Tipperary 1850–1891* (Dublin, 1983).

INTRODUCTION

1 J. Selwyn Schapiro, *Anti-clericalism* (London, 1967); V. M. Arbeloa, *Socialismo y anti-clericalismo* (Madrid, 1973) and René Remond, *L'Anticléricalisme en France de 1815 à nos jours* (Paris, 1976).

2 David Moriarty to William Monsell, 2 March 1868, quoted in Corish, 'Political Problems', p. 4.

3 Francis S. L. Lyons, *Ireland since the Famine* (London, 1971), p. 120, quoting from the *Freeman's Journal*, 10 March 1867.

4 Odo Russell to the Earl of Clarendon, 10 January 1870, in Noel Blakiston (ed.), *The Roman Question: Extracts from the Despatches of Odo Russell from Rome, 1858–1870* (London, 1962), p. 381.

5 Cullen to Patrick Moran, 2 March 1865, no. 43, cited in Norman, *The Catholic Church and Ireland*, p. 91: 'The Fenians are coming out in their true colours. In Tipperary they abused and insulted the priests – so much the better as some of the priests there were rather bitten with Young Irelandism.'

6 When I speak about 'the Church' in the text, I am referring to the Roman Catholic Church. I do so without any intended disrespect to the other Christian churches. Moreover, I generally use the term 'Church' in the restrictive pre-Vatican II sense to mean *the hierarchy*. Where the broader '*People of God*' sense is intended, the meaning will be clear from the text.

7 A good start has been made in this area by Brian Titley, *Church, State, and the Control of Schooling in Ireland 1900–1944* (Kingston and Montreal, 1983).

CHAPTER 1. WILLIAM WALSH AND THE ANGLO-VATICAN TRADITION

1 James Joyce, *A Portrait of the Artist as a Young Man* (New York, 1969) pp. 29–39.

2 *Ibid.*, p. 39.

3 Walsh to Kirby, 3 July 1888, no. 219 (Kirby papers, Irish College, Rome). For the politics of Home Rule and the land question, see Francis S. L. Lyons, *Parnell*, Irish Historical Series pamphlet, no. 3 (Dublin, 1965), p. 21; by the same author, *Parnell* (London, 1977) and *John Dillon* (London, 1968). One of the best works on the period remains Conor Cruise O'Brien, *Parnell and his Party* (London, 1957); see also Joyce Marlow, *Captain Boycott* (London, 1973) and Joseph V. O'Brien, *William O'Brien and the course of Irish Politics 1881–1918* (Berkeley, 1976).

4 Walsh to Kirby, 28 January 1891, no. 54 (Kirby). Chris J. Woods, 'The General Election of 1892: the Catholic Clergy and the Defeat of the Parnellites' in Francis S. L. Lyons and R. A. J. Hawkins (eds.), *Ireland under the Union: Varieties of Tension: Essays in Honour of T. W. Moody* (Oxford, 1980), pp. 289–320.

5 See Larkin, *The Roman Catholic Church and the Plan of Campaign*; J. E. Ward, 'Leo XIII, the Diplomatic Pope', *Review of Politics*, 27 (1966), pp. 47–61; Arturo Jemolo, *Church and State in Italy, 1850–1915* (Oxford, 1960).

6 Walsh to Kirby, 3 July 1888, no. 219 (Kirby).

7 Walsh to Kirby, 28 January 1891, no. 54 (Kirby).

8 Logue to Kirby, 29 August 1889, no. 321, and Walsh to Kirby, 26 October 1891, no. 572 (Kirby).

9 Walsh to Kirby, 9 March 1889, no. 86 (Kirby). Since the research for the book was completed the following volume appeared: Emmet Larkin, *The Roman Catholic Church and the Plan of Campaign in Ireland 1886–1888* (Cork 1978).

10 Patrick J. Walsh, *William J. Walsh, Archbishop of Dublin* (Dublin, 1928) and Sir Shane Leslie, 'Archbishop Walsh', in Conor Cruise O'Brien (ed.), *The Shaping of Modern Ireland* (Dublin, 1960), pp. 98–107: Leslie writes that 'no modern prelate in Ireland has influenced the history of his times and the future of Irishmen more than Walsh'. The Errington mission to block the appointment of Walsh is best documented in Chris J. Woods, 'Ireland and Anglo-papal relations, 1880–1885', *Irish Historical Studies*, 18 (1972), pp. 29–60. After Errington had failed, for which he was rewarded with a baronetcy by Gladstone, Norfolk also made an unsuccessful bid to halt the appointment. A letter was also drafted to William White, Minister at Bucharest, to go to Rome also.

11 Sir Shane Leslie, 'Michael Logue', *Dictionary of National Biography*, 1922–30, pp. 516–517.

12 Fr Michael Curran memorandum, written for the Minister for External Affairs, Desmond FitzGerald, April 1923 (Desmond FitzGerald papers, in possession of his son, Dr Garret FitzGerald, Dublin). Curran had served as personal secretary to Archbishop Walsh for a number of years and reflected the views of his mentor.

13 Michael J. O'Riordan, *Catholicity and Progress in Ireland* (London, 1906), and Sir Horace Plunkett, *Ireland in the New Century* (London, 1904).

14 Michael J. O'Riordan, *La lotta per la libertà in Irlanda e in Inghilterra* (Rome, 1910). This is an interesting pamphlet which was first given as a public lecture in Rome. Cardinals Mariano Rampolla del Tindaro and Antonio Agliari were in the audience.

15 John Hagan, *Home Rule: L'autonomia Irlandese* (Rome, 1913); the name is very interesting when one looks at Hagan's translation of Home Rule. In fact, Hagan became quite adept in the art of free translation later on; see also *Catholic Bulletin*, vol. 20 (April 1930) and vol. 6 (July 1916). Hagan was a scholar who often allowed himself to be drawn into the writing of material which was very far below his professional capacity. An example is the document written in 1921, 'dedicated to the memory of my fellow soldiers of the army of the republic . . . martyrs for human liberty and Ireland's independence, Feast of the Apparition of Our Lady Immaculate, 7th year of the republic. Peace Negotiations: 1648–1921, a Parallel' (Hagan papers, Irish College, Rome).

16 John J. Silke, *Relics, Refugees and Rome* (Rome, 1977), p. 86.

17 Hagan memorandum on the role of the Rector of the Irish College, undated, c. 1920. The Hagan papers, which are in the Irish College, Rome, have not been catalogued.

18 Michael Curran memorandum for FitzGerald (Desmond FitzGerald papers).

19 Hagan memorandum (Hagan).
20 Robert A. Graham, *Vatican Diplomacy, a Study of Church and State on the International Plane* (New Jersey, 1959). For general background to Anglo-Vatican relations see Thomas E. Hachey (ed.), *Anglo-Vatican Relations, 1914–1939* (Confidential annual reports of the British ministers to the Holy See) (Boston, 1972); Sir Alec Randall, 'British Diplomatic Representation at the Holy See' *Blackfriars*, vol. 37 (September 1956), pp. 356–63; Sir Stephen Gaselee, 'British Diplomatic Relations with the Holy See', *The Dublin Review*, vol. 408, pp. 1–19; Harold Temperley, 'George Canning, the Catholics and the Holy See', *The Dublin Review*, vol. 386, p. 1–12; William A. Renzi, 'The Entente and the Vatican during the period of Italian Neutrality, August 1914–May 1915', *The Historical Journal*, vol. 13, no. 3 (1970), pp. 491–508; J. Derek Holmes, *More Roman than Rome: English Catholicism in the Nineteenth Century* (London, 1978); and Blakiston (ed.), *The Roman Question*, p. 381.
21 Graham, *Vatican Diplomacy*, p. 74; see also *British Foreign Office List*, 1940, pp. 489–90.
22 Lt.-Col. Charles à Court Repington, *The First World War, 1914–1918*, diary, vol. 2 (London, 1920), p. 451; the author of the remark was Philip Langdon, a well-informed Benedictine who was secretary to Cardinal Gasquet. Repington was a war correspondent with *The Times*. He described Gasparri as the 'domineering influence in the Vatican'.
23 Michael Curran to Bishop O'Donnell, 14 March 1923 (Archdiocesan Archives, Armagh, Cardinal O'Donnell papers). The Cardinal whom Curran referred to was Merry del Val. But, according to Charles Ledre, 'Merry del Val', *Catholic Encyclopedia*, p. 693, 'politically the influence of the Secretary of State ended with the death of Pius X'. The others, Stanley and Langdon, will be introduced later in the text.
24 Gasquet died in 1929; the *Downside Review*, no. 134, vol. 47 (May 1929), is devoted to an appreciation of the Cardinal. It contains a list of his writings, pp. 147–9; see also Urban Butler, 'Cardinal Gasquet in Rome', p. 151.
25 Benedict Knypers, 'Cardinal Gasquet in London' *ibid.*, p. 145.
26 Sir Shane Leslie, *Cardinal Gasquet* (London, 1953), pp. 91–2.
27 Mgr McDaid interview. Langdon told McDaid that Hagan had exaggerated the influence and reach of Gasquet as an agent of the British in Rome (the late Mgr McDaid was a former Rector of the Irish College).
28 Hagan to Gasquet, 29 October 1914 (Hagan).
29 Gasquet to Hagan, 30 October 1914.
30 Leslie, *Cardinal Gasquet*, p. 15.
31 *Ibid.*, p. 247.
32 *Ibid.*, p. 249; this may have referred to the archdiocese of Tuam in 1918.
33 William Cardinal O'Connell, *Recollections of Seventy Years* (Boston, 1934). This book gives a fairly good account of the Irish influence in the American Church. T. J. Kiernan, *The Irish in Australia* (London, 1953) is a more general account by a former Irish ambassador to Australia of the impact of the Irish in the new world. Corish (ed.), *A history of Irish Catholicism*, vol. 6, parts 1–7 also takes up the same theme for the United States, Canada,

South Africa, South America, Australia, New Zealand, Great Britain.

34 Peter O'Dwyer, *Peter E. Magennis, Priest and Patriot* (Dublin, 1978): this is a work produced in a limited edition by a historian member of his order. It is in no sense a full biography but it is the most comprehensive study of the man to date and perhaps Dr O'Dwyer will extend it soon. See also J. E. McGrath, 'Fr Magennis, Carmelite', in *Whitefriars*, vol. 3, no. 10 (1937), pp. 303–5.

35 De Valera to O'Dwyer, quoted in O'Dwyer, *Peter E. Magennis*, pp. 101–2.

36 Hagan to O'Donnell, 10 January 1924 (Cardinal O'Donnell papers, AAA).

37 Interview with the youthful Bro. Price, who has been in Marcantonio Collonna since 1920 and who numbers Cardinals Benelli and Papalardo among his former pupils of English.

38 *Ibid.*

39 John H. Whyte, '1916 Revolution and Religion', in Frank Martin (ed.), *Leaders and Men of the Easter Rising: Dublin 1916* (Dublin, 1967), pp. 220–6; and Roger McHugh, 'The Catholic Church and the Rising', in Owen Dudley Edwards and Fergus Pyle (eds.) *Dublin 1916* (Dublin, 1968) pp. 196–201.

40 Larkin, 'Church, State and Nation': this essay is relevant to this section. It is based on O'Riordan papers at the Irish College, Rome which were not open to this researcher. The political development of the Irish hierarchy is brilliantly traced in Miller, *Church, State and Nation*. Unfortunately, Dr Miller was unable to gain access to some archives.

41 Brian Farrell, 'Labour and the Irish Political Party System: a Suggested Approach to Analysis', *Economic and Social Review*, vol. 1, no. 3 (1970).

42 Dorothy Macardle, *The Irish Republic* (Dublin, 3rd ed. 1968), pp. 919–22; see Cornelius O'Leary, *Irish Elections 1918–1977: Parties, Voters and Proportional Representation* (Dublin, 1979) pp. 7–8; and *Dail Eireann, Minutes of Proceedings 1919–21* (Government Publications), pp. 22–3.

43 Dan Breen, *My Fight for Irish Freedom* (Tralee, 2nd ed. 1964), p. 41.

44 *Ibid.*, p. 39. This bombastic account of the origins of the violence gives an interesting insight into the mind of one of the most efficient and ruthless gunmen of the period. According to a former Fianna Fail TD, one of the RIC men, who left an invalid wife and family, was shot in the back.

45 Miller, *Church, State and Nation*, p. 404.

46 Interview with Dr Freddie Boland, former secretary of the Department of External Affairs and Chairman of the UN Security Council.

47 Congratulating him on his appointment, Patrick J. Walsh of Dublin wrote on 4 January 1920: 'Nobody, of course, knows better than you do the sinister influences which have been working against you. These influences, inspired from Westminster mainly, have been exerted and have been operating in Rome chiefly. But they have not been by any means confined to the sister isle, or to the Eternal City. Much nearer home and within our own gates, there have been influences from quarters which you may easily surmise, most hostile to you, to your policy and to the whole policy of the Irish College in recent years, and especially since the outbreak of the war for the liberation of small and downtrodden nations'. (Walsh to Hagan, 4 January 1920 (Hagan)). Cardinal Logue, who reluctantly

supported Hagan for the post, was never a very strong admirer of the man's political views. On one occasion, Logue raised the matter of a *prelatura* with Pius XI for Hagan, only to learn: 'we have it to be understood that there was strong opposition among leading Cardinals in curia'. At the time, the Pope also complained, according to Logue, 'that he had never been consulted on the appointment' of Hagan (Logue to Archbishop Byrne, 17 December 1923, Archbishop Edward Byrne papers, DAA).

48 Note on archdiocese secretaries: Michael Curran became Vice-Rector of the Irish College in 1920 after serving as secretary for over a decade to Walsh. The Archbishop had three secretaries. The most senior was Paddy Walsh, who later wrote the biography. He served Walsh for fifteen years and later acted as secretary to Edward Byrne. The two other secretaries were Paddy Dunne and Michael Dwyer. The former was trained in Rome and was a close friend of Hagan. In correspondence it is sometimes difficult to determine who is meant by 'My Dear Paddy'. In the mid-1920s, Tom O'Donnell replaced Dwyer, and in 1930 Mgr Glennon took over and remained as secretary until 1945; he was educated in Salamanca (interview with Mgr Glennon, July 1984).

CHAPTER II. THE PAPACY, THE BISHOPS AND THE ANGLO-IRISH WAR, 1919–1921

1 Earl of Longford and Thomas P. O'Neill, *Eamon de Valera*, p. 89. For a recent survey of the period see Sheila Lawlor, *Britain and Ireland 1914–1923* (Dublin, 1983).

2 Longford and O'Neill, p. 89.

3 Sean T. O'Kelly manuscript (private possession); much of the material will be found in the memoirs published in Irish: Padraig Ó Fiannachta (ed.), *Sean T., Sceal a bheatha o 1916–1923* (Dublin, 1973); however, the manuscript does contain some material not included in the published work.

4 Michael MacWhite profile, *Irish Times*, 26 November 1949. Griffith and MacWhite had been friendly for a number of years; the latter sometimes contributed articles to the *Sinn Fein* paper.

5 Andrew Boyle, *The Riddle of Erskine Childers* (London, 1977) and Erskine Childers, *The Framework of Home Rule* (London, 1911).

6 Desmond FitzGerald papers. For details of FitzGerald and 1916 see Mrs Mabel FitzGerald to Walsh, 1916 (laity file), Archbishop Walsh papers (*DAA*), and *Memoirs of Desmond FitzGerald* (London, 1968), pp. 107–80.

7 See Kathleen Napoli McKenna, 'History of the Irish Bulletin' (an unpublished history of the bulletin by the woman who acted as secretary to FitzGerald and typed every copy). She is married to an Italian general and lives in Rome, where she gave me an extensive interview. Also Desmond FitzGerald, Report on Propaganda Department, June 1920, no. 12 (copy in possession of Mrs McKenna Napoli).

8 The Department really took over from the existing Sinn Fein propaganda

unit which was set up in mid-1917; it changed its name to that of Publicity Department in mid-1919; DE 2/10, DE 2/269.

9 McKenna Napoli manuscript; the latter became Minister for Fine Arts.
10 FitzGerald Report, 2 January 1920.
11 O'Kelly manuscript and Ó Fiannachta (ed.), *Sean T.*, p. 134.
12 Michael A. Ledeen, *D'Annunzio a Fiume* (Rome, 1975); Luigi Sturzo archive, Rome. In *Politics and Morality* (London, 1936), pp. 209–10, Sturzo, writing on the question of tyranny, some years after the Anglo-Irish war had ended, quoted the Abbe Magnin's five conditions for a legitimate revolt:

   (1) a tyranny habitual and not transitory;
   (2) grave tyranny endangering the essential good of the nation;
   (3) tyranny plainly such in the general opinion of honest men;
   (4) impossibility of recourse to other means than revolt;
   (5) serious probability of success.

   And he concludes:

   We cannot subscribe to these five conditions. And therefore we cannot hold the armed revolt of Ireland in 1916–21 to have been legitimate, even though historically justified and though all our sympathies as Catholics and as free men supported her claim. The Bishops of Ireland themselves (unlike certain Irish Bishops in America and Australia) were cautious and sought to further pacification, while the Holy See remained neutral.

13 Writer's interview with the late Canon of St Peter's, Mgr McDaid, the Rector of the Irish College during World War II. He was a clerical student at the time and used to take the copy to the Monsignore for the Rector.
14 George Gavan Duffy to Hagan, 31 December 1919 (Hagan).
15 Sean T. O'Kelly to Hagan, 16 October 1919 (Hagan).
16 E. Cerretti, *Il Cardinale Bonaventura Cerretti* (Rome, 1939): this work contains many references to the ecclesiastic's contacts with the Irish as envoy to Washington and in Australia.
17 For a detailed account of the Vatican mission to Paris, see Giovanni Spadolini, *Il Cardinale Gasparri e la questione romana* (Florence, 1972), pp. 225–48 and F. Margiotta Broglio, *Italia e Santa Sede della grande guerra alla conciliazione: aspetti politici e giuridici* (Bari, 1966).
18 Sean T. O'Kelly to Hagan, undated (Hagan): 'Of course, in all these discussions I made the best possible use of the material you and M. J. C. [Michael J. Curran] had given me. I read over both your letters a couple of times before going there, so that I should have all the points very clear and precisely before my mind.'
19 Sean T. O'Kelly to Hagan, 16 October 1919 (Hagan).
20 Confidential source.
21 Charles Townshend, *The British Campaign in Ireland* (Oxford, 1975), p. 214.
22 Lyons, *Ireland since the Famine*, p. 411 and Robert Kee, *The Green Flag* (London, 1972), p. 669. On 19 November 1920, Bishop Cohalan wrote privately on the question of the MacCurtain killing to Mr Dunlop, authorising Joe Devlin, MP, to 'repeat my offer or challenge' in the Commons. This letter is in the Westminster archives where, no doubt, its contents were brought to the attention of Cardinal Bourne. The quotation is

underlined in heavy pencil (Westminster archive, Bourne papers, no. 5/36a). Swanzy was transferred to the North, where he was shot by the IRA on orders from Michael Collins.

23 *Irish Catholic Directory*, 1921, pp. 548–9.

24 *Ibid.*, pp. 499–507 and Walsh to O'Connell, 11 November 1919 (Walsh papers).

25 *Ibid.*, p. 550.

26 O'Kelly manuscript.

27 Magennis file, O'Kelly speech at Gort Muire, Dublin, 21 July 1955. There is a slight discrepancy in the two accounts. The memoirs make no mention of help from Magennis in drawing up the document, although given the close relationship between the two men, it does not seem unlikely.

28 Hagan's handwritten draft, May 1920, plus the draft of Sean T. O'Kelly with a note by the Vice-Rector, Curran, have survived in the archives of the Irish College (Hagan papers). For the background to the Peace Note, see Dragan R. Zivojinovic, *The United States and Vatican Policies* (Colorado, 1978), pp. 75–96.

29 O'Kelly draft, Hagan archive, May 1920: this section is written in Curran's handwriting although it is written in the first person. I have not seen a copy of the actual memorandum presented to the Pope.

30 O'Kelly manuscript. This point was later echoed in a few episcopal pronouncements, and obviously came from the same source. Thus Logue wrote: 'Even in regular warfare, private assassination would be reprobated, condemned and punished . . . If we made a clean fight for freedom . . . we would finally succeed.' Gilmartin of Tuam made the same point when he advised that 'guerilla war was no war, nor was it war to shoot a policeman from behind a wall and run away' – see Miller, *Church, State and Nation*, p. 479.

31 De Salis to Curzon, 18 June 1920, FO 371 C181/181/22. The prelate referred to may have been Hagan although the latter was not a bishop.

32 *Irish Catholic Directory*, 1921, p. 550; see also Desmond Forrestal, *Oliver Plunkett* (Dublin, 1976). Oliver Plunkett was canonised in 1978.

33 De Salis to Curzon, 20 June 1920, FO 371 C181/181/22.

34 *The Times*, 31 May 1920.

35 O'Kelly manuscript.

36 *Irish Catholic Directory*, 1921, p. 519.

37 O'Connell, *Recollections* and interview with Mgr Denis McDaid, former Rector of the Irish College.

38 De Salis to Curzon, 20 June 1920, FO 371 C181/181/22. Salotti had preached a strongly nationalist sermon at a requiem Mass for the late Mgr O'Riordan. De Salis wrote of the incident: 'Mgr. Salotti, a Vatican official, was severely taken to task earlier in the year for participating in a demonstration at the Irish College while the Rector was understood to have been reprimanded by the Pope himself and reminded that he was in Rome. As to this I cannot speak with certainty but, as regards Mgr. Salotti, the blame inflicted on him was rendered public to a certain degree by the address to me of a strongly-worded note, sent within a couple of days of the occurrence.'

39 *Ibid.*

40 O'Kelly manuscript; this is not an entirely satisfactory source. But there is little reason to doubt the substance of the report even if the Pope was not quite so unguarded in reality.

41 De Salis report, FO 371 C15334/8227/22, p. 5; see also Miller, *Church, State and Nation*, p. 469.

42 Rev. Walter A. Ebsworth, *Archbishop Mannix* (Armadale, 1977), pp. 76–90; this is the latest and most complete biography of Mannix to date. While the author describes the subject as 'the greatest churchman of the twentieth century' he remains critical in some places but is quite partisan in others. For a detached assessment, see Patrick O'Farrell, *The Catholic Church in Australia*, pp. 298–353.

43 De Salis report, FO 371 C15334/8227/22/24. For the reaction of Dail Eireann, see DE 2/452, SPO, Dublin.

44 Miller, *Church, State and Nation*, p. 472. When King George V once received Cardinal Gasquet at a royal garden party, the King suggested that Archbishop Mannix should be kept out of politics and given a high place in the Vatican. 'God forbid' was the Cardinal's comment (Leslie, *Cardinal Gasquet*, p. 16).

45 De Salis report, FO 371 C15334/8227/22.

46 De Salis to Curzon, 28 July 1920, FO 371 C1306/692/22.

47 Alexander Cadogan minute, 22 July 1920, FO 371 C1306/692/22.

48 *Ibid.*, 22 July 1920.

49 De Salis to Curzon, 30 July 1920, *ibid*.

50 Alexander Cadogan minute, 7 August 1920, *ibid*.

51 Thomas E. Hachey, 'The Quarantine of Archbishop Mannix: a British preventive policy during the Anglo-Irish troubles', *Irish University Review*, vol. 1, no. 1, Autumn 1970; see also Cardinal Bourne papers and newspaper reports in *The Times* and *The Manchester Guardian*, 9 August 1920.

52 Townshend, *The British Campaign*, p. 214.

53 Moirin Chavasse, *Terence MacSwiney* (Dublin, 1961), pp. 140–90, and Miller, *Church, State and Nation*, p. 461.

54 In a signed, front-page article, *Il Popolo d'Italia* (29 August 1920) had the headline *MacSwiney agonizza. Viva la republica irlandese*; the hunger strike was praised by Mussolini as 'uno stoicismo superbo'. The Partito Popolare used one occasion in the Italian parliament during a debate on the Treaty of Rapallo, in November to introduce a motion in favour of Ireland; Signor Murri shouted 'What about martyred Ireland?' and 'suddenly deputies all over the chamber rose to their feet shouting enthusiastically: "Long live the Irish Republic"' (*Irish Independent*, 7 November 1920). At a meeting in Milan of Catholic Action, in November 1920, further support was pledged to the cause of Ireland. In March, the following year, a closed meeting was held at the Teatro Eliseo in Rome and was addressed mainly by prominent members of the Partito Popolare, including the future leader of the Christian Democrats, Alcide de Gaspari, while the chair was occupied by the brother of Giovanni Montini (Paul VI). The younger Montini was a visitor to the Irish College, and is believed to have been sympathetic to Irish nationalism.

55 *Irish Catholic Directory*, 1921, pp. 556–61.

56 Confidential clerical source; Cardinal Mercier and the Belgian hierarchy sent a letter of public support to the Irish hierarchy. (The text may have been drafted by an Irish cleric living in Belgium.)

57 *The Times*, 26 October 1920.

58 De Salis to Curzon, 12 November 1920, FO 371 C11453/181/22.

59 Murray letter (Hagan); When Moirin Chavasse was researching her biography of Terence MacSwiney in the early 1950s she was assisted anonymously by Curran, who was then a parish priest in Dublin. He was certain that the Gasquet–Langdon–Merry del Val faction was responsible for the attempt to have MacSwiney condemned. Two bodies of the curia had the competence to deal with the matter, the Holy Office and the Sacred Penitentiary. The matter was referred to the latter: 'Only at the last moment did this action reach the ear of a prominent Irish ecclesiastic through the indiscreet remark of an English religious unable to restrain his anti-Irish feelings.' Curran's reminiscence could refer to either himself or Fr Murray. It is probable that more than one Irish clergyman heard the rumours. But Curran, in the absence of Hagan, who was in Ireland, reported to Cerretti on 21 September that no pronouncement should be made before the Irish views were known to the Holy Office. Cerretti, who had daily audiences with the Pope, sent for Magennis; the latter provided the necessary documents 'and in one way and another the intrigue was checked.' Curran also stated that Gasquet had first requested the condemnation from London. He cites Cardinal Silj, cousin of the Cardinal Secretary of State, as his source. He also stated that at a dinner in the Irish College, in 1930, Cerretti mentioned that Benedict was moved by one particular defence of MacSwiney's actions from Mgr Lottini, the Assessor of the Holy Office. According to Curran, Cardinal Giorgi, the Major Penitentiary, was 'most definitely of the opinion that the Lord Mayor's action was justifiable'. Curran also mentions that in mid-December an unsigned article appeared in *Civiltà cattolica* 'which closed the discussion'. It was written by Fr Cappelle SJ, of the Gregorian University and Consultor of many Roman congregations. It should also be observed here that the vigour of the October pastoral might not have been unrelated to the fact that there were rumours in Rome about a possible condemnation of MacSwiney. Hagan would certainly have made that point forcefully. See Chavasse, *Terence MacSwiney*, pp. 158–61 and Curran memorandum, Terence MacSwiney papers, P48c/204(a), Archives Department, UCD.

But Michael Browne, later Bishop of Galway, was also in a good position to evaluate the situation in Rome. In a series of comments on the draft book (Michael Browne to Chavasse, 22 February, 2 March and 5 June 1954, MacSwiney papers P48c Chavasse 123–5), he challenged the Curran interpretation of events just discussed. He argued that events in Rome relating to the MacSwiney case had to be interpreted in the light of the theological debate which took place on the morality of hunger striking, following the death of Thomas Ashe in 1917, in the pages of the *Irish Ecclesiastical Record*, fifth series, vols. 12 and 13, August 1918 to July 1919. The Professor of Theology at Clonliffe College, John Waters, denied the lawfulness of the hunger strike while his counterpart in Maynooth, Patrick

Cleary, defended the proposition in two articles. There was a separate debate in the *Irish Theological Quarterly* later between Drs Fitzpatrick and Kelleher. Browne made the point that the matter was in dispute:

The Holy Office is the Congregation which deals with disputed points of faith and morals. The question of hunger strike was disputed. If it was held to be wrong by the official theologians of Archbishop Walsh of Dublin in 1918–1919 and by many others in good faith and for theological reasons, you should not write as if it were wrong for the Cardinal Sec. of the Holy Office to consider it. That was his duty in canon law. There is no proof that he performed that duty in an unworthy fashion. He gave full freedom to his Undersecretary Mgr Lottini – that is the meaning of Assessor – to defend hunger strike and report in this sense to the Pope. For all you and I know he may have come to that decision himself. In fact it would be most unlikely that the Undersecretary would go diametrically against the Secretary. The Holy See did not make a decision because for one reason it avoids deciding on a particular individual's act: it tries to keep doctrinal decisions to the general level.

Browne further mentioned that her discussion made too much use of the accusations of intrigue and clique: 'It is not right to use anonymous hearsay evidence to denigrate Cardinals, even though English. I have no brief for either Merry del Val or Gasquet. But there is no evidence that the former abused his high office for political purpose, a serious charge that reflects on the whole Curia.' Browne further pointed out that 'we should not pretend that English Catholics are the only nation who tried to influence the Vatican in favour of their national policy and in favour of their national interests; they all do it – English, Germans, Americans, French and *ourselves*'. He also denied that the article in *Civiltà cattolica* 'closed the discussion'. It was hostile to MacSwiney. He described it as a 'third-rate foreign article'. In fine, Browne did not feel it correct to represent the debate on the lawfulness of the hunger strike 'as a political move of English Catholics: very many Irish ecclesiastics had doubts in conscience on the matter, for instance Kelly, Archbishop of Sydney' (who was a personal friend of Cardinal Gasquet).

60 Townshend, *The British Campaign*, pp. 129–31; Tom Bowden, 'Ireland', in Michael Elliot-Bateman, John Ellis and Tom Bowden eds., *Revolt to Revolution, Studies in the Nineteenth and Twentieth Century European Experience* (Manchester, 1974), pp. 137–278, provides one of the most detailed and scholarly accounts of these incidents.

61 Hagan to Logue, 9 February 1921 (Logue). Della Torre's letter on the Irish question appeared on the same day.

62 Lloyd George to Bourne, 29 November 1920 (Bourne).

63 Cohalan to Mr Dunlop, 19 November 1920 (Bourne).

64 *Freeman's Journal* and *The Times* (London), 28 November – 20 December 1920; in particular, see 14 and 20 December in both papers. It is impossible to ascertain whether the bishop was reported accurately by both papers. Unfortunately, I am told that Cohalan's private papers have not survived, although rumours continue to persist to the contrary. For details of the burning of Cork, see pamphlet compiled by Alfred O'Rahilly, *Who burnt Cork City?* (Dublin, 1921).

65 Collins to Hales, 12 January 1921 (Hales). Another republican said: 'My

own reaction was one of anger . . . For days I brooded over the decree, knowing full well how deeply religious the IRA were. However, in the event, every active service man in our brigade continued the fight, most priests continued to administer the sacraments, and the IRA practised their religion as before.' When another IRA man, Liam Lynch, was told he might be excommunicated, he laughed and said: 'Old Cohalan had dinner with Strickland, I suppose, before he took the pen in his fist, but nobody minds him now.' (quoted in Cardinal Tomas Ó Fiaich, 'The Catholic Clergy and the Independence Movement', *Capuchin Annual*, 1970, pp. 480–502). The first priest to die was Fr Michael Griffin of the diocese of Clonfert on 14 November 1920; a second Cork priest, Fr James O'Callaghan, was killed on 15 May 1921. The late Bishop of Ferns, Donal Herlihy, was shot and wounded by soldiers when he was a boy.

66 *Freeman's Journal*, 14 and 16 December 1920; in an editorial, the paper said the murder would 'send a thrill of horror through Ireland'.

67 *Freeman's Journal*, 22 November–2 December 1920 and *Irish Catholic Directory*, 1921, pp. 541–4.

68 Roger Sweetman memoir (in possession of his son, Fr Michael Sweetman SJ).

69 Curzon minute, 10 December 1920, FO 371 C13755/181/22.

70 Eyre A. Crowe to de Salis, 13 December 1920, *ibid*. The Foreign Office wanted corporate action by the bishops which might reflect the headline set by Cork, who had just issued his statement on excommunication: 'I need not tell you – who are an Irishman – what effect such action would be on your country', Crowe said to de Salis.

71 Eyre A. Crowe to de Salis, 13 December 1920.

72 De Salis to Curzon, 13 December 1920, FO 371 C13755/181/22.

73 De Salis to Curzon, 12 November 1920, FO 371 C11453/181/22.

74 Miller, *Church, State and Nation*, pp. 467–77; a letter from Conor Clune's employer, Edward E. Lysaght, appeared in the *Freeman's Journal* on 30 November. He was at pains to dismiss the allegation that Clune was involved in Sinn Fein. He said that he was employed as a clerk and had never been a member of the IRA. Clune had come to Dublin only at the last minute as a replacement for another employee. Clune was not using the trip as a cloak for other business. The notebook found on him 'was solely concerned with my affairs', while notes relating to the procuring of passports referred to the applications of Mr and Mrs Lysaght who were travelling to the South of France. It is most likely that the youth's uncle, Archbishop Clune, was made aware of his nephew's innocence and the fact that he was shot in dubious circumstances.

75 Reminiscences of Mgr John T. McMahon, *Clare Champion*, 24 and 30 June, 7 July 1972; see also *Saturday Record*, 22 June 1935. (I am grateful to Bishop Michael Harty and Fr Ignatius Murphy for making this information known to me.)

76 O'Kelly to Hagan, 11 January 1921 (Hagan).

77 Hagan to O'Donnell, 25 January 1921 (O'Donnell). For an account of Clune's visit to Ireland, see also Timothy M. Healy, *Letters and Leaders of my Day* (London, 1928), vol. II pp. 634–5.

78 Hagan to O'Donnell, 25 January 1921 (Hagan).

79 Hagan to Logue, 24 January 1921 (Logue).

80 Murray to O'Kelly, 19 February 1921 (Hagan).

81 Mannix lived a 'subdued' life in London, but it was not subdued enough for some of the English hierarchy. Even the pro-Irish Amigo was quite concerned about the flourishes of rhetorical nationalism indulged in by Mannix and on one occasion he wrote to the Bishop of Portsmouth posing the question 'can't something be done to stop Mannix?' (Amigo papers). Every effort was made to get him to modify his language. Cardinal Bourne arranged for him to meet the editor of *The Times*, Wickham Steed. The latter believed that it was a mistake to stop Mannix going to Ireland. There, the actions of his fellow countrymen would have forced him to modify his attitude. The meeting was not a success. Mannix did 'not appreciate the inexpediency of talking in a semi-propagandist way to reporters instead of making his position clear in a statesmanlike way by considered utterance' (letters of 10 and 12 August 1920, Westminster archive Bourne papers, no. 5/6a). The following year, when Mannix was given a farewell dinner in London by members of the clergy, a Fr Basil Barton commented to Bourne's secretary, Jackman, that Cotter of Portsmouth had run the Mannix campaign: 'What a prelate does in his own diocese is, of course, his own concern . . . but [he] has also taken the opportunity to let his political tongue run riot about His Eminence.' As regards a presentation and a dinner 'there's only one presentation I would willingly make, and that is, the gift of a railway ticket to Portsmouth, coupled with the pious hope that His Lordship remain there' (28 April 1921, Westminster archive Bourne papers, no. 5/6a).

87 Another F.O. official's minute, 22 May 1921.

83 Patrick Lennon diary entry, Melbourne 2 July 1963. See also Memorandum of Mannix's visit to Pope drawn up by Hagan, 4 April 1921 (Hagan).

84 *Irish Catholic Directory*, 1922, pp. 592–3.

85 Sean T. O'Kelly to Hagan, 27 May 1921 (Hagan). In an earlier letter on 6 May O'Kelly had written: 'so once again English influence at the Vatican has been too strong to allow of their expressing an opinion of the shocking immoralities and brutalities being inflicted by Protestant England on Catholic Ireland'.

86 Lord Curzon minute, 31 May 1921.

87 Another F.O. official's minute, 22 May 1921.

88 *Ibid.*

89 D. O'Hegarty to de Valera, 24 February 1921 (SPO, DE 2/396). I am grateful to Professor T. Desmond Williams and Brian Farrell of UCD for drawing attention to this file.

90 De Valera to Hegarty, 4 March 1921, DE 2/396, DE 2/3, DE 2/314.

91 Confidential clerical source.

92 Miller, *Church, State and Nation*, pp. 480–2.

93 President to Publicity Department, 16 June 1921, CO 904/23(7), PRO (London), partially quoted in Miller, *Church, State and Nation*, p. 483. This was one of the many documents taken in a raid on de Valera's home in

Blackrock, on 22 June 1921. The captured documents also included a letter from Hagan to Cait O'Kelly.

94 Confidential clerical source.

95 Miller, *Church, State and Nation*, p. 483.

96 *Ibid.* There is some doubt about this; I have not found any elderly priest in what was the diocese of Ross to confirm this view of Kelly. The political views of Kelly can be determined from his correspondence with the influential and widely respected Rector of the Irish College in Paris, Patrick Boyle, CM. From his letters – which are short but descriptive – the Bishop appears to have been pro-Home Rule and also pro-British. He realised the dangers of postponing the move indefinitely: on 10 September 1914, he wrote to Boyle: 'I wish the government would decide the Home Rule issue. The physical force party are now pro-German and are working earnestly on the old hatred of England on the part of young Irish men. We live in troubled times. Money has become the God, not only of the wicked, but, to a large extent, of the good.' On 22 June 1916, he wrote from the Gresham Hotel, Dublin: 'I never saw Ireland so disunited. I cannot forecast the issue – some of the probable issues I tremble to contemplate with horror. Let us hope and pray.' After the failure of the Irish Convention, he wrote, on 24 May 1918: 'Everything was full of hope and lightness for our country. Today all is gloom and darkness – all the old evils are loose. I am sorry Lord Berty has left. I never met Lord Derby. See our friend Sir Eyre Crowe in today's papers.' Kelly wrote after general elections on 6 January 1919: 'All Ireland declared itself Sinn Fein . . . This day last year in the convention we had a splendid settlement in our hands. Now our [side] threw it away'. In another letter (26 October 1920) he spoke of the chaos in Cork and particularly in his own diocese. Of one incident, 'some blackguards fired at the police'. On 10 July 1920 he quotes a clerical source which blames 'pure communism' for conflict in Cork. It is not unreasonable to conclude that Kelly would have been vigorously opposed to de Valera and Sinn Fein on the basis of the above correspondence. Whether he would have gone as far as breaking the confidentiality rule at an episcopal meeting remains a matter for speculation. In the circumstances, it seems unlikely but not out of the question. It should be noted that Kelly *was* Second Secretary of the episcopal Standing Committee.

97 *Irish Catholic Directory*, 1922, pp. 594–5.

CHAPTER III. THE HIERARCHY AND THE TREATY

1 P. F. Quinlan interview; the late Captain Quinlan was in a good position to judge. He was active in the North Cork area.

2 For the nationalist view of the Truce negotiations see *Official Correspondence relating to the Peace Negotiations June–September 1921* (Dublin, 1921).

3 Statement of American Catholic hierarchy, *Irish Catholic Directory*, pp. 597–8.

4 O'Kelly to Hagan, 4 November 1921 (Hagan).

5 *Ibid.*, 17 November 1921.

6 Gavan Duffy to Hagan, 1 December 1921 (Hagan).

7 Confidential source.

8 Statement of bishops, 13 December 1921, *Irish Catholic Directory*, 1922.

9 Logue to Hagan, 10 December 1921 (Hagan).

10 Curran to Byrne, 14 December 1921 (Byrne).

11 Memorandum drawn up by Hagan and dated 7 December(?); but because it has a reference to a letter written by Fogarty (dated 31 December) it would appear to be a revised version of the earlier document to Borgongini Duca.

12 Curran to Byrne, 14 December 1921 (Byrne).

13 Sean T. O'Kelly to Hagan, 21 December 1921 (Hagan).

14 Fogarty to Hagan, 31 December 1921 (Hagan).

15 Gilmartin to Hagan, 19 January 1922 (Hagan).

16 Hallinan to the press, 31 December 1921, *Irish Catholic Directory*, 1922, p. 541.

17 Logue preaching in Armagh, 1 January 1922, *Irish Catholic Directory*, 1922, p. 542.

18 De Valera to Hagan, 13 January 1922 (Hagan).

19 This was not a popular contemporary view of de Valera.

20 *Irish Catholic Directory*, 1923, p. 544.

21 Hagan to Byrne, 7 October 1921 (Byrne).

22 Robert Aubert, *The Church in a Secular Age*: vol. 5, *The Christian Centuries* (London, 1978), p. 545. This authoritative work is one of the most critical accounts of recent Catholic Church history to have been written. The conclave, which opened on 3 February, was dominated by two opposing groups. There was a strong conservative school wishing for a return to the rigid ecclesiastical policies of Pius X and there were those who wanted a continuation of the more open policy of the late Pope. The second group favoured Gasparri and his votes reached twenty-four in the first ballot. The first group opted initially for Merry del Val, but when his votes stuck at seventeen they switched to La Fontaine, patriarch of Venice, who in turn soon reached a ceiling of twenty-two. On the ninth ballot, votes began to go to Damiano Achille Ratti. He was elected on 5 February by forty-two votes out of fifty-four.

23 Hagan to Byrne, 21 February 1923 (Byrne).

24 Hansjakob Stehle, *Eastern Politics of the Vatican 1917–1979* (Ohio, 1981), pp. 11–33; *Catholic Encyclopedia*, s.v. Pius XI; William Telling, *The Pope in Politics: the Life and Work of Pius XI* (London, 1937); Denis Gwynn, *Pius XI* (London, 1932); Philip Hughes, *Pope Pius XI* (London) and Mgr R. Fontanelle, *Pope Pius XI*, (English translation, London, c. 1933).

25 Hagan to Byrne (not sent), 7 February 1922 (Hagan).

26 Byrne to Hagan, 2 February 1922 (Hagan).

27 Details of exchanges between the Department of Foreign Affairs and Count O'Kelly, in Rome, can be found in the following references: Cabinet files S5/857A (SPO, Dublin); Count O'Byrne to Gavan Duffy, no. 1, 23 February 1922; *ibid.*, no. 2, 28 February 1922; and Gavan Duffy to Count O'Byrne, no. 38, 15 March 1922 (FitzGerald).

28 Hagan to Byrne, 22 March 1922 (Byrne).

29 Curran to Byrne, 5 April 1922 (Byrne); Ireland became a republic in 1949.
30 Fogarty to Hagan, 11 April 1922 (Hagan).
31 O'Donnell to Hagan, 10 April 1922 (Hagan).
32 Logue to Byrne, 5 April 1922 (Byrne).
33 *Ibid.*, 15 April 1922.
34 *Freeman's Journal*, 28 April 1922.
35 *Ibid.*, 29 April 1922; despite the attack on the paper in which the entire printing press was destroyed, the *Freeman* managed to publish a stencilled edition for a number of weeks. Cartoons depicted a comely Cathleen Ni Houlihan suffering indignities and rebuffs from 'republicans'. The paper also carried on a fierce cartoon campaign against Sir Henry Wilson.
36 The turnout was very high in cities like Dublin, Cork, Limerick and Waterford. The *Freeman's Journal* was scathing in its criticism of the republicans. One cartoon showed two 'gunmen' looking out from the Four Courts at the throng of organised labour.
37 Confidential source.
38 *Ibid.*
39 *Ibid.*
40 *Freeman's Journal*, 27 April 1922.
41 *Ibid.*
42 Byrne to Hagan, 1 May 1922 (Hagan).
43 Brian Farrell, 'Drafting of Irish Free State Constitution' (in four sections, *The Irish Jurist*, vol. 6, new series (1970), pp. 115–40, pp. 343–56; Vol. 7, new series (1971), pp. 111–35, pp. 345–58. Kennedy acted for the Provisional Government (see section 1, p. 130). Byrne of Dublin did not feel overly concerned; there was no need for the Church to supervise the drafting of the constitution. There was no real conflict of interest or ideology.
44 Confidential source.
45 Curran to Hagan, 20 June 1922 (Hagan).
46 T. Desmond Williams interview with W. T. Cosgrave. The sentence quoted is a paraphrase of the points made by Cosgrave as recorded by the most eminent of Irish historians.
47 Curran to Hagan, 28 and 29 June 1922 (Hagan).
48 Gavan Duffy speech (Gavan Duffy papers).
49 Curran to Hagan, 28 and 29 June 1922 (Hagan).
50 *Ibid.*
51 J.F. D'Alton to Hagan, 1 July 1922 (Hagan).
52 Curran to Hagan, 10 July 1922 (Hagan).
53 *Ibid.*
54 Maurice Moynihan, *Speeches and Statements by Eamon de Valera 1917–1973* (Dublin, 1980), p. 107.
55 John Moher, a former Fianna Fail TD, was a close friend of Sean Moylan, who had played a leading role in the IRA from 1919 to 1921. The latter was in Dublin with Liam Lynch. They were staying at Wynns hotel. Both men tried to stop the fighting and visited the Chief of Staff, General Mulcahy, to urge restraint. He, according to Mr Moher, 'wiped the floor with them'. They then went to Kingsbridge, and got the train as far as Naas, com-

mandeered a car belonging to a retired colonel, and stopped off at a 'Free State' barracks in Kilkenny where they were given a meal and a fill of petrol. They went to Limerick, where Moylan tried to work out a truce with the commander Denis Hannigan. But it broke down soon after. Moher said that Moylan was very anxious to avoid civil war and he did everything he could to stop hostilities. But within weeks of the outbreak of violence, Moylan was conscious of a bitterness which had never before existed. Houses which he had used when 'on the run' were closed to him. Lynch, unlike Moylan, was not a politician. He was quite fanatical. But he was as confused as Moylan at the outbreak of hostilities. Lynch had worked in hardware stores in Fermoy and Mitchelstown. He was a member of the AOH and had been greatly affected by the death on hunger strike of Michael Fitzgerald (John Moher interview, October 1982).

56 Interview with the distinguished Irish diplomat, Dr Con Cremin, 1983. Frank Aiken, according to Dan Bryan, was being supplied by GHQ up to the attack on the Four Courts.

57 Griffith's private secretary, Kathleen McKenna Napoli, was convinced that this was brought on by the strain of work and by the tensions which existed between strong personalities inside the Provisional Government.

58 T. Desmond Williams, profile, *Irish Times* (undated), 1956. Unfortunately, Cosgrave has not yet been the subject of a major biography. It is to be hoped that Maurice Manning will soon complete his work in this area. But it will be impossible to surpass this brilliant description by Professor Williams of a politician who has not received his due recognition: 'If any man can claim outstanding credit for the evolution of a society which is at once conservative and yet also "liberal" in its constitution, it is William T. Cosgrave . . . because he, more than any other of his colleagues, impressed in unobtrusive fashion the traditional pattern of the old upon the new Ireland which he was called upon to lead at its most critical turning point.' I am deeply indebted to Professor Williams for providing me with interview notes which he made with the late W. T. Cosgrave.

59 O'Kelly to Hagan, 26 August 1922 (Hagan).

60 Mulcahy to Hagan, 2 September 1922 (Hagan).

61 Hagan received some correspondence from Mellowes and O'Connor which was not disheartening: 'You will find that he is at one with us in a passionate longing that the section of our countrymen now in arms against the Republic should end the senseless and criminal strife and unite us in its defence against the common enemy whose devilish machinations have, by the aid of the powerful and corrupt press in this country, stampeded them into continuing the war which the British forces hitherto failed to make effective.' (6 September 1922).

62 O'Doherty to Hagan, 11 November 1922 (Hagan).

63 SPO S1792.

64 *Irish Times*, 11 October 1922.

65 Moynihan, *Speeches and Statements*, p. 108.

66 *Dail Debates*, vol. 1, col. 2267, 17 November 1922.

67 Andrew Boyle, *The Riddle of Erskine Childers* (London, 1977) and Terence

de Vere White, *Kevin O'Higgins* (London, 1948), pp. 124–8.

68 O'Donnell to Hagan, 25 November 1922. As the policy of executions progressed, O'Donnell himself was to suffer because of the general attitude of the Church towards republicans: 'My native home and everything in it was burned down on the night of St Patrick's day with considerable harshness or cruelty to the inmates, as a reprisal [for Free State executions at Drumboe]'. As it turned out, O'Donnell had, when he heard of the planned executions, spent 'the entire evening' and managed after 'hours' to make 'telephonic communication with Dublin and sent most earnest representations against the executions' (Hagan).

69 Hagan to Byrne, 2 December 1922.

70 The communiqué read:

The execution took place this morning at Mountjoy Jail of the following persons taken in arms against the Irish Government: –

| RORY O'CONNOR, | JOSEPH McKELVEY, and |
| LIAM MELLOWS, | RICHARD BARRETT, |

as reprisal for the assassination on his way to Dail Eireann on the 7th December of Brigadier Sean Hales, TD and as a solemn warning to those associated with them who are engaged in a conspiracy of assassination against the representatives of the Irish people. (*Irish Times*, 9 December 1922).

71 Magennis to Hagan, 9 December 1922.

72 On the eve of the executions, the Archbishop had gone to plead with Cosgrave not to carry out the decision of the Executive Council. But he was not listened to despite the personal bond of friendship between the two men. (The writer is grateful to Professor T. Desmond Williams for the information which was given to the latter in an interview with W. T. Cosgrave.)

73 Byrne to Cosgrave, 10 December 1922 (Byrne). It is not clear whether this letter was ever sent. No copy has been found in government archives.

74 Interview with Bishop Dunne, Dublin, June 1981. On 8 December 1922 the Dail was the scene of heated exchanges. The four executed men had been in custody for five months. 'I am almost forced to say that they have killed the new state at its birth. I cannot imagine that anyone who is thinking in terms of anything but vengeance can defend this action . . . There is no pretence of legality. There is not even the trial guaranteed under the rules authorised. The offence these men committed was an offence commited before July' (Tom Johnson). Gavan Duffy asked repeatedly 'How long is this Corsican vendetta to contunue? These men who were executed this morning were your prisoners of war – prisoners for several months – and they are put to death because somebody else killed Sean Hales, and put to death by a Government . . . You stand self-condemned on your own Constitution.' (*Dail Debates*. vol. 2, cols. 49–51, 8 December 1922). Johnson engaged in a long correspondence with Cosgrave, on the executions. Johnson had heard that the first the parents of the four men, executed on 17 November, knew of the event was when they read the evening newspapers. Cosgrave replied that in future efforts would be made to communicate with the relatives by wire *after* the executions had taken place. Cosgrave turned down a request

for trials to be held in public or for the proceedings to be published in the press.

Over seventy were ultimately executed by the government during the Civil War. The remains were buried in barracks or prison grounds. Efforts by relatives to have the remains handed over to them failed. In 1924, when government troops evacuated certain barracks throughout the country orders were given by the Commander-in-Chief, General Eoin O'Duffy, that it was 'necessary that the remains of executed Irregulars interred therein should be exhumed and re-interred at the nearest permanent post' (SPO S1884).

75 *Irish Times*, 18 September 1981.
76 Mr Liam Cosgrave to author, 15 November 1983.
77 This is speculation on my part. But in a letter to Dublin, Hagan identified O'Higgins, in particular, as 'not the man of the hour'. Fresh from his failed peace mission to Dublin, the Rector argued that the latter was 'out for a diehard policy in which he has been able so far to drag a few lesser lights with him'. He had much greater confidence in Mulcahy and Cosgrave. So, too, had Byrne. Yet, according to Ernest Blythe, O'Higgins asked at the Executive Council meeting at which the decision to execute the four was taken: 'is there no other way?' O'Connor had been best man at O'Higgins' wedding. (Blythe interview in film, *Ireland: the Making of the Republic*, 1975.) But that did not mean that O'Higgins opposed the executions policy generally. As a lawyer, however, he must have been aware of the illegality of shooting men without trial 'as a reprisal'. In the context of this debate, it is relevant to quote the well known views of Professor T. Desmond Williams on the war. It is worth noting that he does not hold that 'extremism' was the monopoly of any one side:

All wars are the product of indecision, chance, misunderstanding, and personal will. They come from the environment in which people work and the conviction of those in power. The war under discussion might have started earlier, or later. In either case, the outcome for Ireland would have been different. Perhaps the extremists on both sides alone knew their own minds and the contingent situation better than those of more moderate opinions. But moderation, reluctance to engage in a war with one's own countrymen may be of greater value than the confidence and arrogance of those who see right and wrong too clearly. The balance between the forces of liberty and order may have depended upon those who found it hardest to decide between black and white, even if muddle and panic deriving from these decisions greatly contributed to the origins and conduct of this particular war. A full state of war lasted for nearly a year, but its after-effects for much longer. (T. Desmond Williams, 'From the Treaty to the Civil War', in T. Desmond Williams (ed.), *The Irish Struggle* (London, 1966), pp. 127–8).

CHAPTER IV. THE VATICAN AND THE CIVIL WAR

1 Hagan to Byrne, 13 November 1922 (Byrne).
2 Confidential memorandum accompanying letter of 13 November, and sent

by hand. Only one copy was made, and Hagan asked Byrne to show it to O'Donnell and other interested parties. Hagan also wrote to O'Donnell saying that he had sent an important communication to Byrne which might interest him (Hagan to O'Donnell, 14 November 1922 (O'Donnell)). The memorandum is to be found with the letter to Byrne.

3 Logue to Byrne, 22 November 1922 (Byrne). The letter was an implied criticism of Hagan's role in Rome.

4 *Ibid.*

5 *Ibid.*

6 Hagan to Borgongini Duca, 13 November 1922 (Hagan).

7 Byrne to Hagan, 28 November 1922 (Byrne). Italian translation in Hagan papers. (On 13 November, Hagan tried to persuade both Byrne and O'Donnell to travel to Rome for the Consistory on 12 December 1922.)

8 Hagan to Byrne, 24 November 1922 (Byrne).

9 *Ibid.*, 28 November 1922.

10 *Ibid.*, 22 November 1922.

11 *Ibid.*, 28 November 1922.

12 *Ibid.*, 4 December 1922.

13 Con Murphy to Hagan, December 1922 (Hagan). The Executive Council discussed Murphy's application for a passport for Rome on 4 October 1922 and granted his request (SPO 1792).

14 Curran to 'Carissimo' (possibly Paddy Dunne, secretary to the Archbishop), 4 January 1923 (Byrne).

15 Bishop Amigo of Southwark to Hagan, 10 December 1922 (Hagan).

16 Curran to 'Carissimo', 4 January 1923 (Byrne).

17 Logue to Byrne, 21 January 1923 and Logue to Byrne, 17 December 1923 (Byrne).

18 Confidential clerical source. The matter was brought, at Gasparri's request, before the Standing Committee of bishops in January. 'This step is a new departure, and you can easily grasp the importance of it.' (Hagan to Paddy Dunne (secretary of Byrne), 23 January 1923, DAA Byrne papers. In the same letter, Hagan said he was glad that no episcopal pronouncement was made: 'Apparently emanations of that kind do not produce much effect.'

19 Fogarty to Hagan, 10 January 1923 (Hagan).

20 Fr Fred Morrissey, James St., Dublin, to Hagan, 20 February 1923 (Hagan).

21 *Ibid.*, Col. Dan Bryan, who was in the arresting party, is unaware of such details, which would indicate that it was priestly gossip.

22 Dr McCaffrey to Logue, 2 March 1923 (Logue).

23 Hagan to Art O'Brien, 13 February 1923 (Hagan).

24 Sir Anthony Rhodes gives a highly coloured account of the 'Marquis McSweeney' who obtained a high post at the Vatican during the First World War: 'It was subsequently discovered that he too was not a nobleman, but an Irish butcher's son who had married the Brazilian heiress, Cavaleranti de Albuquerque. He became suspect to the British Embassy because, having divorced the Brazilian lady, he married Her Highness Countess Anna von Schlitz, a relative of the German Kaiser. The English diplomats in Rome became convinced that this "Marquis McSweeney" was working for the German Secret Service, while protected by his official

status at the Vatican.' Sir Anthony had earlier referred to Count Kelly (*sic*) as a 'member of the Third International'. Sir Anthony Rhodes, *The Power of Rome in the Twentieth Century: The Vatican in the Age of Liberal Democracies, 1870–1922* (London, 1983), p. 157; this chapter is colourfully entitled 'The Irish Bane'.

25 Hagan to Dublin, 23 January 1923 (Byrne).
26 Hagan to Dublin, 2 February 1923 (Byrne).
27 Hagan memorandum on Luzio mission (Byrne).
28 *Freeman's Journal* telegram, 7 March 1923 (Hagan).
29 Hagan to Byrne, 7 March 1923 (Byrne).
30 *Ibid.*
31 Hagan memorandum (Byrne).
32 *Ibid.*
33 Hagan to Byrne, 8 March 1923 (Byrne).
34 *Ibid.*
35 Hagan to Byrne, 12 March 1923 (Byrne).
36 Hagan to Byrne, 8 March 1923 (Byrne).
37 Hagan to Byrne, 12 March 1923 (Byrne).
38 Curran to O'Donnell, 14 March 1923 (O'Donnell).
39 *Ibid.*; see also Curran memorandum to the Minister of External Affairs, 24 April 1923 (FitzGerald). This memorandum is difficult to date precisely and cannot be fitted with certainty into the chronology of the Luzio visit. But the arguments used, even if they relate to a different period, throw additional light on the Vice-Rector's thinking on this matter. Curran suggested that a permanent delegate or nuncio 'may be a source of trouble to us'. But 'at the right time it may be met in a way that will be useful and honourable to us', he added. If the possibility arose, the government was to insist 'that such a representative should be an Irish and not an Italian ecclesiastic'. The reason was that 'any Italian will be open to English influence whether exercised in London or in Rome. Only an Irish ecclesiastic can at the same time be loyal to the interest of the Holy See and Ireland.' In Rome, Curran argued that the Irish Church, which also included America, Australia and South Africa, was without a delegate: 'Our Catholic populations overseas entitle us to be the authoritative spokesman of Irish- and English-speaking Catholics. The English have successfully arrogated to themselves this position. It is a usurpation which can only be effectively displaced by the appointment of competent Irishmen to the Curia and Congregations.' An obvious first step to strengthen the Irish position in Rome was to 'demand and secure a Cardinalate in Dublin. The present position is absurd for many reasons, and not confined to the one fact that Armagh is not at the moment within the jurisdiction. Where the seat of Government is the Cardinal should be. The sooner this is in effect the better.' Curran also made points about the change in the system of electing bishops which would be necessitated by the appointment of a nuncio in Dublin.
40 Marquis MacSwiney to Desmond FitzGerald, 28 May 1923 (FitzGerald).
41 Theo Russell to Curzon, 12 March 1923, FO 371 C5143/443/22.
42 Theo Russell to Curzon, 17 March 1923, FO 371 C5027/443/22.

43 Magennis himself had given this version of the mission's origins to Sean MacBride; interview with writer, 22 July 1978. It has not been possible to confirm this account from sources inside the order.

44 Theo Russell to Curzon, 17 March 1923, FO 371 C5027/443/22.

45 A copy of this message was sent on to Dublin and may well have helped confirm the growing suspicion there that the envoy was in fact republican in his sympathies (SPO. S2198).

46 Interview with Bishop Dunne, former private secretary to Archbishop Byrne. Both men were in Rome in 1924, and the Pope said to Byrne that he realised the mission was a failure from the time he heard that Luzio had not visited the Archbishop of Dublin before going to Armagh.

47 Lionel Curtis (Under-Secretary in charge of Southern Ireland at the Colonial Office) minute, 24 April 1923, FO 371 C7401/443/22.

48 *Ibid.* The Russell telegram was sent by the Colonial Office to Dublin. The Free State had its suspicions partially confirmed that Luzio was there to scrutinise the behaviour of the Irish government. The feeling that the Vatican was putting the Irish government on trial was an exaggerated feeling, but it was one which did not put either Cosgrave or his cabinet colleagues in the mood to treat the unfortunate envoy, Luzio, with the respect his mission probably deserved. It would also appear that the Free State was misled into thinking that Luzio was in some sense a personal friend of de Valera's and therefore likely to be sympathetic to the 'irregulars'. In fact Luzio, as subsequent events proved, was far from being on the side of de Valera. He wanted to bring about an end to the hostilities and set about it in a manner calculated to cause maximum offence to Church and State. In this case the pride of both parties, for differing reasons, was easily wounded, which was so much the worse for Luzio. Gasparri himself could not have effected a peaceful reconciliation at that stage. The Free State knew that it had won and was preparing to teach the 'irregulars' a lesson.

49 O'Donnell to Hagan, 21 March 1923 (Hagan).

50 Cait O'Kelly to Hagan, 13 April 1923 (Hagan).

51 *Ibid.*

52 De Valera to Hagan, 19 May 1922 (Hagan).

53 *Ibid.*

54 *Freeman's Journal*, 18 April 1923.

55 Theo Russell to Curzon, 1 May 1923, FO 371 C8133/443/22.

56 A Peace Committee, composed of three pro- and three anti-Treaty delegates, was set up in December and some of its members were instrumental in getting Luzio to intervene by lobbying the Dublin, Cork and Limerick corporations at his request to issue an invitation to the Monsignore to use his good office to halt the violence: see Mr O'Keefe, 'A peace Effort in the Civil War', *Irish Times*, 1 April 1975.

57 Memorandum from the Assistant Legal Secretary, 19 April 1923, entitled 'Mgr. Luzio and the Northern Question', p. 5 (SPO S2198). The memorandum, which was circulated to each member of the Executive Council, also concentrated on the effect the visit would have on Northern public

opinion. Northern unionist opinion, the memorandum said, had always been 'definitely and quite genuinely and honestly afraid of papal interference in the secular affairs of Ireland'. The Assistant Secretary had in mind the dread of the 'Power of Rome', the 'Whore of Babylon', as the street-corner evangelists put it. That was the real basis of the anti-union sentiment amongst the rank and file in the Six Counties. For years a favourite theme of the Northern papers had been the 'malign influence and hidden power of Rome'. The cry of 'No Pope' had always been the most potent rallying cry and often 'the Orange mass remains immobile until the high Priests of the Order raise, Mohammed-like, the bogey of the "Roman Danger"'.

58 *Freeman's Journal*, 18 April 1923.
59 Logue to Hagan, 24 April 1923 (Hagan).
60 *Freeman's Journal*, 23 April 1923.
61 Lionel Curtis minute, 24 April 1923, FO 371 C7401/443/22.
62 Executive Council minutes, G/2 C1/93, 24/4/1923.
63 Lionel Curtis minute, 24 April 1923, FO 371 C7401/443/22.
64 Executive Council minutes, G/2 C1/93, 24/4/1923.
65 *Ibid.*, G/2 C1/89, 23/4/1923 (SPO).
66 Interview by writer with Tommy Mullins, who was responsible for taking Luzio on his rounds.
67 Italian Royal Consuls in Dublin, no. 704/39, 20 April 1923 (A.S.M.A.F. serie 1919–30; pacco 1196, fac. 4744).
68 Official department minutes of Rome trip signed by S. P. Breathnach (Joseph Walshe), May 1923 (FitzGerald).
69 *Ibid.*
70 Executive Council minute, G/2 C1/99, 5/5/1923.
71 Paddy Walsh to Hagan, 23 May 1923 (Hagan).
72 De Valera to Hagan, 19 May 1923, *ibid.*
73 Logue to Hagan, 22 May 1923, *ibid.*
74 De Valera to Hagan, 19 May 1923, *ibid.*
75 Theo Russell to Curzon, 1 May 1923, FO 371 C8133/443/22.
76 Hagan to Byrne, 25 May 1923 (Byrne).
77 Hagan to Mannix, 5 October 1923.
78 This remark may be apocryphal, but may not have been far from the dejected would-be peace-maker's secret thoughts.

CHAPTER V. CUMANN NA NGAEDHEAL AND THE QUEST FOR LEGITIMACY

1 Hagan to O'Donnell, 10 January 1924 (O'Donnell).
2 O'Donnell became Cardinal on 19 November 1924 (Appendix I). Hagan was bitterly upset at the time. He said that he had been quite wrong in his analysis of Irish history:
   I have been expounding a theory to which my historical studies had led me, to the effect that there never existed in Ireland anything in the shape of a really national spirit or any consciousness of an Irish nation, but that we are merely a

conglomeration of clans, each of which looked not beyond its nose, and all of which pursued their own individual interests alone ready at any moment to betray the others if by doing so they could hope to satisfy cupidity, jealousy, hate, and other similar passions. But I freely confess that I made one mistake. I thought that education and increased knowledge a couple of years ago had brought forth a new Ireland with lofty ideals and without any of the mainsprings of action such as vitiated the land of old. I never made a greater mistake; and when I think of it I am surprised at myself for not seeing that a land where the two Hughes tried and failed was not likely to afford a fertile field in which lesser men could in baser ages be expected to produce a better crop.

3 Out of a total of 153 seats, Labour got fourteen, Farmers took fifteen, and sixteen independents were elected; Labour, Farmers and independents together got one more seat than the anti-Treaty party's showing of forty-four. It was quite clear that a sizeable section of the electorate felt, as de Valera had intimated to Hagan, like saying 'a plague on both your houses' to Cosgrave and the republicans.

4 Cosgrave to Byrne, 28 October 1923 (Byrne): the intervention was partially made at the request of a Dublin publisher, Mr O'Keefe of Duffy & Co.

5 Byrne to Cosgrave, 28 October 1923 (Byrne).

6 Cosgrave to Byrne, 12 October 1923 (Byrne).

7 T. Desmond Williams, Cosgrave profile, *Irish Times*, 1956.

8 Walshe left no private papers. The Department files are not open to historians but it has been possible to formulate this profile from a number of printed and oral sources. There is more extensive treatment of the subject in my 'Department of Foreign Affairs' in Zara Steiner (ed.), *The Times Foreign Offices of the World* (London, 1982), pp. 276–295, which cites some British sources, in particular a profile of Walshe by Sir John Maffey. I have also been helped in trying to understand the complex character of this man by Professor T. Desmond Williams, Dr Freddie Boland, Dr Con Cremin, Mr Frank Aiken and Dr Conor Cruise O'Brien.

9 Whyte, *Church and State*, pp. 36–7; Michael Adams, *Censorship: the Irish Experience* (Alabama, 1968).

10 SPO S4127. There was no provision for divorce in Irish law. The Matrimonial Causes Act of 1857 was never extended to Ireland. The only other course open to couples was the costly and lengthy procedure of private bill in parliament. White, *Kevin O'Higgins*, p. 116; see also Gerard Fitzgibbon-memorandum, 5 February 1925, SPOS 4127.

11 Hugh Kennedy to Cosgrave, 15 February 1923, SPO S4127.

12 C. S. Duggan to Cosgrave, 20 March 1923; the latter concluded: 'I think you may take it therefore, that the Church will strenuously resist any legislation providing for divorce even for non-catholics. I take it that the result of the absence of facilities for divorce in this country would be that persons desiring such facilities would leave Ireland and become domiciled in some other country in which they are available. The archbishop's view is that Ireland would not lose anything by this.'

13 Byrne to Duggan, 10 October 1923, enclosing confidential memorandum and resolution of bishops (SPO S4127).

14 Cosgrave to James Downey, Bishop of Adara and Coadjutor Bishop of Ossory, 21 September 1925, SPO S4127.

15 SPO S4127.

16 *Ibid.*

17 Michael J. Browne to Hagan, 23 July 1924 (Hagan). Browne may have been referring to such remarks from members of the hierarchy as the statement of the Bishop of Galway, O'Doherty: 'the dances indulged in were not the clean, healthy National Irish dances. They were, on the contrary, importations from the vilest dens of London, Paris and New York; direct and unmistakable incitements to evil thoughts, evil desires and grossest acts of impurity. For the average individual these fast dances were immediate occasions of sin.' (*Irish Catholic Directory*, 1925, p. 563).

18 *Connacht Tribune*, 7 June 1924.

19 Sean T. O'Kelly to Hagan, 17 June 1924. Gilmartin may have been upset because one of his number broke political ranks with many of his fellow bishops. But it may have been more than that. Gilmartin may have been more upset because one of the youngest of their bench had entered politics in a public, partisan manner. Irish bishops had been publicly involved in politics before independence. But independence and the Civil War ended that practice as far as the hierarchy were concerned. There was a good example of that attitude in April–May 1923. A decision was taken at the Cumann na nGaedheal general council meeting on 14 April that there should be a public appeal for funds and that Fogarty of Killaloe should be asked to act as a trustee. The bishop's reply was read to a Standing Committee meeting on 25 May: 'His lordship stated that while he was wholly in sympathy with the objects of the Organisation, he felt sure the committee would understand that the time had now arrived for clergy not to take a prominent part. He preferred not to act as a trustee but would of course subscribe when the appeal was issued.' (Cumann na nGaedheal minute book, p. 39, Archives Department, UCD).

20 Browne to Hagan, 24 July 1924 (Hagan).

21 Dignan to Hagan, 3 December 1924 (Hagan).

22 Browne to Hagan, 17 December 1924 (Hagan). This was a particularly disturbed year of Cosgrave's government. There was serious disruption in the army.

23 Interviews with Mgr McDaid, former Rector of the Irish College in Rome, Alexander J. McCabe, former Rector of the Irish College in Salamanca and with many clergymen who were students there in the 1920s.

24 Sinead de Valera to Hagan, 25 April 1926 (Hagan).

25 Hagan to Mannix, October 1923 (Hagan).

26 Hagan to de Valera, 31 May 1925 (Hagan).

27 *Ibid.*

28 Sean T. O'Kelly to Hagan, 30 November 1925; O'Kelly also made reference to the 'red hat' for O'Donnell: 'When I was on the sea, I read of the announcement about Armagh, and I was very pleased, and doubly pleased that the honour did not go to my own city.' Republicans generally were not over-enthusiastic about the Archbishop of Dublin.

29 *Ibid.*

30 Browne to Hagan, 20 December 1925 (Hagan). In the same letter Browne writes that 'Cardinal O'Donnell's appointment "has not set the Liffey on fire". People here do not feel quite sure of the line he will take; not so sure as if another had been appointed.'

31 Sean MacBride interview.

32 Mgr McDaid interview. He was told of the incident by the employee in question.

33 Longford and O'Neill, *Eamon de Valera*, pp. 242–3. Peter Pyne, 'The Third Sinn Fein Party 1923–1926', *Economic and Social Review*, vol. 1, No. 1, pp. 29–50 and vol. 1, no. 2, pp. 229–57.

34 This observation is derived from the general correspondence in the O'Donnell and Hagan papers.

35 These views are partially supported by the opinions of Professor T. Desmond Williams.

36 O'Kelly to Hagan, 21 December 1927 (Hagan).

37 White, *Kevin O'Higgins*. At the time both the Minister for Education and the Minister for Defence were ill, and President Cosgrave and the Minister for Industry and Commerce, Patrick McGilligan, were suffering from fatigue.

38 *Irish Catholic Directory*, 1928, pp. 592–3. The funeral Mass was celebrated by the Archbishop of Dublin, assisted by four other Catholic bishops.

39 Joseph Walshe Memorandum, 18 July 1927, Patrick McGilligan papers, Box C5(B), Archives Department, UCD (I am indebted to Ronan Fanning of UCD for drawing my attention to this document). Walshe discounted 'as easily palliated' considerations of the possible alienation of Protestants in the Six Counties and 'possible jealousies and intrigues centering around a Nuncio in Dublin'.

40 Walshe did not raise the Dignan case but I am sure the Bishop's remarks had not gone unnoticed by him.

41 Walshe memorandum.

42 *Catholic Bulletin*, vol. 13, December 1923, p. 864; *Il Secolo*, 1 September 1923, carries an extensive article on the history of the saint's activities in Italy.

43 Confidential clerical source.

44 In 1925, the Governor General, Timothy M. Healy, wrote to his sister-in-law, Annie, from Rome: 'Yesterday, we visited the graves of O'Neill and O'Donnell. The Chiefs must have been held in honour to get sepultures near the spot where St Peter was crucified . . . *The heads of the Irish orders here all resent the politics of the Irish College and instead of being a centre as formerly they avoid it.*' (my italics; 27 May 1925, P6/A/126, Healy/Sullivan family papers, Archives Department, UCD).

45 O'Kelly to Hagan, 11 December 1927. Apart from the accuracy of the conversation, it demonstrated that O'Kelly – probably through membership of the Catholic Truth Society – was in a position to meet the Archbishop of Tuam to discuss political matters.

46 Browne to Hagan, 31 December 1927 (Hagan).

47 Hagan to Byrne, 8 February 1928 (Byrne): 'Cardinal Bourne stayed with

the Redemptorists while in Rome. It could be interpreted that the latter was trying to land his own candidate, Murray, in Armagh. He [a contact] had much to say all going to give the impression that the chief is taking a personal interest in the appointment . . . and finally that what is being sought for is a man who will be not only good for Catholic Ireland but not bad for Protestant England. [Handwritten in margin is the following.] I also gather from him that the English ambassador is not idle. I assume that it is not necessary for me to dot the i's and cross the t's.'

48 Murray to Hagan, 3 May 1928 (Hagan).
49 Browne to Hagan, 8 November 1926 (Hagan).
50 FitzGerald papers and Keogh, 'Department of Foreign Affairs'.
51 Confidential clerical source. It is not possible to ascertain the exact date of the request.
52 Sir H. Batterbee minute, FO 627 U176/78/750.
53 Foreign Office Memorandum on inter-departmental meeting of 4 April 1929, at which Sir Hubert Montgomery, Sir H. Batterbee, Joe Walshe and Orme Sergeant attended, FO 627 U199/78/750 and FO 627 U137/78/750.
54 *Ibid.*
55 Walshe to Assistant Secretary of External Affairs, 20 April 1929, SPO S5/857A. The memorandum was circulated to the Executive Council.
56 Inter-departmental memorandum.
57 Sir H. Montgomery to Chilton, 8 April 1929, FO 627 U244/78/750.
58 Chilton to Sir H. Montgomery, 20 April 1929, FO 627 U245/78/750.
59 Chilton to Montgomery, 19 April, 1929, FO 627 U244/78/750.
60 Inter-departmental memorandum.
61 Walshe memorandum, 20 April 1929, SPO S5/857A.
62 Chilton to Montgomery, 1 May 1929, FO 627 U274/78/750. Before leaving Rome, McGilligan and his wife, accompanied by Walshe, saw Mussolini at the Palazzo Chigi. The Duce was dressed in rough riding gear and was seated at the far corner of a vast room leaving the visitors a full ninety feet to walk to him. McGilligan conveyed the 'good wishes of the President and the government to the Duce'. Mrs McGilligan asked him for a signed photograph of himself, and the Duce seemed 'highly pleased at the request and complied right away'.
63 Chilton to Kopple, 22 March 1929, FO 627 U175/78/750.
64 Sean T. O'Kelly to Hagan, 3 March 1929 (Hagan).
65 *Ibid.*, 8 May 1929.
66 Walshe memorandum to cabinet, 21 May 1929, SPO S5/857A.
67 Sir H. Batterbee minute, 17 May 1929, FO 627 U305/78/750.
68 It would appear that Walshe supplied the information to his Minister on the basis of a telephone conversation with the Vatican's Under-Secretary of State, Mgr Borgongini Duca. The latter, according to Walshe, had given him a verbal undertaking promising that diplomatic contact would be established to comply with the request of the Irish. When Walshe had been in Rome earlier in the year, he had received a promise from the same Vatican official that 'a chargé d'affaires would be sent to the Celebrations'. *Dail Debates*, vol. 30, cols. 796–821, 5 June 1929.

69 Profile of Charles Bewley in the *Isis*, no. 440, 18 June 1910, p. 459; see
    also Charles Bewley's unpublished autobiography in possession of his
    brother. This work was written after the war when he had left the Irish
    diplomatic service and shows signs of considerable retrospection, which
    makes it somewhat unreliable as a source. (I also interviewed Professor
    Daniel Binchy, who was extremely helpful and encouraging.)
70 Sir H. Montgomery minute, 7 June 1929, FO 627 U355/78/750.
71 Bewley memoir, pp. 91–2.
72 Joseph Walshe to Patrick McGilligan, 16 June 1929, official report
    (McGilligan papers; these files are in the possession of Mr Maurice
    Manning, UCD, who kindly allowed me to consult them).
73 *Exposition of the Malta Question, with documents* (Vatican, 1930). This
    gives the Church side of the controversy. Peter C. Kent, *The Pope and the
    Duce* (London, 1981), pp. 73–95.
74 Walshe to McGilligan, 16 June 1929. (See note 72).
75 *Ibid.*
76 *Pro-memoria* written after Walshe's meeting with Gasparri.
77 Walshe to McGilligan, 16 June 1929. (See note 72).
78 Walshe to McGilligan, 16 June, official report. (*Ibid*).
79 *Ibid.*; a personal letter of the same date to 'my dear Paddy'.
80 *Ibid.*
81 *Ibid.*
82 *Ibid.*, 19 June 1929, official report.
83 *Ibid.*, 22 June 1929, official report.
84 *Ibid.*, 16 June 1929, personal letter.
85 Bewley memoir, p. 93.
86 Curran to Hagan, 13 June 1929 (Hagan).
87 Curran to P. Dunne, 18 June 1929 (Byrne).
88 Curran to Hagan, 13 June 1929 (Hagan).
89 Walshe to McGilligan, 17 June 1929. Three years later Walshe was to
    renew his friendship with de Valera and maintain a close working
    relationship with the President until he became the first Irish ambassador
    to the Vatican in 1946.
90 Bewley memoir, p. 90.
91 Walshe to McGilligan, 17 January 1929. (See note 72).
92 Curran to Hagan, 19 June 1929 (Hagan).
93 *Ibid.*
94 Walshe to McGilligan, 22 June 1929. (See note 72).
95 *Ibid.*, undated but probably sometime in September: there is also mention
    of the Minister for Local Government and Public Health visiting Rome at
    that time (McGilligan).
96 Bewley to Walshe, 21 September 1929. (See note 72).
97 FO 627 U631/78/750. McGilligan seems to have had no understanding of
    the weakness of the British position at the Vatican. Strickland had been
    declared *persona non grata* by the Vatican in July 1929. The following
    year, the British had reduced the status of the Legation by withdrawing
    their Minister (Kent, *The Pope and the Duce*, pp. 88–9).

98 Minute by Orme Sargent, 24 October 1929 (*Ibid*).
99 Randall to the Foreign Office, 24 October 1929, FO 627 U646/78/750.
100 Hagan to MacRory (MacRory).
101 *Ibid*.: the hierarchy did not want to risk undue political interference on that appointment through a nuncio.
102 Hagan to Dublin, 27 November 1929 (Byrne). As a fall-back position, it is believed that the bishops proposed the respected Fogarty of Killaloe as a nuncio (confidential clerical source).
103 *Irish Independent, Irish Times* and *Daily Sketch*, 17 January 1930. The Department of External Affairs drew up detailed memoranda for the government on protocol for the occasion of the reception. See McGilligan papers, P35b/113, Archives Department, UCD.

CHAPTER VI. COSGRAVE, DE VALERA AND THE CONFESSIONAL CHALLENGE

1 Whyte, *Church and State*, and Miller, *Church, State and Nation*; the latter refers to him once as O'Hagan, p. 462.
2 T. Desmond Williams, Cosgrave profile, *Irish Times*, 1956.
3 Bishop Collier of Ossory report, 1929, presented to meeting of hierarchy, in Maynooth, June 1930; see also Whyte, *Church and State*, pp. 37–8.
4 *Dail Debates*, vol. 35, cols. 539–40, 6 June 1930.
5 T. Desmond Williams, notes on interview with W. T. Cosgrave; for details of O'Brien's career see Sean Reamonn, *History of the Revenue Commissioners* (Dublin, 1981), p. 289.
6 *Dail Debates*, vol. 35, col. 546, 4 June 1930.
7 *Senate Debates*, vol. 13, col. 1759, 20 June 1930–.
8 Williams interview.
9 *Ibid*.
10 An indication of the level of criticism in some extreme lay Catholic circles appeared in *The Catholic Mind*, a journal of limited vision and tolerance. The following extract is from the August 1930 edition:
DEALERS IN FILTH: A CHALLENGE TO THE LAW
The Editor of *The Catholic Mind* on July 7 entered the shop of Hamilton Long & Co., Ltd., Pharmaceutical Chemists, at O'Connell Street, Dublin, and inquired for certain articles well advertised in banned British newspapers.
These articles are used for the purposes of artificial birth-control.
The assistant answered the Editor's query as to the price of the articles, and supplied a box of them, for which half-a-crown was paid. With his purchase in his pocket, the Editor informed the assistant as to his identity, and promised to deal with the sale in this issue of *The Catholic Mind*. This note, therefore, fulfils a promise and exposes a scandal.
Messrs. Hamilton Long & Co. Ltd., are the contractors for various Catholic institutions in Dublin and have, in addition, the patronage of thousands of Catholic families. We conceive it to be our duty in the circumstances, to expose the fact that they deal in filth. We have given in this matter not the least consideration to our position in law. We do not give a straw what our position is, for this, it is our deep

conviction, is a matter in which it is the duty of a Catholic journalist to invoke the Public. If any law protects Messrs. Hamilton Long & Co. Ltd., in this instance it is a rotten law, worthy only of the contempt of honest men. We are prepared to make that plea before a Dublin jury.

   And publicly we denounce Messrs. Hamilton Long & Co., Ltd., to the Minister of Justice (Mr Fitzgerald Kenney, K.C.), and the Chief Commissioner of Police (General Eoin O'Duffy) as being guilty of one of the most serious offences known under the Censorship of Publications Act (Section 17, sub-sections 1, 2 and 3). Enclosed in the box of articles supplied to us was certain 'printed matter' violating this section. (*Catholic Mind*, vol. 1, no. 8 (August 1930), p. 199).

11 Whyte, *Church and State*, pp. 37–43.

12 *Ibid.*

13 Carrigan Committee (as Criminal Law report became known), SPO S5998. The report commented: 'This percentage is the highest recorded and compares with 1.80 per cent for the census triennial period 1870–2. If morality conditions existing among a population of over 4 millions in the period 1871–80 continued to prevail in today's population of less than 3 millions, the official illegitimacy figures for the year 1929 would be less than 1,280' (p. 8).

14 Department of Justice memorandum, SPO S5998.

15 See Whyte, *Church and State*, p. 47 and Jack White, *Minority Report: the Anatomy of the Southern Irish Protestant* (Dublin, 1975) and *Catholic Bulletin*, vol. 21, pp. 100–1 (January, February and March 1931), and *Catholic Mind*, vol. 2, nos. 1 and 2 for a general account. (Government reaction and details of secret Church–State negotiations can be found on files S2547A and B, President's Office, SPO.)

16 *Standard*, 13 December 1930.

17 *Catholic Bulletin*, vol. 21, no. 1, 1931, p. 10.

18 *Ibid.*, p. 3.

19 *Standard*, 3 December 1930. An editorial castigated Fianna Fail and referred to their stand as 'naked secularism'.

20 *Irish Independent*, 7 January 1931.

21 The Fianna Fail weekly, the *Nation*, took the same line as de Valera, but it was less equivocal than the party leader on the question of religion:
   The Irish people are made up of men and women of different religious beliefs and for the majority to insist upon appointments for men and women of their faith only is unjust and anti-national. There must be only one test for the public service, ability to perform the work, and that can only be discovered and recognised through competitive examination or some similar method by which the best wins . . . [lack of knowledge of Irish mentioned] . . . But to declare her unfitted by religion or by the fact that she holds a Trinity degree is to recreate under the cloak of Catholicism the spirit of Ascendancy which cursed this Nation for three hundred bitter years. (*Nation*, 13 December 1930)
   This was a genuflection to the spirit of Wolfe Tone, but those laudible sentiments were not deafening Fianna Fail audiences from Belmullet to Ballina during the dispute.

22 *Catholic Bulletin*, vol. 21, no. 2, p. 143; it is possible that the author of the

article could have been the Jesuit Edward Cahill, who pioneered Catholic Action in Dublin.

23 Minister's note of interview with the Archbishop of Cashel, mid-February 1931, SPO S2547A.

24 Glynn memorandum, SPO S2547A.

25 Keane to Cosgrave, 17 February 1931, SPO S2547A. Two days later Cosgrave sent a reply, in manuscript as usual. It was not his intention to 'endeavour to have questioned the administrative acts of the Archbishop of Tuam in his archdiocese. Rather was I concerned, and earnestly concerned, to seek your assistance in an endeavour to find a way of preventing serious misunderstandings arising.'

26 Keane replied on the 23rd indicating his willingness to take part in discussions 'without perhaps defining the exact capacity in which I act'.

27 The talks were to take place 'as quietly and informally as may be'. That did not prevent 'your being accompanied by one of your colleagues should you so wish'. Cosgrave replied on the 27th that 'Professor O'Sullivan and I shall be at Your Lordship's service either in the forenoon or afternoon of Tuesday next. The afternoon would be more suitable for us – but that does not bind your Lordship in the least. Subject to Your Lordship's permission Col. O'Reilly will call at the Hibernian Hotel, or whatever Your Lordship mentions, at 10.30 a.m. Tuesday to make the appointment and to mention place. Provisionally my house in Templeogue, Professor O'Sullivan's at Terenure, or my office or the Professor's or any other suitable place' (SPO S2547A).

28 Glynn memorandum on Gilmartin interviews, 26 February 1931, SPO S2547A.

29 Glynn memorandum, *ibid.*

30 Gilmartin to Glynn, 27 February 1931, SPO S2547B; it is probable that the Archbishop would not have enjoyed much support for the idea on the bench. A concordat would have brought Dublin closer to Rome and diminished further the independence of the local bishops and clergy.

31 Cosgrave to Gilmartin, 2 March 1931, SPO S2547A.

32 Gilmartin to Sir Joseph Glynn, 3 March 1931, *ibid.*

33 Gilmartin to Cosgrave, 4 March 1931, *ibid.*

34 These are the texts of the two typed notes, which might better be described as 'fragments'. Originally, they were handwritten notes, conceivably scribbled hurriedly before a meeting, possibly the Executive Council. But both were deemed important enough to be typed and placed on file.

35 The toughness within the Executive Council may have been one reason for Cosgrave's change of position. Possibly private reassurance from Keane of Limerick may have been another factor. Cosgrave's colleagues must have realised that the library question was a local issue, as the Archbishop of Cashel had indicated.

36 Cosgrave to Gilmartin, 11 March 1931, SPO S2547A.

37 SPO S2547A.

38 Cosgrave to MacRory, 22 March 1931 (MacRory). See also J. H. Whyte, 'Political Life in the South' in Michael Hurley (ed.), *Irish Anglicanism 1869–*

1969 (Dublin, 1970), pp. 143–53.

39 Memorandum on meeting between Cosgrave and O'Sullivan with Gilmartin, 15 April 1931, SPO S2547A.

40 *Irish Press*, 2 January 1932; the headline of the Fianna Fail paper described the news as a 'sensational development'.

41 *Round Table*, vol. 86 (March 1932), p. 369.

42 Confidential clerical source.

43 Cosgrave to MacRory, 13 August 1931, SPO S5864B; S5864A + B is an extensive dossier of police reports, Department of Justice memoranda and minutes outlining deteriorating social situations in the country.

44 Cosgrave to Byrne, 17 September 1931 (Byrne).

45 Cosgrave to MacRory, 10 September 1931, SPO S5864B; Cosgrave sent a thick dossier to each Catholic bishop consisting of a memorandum 'regarding the activities of certain organisations', a report by the Department of Justice on 'Alliance between Irish Republican Army and Communists', a copy of a Saor Eire pamphlet and other relevant documents. According to another Department of Justice file on the situation in August 1931, there were approximately 1,300 officers and 3,500 rank-and-file members of the IRA: 'the names, addresses and ranks of practically all of these men who are of any importance are known to the police, but, for reasons which will appear, it is not possible to bring them to justice'. (See SPO S5864B, Byrne and MacRory papers.) The files certainly revealed increased activity by the IRA and the radicalisation of rural workers. But did that constitute a 'conspiracy'? The Department of Justice found the exact 'nature and objects' of the 'conspiracy' presented 'considerable difficulty in definition'.

46 For background reading on this topic, see Peadar O'Donnell, *There will be Another Day* (Dublin, 1963); Michael McInerney, *Peadar O'Donnell, Irish Social Rebel* (Dublin, 1975); Peadar O'Donnell, 'The Clergy and Me', *Doctrine and Life*, vol. 24 (October 1974), pp. 539–44. O'Donnell was stoned by a clergyman in Drumsna, County Leitrim in 1933 for his defence of James Gralton, a naturalised American citizen and a communist who ran a dance hall and gave his political views to those who were willing to listen. He was attacked by the *Irish Rosary* as a man sent to study Russia, in 1929. O'Donnell is a rather good example of a man who was not hostile to the Catholic Church, but whose social philosophy was sufficient to draw upon him the wrath of the clergy.

47 See the chapter entitled 'Shades of Republicanism' in Conor Cruise O'Brien, *Herod: Reflections on Political Violence* (London, 1978).

48 Aiken was a blunt plain-spoken man who had helped bring the futile Civil War to a swift conclusion when he became chief of staff of the IRA.

49 De Valera to MacRory, 9 October 1931 (MacRory).

50 *Dail Debates*, vol. 40, col. 325, 16 October 1931.

51 Frank Aiken to Cardinal MacRory, 19 October 1931 (MacRory).

52 *Irish Catholic Directory*, 1932, pp. 622 and 623.

53 Bewley memoir.

54 I have not found evidence of any bishop who was sceptical about the documents. At least one prelate was sufficiently pro-Fianna Fail to allow de

Valera see the memoranda.

55 Tom Johnson to R. J. P. Mortished, 1 November 1931 (Mortished papers, in possession of Mrs Margaret Vanek, Ballinderry House, Rathdrum, County Wicklow). See also Mortished to Johnson, 11 November 1931.

56 I am grateful to Prof Lee for bringing this to my attention.

CHAPTER VII. DE VALERA, FIANNA FAIL AND THE CATHOLIC CHURCH

1 Dulanty to Walshe, External Affairs, 18 January 1932, P35b/115 (McGilligan).

2 *Round Table*, vol. 87 (June 1932), p. 499.

3 James Dillon, filmed interview.

4 Michael Mills interview. A source who had good reason to know about performance in cabinet said that MacEntee was the most voluble and forceful in argument; Lemass was next in line; Oscar Traynor intervened infrequently, but when he did so he was listened to by de Valera, as was the quiet Jim Ryan. Sean T. was 'the elder statesman', Gerry Boland was listened to with some 'impatience', but he was Harry's brother. Aiken was closest to de Valera at a personal level. It would be rash to conclude that de Valera gave responsibility to people in relation to their fidelity to him rather than on the basis of their talent. That was not so. De Valera knew that his ministers reflected different layers of political reality. He was not prepared to put up with mediocrities as long as they agreed with him. On paper he did not have a strong cabinet but, in reality, it proved to be much more determined.

5 T. Desmond Williams interview.

6 Conor Cruise O'Brien interview. I have not found any evidence to support this rumour. It is possible that Walshe was less hostile to that move than he would have been to the withholding of land annuities. On 12 March 1932, three days after he had been elected President of the Executive Council, de Valera received a hand-written note from Walshe: 'Nobody knows and nobody ever shall know from that I have written it', he concluded only a day after both men had had their first meeting of the new administration. That sentence was to characterise Walshe's future relationship with de Valera. It also was to reflect the way he was to run his department. The contents of the letter indicate the calibre of Walshe as an able administrator and his capacity to make a good first impression. He offered sound advice, which was not entirely free of an element of flattery: 'I believe that you can achieve the unity of this country within seven years . . .'. It is not difficult to see why Walshe became an important figure, although not quite as important as he himself might have thought, in the new administration's decision-making process. (SPO S2264).

7 *Round Table*, vol. 90 (March 1933), p. 291. Immediately he came to power de Valera set about abolishing the Governor Generalship. His task achieved, he phoned Buckley: 'You're abolished', he told Buckley. 'And you're one too', came the reply (recounted by Fr Kevin Kennedy).

8 *Round Table*, vol. 89 (December 1932), p. 135.

9 Bewley memoir, p. 102. Thanks to a number of references which were supplied by Dr Deirdre McMahon I was able to confirm many of the view put forward above. Ogilvie Forbes wrote to P.A. Koppel at the Foreign Office on 11 July 1932, reporting that the Cardinal Secretary of State, Pacelli, 'expressed decided disapproval of the Irish Free State Government in declining to invite the Governor General to their reception in honour of the Legate' during the Eucharistic Congress. In general, the Vatican would have much preferred the host of the legate to have been the Cosgrave rather than the de Valera government (FO 627/40/U423/15/750). The Vatican was obviously distressed by some of the unseemly diplomatic behaviour between the Governor General and the Irish government. Another British report speaks of the embarrassment caused by de Valera on insisting on coming to Rome. The Holy See 'earnestly desired the best relations' with Great Britain and Pacelli hoped that the visit 'would not have the effect of prejudicing them in any way. Mr. de Valera had already been informed through the nuncio of the Pope's wish that he should be careful to do nothing before the visit to Rome to embroil himself further with Great Britain . . . and when Mr de Valera came to Rome the opportunity would be taken to impress on him that the Holy See hoped he would moderate his policy towards Great Britain' (FO 371/16810/C2085/22). The visit passed off in an 'atmosphere of civility without much cordiality', which was reflected in the fact that the *Osservatore Romano* refrained from giving 'the usual puff' to the distinguished visitor (FO 371/16811/C5341/2621/22). The relationship between Pacelli and de Valera can only be explored further when the Department of Foreign Affairs opens its files to scholars. See also Deirdre McMahon, *Republicans and Imperialists: Anglo-Irish Relations in the 1930s* (New Haven and London, 1984).
10 *Official Congress Programme* (Dublin, 1932).
11 G. K. Chesterton, *Christendom in Dublin* (London, 1932), p. 16.
12 Bewley memoir, pp. 99–101.
13 Byrne to MacRory, 9 June 1932 (Byrne).
14 *Irish Independent*, 21 June 1932.
15 *Eucharistic Congress Dublin, 1932* (Pictorial Record), also *Sectional Meetings, papers and addresses* (vol. 2 of the *Book of the Congress*); for editorials on the event see the Irish press, 20, 23 and 24 June 1932.
16 Reverend Joseph P. Kelly, parish priest of Athboy, letter to author, 22 December 1982. Dr Kelly was the son of a serving Fianna Fail TD.
17 Bro. Evaristus OFM interview with author.
18 Fr Robert Graham SJ interview with author, Rome.
19 Sean MacEntee interview with author; see also Evelyn Bolster, *The Knights of St Columbanus* (Dublin, 1979).
20 Fianna Fail Parliamentary Party minute book, 28 June, 1933 (Fianna Fail archive).
21 Bewley autobiography, pp. 103–4; and *Il Popolo d'Italia*, 1 June 1933.
22 O'Kelly manuscript.
23 Copies of League documents circulated by the Department of External Affairs, in writer's possession.

24 English translation of address delivered in French by Sean T. O'Kelly, Vice-President, Executive Council to the Cercle Catholique, Geneva, on 4 October 1933.

25 The National Centre Party won eleven seats, Labour eight, Independents eight and independent Labour one.

26 Note made by Minister for Justice following meeting with episcopal delegation, 1 December, 1932.

27 Department of Justice memorandum, 10 November, 1933, S6489A.

28 The law was amended by the Health (Family Planning) Act, 1979, which allowed contraceptives – including condoms – to be sold by chemists on prescription to married couples. It was, as the then Minister for Health, Charles Haughey, said, 'An Irish solution to an Irish problem'. Dail Debates. vol. 312, col. 335, 28 February 1979.

29 It is not clear whether every bishop was sent a copy of the report, following the suggestion of the episcopal delegation to the Minister for Justice in December, 1932.

30 Whyte, *Church and State*, p. 365; Professor Whyte is quite accurate in this surmise about the representation of the hierarchy on the question of dance halls.

31 Longford and O'Neill provide a detailed account of the various influences on the formulation of the Constitution. The Irish version is more complete. For general works on the Constitution see John Kelly, *Fundamental Rights in the Irish Law and Constitution* (Dublin, 1967); Basil Chubb, *The Constitution and Constitutional Change in Ireland* (Dublin, 1978); Basil Chubb, *The Government and Politics of Ireland* (London, 1970), pp. 65–9 and 187–91; Declan Costello, 'The Natural Law and the Constitution', *Christus Rex*, vol. 8 (1954), pp. 201–18; Enda McDonagh, 'Church and State in the Constitution of Ireland', *The Irish Theological Quarterly*, vol. 28 (1961), pp. 131–44; and Desmond M. Clarke, 'Emergency Legislation, Fundamental Rights and Article 28.3.30 of the Irish Constitution', *The Irish Jurist*, vol. 12, new series (1977).

32 The relationship between de Valera and Cahill was never close; de Valera respected the learning of Fr Cahill although he did not share the latter's passionate convictions. Yet when Cahill published *The Framework of a Christian State*, in 1932, de Valera wrote to him (in Irish): 'I am very grateful to you for the gift of the book "The Framework of a Christian State". It is a work that ought to be read and reread, and I expect to find advice and direction in it during the coming years.' De Valera to Cahill, 2 August 1932 (Cahill). The writer is grateful to Dr McGrath and Fr O'Connell of Leeson St for their kindness and cooperation in providing access to this valuable collection of papers.

33 De Valera to Cahill, 19 September 1936. Maurice Moynihan, a civil servant who was particularly close to de Valera, has told the writer he does not believe that Cahill's views were very influential on the President. The Longford–O'Neill biography overstates the Jesuit's role in the process, in my opinion.

34 L.J. Kiernan SJ to Cahill, 16 October 1936 (Cahill): 'It may be that you would

like to add to some of the matters dealt with in this report, or possibly to suggest alternative recommendations. I have no objection to your doing this, but think (1) that this second document ought not be handed in with the first or at least as not forming part of the first; and (2) that since what you recommend will be regarded as emanating from the society, and on the other hand in view of the extreme importance of the matter, I would ask you to submit for censorship to any two you may select of the committee members the document you may propose to hand Mr. De Valera.'

35 Cahill to de Valera, 13 November 1936.

36 The Kiernan letter stated, relating to the committee draft: 'Now, as that document will be the product of the best heads we have in matters of this kind, I think it would be well if it were presented as it stands by your Reverence to Mr. De Valera.' Cahill wrote to de Valera on 13 November, 'sending herewith the further draft articles which I referred to in my letter of 21 October'. The 21 October letter probably contained the committee draft which the Longford and O'Neill biography refers to as the Cahill draft. It seems that there were two separate submissions, one from the committee and one from Fr Cahill. Since the de Valera biography refers to the 'October' draft from Fr Cahill (p. 296), it is obvious that the two submissions were inadvertently attributed to the pen of Cahill exclusively. It is possible that de Valera was not made aware that the Jesuits had set up a special committee on the Constitution.

37 ARTICLE I

Religion

(a) Freedom of religious worship in public and in private is guaranteed to all within the limits of public order and morality.

(b) The Catholic faith, which is the faith of the vast majority of the nation, and which is inseparably bound up with the nation's history, traditions and culture, occupies among religions in our country a unique and preponderant position.

(c) The relations between the Catholic Church and State, in matters that concern both Church and State, shall be determined by an agreement to be entered into with the Holy See. This agreement shall be ratified by the Oireachtas, and after such ratification shall have the force of law.

(d) The relations to the State of other religious bodies within the nation may be determined by an agreement between the State and the official representatives of the bodies in question.

(e) Every religious association recognised by the State may freely manage its own affairs, own and acquire movable and immovable property, administer and dispose of the same, possess and enjoy its revenues and endowments and maintain institutions for religious, educational and charitable purposes.

Cahill used the following sources in his work: The Polish Constitution, 1921, taken from *Select Constitutions of the World*, 2nd edn (Madras, 1934); Austrian Constitution of 1934, *Documentation Catholique*, vol. 32 (1934), col. 78ff; the Portuguese Constitution of 1933 in English translation; *Codex Juris Canonicis; Code of Social Principles* (Catholic Social Guild, Oxford, 1929); Catholic Truth Society booklets; and *The Pope and the People*, a selection of papal encyclicals in English published by the London Catholic Truth Society.

38 PREAMBLE
IN THE NAME, AND UNDER THE PROTECTION OF THE MOST HOLY TRINITY,
FATHER, SON AND HOLY GHOST, AND OF OUR REDEEMER JESUS CHRIST THE
UNIVERSAL KING.

We the people of Ireland being the parent nation of the Irish race, thanking God for having preserved our ancient nation through centuries of persecution and enslavement;

Remembering with gratitude and pride the preserving sacrifices of life, liberty and property, incurred by our people, generation after generation for the sake of country and faith;

Recalling in a special way, the heroic generosity and devotedness of the men who raised the standard of Freedom in 1916;

Seeking now the unity, peace and prosperity of our nation, and the welfare of all its people without distinction of religion or race;

Hereby confirm and proclaim the sovereign rights of the Irish people as a united independent Christian nation.

And in order that our state may flourish in strength, security and peace, and that all its citizens may live in mutual harmony we are resolved and hereby decree to exercise our supreme and sovereign political authority on the basis of the eternal principles of justice, liberty and personal equality in accordance with the precepts and methods laid down on this Preamble and in the following Constitution to which we now give our free and deliberate sanction and approval.

Recognising that all supreme, political and civil authority legislative, executive and judicial and all other moral powers of government come to us from God, we separate, transfer and distribute them to such persons and bodies as are hereinafter described and set up in and by this Constitution; and we moreover acknowledge and declare that all such powers can be exercised in accord with the precepts of the Divine Law of God, natural and positive and that any other exercise of them is and is by us hereby declared null and void and of no moral force.

We guarantee to all the families and all the citizens of the State equally before the law, the full recognition of all their natural and justly acquired rights, and liberty and protection in the exercise of them.

And so with the sacred purpose and intention of ensuring the development of all the spiritual and material resources of the nation, of the glory of God, the welfare of our people and the benefits of mankind we decree and enact this Constitution as the fundamental Law of the Irish State.

39 Longford and O'Neill, *Eamon de Valera*, p. 296.

40 Tomas O Neill and Padraig O Fiannachta, *De Valera* (2 vols., London, 1968–70), vol. 2, p. 335: 'Bhi comhairle agus moltai a bhfail in Dr Mac Uaid i dtaobh alt airithe go dti go raibh an dreacht i mbeal a chlobhuailte.' (Dr McQuaid was on hand to give advice and encouragment on articles right up to the point where the constitution went to the printers.)

41 A comparison of the Irish and English versions of the biography indicates that the former has a number of salient details omitted in the O'Neill and Longford version. See O Neill and O Fiannachta, *De Valera*, vol. 2, p. 335: the Irish text mentions that the religious clause was circulated among friends. But it is certain that McQuaid was not included in that inner circle.

42 If there was a minimum of only nine copies available, most can be

accounted for – de Valera, Walshe, Moynihan, McDunphy, Hearne, O'Donoghue and the Attorney General, Patrick Lynch. The remaining two copies may have gone to Frank Aiken and one other Minister – possibly Sean T. O'Kelly.

43 Preliminary draft, Article 42, pp. 42–3, circulated 'privately' by President, SPO S9715A. Mr. MacEntee said to me that he had not seen that particular article before.

44 See Appendix II for wording. In the late 1940s a group emerged in Dublin known as *Maria Duce* (under the leadership of Mary). It evolved from a discussion group run by Denis Fahey, who was a prolific publicist in the 1930s and 1940s and a member of the same congregation as John Charles McQuaid. Among his many works are to be found such titles as *The Kingship of Christ, according to the Principles of St. Thomas* (Dublin, 1931); *Money Manipulation and Social Order* (Dublin, 1944); *The Mystical Body of Christ in the Modern World* (Dublin, 1935; this work was reissued in 1938 and again in 1939); *The Rulers of Russia* (Dublin, 1938); *The Mystical Body of Christ and the Reorganisation of Society* (Cork, 1945), pp. 148–94. One of the tasks which this radical rightist group set itself was the reform of Article 44, by the substitution of a One, True, Church formula. There have been various suggestions which tie McQuaid to the group (see Gerry Moore, 'The Radical Right in Ireland: Maria Duce', Sociological Association of Ireland, Seventh Annual Conference, 1980). Moore based his contention on a claim by Fahey that he had the support of his religious superiors and the Archbishop of Dublin for *Maria Duce*. That, in turn, lent support to the contention that McQuaid was opposed to Article 44, and he quotes Johnny Feeney, *John Charles McQuaid: the Man and the Mask* (Cork, 1974), p. 35. The latter argues that although McQuaid did not *recognise* the group, he shared Fahey's views on Article 44. Feeney does not quote any source. Moore's reasoning is quite defective. It is not sufficient to accept the unconfirmed statement of a partisan figure like Fahey to determine McQuaid's attitude towards *Maria Duce*. A firm indication of how McQuaid viewed the group can be determined by the fact that he refused to assign them a chaplain and instructed them to change their name in 1954; see Roland Burke Savage, 'The Church of Dublin, 1940–1965: a Study of Most Reverend John Charles McQuaid, DD', *Studies*, vol. 54, no. 216 (Winter 1965), p. 334.

45 O Neill and O Fiannachta, *De Valera*, vol. 2, p. 335.

46 MacEntee interview.

47 Longford and O'Neill, *Eamon de Valera*, p. 296 and O Neill and O Fiannachta, *De Valera*, vol. 2, p. 335.

48 MacRory draft (MacRory).

49 Longford and O'Neill, *Eamon de Valera*, 296–7 and O Neill and O Fiannachta, *De Valera*, vol. 2, pp. 335–6.

50 Moynihan interview.

51 The historical origins of the expression 'the state recognises the special position . . .' is very interesting in the Irish context. Professor T. Desmond Williams was told by de Valera that he had arrived at that particular formula independently of outside sources. Yet the same term, according to

Professor Williams, is to be found in a document by Pius VII criticising the 1814 French Constitution – a document which had been sent to the President by McQuaid in February 1937. In 1955, de Valera wrote to the Director of Radio Eireann to dispute a claim made in a broadcast that the idea came from the French concordat of 1801 (*Irish Times*, 14 October 1955). O Neill and O Fiannachta, *De Valera*, vol. 2, p. 335, suggests that an early draft proposal from Fr Cahill may have influenced the President. Although I have not seen Fr Cahill's original draft, which must be in the de Valera papers still closed to researchers, a rough Cahill copy of what might have been the submission at a very early stage of preparation does contain the words 'UNIQUE AND (ALTOGETHER SPECIAL)'. The interesting point is that the two words in brackets are crossed out.

52 George Seaver, *George Allen Fitzgerald Gregg, Archbishop* (Dublin, 1963). Gregg is supposed to have been strikingly similar to de Valera when they were both younger men. In the summer of 1922, just after the outbreak of the Civil War, Dr Gregg was visiting friends at a hotel in Greystones, a seaside suburb of Dublin. A Free State officer followed him to the hotel and asked him his name: 'I am the Archbishop of Dublin', came the reply. But the officer then asked for identification and he was shown some letters. That did not satisfy him either. The matter was cleared up a little later on. It transpired that the officer's suspicions were aroused when the Archbishop, quite by accident, had asked directions from a boy at the station who happened to be one of de Valera's sons. (Seaver, pp. 123–5.)

53 Minute by MacRory on a letter from de Valera, 29 May 1937 (MacRory). Traditionally, the term 'Church of Ireland' was a stronger source of contention between the Anglican Church and the Presbyterians. But I have no evidence to support the view that in 1937 the wording resulted in protests from the Presbyterians. MacRory got support on this question from the Jesuit P.J. Gannon. He wrote to the Cardinal on 9 June 1937, explaining that he did not want to send a letter to the papers urging a change in the wording of the article, as it would only provoke controversy and make it appear 'as dictation from our side to involve the C. of I. in some *diminutio capitis*'. Instead, Gannon said he had written a 'careful and I hope diplomatic note to Dev. explaining all that the title logically involved' and suggested a redrafting of the 'offending paragraph' so as 'to grant toleration in general terms refraining from explicit reference to Jews or the sects (this would be everyway the best procedure).' The other alternative outlined by Gannon was a slight alteration such as 'the state acknowledges as religious bodies within the law the institutions known as etc.,'. De Valera had not answered when he wrote to the Cardinal and 'from his character I hardly expect him to be moved by anything I write especially as he seems unmoved by your Eminence's immense authority. Still every little counts and I hope I have done no harm. Hoping you are keeping well in spite of the responsibilities resting on you.' (MacRory papers).

54 See Appendix II.

55 O Neill and O Fiannachta, *De Valera*, vol. 2, p. 337.

56 Moynihan interview.

57 Interview with Mgr McDaid.

58 Professor Geoffrey Hand, nephew of the envoy, to author.

59 MacRory minute on letter from de Valera, 29 May 1937 (MacRory).

60 McElligott memorandum; for a profile of McElligott see Thomas K. Whitaker, *Interests* (Dublin, 1983), pp. 287–90.

61 In 1981 MacEntee told the *Sunday Times* that Articles 2 and 3 of the Constitution would not have been drafted in their present form had de Valera realised that they would alienate the Unionists. MacEntee said 'If we could have done it again, we would have added "by free consent of the people".' He added 'Nobody dreamed unity could be achieved any other way. We didn't think the addition was necessary.' (*Sunday Times*, 1 November 1981).

62 McElligott memorandum.

63 Moynihan to all departments, 23 April 1937, SPO S10160.

64 McElligott memorandum, 24 April 1937.

65 M. McDunphy to Department secretaries etc., 24 April 1937, SPO S10160. List of proofs in S9830.

66 Minute of the Executive Council, 23 and 27 April 1937, SPO G2/14.

67 Gerry Boland interview, *Irish Times*, 11 October 1968.

68 MacEntee interview, 22 March 1979.

69 Minute SPO S9830.

70 *Irish Press*, 17 May 1937 (see Appendix II for further press comment).

71 MacRory to de Valera, 9 May 1937, SPO S9852.

72 Jacob Slomner to de Valera, 4 May 1937, SPO S9852.

CONCLUSION

1 Joyce, *A Portrait of the Artist as a Young Man*, p. 39.

2 Joseph Lee, *The Modernisation of Irish Society* (Dublin, 1979), p. 114.

3 Conor Cruise O'Brien, *Parnell and his Party*, p. 297; and by the same author, with Maire MacEntee, *A Concise History of Ireland* (New York, 1972), pp. 123–4.

4 C.J. Woods, 'The general election of 1892', p. 300.

5 Bishop of Cork, O'Callaghan, to Kirby, 27 December 1890, no. 482 (Kirby).

6 Walsh to Kirby, 28 January 1891, no. 54 (Kirby).

7 Owen Chadwick, *The Secularisation of the European Mind in the Nineteenth Century* (Cambridge, 1977), p. 129.

APPENDIX I

1 Whyte, 'The Appointment of Catholic Bishops', pp. 12–32.

2 *Ibid.*

3 *Ibid.*, p. 29; the diary is in private possession and is an excellent source for nineteenth-century religious history.

4 Confidential clerical source.

5 This section of the appendix is based largely on a memorandum drawn up for the author by a private clerical source.

6 Whyte, 'The Appointment of Catholic Bishops', p. 2.

BIBLIOGRAPHY

NOTE ON SOURCES

It may come as a surprise to non-Irish readers that the files of the Department of Foreign Affairs – with a few known exceptions – are not open to researchers. Unlike most EEC countries, where a thirty-year rule – or lower – is in operation, Ireland has yet to update its legislation governing official archives. (An Archives Bill has been in draft form since 1977.) Unlike the Department of Foreign Affairs, the Department of the Taoiseach operates under a thirty-year rule. Dr Ronan Fanning has written a *History of the Department of Finance* with access to many files. Some other government departments have also granted limited access to *bona fide* researchers. It is regrettable that modern Irish history has to be written circuitously, looking at the mirror image of British and American official sources. Notwithstanding the limitations, it is still possible to write comprehensively. The related themes of Irish–Vatican and Church–State relations might appear to be difficult topics to tackle without official Department of Foreign Affairs sources. Happily, that has not proved to be the case. The private papers of most of the state's early Ministers of Foreign Affairs are available (de Valera's archive is the exception). Moreover, some Iveagh House memoranda surface in Taoiseach Departmental S files. Retired diplomats are willing to talk about their early careers and about the personalities responsible for setting up the Department of Foreign (External) Affairs. But it is unfortunate – and perhaps unfair sometimes – to have to rely so heavily on non-Irish sources to form a judgement about Joseph Walshe and other leading members of his department. Irish files might prove more reliable in this regard. But apart from limited official files and a large collection of personal papers, I was fortunate to secure access to ecclesiastical files, which have proved to be a major source for the period. In particular, I would like to mention the central importance of the John Hagan, Michael Logue and Edward Byrne collections. Altogether, the sources consulted in the writing of this work have proven to be rich and revealing. It is doubtful if the official files of Iveagh House will substantially alter the main argument of this book.

PRIMARY SOURCES

State Paper Office, Dublin
Dail Eireann papers

Irish Executive Council minutes
Department of Taoiseach S files

Public Record Office of Ireland, Dublin
General Files

Public Record Office, London
Cabinet minutes
Cabinet memoranda
Dominions Office papers
Foreign Office papers
Irish Office papers

National Archives, Washington
Department of State records
American legation (Dublin) papers

Vatican Archives
Propaganda papers

Italian State Archive, Rome
Archivio centrale dello stato (Irish file)
Archivio storico del ministero degli affari esteri (Irish file)

Department of Taoiseach
S files relating to the drafting of the 1937 Constitution

PRIVATE PAPERS
Southwark Archdiocesan Archive, London
Amigo papers

Family possession, Dublin
Charles Bewley memoir

Archives Department, University College Dublin
Ernest Blythe papers

Westminster Archdiocesan archive
Francis Bourne papers

Irish College, Paris
Patrick Boyle papers

Archdiocesan Archive, Dublin
Edward Byrne papers

Jesuit archives, Dublin
Edward Cahill papers

Archdiocesan archives, Dublin and Armagh and Irish College, Rome
Paul Cullen papers

Cork Archives
Liam de Róiste diaries

Family possession, Dublin
James Douglas memoir

Family possession, Dublin
Desmond FitzGerald papers

National Library of Ireland, Dublin
Frank Gallagher papers

Family possession, Dublin
George Gavan Duffy papers

Irish College, Rome
John Hagan papers

Family possession, Cork
Donal Hales papers

Hoover Institution, Stanford
Healy papers

Archives Department, University College Dublin
T.M. Healy papers

National Library of Ireland, Dublin
Tom Johnson papers

Irish College, Rome
Tobias Kirby papers

National Library of Ireland, Dublin
Shane Leslie papers

Family possession, Dublin
Sean Lester journal

Archdiocesan Archives, Armagh
Michael Logue papers

In the possession of the author
Alexander J. McCabe journal

Public Record Office of Ireland, Dublin
Frank MacDermot papers

National Library of Ireland, Dublin
Joe McGarrity papers

Archives Department, University College, Dublin, and in the possession of Mr Maurice Manning, TD
Patrick McGilligan papers

In the possession of the author, Rome
Kathleen McKenna Napoli papers

Archdiocesan Archives, Armagh
Joseph MacRory papers

Archives Department, University College, Dublin
Terence MacSwiney papers

Family possession, London
John Maffey (Lord Rugby) papers

Carmelite archives, Dublin, New York and Rome
Peter Magennis papers

Family possession, Wicklow
R. J. P. Mortished papers

National Library of Ireland, Dublin
William O'Brien papers

Archdiocesan Archives, Armagh
Patrick O'Donnell papers

Family possession and National Library of Ireland, Dublin
Sean T. O'Kelly papers

Diocesan Archives, Killarney
John O'Sullivan journal

Instituto Luigi Sturzo, Rome
Luigi Sturzo papers

Family possession, Dublin
Roger Sweetman Manuscript

National Library of Ireland, Dublin
Liam Walsh manuscript

Archdiocesan archive, Dublin
William Walsh papers

POLITICAL PARTIES
Labour Party headquarters, London
British Labour Party papers

Archives Department, University College Dublin
Cumann na nGaedheal (later Fine Gael)

Fianna Fail headquarters, Dublin
Fianna Fail Archives

Labour Party headquarters, Dublin
Irish Labour party papers

PARLIAMENTARY SOURCES
Dail Eireann Debates
Seanad Eireann Debates
House of Commons, Westminster, Debates
Italian Parliamentary Debates

WORKS OF REFERENCE
Catholic Encyclopedia
J. S. Crone, *A Concise Dictionary of Irish Biography* (Dublin, 1928)
A Dictionary of Irish Biography
Dictionary of National Biography
Irish Catholic Directory
Keesing's Contemporary Archive
Magill Book of Irish Politics, 1983
New York Times Index
Saorstat Eireann Official Handbook
Thoms Directory
Times Index
Who's Who
Who Was Who

OFFICIAL REPORTS
Reports of Commission on Vocational Organisation, 1943
    Emigration and other Population Problems, 1956
    Inquiry into Banking, Currency and Credit, 1938

NEWSPAPERS

Daily Press:
Belfast Telegraph
Cork Examiner
Corriere della sera

Freeman's Journal
Il Popolo
Irish Independent
Irish Press
Irish Times
New York Times
Osservatore Romano
Popolo d'Italia
The Times (London)

Weekly Press:
An Phoblacht
An t-Oglach
Irish Bulletin
Irish Catholic
Irish People
Irish Worker
Irish Workers Voice
Kilkenny People
Labour News
The Nation
Protestant Telegraph
Republican Congress
Standard
Sunday Independent
Sunday Press
United Ireland
United Irishman
Voice of Labour
Watchword
Waterford Standard
Waterford Weekly Star

Journals and reviews:
An Cosantoir
The Bell
Blackfriars
Capuchin Annual
Catholic Bulletin
Christus Rex
Civiltà cattolica
Concilium
Contemporary Review
Cross
Doctrine and Life
Downside Review

Economist
Furrow
Hibernia
Illustrated London News
Ireland To-day
Irish Catholic Pictorial
Irish Ecclesiastical Record
Irish Mind
Irish Monthly
Irish Rosary
Irish Statesman
Irish Theological Quarterly
Journal of Ecclesiastical History
Leader
New Statesman
Round Table

SECONDARY SOURCES

Adams, Michael, *Censorship: The Irish Experience* (Alabama, 1968).
Alix, Christine, *Le Saint-Siège et les Nationalismes en Europe 1870–1960* (Sirey, 1962).
Andrews, C. S., *Man of No Property* (Cork, 1982).
    Dublin Made Me (Cork, 1979).
Anon, *Eucharistic Congress* (Dublin, 1932) (Pictorial Record).
Anon, 'Sectional Meetings, Papers and Addresses', vol. 2 of the *Book of the Congress* (Dublin, 1932).
Arbeloa, V. M., *Socialismo y anti-clericalismo* (Madrid, 1973).
Aubert, Robert, *The Church in a Secular Age: vol. 5, The Christian Centuries* (London, 1978).
Bennett, Richard, *The Black and Tans* (London, 1959).
Bew, Paul, Peter Gibbon and Henry Patterson, *The State in Northern Ireland 1921–72* (Manchester, 1979).
Blakiston, Noel (ed.), *The Roman Question: Extracts from the Despatches of Odo Russell from Rome, 1858–1870* (London, 1962).
Blanchard, Jean, *The Church in Contemporary Ireland* (Dublin, 1963).
Blanshard, Paul, *The Irish and Catholic Power* (London, 1954).
Bolster, Evelyn, *The Knights of St Columbanus* (Dublin, 1979).
Bowman, John, *De Valera and the Ulster Question 1917–73* (Oxford, 1982).
Bowyer Bell, J., *The Secret Army: A History of the I.R.A., 1916–1970* (London, 1972).
Boyce, George D., *Nationalism in Ireland* (Dublin, 1982).
Boyle, Andrew, *The Riddle of Erskine Childers* (London, 1977).
Breen, Dan, *My Fight for Irish Freedom* (Tralee, 2nd ed. 1964).
Brennan, Michael, *The War in Clare, 1911–1921* (Dublin, 1980).

Broglio, F. Margiotta., *Italia e Santa Sede della grande guerra alla conciliazione: aspetti politici e giuridici* (Bari, 1966).

Brown, Terence, *Ireland, A Social and Cultural History 1922–79* (London, 1981).

Browne, Kevin J., *Eamon de Valera and the Banner County* (Dublin, 1982).

Buonaiuti, Ernesto, *Impressions of Ireland*, English translation (Dublin, 1914).

Cahill, Edward, *The Framework of a Christian State* (Dublin, 1932).

Camp, Richard L., *The Papal Ideology of Social Reform* (Leiden, 1969).

Carty, R. Kenneth, *Party & Parish Pump – Electoral Politics in Ireland* (Ontario, 1981).

Cerretti, E., *Il Cardinale Bonaventura Cerretti* (Rome, 1939).

Chadwick, Owen, *The Secularisation of the European Mind in the Nineteenth Century* (Cambridge, 1977).

Chavasse, Moirín, *Terence MacSwiney* (Dublin, 1961).

Chesterton, G. K., *Christendom in Dublin* (London, 1932).

Childers, Erskine, *The Framework of Home Rule* (London, 1911).

Chubb, Basil, *The Government and Politics of Ireland* (London, 1970).

The Constitution and Constitutional Change in Ireland (Dublin, 1978).

Clarke, Desmond M., 'Emergency Legislation, Fundamental Rights and Article 28.3.30 of the Irish Constitution', in *The Irish Jurist*, vol. 12, new series (1977).

Cohan, Al, *The Irish Political Elite*, Studies in Irish Political Culture 4 (Dublin, 1972).

Concannon, Thomas (Mrs), *The Blessed Eucharist in Irish History* (Dublin, 1932).

Connolly, Sean J., *Priests and People in Pre-Famine Ireland* (Dublin, 1982).

Coogan, Tim Pat, *The I.R.A.* (New York, 1970).

The Irish: A Personal View (London, 1975).

Corish, Patrick J., 'Gallicanism at Maynooth: Archbishop Cullen and the Royal Visitation of 1853' in Art Cosgrove and Donal McCartney (eds.), *Studies in Irish History presented to R. Dudley Edwards* (Dublin, 1979), pp. 176–89.

'Political Problems 1860–1878', *A History of Irish Catholicism*, vol. 5, nos. 2 and 3 (Dublin, 1967).

Corish, Patrick J. (ed.), *A History of Irish Catholicism*.

Daly, Gabriel, *Transcendence and Immanence: a Study in Catholic Modernism and Integralism* (Oxford, 1980).

Davis, Richard, *Arthur Griffith and Non-Violent Sin Féin* (Dublin, 1974).

Deasy, Liam, *Towards Ireland Free – the West Cork Brigade in the War of Independence 1917–1921* (Dublin, 1973).

Delzell, Charles E. (ed.), *The Papacy and Totalitarianism between the Two Wars* (New York, 1974).

Durey, Michael, 'The Survival of an Irish Culture in Britain, 1800–1845', *Historical Studies*, vol. 20, no. 78 (April, 1982), pp. 14–35.

Dwyer, T. Ryle, *De Valera's Darkest Hour 1919–1923* (Cork, 1982).

Ebsworth, Walter A., *Archbishop Mannix* (Armadale, 1977).

Edwards, Ruth Dudley, *James Connolly* (Dublin, 1981).

Elliot-Bateman, Michael, John Ellis and Tom Bowden, *Revolt to Revolution*, Studies in the Nineteenth and Twentieth Century European Experience, (Manchester, 1974).

Fahey, Denis, *The Kingship of Christ, According to the Principles of St Thomas* (Dublin, 1931).

Money Manipulation and Social Order (Dublin, 1944).

The Mystical Body of Christ in the Modern World (Dublin, 1935).

The Mystical Body of Christ and the Re-Organisation of Society (Cork, 1945).

Fanning, Ronan, *Independent Ireland* (Dublin, 1983).

The Irish Department of Finance (Dublin, 1978).

Farrell, Brian, 'The Drafting of Irish Free State Constituion' (in four sections), *The Irish Jurist*, vol. 6, new series (1970); vol. 7, new series (1971).

'Labour and the Irish Political Party System, a suggested Approach to Analysis' in *The Economic and Social Review*, vol. 1, no. 3, 1970, pp. 477–502.

Séan Lemass (Dublin, 1983).

Chairman or Chief? The Role of Taoiseach in Irish Government (Dublin, 1971).

Feeney, John, *John Charles McQuaid: The Man and the Mask* (Cork, 1974).

Fenech, Dominic L., 'Britain's Relations with the Vatican 1880–1922' (unpublished dissertation, University of Oxford, 1977).

Fennell, Desmond (ed.), *The Changing Face of Catholic Ireland* (London, 1968).

Fitzpatrick, David, 'The Geography of Irish Nationalism 1910–1921', *Past and Present*, (February 1978), pp. 113–44.

Fontanelle, R., *Pope Pius XI* English translation (London, *c.* 1933).

Forester, Margery, *Michael Collins: The Lost Leader* (London, 1971).

Forrestal, Desmond, *Oliver Plunkett* (Dublin, 1976).

Gallagher, Michael, *Electoral Support for Irish Political Parties 1927–1973*, Sage Professional Paper, (London, 1976).

Garvin, Tom, 'Defenders, Ribbonmen and Others: Underground Political Networks in Pre-Famine Ireland' *Past and Present*, no. 96 (August 1982), pp. 113–55.

The Evolution of Irish Nationalism (Dublin, 1981).

Gaselee, Stephen, 'British Diplomatic Relations with the Holy See', *The Dublin Review*, no. 408 (January 1939), pp. 1–19.

Graham, Robert A., *Vatican Diplomacy, A Study of Church and State on the International Plane* (New Jersey, 1959).

Greaves, C. Desmond, *Liam Mellowes and the Irish Revolution* (London, 1971).

Gwynn, Denis, *Pius XI* (London, 1932).

Hachey, Thomas E. (ed.), *Anglo-Vatican Relations 1914–1939* (Confidential annual reports of the British Ministers to the Holy See) (Boston, 1972).

'The Quarantine of Archbishop Mannix: a British Preventive Policy during the Anglo-Irish Troubles', *Irish University Review*, no. 1 (Autumn 1970).

Hagan, John, *Home Rule: L'Autonomia Irlandese* (Rome, 1913).

Harkness, D, W., *The Restless Dominion: The Irish Free State and the British Commonwealth of Nations 1921–31* (London, 1969).

Hogan, Robert, *After the Irish Renaissance – A Critical History of the Irish Drama since 'The Plough and the Stars'* (Minneapolis, 1967).

Holmes, Derek J., *More Roman than Rome: English Catholicism in the Nineteenth Century* (London, 1978).

Hughes, Philip, *Pope Pius XI* (London, 1937).

Hurst, Michael, *Parnell and Irish Nationalism* (London, 1968).

Jemolo, Arturo, *Church and State in Italy, 1850–1915* (Oxford, 1960).
Johnson, Paul, *History of Christianity* (London, 1978).
Joyce, James, *A Portrait of the Artist as a Young Man* (New York, 1969).
Keatinge, Patrick, *A Place Among the Nations: Issues of Irish Foreign Policy* (Dublin, 1978).
  The Formulation of Irish Foreign Policy (Dublin, 1973).
Kee, Robert, *The Green Flag* (London, 1972).
Kelly, John, *Fundamental Rights in the Irish Law and Constitution* (2nd ed., Dublin, 1967).
Kent, Peter C., *The Pope and the Duce* (London, 1981).
Keogh, Dermot, 'Department of Foreign Affairs' in Zara Steiner (ed.), *The Times Foreign Offices of the World* (London, 1982), pp. 276–95.
Kiernan, T. J., *The Irish in Australia* (London, 1953).
Larkin, Emmet, *The Making of the Roman Catholic Church in Ireland 1850–1860* (Chapel Hill, 1980).
  The Roman Catholic Church and the Creation of the Modern Irish State 1878–1886 (Dublin, 1975).
  The Roman Catholic Church and the Plan of Campaign in Ireland 1886–1888 (Cork, 1978).
  The Roman Catholic Church in Ireland and The Fall of Parnell 1888–1891 (Chapel Hill, 1979).
  'The Devotional Revolution in Ireland 1850–1875' in James Walsh and Larry McCaffrey (eds.), *The Historical Dimensions of Irish Catholicism* (New York, 1976), pp. 625–52.
  'The Roman Catholic Hierarchy and The Fall of Parnell', *Victorian Studies*, vol. 4 (June 1961), pp. 315–36.
Lawlor, Sheila, *Britain and Ireland 1914–1923* (London, 1983).
Ledeen, Michael A., *D'Annunzio a Fiume* (Rome, 1975).
Ledre, Charles, 'Merry del Val' in *New Catholic Encyclopedia*.
Lee, Joseph., *The Modernisation of Irish Society* (Dublin, 1979).
Lee, Joseph and Ó Tuathaigh, Gearoid, *The Age of de Valera* (Dublin, 1982).
Leslie, Shane, 'Archbishop Walsh', in Conor Cruise O'Brien (ed.), *The Shaping of Modern Ireland* (Dublin, 1960), pp. 98–107.
  Cardinal Gasquet (London, 1953).
  'Michael Logue' in *Dictionary of National Biography, 1922–1930*.
Longford, Earl of and Thomas P. O'Neill, *Eamon de Valera* (London, 1970).
Lyons, F. S. L., *Culture and Anarchy in Ireland 1890–1939* (Oxford, 1979).
  Ireland since the Famine (London, 1971).
  Parnell (London, 1977).
  Parnell Irish Historical Series pamphlet, no. 3 (Dublin, 1965).
  The Fall of Parnell (London, 1960).
Macardle, Dorothy, *The Irish Republic* (Dublin, 3rd ed. 1968).
McCarthy, Michael J. F., *Priests and People in Ireland* (Dublin, 1903).
McColgan, John, 'Partition and the Irish Administration', *Administration*, vol. 28, no. 2, 1980, pp. 147–83.
MacCurtain, Margaret and Donncha Ó Corráin, *Women in Early Irish Society: The Historical Dimension* (Dublin, 1978).

McDonagh, Enda, 'Church and State in the Constitution of Ireland', *The Irish Theological Quarterly*, vol. 28 (1961), pp. 131–44.

MacDonagh, Oliver, *States of Mind: A Study of Anglo-Irish Conflict 1780–1980* (London, 1983).

MacDonald, Malcolm, *People and Places* (London, 1969).

Titans and Others (London, 1972).

MacEntee, Sean, *Episode at Easter* (Dublin, 1966).

McGrath, J. E., 'Fr Magennis, Carmelite', in *Whitefriars*, vol. 3, no. 10 (1937), pp. 303–5.

MacGreil, Michael, *Prejudice and Tolerance in Ireland* (based on a survey of Intergroup attitudes of Dublin adults and other sources) (Dublin, 1978).

McHugh, Roger, 'The Catholic Church and the Rising', in Owen Dudley Edwards and Fergus Pyle (eds.), *Easter 1916* (Dublin, 1968).

McInerney, Michael, *Peadar O'Donnell, Irish Social Rebel* (Dublin, 1975).

McMahon, Deirdre, *Republicans and Imperialists: Anglo-Irish Relations in the 1930s* (New Haven and London, 1984).

Manning, Maurice, *Irish Political Parties: an Introduction*, Studies in Irish Political Culture, 3 (Dublin, 1972).

The Blueshirts (Dublin, 1970).

Marlow, Joyce, *Captain Boycott and the Irish* (London, 1973).

Meenan, James, *The Irish Economy since 1922* (Liverpool, 1970).

'From Free Trade to Self-Sufficiency', in Francis MacManus (ed.), *The Years of the Great Test* (Cork, 1967).

Memoirs of Desmond FitzGerald 1913–1916 (London, 1968).

Miller, David W., *Church, State and Nation in Ireland 1898–1921* (Dublin, 1973).

'Irish Catholicism and the Great Famine', *Social History*, vol. 9 (1975), pp. 79–98.

Mitchell, Arthur, *Labour in Irish Politics 1890–1930* (Dublin, 1974).

Moody, T. W. and Martin, Frank X., *The Course of Irish History* (Cork, 1967).

Moynihan, Maurice, *Speeches and Statements by Eamon de Valera 1917–1973* (Dublin, 1980).

Murphy, John A., *Ireland in the Twentieth Century* (Dublin, 1975).

'Priests and People in Modern Irish History', *Christus Rex*, vol. 20, no. 3 (1969), pp. 235–59.

Newsinger, John, ' "I Bring Not Peace but a Sword": The Religious Motif in the Irish War of Independence', *Journal of Contemporary History*, vol. 13 (1978), pp. 609–28.

'Revolution and Catholicism in Ireland 1848–1932', *European Studies Review*, vol. 9, no. 4 (October 1979), pp. 457–80.

Nolan, Michael, 'The Influence of Catholic Nationalism on the Legislature of the Irish Free State', *The Irish Jurist*, vol. 10, new series (1975), pp. 128–69.

Norman, Edward R., *The Catholic Church and Ireland in the Age of Rebellion* (London, 1965).

O'Brien, Conor Cruise, 'Church, State and Nation', *Furrow*, vol. 26, no. 2 (February 1975), pp. 77–87.

States of Ireland (London, 1972).

Herod: Reflections on Political Violence (London, 1978).

Parnell and his Party, 1880–1890 (Oxford, 1957).

O'Brien, Conor Cruise and Maire MacEntee, *A Concise History of Ireland* (New York, 1972).

O'Brien, Conor Cruise (ed.), *The Shaping of Modern Ireland* (London, 1960).

O'Brien, Joseph V., *William O'Brien and the Course of Irish Politics 1881–1918* (Berkeley, 1976).

O'Connell, William (Cardinal), *Recollections of Seventy Years* (Boston, 1934).

O'Connor Lysaght, D. R., *The Republic of Ireland* (Cork, 1970).

O'Donnell, Peadar, *There will be Another Day* (Dublin, 1963).

'The Clergy and Me', *Doctrine and Life*, vol. 24 (October 1974), pp. 539–44.

O'Dwyer, Peter, *Peter E. Magennis, Priest and Patriot* (Dublin, 1978).

O'Farrell, Patrick, *The Catholic Church in Australia* (Melbourne, 1977).

'Whose Reality? The Irish Famine in History and Literature', *Historical Studies*, vol. 20, no. 78 (April 1982), pp. 1–13.

Ó Fiaich, Tomas, 'The Catholic Clergy and the Independence Movement', *Capuchin Annual*, 1970, pp. 480–502.

Ó Fiannachta, Padraig (ed.), *Sean T., Sceal a bheatha 1916–1923* (Dublin, 1973).

O'Hegarty, P. S., *The Victory of Sinn Féin* (Dublin, 1924).

Oldmeadow, Ernest, *Francis Cardinal Bourne* (2 vols., London, 1944).

O Neill, Tomas and Padraig O Fiannachta, *De Valera* (2 vols., London, 1944).

O'Leary, Cornelius, *Irish Elections 1918–1977: Parties, Voters and Proportional Representation* (Dublin, 1979).

Oliveri, Mario, *The Representatives: the Real Nature and Function of Papal Legates*, English translation (Gerrards Cross, 1980).

O'Rahilly, Alfred, *Thoughts on the Constitution*, (Dublin, 1938).

Ó Riordain, John J., *Irish Catholics: Tradition and Transition* (Dublin, 1980).

O'Riordan, Michael J., *Catholicity and Progress in Ireland* (London, 1906).

O'Shea, James, *Priest, Politics and Society in Post-Famine Ireland: A Study of Co. Tipperary 1850–1891* (Dublin, 1983).

Pakenham, Frank, *Peace by Ordeal: The Negotiation of the Anglo-Irish Treaty 1921* (London, 1962); see also under Longford, Earl of.

Paul-Dubois, L., *Contemporary Ireland* (Dublin, 1908).

Plunkett, Horace, *Ireland in the New Century* (London, 1904).

Pyne, Peter, 'The Third Sinn Féin Party 1923–26' *Economic and Social Review*, vol. 1, no. 1, 1969, pp. 29–50 and vol. 1, no. 2, 1970, pp. 229–57.

Randall, Alec, *Vatican Assignment* (London, 1957).

'British Diplomacy and The Holy See 1555–1925', *The Dublin Review*, no. 482 (1959–60), pp. 291–303.

British Diplomatic Representation at the Holy See, *Blackfriars*, vol. 37 (September 1956), pp. 356–363.

Reamonn, Sean, *History of the Revenue Commissioners* (Dublin, 1981).

Rémond, René, *L'Anticléricalisme en France de 1815 à nos jours* (Paris, 1976).

Renzi, William A., 'The Entente and the Vatican During the Period of Italian Neutrality, August 1914–May 1915', *The Historical Journal*, vol. 13, no. 3 (1970), pp. 491–508.

Repington, Charles à Court, *The First World War 1914–1918*, Diary, vol. 2 (London, 1920).

Rhodes, Sir Anthony, *The Power of Rome in the Twentieth Century: The Vatican in the Age of Liberal Democracies 1870–1922* (London, 1983).
Rumpf, Erhard and Anthony L. Hepburn, *Nationalism and Socialism in Twentieth Century Ireland* (Liverpool, 1977).
Ryan, William P., *The Pope's Green Island* (London, 1912).
Savage, Roland Burke, 'The Church in Dublin 1940–1965: A Study of Most Reverend John Charles McQuaid, DD', *Studies*, vol. 54, no. 216 (Winter 1965), p. 334.
Schapiro, J. Salwyn, *Anti-Clericalism* (London, 1967).
Seaver, George, *George Allen FitzGerald Gregg, Archbishop* (Dublin, 1963).
Shaw, Francis, 'The Canon of Irish History: A Challenge', *Studies*, vol. 61, no. 242 (Summer 1972), pp. 120–37.
Silke, John J., *Relics, Refugees and Rome* (Rome, 1977).
Spadolini, Giovanni, *Il Cardinale Gasparri e la questione romana* (Florence, 1972).
Stehle, Hansjakob, *Eastern Politics of the Vatican 1917–1979* (Ohio, 1981).
Sturzo, Luigi, *Politics and Morality* (London, 1936).
Telling, William, *The Pope in Politics: The Life and Work of Pius XI* (London 1937).
Temperley, Harold, 'George Canning, The Catholics and The Holy See', *The Dublin Review*, vol. 386, pp. 1–12.
Titley, Brian, *Church, State, and the Control of Schooling in Ireland 1900–1944* (Kingston and Montreal, 1983).
Townshend, Charles, *The British Campaign in Ireland* (Oxford, 1975).
Van Voris, Jacqueline, *Constance de Markievicz: In the Cause of Ireland* (Amherst, 1967).
Wall, Maureen, 'The Rise of a Catholic Middle Class in Eighteenth-Century Ireland', *Irish Historical Studies*, vol. 11, no. 42 (September 1958), pp. 91–115.
Walsh, Patrick J., *William J. Walsh, Archbishop of Dublin* (Dublin, 1928).
Ward, Alan J., *Ireland and Anglo-American Relations 1899–1921* (London, 1969).
Ward, J. E. 'Leo XIII, The Diplomatic Pope', *Review of Politics*, vol. 27 (1966).
Whitaker, Thomas K., *Interests* (Dublin, 1983).
White, Jack, *Minority Report: The Anatomy of the Southern Irish Protestant* (Dublin, 1975).
White, Terence, de Vere, *Kevin O'Higgins* (London, 1948).
Whyte, John H., *Church and State in Modern Ireland 1923–1979* (Dublin, 1980).
 '1916 Revolution and Religion' in F. X. Martin (ed.). *Leaders and Men of the Easter Rising: Dublin 1916* (Dublin, 1967), pp. 220–6.
 'Political Life in the South' in Michael Hurley (ed.), *Irish Anglicanism 1869–1969* (Dublin, 1970), pp. 143–153.
 'The Appointment of Catholic Bishops in Nineteenth Century Ireland', *Catholic Historical Review*, vol. 58 (April 1962).
Williams, T. Desmond, *Secret Societies in Ireland* (Dublin, 1973).
Williams, T. Desmond (ed.), *The Irish Struggle* (London, 1966).
Woods, Chris J., 'The General Election of 1892: The Catholic Clergy and the Defeat of the Parnellites' in S. L. Lyons and R. A. J. Hawkins (eds.),

Ireland Under the Union: Varieties of Tension: Essays in honour of T.W. Moody (Oxford, 1980), pp.289–320.

'Ireland and Anglo–Papal Relations 1880–1885', *Irish Historical Studies*, vol. 18, no. 69 (March 1972), pp. 29–60.

Younger, Carlton, *Ireland's Civil War* (London, 1968).

Zivojinovic. Dragan R., *The United States and Vatican Policies* (Colorado, 1978).

INDEX